Managing Social Media Practices in the Digital Economy

Shirin Alavi
Jaypee Institute of Information Technology, India

Vandana Ahuja
Amity Business School, Amity University, Noida, India

A volume in the Advances in Marketing, Customer Relationship Management, and E-Services (AMCRMES) Book Series

IGI Global
DISSEMINATOR OF KNOWLEDGE

Published in the United States of America by
IGI Global
Business Science Reference (an imprint of IGI Global)
701 E. Chocolate Avenue
Hershey PA, USA 17033
Tel: 717-533-8845
Fax: 717-533-8661
E-mail: cust@igi-global.com
Web site: http://www.igi-global.com

Library of Congress Cataloging-in-Publication Data

Names: Alavi, Shirin, 1980- editor. | Ahuja, Vandana, editor.
Title: Managing social media practices in the digital economy / Shirin Alavi and Vandana Ahuja, editors.
Description: Hershey : Business Science Reference, 2019. | Includes bibliographical references and index. | Summary: “”This book facilitates an understanding of diverse social media tools and platforms and their impact on society, business, and the economy and illustrates how online communities can benefit the domains of marketing, finance, and information technology”--Provided by publisher”-- Provided by publisher.

Identifiers: LCCN 2019037753 (print) | LCCN 2019037754 (ebook) | ISBN 9781799821854 (hardcover) | ISBN 9781799821861 (paperback) | ISBN 9781799821878 (ebook)
Subjects: LCSH: Information technology--Economic aspects. | Marketing--Technological innovations. | Social media--Economic aspects. | Social media--Social aspects.
Classification: LCC HC79.I55 M364 2019 (print) | LCC HC79.I55 (ebook) | DDC 302.23/1--dc23
LC record available at https://lccn.loc.gov/2019037753
LC ebook record available at https://lccn.loc.gov/2019037754

This book is published in the IGI Global book series Advances in Marketing, Customer Relationship Management, and E-Services (AMCRMES) (ISSN: 2327-5502; eISSN: 2327-5529)

British Cataloguing in Publication Data
A Cataloguing in Publication record for this book is available from the British Library.

Advances in Marketing, Customer Relationship Management, and E-Services (AMCRMES) Book Series

ISSN:2327-5502
EISSN:2327-5529

Editor-in-Chief: Eldon Y. Li, National Chengchi University, Taiwan & California Polytechnic State University, USA

MISSION

Business processes, services, and communications are important factors in the management of good customer relationship, which is the foundation of any well organized business. Technology continues to play a vital role in the organization and automation of business processes for marketing, sales, and customer service. These features aid in the attraction of new clients and maintaining existing relationships.

The Advances in Marketing, Customer Relationship Management, and E-Services (AMCRMES) Book Series addresses success factors for customer relationship management, marketing, and electronic services and its performance outcomes. This collection of reference source covers aspects of consumer behavior and marketing business strategies aiming towards researchers, scholars, and practitioners in the fields of marketing management.

COVERAGE

- Cases on CRM Implementation
- Mobile CRM
- Online Community Management and Behavior
- B2B marketing
- Mobile Services
- Customer Relationship Management
- CRM and customer trust
- Web Mining and Marketing
- E-Service Innovation
- Text Mining and Marketing

IGI Global is currently accepting manuscripts for publication within this series. To submit a proposal for a volume in this series, please contact our Acquisition Editors at Acquisitions@igi-global.com or visit: http://www.igi-global.com/publish/.

The Advances in Marketing, Customer Relationship Management, and E-Services (AMCRMES) Book Series (ISSN 2327-5502) is published by IGI Global, 701 E. Chocolate Avenue, Hershey, PA 17033-1240, USA, www.igi-global.com. This series is composed of titles available for purchase individually; each title is edited to be contextually exclusive from any other title within the series. For pricing and ordering information please visit http://www.igi-global.com/book-series/advances-marketing-customer-relationship-management/37150. Postmaster: Send all address changes to above address.

Titles in this Series

For a list of additional titles in this series, please visit:
https://www.igi-global.com/book-series/advances-marketing-customer-relationship-management/37150

Handbook of Research on Retailing Techniques for Optimal Consumer Engagement and Experiences
Fabio Musso (University of Urbino Carlo Bo, Italy) and Elena Druica (University of Bucharest, Romania)
Business Science Reference • © 2020 • 571pp • H/C (ISBN: 9781799814122) • US $285.00 (our price)

Handbook of Research on Contemporary Consumerism
Hans Ruediger Kaufmann (University of Applied Management Studies Mannheim, Germany & University of Nicosia, Cyprus) and Mohammad Fateh Ali Khan Panni (City University, Bangladesh)
Business Science Reference • © 2020 • 361pp • H/C (ISBN: 9781522582700) • US $285.00 (our price)

Improving Marketing Strategies for Private Label Products
Yusuf Arslan (Sakarya University, Turkey)
Business Science Reference • © 2020 • 383pp • H/C (ISBN: 9781799802570) • US $195.00 (our price)

Digital Marketing Strategies for Tourism, Hospitality, and Airline Industries
José Duarte Santos (Instituto Superior Politécnico Gaya, Portugal) and Óscar Lima Silva (Instituto Superior Politécnico Gaya, Portugal)
Business Science Reference • © 2020 • 267pp • H/C (ISBN: 9781522597834) • US $225.00 (our price)

Exploring the Power of Electronic Word-of-Mouth in the Services Industry
Sandra Maria Correia Loureiro (Instituto Universitário de Lisboa, Portugal) and Hans Ruediger Kaufmann (University of Applied Management Studies, Germany)
Business Science Reference • © 2020 • 463pp • H/C (ISBN: 9781522585756) • US $265.00 (our price)

IGI Global
DISSEMINATOR OF KNOWLEDGE

701 East Chocolate Avenue, Hershey, PA 17033, USA
Tel: 717-533-8845 x100 • Fax: 717-533-8661
E-Mail: cust@igi-global.com • www.igi-global.com

Editorial Advisory Board

Table of Contents

Detailed Table of Contents

Social media marketing is a new form of communication between firms and consumers. The interactive nature of social media platforms enables consumers to share their perceptions about firms by creating their own content in various forms. Besides, firms are able to attract and engage with consumers through creating effective content on their social media channels. Both user-generated content (UGC) and firm-generated content (FGC) have a significant role in firm performance and consumer behavior. However, the previous studies have mostly focused on the effects of UGC and addressed the issue from the consumer side. Therefore, as distinct from existing studies, the study at hand addresses the specific effects and benefits of UGC and FGC from both the firm and consumer sides, within a theoretical framework. In addition, based on the findings of the reviewed studies, the chapter presents some practical implications for business.

Several studies have approached the link between social media and e-commerce with different lenses, however, the study of motivations for sharing content specifically from e-commerce websites into social media has not been thoroughly approached and provides fertile ground for further exploration. This chapter uncovers which motivations serve as a background for individuals sharing intentions of e-commerce content. After a focus group with 7 individuals, results indicate participants focus more on intrinsic rewards than extrinsic ones when sharing, that self-interest is more predominant than reciprocity as a motivator for sharing, one-to-one exchanges are the preferential direction of exchange. Also, websites with cleaner designs and higher usability positively impact sharing intentions, experiences tend to be more likely shared than physical products, and participants are purposeful in their selection of sharing channels.

This chapter examines the usage of social media in predicting consumer buying process. A mixed method approach has been applied, a cross sectional survey and in-depth interviews were conducted in three universities in Ghana. The responses were collected from individuals in the age group of 18 -30. Data was analysed using Logistics Regression and Thematic analyses. The findings revealed that the social media behaviour of young consumers could significantly influence their behaviour at the pre-purchase information search and evaluation levels. The findings suggest young consumers are more likely to use social media for marketing activities such as purchasing, hence industries should redirect more activities towards this digital channel. This implies that social media is driving young consumers into e-commerce and that presents a huge opportunity for business and marketers.

The digital economy is changing the way business is done and is showing tremendous potential for organisational progress and global influence.As innovative products and service offerings make the world more competitive,if created properly, digital connectivity will be able to provide new business models and faster entries into global markets (Anderson, Wladawsky-Berger,2016).This gives rise to important issues pertaining to consolidation of practices, implementation of relevant issues across global companies, and many more. Appropriate answers can be searched for these questions in the international research databases on the digital economy like Scopus and Web of Science. Research contributions of authors demonstrating scientific completeness are of great important here. Also important are databases that have been adequately cited.

Popularity of social media is increasing day by day and there are thousands of social media platforms on the internet with different features. This chapter discusses the term social media in general and examines its evolution in detail from the beginning of the first e-mail to today. Authors explore the terms pertaining to the domain of Social Network Sites (SNS) which are considered as one of the most used forms of social media. Authors present a discussion about a popular topic "SNS addiction" and examine its characteristics with a brief literature review. Accordingly, despite the fact that excessive use of social network sites cannot be formally accepted as a behavioral addiction; shy and young, extroverted, and neurotic women with no relationship are more likely to develop addictive behaviors towards social media.

Foreword

It gives me great pleasure to write a foreword for this book on *Managing Social Media Practices in the Digital Economy*. The editors have chosen an interesting field as a large number of organizations are embracing the world of social media and using it to reach out to the world. This "reaching out" is helping firms gather user preferences, build consumer profiles and develop brand recognition. Social media sites and platforms add significant value to business activities, including market research, co-creation, new product development, and brand and customer management. Understanding and correctly incorporating these tools into daily business operations is essential for organizational success.

The editors of this book have compiled 11 chapters that provide a unique and interesting reference resource for understanding diverse social media tools and platforms and their impact on society, business, and the economy as a whole. The book features research on topics such as mobile technology, service quality, content marketing, and consumer engagement. The material in this book is equally relevant for managers, managing directors, executives, marketers, industry professionals, social media analysts, academicians, researchers, and students.

Social media is an amalgamation of virtual channels, tools and platforms that enable people to come together in a virtual setting to collaborate, communicate, and/or share content. The term *social* captures the idea that user generated content can be shared and communities or cliques can come together for information sharing and exchange of ideas. Social Networking Platforms, Blogs, Online Communities and Mobile Apps are the most significant social media tools used by businesses. Social media is utilized by businesses for the purpose of brand management, triggering sales, collecting customer intelligence, managing organizational reputation, building consumer brand relationships, understanding competitors, targeted advertising, analytics, and for online payments and shopping.

Industry leaders need to revisit their social media practices in order to capitalize on emergent technology trends such as Virtual Reality, Artificial Intelligence and Internet of Things. Disruptive innovations like chatbots and voice technologies are fast challenging text based systems. As per Gartner, organizations need to be more fluid and functional. Paid social advertising is significant for enhancing reach and consumer engagement.

The democratization of content and the emergence of new typologies and formats is driving the need for organizations to innovate. Facebook's thumbstoppers, Snapchat's stories, and Instagram's picturesque approaches are giving rise to new techniques of communication between organizations and associated stakeholders.

The biggest reason for the emergence of this wave of social media is the fluctuation and transformation in social trends at a global level. Convenience and collaboration are the two key drivers in individual adoption of information technology in general and social media tools in particular. Use of these tools for commercial practices, making payments, playing online games, retrieving information, keeping abreast of current affairs, etc. is on the rise.

The use of chatbots in social media marketing is further influencing the social media app world and messaging apps like Wechat, WhatsApp, Slack, Apple iMessage, and Facebook Messenger are growing at a fast pace, making it easier for users to search content and enhance personalization. Special bot personalities and interactive abilities add a unique flavor to bring these user interactions to life, giving new twists to the social media ecosystem.

While the dynamic nature of this field makes it challenging to provide a comprehensive overview of the social media ecosystem, this book definitely presents a fresh perspective and an interesting start. This book undeniably provides a good comprehensive beginning in a space that has numerous emerging trends. I am confident that you will obtain great insights in reading the various chapters in this book.

I wish the editors all the best for this successful endeavor.

Deepak Khazanchi
University of Nebraska, Omaha, USA

Deepak Khazanchi is Associate Dean for Academic Affairs, Professor of Information Systems and Quantitative Analysis and Community Engagement & Internationalization Officer in the College of Information Science and Technology at the University of Nebraska Omaha. His research interests include virtual-project management, virtual teams in crisis settings, Intelligent Project Management (ML/AI & PM), and B2B assurance services in extended enterprise environments.

Preface

INTRODUCTION

In the contemporary world, the advent of digitization has transformed the way organizations function. Technology has permeated every single organizational domain and subsequently, disruptive changes have ushered in new organizational cultures, working styles and mannerisms. The world of the internet has pushed virtualization into every facet of individual lives-both personal and organizational.

Social media is a very important ambit in this technology driven world. It has completely transformed the manner in which brands and consumers communicate among themselves. The new tools and approaches provided by Social Media can be applied to all industry verticals. But it is imperative for businesses to learn and adopt the correct social media practices that are consistent with the requirements of their industry vertical and business plan. By adopting apt social media practices the organizations will be able to carve a niche for themselves. This book on "Managing Social Media Practices in a Digital Economy" incorporates the core foundations and techniques for creating a widespread and effective social media marketing plan. In the contemporary times social media platforms are dedicated to understand their customers more intensely and fulfil their every need. For majority brands that aspire to achieve excellent ratings in customer experience management it is crucial to stay connected with their customers and understand customer-driven social media trends and the technologies that enable them. An organization can do step wise planning for enhancing its social media presence. In order to attain this organizations and marketers face unprecedented opportunities and challenges. For this it is important to identify the impact of current presence and competition on the social web. This has to be further supported by the establishment of goals and various strategies to achieve them. In this book an effort has been made to identify various social media trends and practices that are prevalent in the modern times. These trends are primarily related to technology, most significant social media platforms, content and content categorization and the various stakeholders who use these platforms in their day to day lives. In many instances the consumers are driving the content on social media platforms so the marketers cannot simply transmit their own sequence of events. The online ratings and reviews on various social media platforms affirm that the customers are very vocal about their experiences. In the past these brands have never invested so much power in the hands of consumers in shaping their reputation and goodwill and neither the consumers had an opportunity to connect and bond with their favorite brands so closely. Customer advocacy through online medium remains a very powerful approach for enhancing brand affinity. According to current statistics majority of consumers value recommendations from peers and family over all forms of paid advertising. The data of American Marketing Association further supports this. Thus, we see that brands across all industry verticals have recognized the significance of consumer evangelism. The brands have to be really vigilant at the time of fabricating content with respect to cost of production and ratio of production to distribution. One more important requirement is that the present-day consumers want participation in social media platforms, they are no more willing to be just mere onlookers. The content that is shared online should be medium not too long and should include infographics, videos and link posts that could be circulated as a targeted Facebook or Instagram content. Influencer centered campaigns are almost bread and butter for all brands. The online trust and credibility that these influencers have gathered is stupendous. Most adult population in all countries trust and follow influencers sometimes more than the brand itself. As consumers in recent times do both product research and purchase simultaneously, the search engine optimization is a necessity. It is important for brands to know that whether consumers have visited shopping sites or popular social platforms like Instagram, Pinterest or Snapchat as this will give insights to organization that which sites enable consumers to locate the brand and which are driving sales. Organizations should also draw insights from organic search reports and pay per click category campaigns and identify those sites that drive traffic the brand site; for example, a fast-moving consumer goods brand will want to test social sites like Pinterest and shopping sites like Amazon. The brands have also recognized the importance of voice technology as a high-end marketing tool. Consumers want to be heard but in order to harness the power of voice organizations have to investigate voice search queries and tie up with call centers. Marriott International and Axe are among the brands that have moved beyond mere experimentation to building standalone campaigns around the technology. Maybe it is time to listen in.

The internet has also enabled individuals to become more social. Interestingly, this socialization has ushered in more ways by which organizations and individuals can make use of the internet for social, economic and business benefit.

Each industry vertical-automobile, banking, financial institutions, FMCG sector, hospitality industry, healthcare and pharma, apparel, Information technology, Media and entertainment etc., has crafted a significant social media presence for itself. These organizations have developed a virtual profile for themselves across several social media platforms including Facebook, Instagram and Twitter.

Benefits to the social, economic and business domains are listed below:

Social Benefits

- *Maintain Customer Relationships*
  Brands are using social media to maintain consumer relationships, engage consumers and build an affinity between brands and consumers. As organizations share content which may be of interest to consumers, they are able to get consumers to like, share and comment on that content. This way, consumers unwittingly get engrossed in a conversation with the brand and move from a state of mere engagement to a state of involvement with the brand. Consumer-brand resonance deepens as consumers identify brand related content on social media, which is in sync with their thoughts and belief systems. This eventually induces brand likeability and helps in sustaining long term consumer-brand relationships.
- *Use Opinion Leaders for Influencer Marketing*
  Influencers include individuals, organizations and people who possess an expert level of knowledge and at the same time, possess a social clout and the ability to influence others. Social media makes use of this individual clout to stimulate the choices and brand affinity of other individuals or consumers. These influencers generate positive social media content, which when amplified, serve as testimonials for a brand or consumer. These include authoritative individuals, activists, connected trendsetters and trusted persons who are respected by their communities and exercise influence over their cliques and groups. This way social media becomes a subtle medium which persuades the audience to believe or adopt a particular point of view, often with the agenda of encouraging purchase behavior.
- *Generate Goodwill for the Brand*
  A large number of organizations are showcasing their corporate social responsibility endeavors, through their social media activity. These endeavors create an image of a responsible, emotional and humane brand, interested in working towards the upliftment and wellbeing of society at large. This helps an organization usher in positivity for its image and brand personality and generates goodwill for the brand. Research has already proven that these measures contribute to the brand equity of an organization, in the long run.

Economic and Business Benefits

- *To Beat Competition*

  It is essential for organizations to keep a track of the social media accounts of their competitors. This helps them to gauge the consumer sentiments with respect to the products of their competitors. Any shortcoming in the product and service of their competing organization can help the companies to improve their own product and service which in turn would help them to address and acquire new customers.
- *Humanize Brand and Relationship Building*

  In order to retain existing customers and acquire new customers it is essential to demonstrate the human side of your brand in terms of embracing strong brand values that are in interest of all-important stakeholders like employees and customers. Social media offers ample opportunities to build relationships and promote consumer evangelism. Social media advocacy programs also go a long way in relationship building
- *Build Brand Awareness and Reputations*

  With the increase in number of online shoppers and internet surfers almost half of the world's population is using social media platforms. Almost all the organizations are using these to reach highly targeted potential customers. Organizations have data repository of innumerable individuals who have online presence on these platforms. Organizations can build themselves as thought leaders in order to enhance consumer trust.
- *Boost Brand Visibility*

  Social media helps in enhancement of brand awareness as the information related to brand is propagated very quickly among millions of social media users. Social media is a sustainable and effective way to communicate with the consumer base and attract prospective consumers or clients.
- *Recruitment*

  Social media is increasingly used by organisations to launch hiring campaigns. Various professional networks like LinkedIn are devoted to attracting the skilled personnel in various organizations.
- *Generate Leads and Boost Sales*

  Lead generation is an important contribution of social media towards business. Many social networks offer advertising formats specifically designed to collect leads. Social media accounts are a critical part of sales pipeline management of an organization in the contemporary times. The number of people using social media has grown by leaps and bounds. As a result social sales tools have also evolved. Now social networks have become increasingly important for product search and electronic commerce. Social selling is a critical tool for various sales professionals.

- *Increase Website traffic*
  One of the key ways to drive traffic to your website are social media posts and ads. The content that is shared from the blog or website to the respective social channel is a great way to incite readers. Participation in various social chat platforms can also be a great way of increasing traffic to your website. The companies should try to offer more value on chat rather than just promoting their products and services.

The above benefits have crafted well defined roles for social media enthusiasts and practitioners in organizations. These include:

- *Social Media Managers*
  They are responsible for generating and propagating social media content directed towards consumer engagement and creation of an interactive relationship between consumers and the company. They have to work in sync with the corporate marketing goals, generate monthly reports on emerging social media trends, develop social media calendars, monitor organizational social media accounts, amplify consumer reviews and testimonials, and contribute to the long term social media strategic plans of the organization.
- *Social Media Strategists*
  They are experts in the domain of social media who are responsible for planning and developing an organization's social media strategy. The objective is to enhance the online presence of the organization in terms of brand visibility. Additionally, they also oversee the implementation of the digital marketing efforts of an organization, including those activities directed towards generating greater volumes of web traffic.
- *Social Media Specialists*
  These individuals are responsible for developing and implementing the organizational social media strategy, to enhance the virtual presence and advance the marketing and sales efforts of the company. The role requires the development of Key Performance indicators and management of social media content effectively to ensure that the organization stays ahead of competition. Social media specialists are expected to measure the success of respective campaigns, identify best industry practices in the realm of social media, and use social media analytics to provide actionable information to the Marketing, Sales and Product Development teams. Additionally, specialists also monitor the search engine optimization activities of the company to ensure best results.

- *Community Managers*
  Social media community managers are responsible for developing online communities around a brand by participating in online conversations, listening to customers, engaging individuals, and acting as brand advocates. They further spur other individuals to become consumer evangelists,
- *Content Managers*
  are responsible for creating content for social media campaigns. The have excellent command over language and possess graphic designing skills to create the required content campaigns. They are also responsible for content optimization. This is achieved by identifying which content marketing strategies work best for the organization with regard to increase in traffic and consumer engagement.
- *Digital Marketing Managers*
  They are responsible for Search engine marketing and search engine optimization to ensure superior performance of an organization's virtual assets-these include the organizational websites, and any other social media presence created by the organization. They ensure that the organizational website performs well with regard to any search queries performed by the consumers. Better keyword management and planned keyword advertising activities aid in the process. These individuals are responsible for banner ads, pop ups and a variety of other activities directed towards optimizing the virtual presence of the companies and increase traffic on all the organizational web pages. These individuals aim at enhancing the efficiency and revenue benefits leveraged by an organization from its online presence.
- *Social Media Analysts*
  These individuals monitor the social media presence of an organization to identify top performing social media content. They are responsible for extracting actionable information from the vast realms of social media data that is collected and processed by them, using social media analytical tools. They analyze campaign performance, most important influencers, consumer sentiment and online reputations of organizations and individuals. They are responsible for signaling the need of corrective action, as and when required by the organization. Their analysis on consumer data-demographic, geographical and preferential, aids organizations in their consumer segmentation and targeting activities and helps in better brand positioning. They can also help in keeping abreast of competitors' activities and help organizations in the strategic planning activities.

This book has 11 chapters in all.

The first chapter on *An Evaluative Framework for the Most Suitable Theory of Mobile Learning* describes how there has been a significant shift in the focus of usage of Information Communication Technology and associated tools in the field of education. The chapter explains how there is a shift from e-learning to mobile learning. This has happened as mobile devices are ubiquitous tools which offer technological and pedagogical advantages to consumers and students at affordable rates. The chapter emphasizes on how the potential of these mobile tools can be utilized effectively by teaching-learning communities across several South Asian developing nations.This chapter outlines an evaluative agenda of contemporary theories of learning and suggests a most suitable theory of learning which can be leveraged to promote mobile learning in order to promote access of education in the developing nations.

The second chapter on *Promotion of Tourism Using Social Media* highlights effective social media practices across the tourism sector. As customer preferences evolve and more and more individuals find travelling an enjoyable activity, social media has found a very significant application in the tourism sector. This chapter uses examples from India, to highlight how diverse social media platforms are contributing effectively, to the revenue generated by the tourism sector. The chapter details the evolving backdrop of the tourism sector and traces the emergent role of social media in the growth of this sector. The chapter also proceeds to explain how travel research, customer service levels, social sharing, travel agencies and loyalty programs, now constitute the tourism fabric across the globe. After listing the needs of a typical traveller, the chapter discusses how ability of social media content to generate consumer engagement, popularity and characteristics of social media content and credibility of information on the social platforms are the three important pillars of social media for the tourism industry and delineates the various social media platforms, tools and communities relevant to the travel and tourism industry.

The third chapter on *A Content Marketing Framework to Analyze Customer Engagement on Social Media* focuses on the various dimensions of social media content that aid the process of consumer engagement. It details how the content types-Image, Link and Videos impact the likes, comments and shares on social media, which are indicative of level of consumer engagement. The chapter also traces how time frame of content postage and message interactivity are two key players which govern the level of consumer engagement and social media. Post appeal, length of content title, and the day of the week when the content has been posted further, have a distinct impact on the level of consumer engagement. By evaluating each of these variables, organisations which are making use of social media for consumer engagement, can create monthly social media calendars and plan their social media activity accordingly. Additionally, by making use of the right social media vehicles, organizations can derive greater productivity from their social media resources and efforts. A structured, well defined approach to content marketing can help organizations make optimal usage of their social media presence. Successful consumer engagement is the precursor to long term consumer brand relationships.

The fourth chapter on *A Literature Review of Social Media for Marketing: Social Media Use in B2C and B2B Markets* focuses on the changes in the ways B2B and B2C marketers communicate with the consumers, and create content for consumption by organizational consumers and employees and positively impact brand awareness, brand image, sales and consumer brand relationships. As per latest data received form the Content Marketing Institute(CMI, 2018), it is observed that over 92% of marketers in the B2B segment prefer to use social network sites and content in place of traditional marketing methods to connect with all their stakeholders including customers, vendors, employees, suppliers etc., to develop synergistic relationships based on trust.

The fifth chapter on *How do Firm and User Generated Contents Benefit Firms and Affect Consumers-A Literature Review*, focuses on how the era of virtualization and consumer generated content has made it imperative for organizations to connect with prospective consumers in online environments. Social media campaigns by brands provide additional touch points for organizations to share their perspectives and thoughts with consumers. Tangible on intangible stimulus from these touch points aids in the formulation if brand-consumer relationships and triggers consumer engagement. Well planned content marketing activities use consumer pull techniques and enhance brand visibility. In a subtle fashion, these brands communicate the brand identity to the consumer. Corporate social responsibility endeavors generate goodwill and create a humane impression of the brand. Storytelling techniques propagate brand personality and strengthen brand image. This chapter reveals the benefits of consumer generated as well as firm generated content and crafts a framework which will be useful for corporate practitioners.

The sixth chapter on *Social Media and E-commerce: a Study on Motivations for Sharing Content From E-commerce Websites* focuses on identifying user motivations for sharing product specific information on diverse social media channels. This subject is quiet relevant to organizations in the e-commerce sector to enhance content shareability. As per this chapter, intrinsic motivation is more significant in this context, specially as compared to extrinsic motivation prompted by external rewards. It is the individual's inner mind that prompts him to indulge in these activities. Dissatisfaction with an organization or brand as well as reciprocity and self-interest were key drivers of individual motivation to indulge in these activities. Additionally, the chapter proceeds to discuss how an aesthetic website design can have a positive impact on the consumer perceptions and subsequent actions. It also states that sometimes people are only interested in sharing experiences and the associated websites get shared and subsequently garner the desired visibility.

The seventh chapter on *Empowering the Economic Impact of Virtual Communities: Managing Trust in the Sharing Economy* focuses on the emergence of online communities as valuable sources of communication and trustworthy environments for idea sharing and interaction with peers. Trustworthiness in collaborative environments is a precursor to product consumption, as uncertainties are reduced through a conscious effort by products and brands. As brands touch base with consumers across their experiences, emotions and interests, cliques develop and this human need to exchange thoughts, goods and services, has given birth to this era of a digital economy. Social networks are increasing the degree of transparency available to individuals in relationships and transactions. The chapter examines trust issues in the context of a sharing economy and proceeds to explain the associated economic effects. The chapter further traces the relationship between culture and trust as well as the concepts of risk and reliability. It is vital to evaluate the level of risk taking ability as well as risk aversion of individuals and consumers, to understand the corresponding impact of the same in a sharing economy. Reliability has further given birth to the trend of peer to peer trade which utilizes the benefits of collaborative consumption which leads to the development of new perspectives about the sharing economy.

The eighth chapter on *Social Media: Concept, Role, Categories, Trends, Artificial Intelligence and the Impact on Youth and Careers* traces the advancement of social media and the resulting career related opportunities available to the youth today. A proper channelization of the domain by academia can result in providing the youth with the relevant qualifications for appropriate jobs. Social media as a field can be taught in the Media and Journalism domains, the Humanities arena, the Management world as well as Graduate and Undergraduate programs in science and technology. This chapter details the various facets of social media and links them with the various roles available to the youth along with the job descriptions and eligibility requirements.

The ninth chapter on *Social Media Usage in the online Consumer Decision Process and Buying Behaviour* details a research study carried out in three universities in Ghana which revealed that social media activity of young consumers needs to be studied in detail as this can significantly predict consumer behavior. The findings suggest that social media presents a huge opportunity for business and marketers and young people are more likely to use social media for business and marketing, hence businesses should redirect their efforts towards these digital channels.

The tenth chapter on *Methods of Published Articles on Digital Economy: Analysis and Reflections on Databases Scopus and Web of Science*, focuses on digitization and subsequent impact on the availability of information to researchers, scholars and practitioners. The chapter focuses on the multidisciplinary databases of Scopus and Web of Science and elucidates how their superior quality delivers rigorous insights and detailed coverage empowers research performance. The chapter proceeds to explain how this drives organizations, academicians, researchers and individuals to arrive at better decisions.

The eleventh chapter on *Social Network Sites (SNS) and Their Irrepressible Popularity: Can They Really Cause an Addiction?* traces the evolution of social media and proceeds to generate a classification of social media tools into communication, collaboration and multimedia tools. The chapter commences with the argument that the primary cause for the popularity of social media is its regular updation, multiple utility and open source genre. The authors cite the work of Mayfield to outline the five common characteristics of social media platforms viz. participation, openness, conversation, community and connectedness. The chapter proceeds to delve deeper into issues pertaining to self-representation and explores the aspects of over indulgence in this domain. The chapter reiterates the need to retain an optimum balance between adoption of social media for personal or business purposes and over indulgence in the medium to prevent addiction to the same. The concerns towards addiction stem from the emergence of several instances where over use or over participation in the medium has caused obsession with the same, resulting in an over dependence on the virtual world.

Exchange of dialogue and ideas aids in the dissemination of knowledge. The uniqueness of this book lies in the diversity of the individuals who have participated in the formulation of the chapters of the book. A vast geographical expanse, leading to disparate ideas and a multitude of different viewpoints makes this a distinctive resource. This book will serve as a premier reference resource and will be useful to practitioners, academicians and research professionals.

The editors will specifically like to thank each and every member of the Editorial Review Board of the book. A well-defined editorial process of proposal solicitation and selection and a rigorous peer review process have helped the editors in ensuring that only quality, original content finds its way into the book. A mélange of disparate view points have given this book a freshness of ideas which are of value to a varied set of researchers, academicians and corporate practitioners. The editors would also like to thank all the chapter authors as well as all other individuals who have participated in the process of development of this reference resource. Additionally, the editors would like to thank Prof. Deepak Khazanchi, Associate Dean, College of IS&T, University of Omaha, Nebraska, USA, for contributing a very strong foreword for the book.

Chapter 1
An Evaluative Framework for the Most Suitable Theory of Mobile Learning

Niti Mittal
Jaypee Institute of Information Technology, India

Monica Chaudhary
https://orcid.org/0000-0002-8344-1447
S. P. Jain School of Global Management, Sydney, Australia

Shirin Alavi
https://orcid.org/0000-0001-8743-6701
Jaypee Institute of Information Technology, India

ABSTRACT

The focus of ICT in education has shifted from e-learning to mobile learning as mobile devices offer many technological and pedagogical affordances coupled with their affordability. It is imperative to say their potential can be leveraged efficiently in teaching-learning communities in developing countries in general and South-Asian countries in particular. To ensure its successful implementation a theory of mobile learning is required. This chapter draws an evaluative framework of existing theories of learning and proposes the most suitable theory of learning which can be leveraged to promote mobile learning to promote access of education in the developing nations.

DOI: 10.4018/978-1-7998-2185-4.ch001

INTRODUCTION

Mobile learning is a buzzword in technology-enhanced learning domain. It is an emerging trend in schools and in higher education not only in the developed nations but developing nations as well. In the past decade the focus of ICT in education has shifted from e-learning to mobile learning or m-learning. This shift can be attributed to high cost of computers and laptops and unprecedented affordances of mobile technologies in terms of technology and cost. The report prepared by Deloitte for GSMA to assess the impact of mobile telephony on economic growth of developing nations suggests that mobile devices are the best or the only option for internet in the developing nations (Deloitte/GSMA Report, 2012). With the naissance of Web 2.0 the way knowledge is received and shared has gone an unprecedented change.

Mobile learning supports problem-based learning, personalized learning, context-based and situated learning etc. The literature supports the capacity of mobile learning to augment traditional learning methods. Despite this, mobile learning lags behind in its full-scale implementation. This can be attributed to the fact that mobile learning is considered only as a tool for delivering education. But mobile learning is not a tool but 'a method of teaching'. Therefore, we need a theory of mobile learning to pave way for its successful implementation and realization of its potentialities in the world especially in developing nations where GDP and per capita income is low. What, when, where and how of learning have intrigued mankind since the beginning and many theories of learning have been advanced over the last 2500 years since Confucius, but almost all have been predicated on the assumption that learning occurs in a school classroom under the supervision of a teacher. But none of the theories that have been proposed throw a direct light on the mobility of the learner, which is the necessary requirement of new age learners. Meeker (2014) states that mobile internet traffic already constitutes more than twenty five percent of global traffic. In the developed world people already own one or more smart devices like mobile phones and tablets and they are using their mobile phones in preference over other devices to access information, build knowledge and share understanding.

When we talk of mobile learning what exactly we are talking about? Is it the learner who is mobile or is it the technology which is mobile? Since books and laptops being portable can be taken along with the learner. Do these constitute mobile learning? Puentedura (Pegrum, 2014a) has elaborated over this anomaly in a concise manner. He has stated that "a useful rule of thumb for differentiating portable from truly mobile devices is that the former are typically used at point A, powered down and moved, then opened up at point B, while the latter are used at point A, point B and everywhere in between without stopping." This differentiation highlights 'always on' characteristics of mobile devices. Thus, mobile devices are not only portable but are also light weight which makes them easier to carry even at marketplaces, they are ubiquitous because of the low cost as compared to desktops and laptops. They confer flexibility to the learners as they are wireless and they have the largest percentage of ownership both in the developed and developing countries. Mobile devices include simple mobile phones, smartphones, PDAs, Mp3 players, iPods, iPads, e-book readers, tablets and mini pads as well as emerging devices like fitness bands, smart watches, smart glasses. As the number of mobile device owners is rising both in the developed and developing nations, institutes can initiate a BYOD (Bring Your Own Device) concept. BYOD initiative will reduce the hardware cost of the institutes and maximizes the affordances of mobile devices because many individuals upgrade their devices more often than the institutions do (Pegrum, 2014b). Needless to say their potential can be leveraged efficiently in teaching-learning communities in developing countries in general and South-Asian countries in particular. In India, in order to popularize mobile learning Akash tablets have been given to college students and the government has launched digital India campaign in order to bridge urban rural divide. Add a final comment to conclude the para.

Having an effective theory to guide mobile learning practices in formal education will enable teachers in curriculum development and its implementation. This chapter is an attempt to provide a framework for elucidating the most suitable theory of mobile learning.

BACKGROUND

Research Goals

There is an upsurge in the use of educational technology in general and mobile learning in particular in formal educational setting. Online learning, flipped classrooms, blended learning, hybrid learning are some of the common terms which are being used while integrating technologies in the classroom. This blending of technology has not only created new learning environment but has also created opportunity for the teachers to re-evaluate the instructional model and the learning theories they use in content-delivery and teaching the students. The mere usage of mobile technology to deliver the content does not constitute mobile learning. Any new method of teaching if grounded in theory of learning will bring in the desired results. Thus, the critical analysis of the prevalent learning theories with respect to their integration in mobile learning is crucial. Through this paper we sought to determine the most suitable learning theory in which to ground the mobile learning. This has been achieved systematically by first identifying the parameters of mobile learning through literature review and then analyzing the identified parameters in the light of learning theories. The research questions which have guides this research are as follows:

1. To identify the unique features of mobile learning which are used in classroom teaching and are postulated as crucial for new-age learners.
2. To identify the learning theory that suits best and caters to the unique features of mobile learning?

Rationale of the Study

Sharples et al. (2005a) postulated that almost all the theories proposed since the time of Confucius assume that learning takes place inside the four walls of classroom mediated by the teacher. But the educational landscape has metamorphosed since then. The new age learning has shifted from teacher-centered, authoritative and physical-space bound learning to student-centered, learner-autonomous and anytime anywhere learning paradigm. Mobile learning transcends the physical limitations of time and space. It caters to personalized, ubiquitous, independent and work-based learning. It has the capacity to meet the demands of new age learners. In order for mobile learning to become the future of formal learning, the practice must be rooted in theory. This article draws on various existing theories of learning and examines which theory could be best used for mobile learning principles. We need a theory for mobile learning because mobile learning offers unique features and is positioned separately from the traditional teaching practices. The theory to be of value must account for contemporary practices (Sharples et al., 2005b). In the light of above discussion we have taken major learning paradigms behaviorism; cognitivism; constructivism and connectivism to analyze the best suited theory of mobile learning.

REVIEW OF LITERATURE

What is Learning?

Learning is the most important concept in the fields of psychology and Education. Each individual is born with native tendencies which determine his responses towards the environment. He is being constantly acted upon by the environment and he responds towards it which creates an action-reaction- behavior. And all such action- reaction- behavior involves changes and modifications in the individual as well as some changes in the environment. This change or modification in the behavior of the individual is called learning. What man learns is the function of his innate nature and the environment in which he lives. It is the key process in human behavior. It is a continuous process. It may not be directly observable but it is universal and permanent change. The simplest and the most comprehensive definition of learning is "the change in behavior". Learning is inevitable, essential and ubiquitous. Alexander et al. (2009a) have compared learning to the river system and assert that it is insufficient to proffer a working definition of learning but essential to map out the criteria dimensions of learning and a description of the complex interactions among the dimensions that form the basis of a learning system. They have highlighted nine dimensions of learning: learning is change; learning is inevitable, essential, and ubiquitous; learning can be resisted; learning may be disadvantageous; learning can be tacit and incidental as well as conscious and intentional; learning is framed by our humanness; learning refers to both a process and a product; learning is different at different points in time and it is interactional. Based on the above dimensions, they defined learning as:

a multidimensional process that results in a relatively enduring change in a person or persons, and consequently how that person or persons will perceive the world and reciprocally respond to its affordances physically, psychologically, and socially. The process of learning has as its foundation the systemic, dynamic, and interactive relation between the nature of the learner and the object of the learning as ecologically situated in a given time and place as well as over time.

What Differentiates Mobile Learning from Learning?

Sharples et al. (2005c) have drawn a line between learning and mobile learning, According to them in mobile learning "It is the learner that is mobile, rather than the technology; Learning is interwoven with other activities as part of everyday life; Learning can generate as well as satisfy goals; The control and management of learning can be distributed; Context is constructed by learners through interaction; Mobile learning can both complement and conflict with formal education; Mobile learning raises deep ethical issues of privacy and ownership". It is now evident that while traditional learning is teacher-directed, and product-oriented, the mobile learning is student-centered as well as process-oriented. In mobile learning the focus is on active engagement of students and how they come to acquire the knowledge. Thus, mobile learning focuses on mobility of not only the devices but of the learner as well as learning experiences. Pegrum (2014b) has defined three levels of mobility, which are as follows:

1st Level

Only the Devices are Mobile: The teacher may allow the students to use tablet in the classroom which can be taken to another classroom (mobility of the device). He will ask the student to solve the quiz given in the educational app. But in this case the student is sitting at his desk. The teacher is only providing the information.

Although some online networking is possible, the learner and his learning experiences are not mobile. This is just information transmission to the students or behavioristic approach of teaching.

2nd Level

The Devices and the Learners are Mobile: In the second case the same teacher may ask his students to browse more information online related to the topic and share that information with his peers while moving with their tablets in the classroom. Here the learner as well as the device is mobile but not the learning experience because the there is space constraint (inside the classroom). This approach of learning is more constructivist in nature because it fosters interaction and collaboration.

3rd Level

The Devices, the Learners and the Learning Experience are Mobile: Now the teacher may ask the students to move freely to visit the market places, museums and see the buildings, photograph them, annotate the pictures with building's name and information about them and share the pictures online before commenting on their peers' photos. Here the learning experiences are also mobile because the constraint of space has been removed. Their construction of learning is "situated and embodied". This approach of learning is the most sophisticated and the most suitable method of learning as the constraint of time and place has diminished (Pegrum, 2014c). Mobile learning (ML) is characterized by the mobility at all the three levels. It can be depicted as given in the Figure 1.

Figure 1. Mobile learning: learner, devices and learning experiences all are mobile

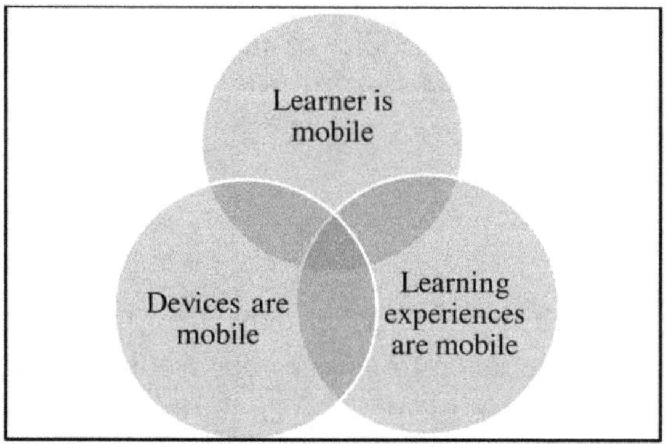

Learning Theories

Various theories of learning have been advanced to explain the nature of learning process add reference. The theories can be broadly grouped under three broad categories: Behaviorism, Cognitivism and Constructivism. With the advancement of digital technology in education system a new theory of learning has been proposed for new-age learners by George Siemens in the year 2005. It is called connectivism (Siemens, 2005). Behaviorism, cognitivism, and constructivism theories are most often utilized in the creation of instructional environments. These theories, however, were developed in a time when learning was not impacted through technology. Over the last twenty years, technology has reorganized how we live, how we communicate, and how we learn. Learning needs and theories that describe learning principles and processes should be reflective of underlying social environments. Vaill (1996) emphasizes that "learning must be a way of being – an ongoing set of attitudes and actions by individuals and groups that they employ to try to keep abreast of the surprising, novel, messy, obtrusive, recurring events."

Behaviorism

Skinner (1968) is the leading theorist of behaviorist school of learning. According to him learning is function of change in the explicit behavior which occurs as result of the human being's response towards environmental stimuli. The driving force for the behavior and development is external and does not originate inside the human being. Behaviorism is actually a stimulus-response theory of learning and behavioristic school of thought considers knowledge as arising from stimulus-response repertoire where any learning that takes place occurs outside the individual and the cognitive function of an individual does not play any role. Reinforcement plays a crucial role in learning. There are two types of reinforcement- positive and negative. Skinner (1968) defined positive reinforcement as creating 'situations which a person likes' and negative reinforcement as 'removing any situation he doesn't like'. Bullock (1982) described main tenets of behaviorism which are: *objectivism* (that is, human behavior is analyzed in terms of observable external events); *environmentalism* (environment plays a significant role in determining human behavior); and *reinforcement* (where the consequences of our actions determine the subsequent behaviors).The main argument raised against behaviorism was that it ignores the cognitive and innate abilities of the learner and recognizes the external stimuli as the driving force of learning. Behaviorism also ignores the socio-cultural aspect like communication in the classroom, project work, group work etc. which must be incorporated in it (Hassan, 2011). According to Keskin & Metcalf (2011) the focus of behaviorist theory in mobile learning is information and content delivery by text messages;

language learning listening and speaking practice through test and quiz tool and feedback through Mobile Response System.

Cognitivism

Cognitivism gained momentum in the late 1950s as a counter attack towards behaviorism, which relied upon overt or observable behavior as the determinant of human learning. The cognitivists emphasized the role of internal mental processes and how mind works during the process of learning. There was increased concern towards cognitive processes such as thinking, problem solving, language, concept formation and information processing. Cognitive theories focus on students' learning process that is; how the information is received, organized, stored, and retrieved by the mind. "Learning is concerned not so much with what learners do but with what they know and how they come to acquire it"(Jonassen, 1991). The learner is viewed as an active participant in the learning process. Piaget (year) believed that there are four propellants of mental development. Each one of them is important because it is the interaction of these factors that result in cognitive development. The first factor is *maturation* of nervous system and endocrine system which provide physical capability. Second, *experience* as experienced by the learner. Third, *social interaction* and the fourth is internal self-regulatory mechanism of the learner (Webb, 1980). Cognitivism was propagated as a strong attack against the objectivism as proposed by behavioristic school of thought. Cognitivism holds the view that knowledge is subjective i.e. the learner constructs knowledge based on his own experiences.

Constructivism

Constructivism is an umbrella term used to cover the ideas of Piaget, Vygotsky, Bruner, and Bandura regarding how people learn. It is the confluence of cognitivism and social aspects of learning. The constructivists emphasize the role of conversation in learning apart from knowing how the mind works or processes the information. Constructivist theories propose that individuals construct knowledge actively and knowing is an adaptive process. According to constructivists, people learn through their subjective experiences. The students build new knowledge upon the existing schema or past experiences which they bring to the classroom. Thus, according to the proponents of constructivism, knowledge is an accumulative process and children are the active participants in the construction of knowledge. Behavior and cognitive processes are no longer the core constructs through which learning can be explained. The factors like time, situatedness, reciprocity between individuals and cultural practices have been envisaged as other important factors by the researchers. There are many different types of constructivism like cognitive, critical, radical, and social.

But the underlying feature of all the theories is that the learners, 'construct their own knowledge' (Sener, 1997; Boghossian, 2006). The advent of web 2.0 technologies and the ever increasing share of space that the students now hold in virtual learning environment, self-advocates the reinterpretation of constructivism as a new- age learning theory for 21st century learners. The idea of 'communication' as a key factor in the construction of knowledge is being supported by mobile technologies. We can say that mobile learning with all the potentialities for social interaction and conversation using social networking sites, mailing features, collaborative tools etc. can be a harbinger or reviver of constructivism in education. Lock and Johnson (2018) also reiterated the need of online music learning design to be grounded in social constructivist framework to guide how technology can be used for best outcomes.

Connectivism

Connectivism can be aptly described as the learning theory for the digital age. In the advancing technology era the knowledge is being constantly generated and is stored in the cyber space. The learner can derive this knowledge through specialized connections within a community. The learner creates their own social networks which have the potential to create unexpected outcomes. The knowledge acquisition depends on the learner's ability to integrate with his or her own learning environment. This theory is based on chaos theory or complexity zone which entails "finding meaning or making sense out of a random and unpredictable set of variables" (Marais, 2010). Connectivism can be used to create and evaluate learning that happens via social networking sites and online communities (Siemens, 2004; Downes, 2007a). The main underlying assumption in this theory is that knowledge is distributed and "can reside outside of ourselves" (Siemens, 2005, p. 8). Downes (2007b) asserts that "knowledge is distributed across a network of connections, and therefore learning consists of the ability to construct and traverse those networks". Learning within the connectivist framework consists of both interaction and cognitive engagement. The interaction takes place between other humans and network sources which result in building connections and network formation (Wang et al., 2014). Collaboration is the key word in connectivist paradigm. The learners collaborate through group activities and the members help each other in realizing their goals. Thus, knowledge is acquired through interactions (Garcia & Ferreira, 2014). Siemens (2004) outlines eight principles of connectivism:

- Learning and knowledge rest in a diversity of opinions.
- Learning is a process of connecting specialized nodes or information sources.
- Learning may reside in non-human appliances.
- Capacity to know more is more critical than what is currently known.

- Nurturing and maintaining connections is needed to facilitate continual learning.
- Ability to see connections between fields, ideas, and concepts is a core skill.
- Currency (accurate, up-to-date knowledge) is the intent of all connectivist learning activities.
- Decision-making is in itself a learning process.

Connectivism assumes that the knowledge resides in the networks. Therefore, technology plays an important role in connectivist learning. Blogs, wikis, discussion forums, social networks exemplify connectivism paradigm. The four components of connectivism are social interaction, collaborative activity, participation and the distinguishing factor 'networking'. Thus, there is one more aspect to connectivism and that is non-human resource: networking. Technology plays an important role in assisting the learner to construct knowledge (Ng'ambi, 2013). Greenhow (2009) stated that "Knowledge is decentralized, accessible and co-constructed among a broad base of users" through discussion and participation in the Web 2.0 environment.

Mobile Learning in South Asian Countries

The international development community emphasizes the role of education in improving socio-economic development in South Asia. The tertiary education in South Asian countries faces the issue of students' enrolment. The inequalities in education pose barriers in developing world and the how to deliver cost-effective and quality education remains the problem (Valk et al., 2010a). The researchers' community considers mobile phones as a viable solution to tackle the problem of unequal access of education. Mobile phones are at the forefront of ICT solutions for education due to their low cost, increased functional capabilities, portability and enhanced data transfer capabilities. Valk et al. (2010b) support mobile devices as a tool for advancing education in developing countries. They build their argument on the premises that mobile phones are the most prominent ICT tools and the penetration rate of these devices is rising. Samrajiva and Zainudeen (2008) posit that mobile phone ownership is more prominent in lower socio-economic segment of the society. In addition, mobile phones require less sophisticated physical infrastructure like roads and wires as they work on radio spectrum. Therefore they have been termed as 'leapfrogger' by the Economist (2008). Many developing countries are investing in installation of mobile phone networks instead of fixed telephone infrastructure (Motlik, 2008; Traxler & Dearden, 2005). Thus, mobile learning can prove to be a potential tool for expansion of education in developing countries. Mobile learning projects have been undertaken in many developing countries of Europe, Asia Pacific and North America. But the number of projects is fewer in number in Asia Pacific region. Valk et al. (2010c) conducted case studies on six mobile learning projects in Philippines, Mongolia, Bangladesh, Thailand and India. They conducted case studies on two mobile learning projects in Bangladesh (Islam et. al, 2005; Pouezevara & Khan 2007). The former project was initiated with the aim of determining how mobile phones can be used to introduce the concept of *interactivity* in distance education model. It simulated typical distance education programme over television network with an additional advantage of interaction between the course instructor and the learner. The interaction was mediated via SMS. This experimental study revealed that mobile learning is at least as effective as face-to –face learning and thus mobile phones can be used to tackle the problem of access to education in Bangladesh. In the case study of the project "Improving Literacy in Rural India: Cellphone Games in an After School Program" carried out by Kam et al. in 2009. The authors (Valk et al., 2010) findings contradict the potential benefits of mobile learning but they assert that these finding imply that there is need to redesign the software used to teach the students. The project "Learning Communities Enabled by Mobile Technology: A Case Study of School-Based, In-Service Secondary Teacher Training in Rural Bangladesh" aimed to determine whether mobile phone-supported distance education could serve as an effective modality for in-service secondary teacher training in Bangladesh. The findings of this project depicted favorable results with respect to the use of mobile phones as it proves to be less costly and flexible. The proponents of new learning or learning for new age learners assert that mobile learning is beneficial for new age learners because it caters to individual and personalized learning. It caters to diverse learner background as the learner can optimize learning according to his needs and time. He can access information and choose to build on his current understanding until he gains mastery over the concept. Sharples (2005d) further highlights its relevance by stating that mobile learning helps in 'impromptu' learning contexts. The learning can take place 'anytime' 'anywhere'. This aspect is particularly useful for those learners who have to juggle between the traditional classrooms and job responsibilities. The portable and connected nature of these devices renders them most suitable option for advancing education in South Asian countries. Their ability to support lifelong learning also increases their value. Sharples (2007) claims that mobile learning exerts democratizing effect because it is a learner-centered strategy as the learner can choose when and where to access information and build his knowledge rather than being mere recipient of information passed by the teacher. The demand for mass education and globalization combined with technological changes has far reaching implications for higher education.

Student Online Communities for Learning

According to Wenger et al. (2002) a Community of Practice is 'a group of people who interact, learn together, build relationships, and in the process develop a sense of belonging and mutual commitment'. The three key dimensions of CoP are mutual engagement, joint enterprise, and shared repertoire (Wenger, 1998). These dimensions help to develop a shared learning experience with a rich array of resources including meaningful stories, tools, and possible ideas or solutions for dealing with problems. Higher education system views community as essential to support collaborative learning and promote higher learning skills (Garrison & Hanuka, 2004). The concept of online communities was given by Lave & Wenger in 1999. The community can be purely online, face-to-face or blended community. Wenger emphasized social aspect of education. According to him the value of education lies in social participation and active involvement in community. Communication, Collaboration and Co-creation are the three Cs which characterize learning communities. The communities can be Professional learning communities (PLCs), Students Learning Communities (SLCs) or Communities of Practice (CoP). With the emergence of new internet technologies, there has been a change in a way the users communicate with each other and share information. It has resulted in a scope for new strategies for teaching and learning focusing on the "online *networked learning tools* to create better, more functional learning communities" (Cheng, 2013a). Salmon (2001) wrote, "Learning is built around learning communities & interaction, extending access beyond the bounds of time and space, but offering the promise of efficiency and widening access. Think of individuals as nodes on a network!" Learning communities thrive on networked learning model, which is again closely associated with connectivism theory (Cheng, 2013b) that focuses mainly connection-building between the learners so that they can learn and collaborate efficiently. The role of the teacher in these virtual communities is that of a facilitator. The students pose problem and the ensuing discussion that flows around the topic of interest helps in solving the problem through collaborative efforts of community members.

Research Methodology

Firstly, the unique parameters of mobile learning (ML) were identified through detailed review of literature. We examined twenty peer-reviewed Scopus-indexed research articles about mobile learning and its distinguishing features. Through careful investigation we distilled twenty salient features and advantages which the authors have stated to be chief characteristics of mobile learning environment. These features of mobile learning have been termed as technological and pedagogical affordances by the researchers. We have clubbed these affordances together and named them parameters of mobile learning (exhibited in Table 1). The next phase of the research involved critical examination of the learning theories and their principles with respect to these ML parameters. While making detailed analysis of the learning theories the following framework was kept in mind:

- The epistemological basis of the learning theories.
- The principles of the learning theories.
- The ways in which these theories support mobile learning.

After thorough investigation of principles of theories of learning they were analyzed with respect to the parameters whether the particular theory supports the parameter. The mark 'X' has been put in the column to show the particular theory supports the parameter. The final evaluation grid is exhibited below (Table 1).

SOLUTIONS AND RECOMMENDATIONS

The evaluation grid (Table 1) shows that behaviorism theory of learning supports three features, Cognitivism theory of learning supports four, constructivism supports eighteen and connectivism theory of learning supports all the twenty parameters of mobile learning. Upon evaluation it is revealed that the unique features of connectivism are its ability to construct and traverse the networks of knowledge, which are diverse and autonomous and integrating informal learning with formal education. Diversity within a network helps in gaining different perspectives and different viewpoints of the members which helps in production of new knowledge. The open structures of these networks facilitate easy movement from one network of learning to other. This presents knowledge in multiple dimensions and the learner constructs the knowledge by assessing the whole situation. Thus connectivism aids in holistic knowledge development. The learning theory of connectivism and mobile learning complement each other as mobile technologies allow 24X7 Wi-Fi connectivity which facilitate knowledge distribution and sharing over networks.

The essence of mobile learning lies in connectivity with the peers, teachers and the content. Therefore, we propose that teachers must understand the underlying principle of connectivism and integrate its principles in the instructional design. In order to understand the essence of connectivism, the teachers should build their knowledge starting from the theory of behaviorism because the learning theories are not completely isolated from each other but are an improvement over their predecessors. While behaviorism can be applied in achieving lower level teaching objectives of knowledge and awareness, the connectivist theory will help in attaining mastery learning of the concept. The traditional teaching-learning methods are largely

Table 1. The final evaluation grid

S. NO.	Parameters of Mobile Learning	Sources	Behaviorism	Cognitivism	Constructivism	Connectivism
1.	Flexibility Of Learning	Ally & Prieto-Blázquez (2014); Kearney et al. (2012)			X	X
2.	User Friendliness Of The Learning Strategy	Huang et al. (2012)			X	X
3.	Learner Control Of The Learning Process	Nortcliffe & Middleton (2010)			X	X
4.	Enhancing Learner Motivation For Learning	Hwang & Pu (2014)	X	X	X	X
5.	Provides Authentic Learning Context (Inside Or Outside The Classroom)	Hwang et al. (2011)			X	X
6.	Promotes Flexible And In-Depth Thinking	Barak & Levenberg (2016); Hwang et al. (2011)		X	X	X
7.	Share Resources	FernáNdez-LóPez et al. (2013)			X	X
8.	Engage In Co-Construction Of Knowledge	Lin et al. (2013); Lan et al. (2012)			X	X
9.	Find And Build Groups And Communities Of Practice	Barker et al. (2005)			X	X
10.	Integrating Informal Learning With Formal Education	Wong & Looi (2011)				X
11.	Supports Activity-Oriented Learning	Kurti et al. (2008)			X	X

continued on following page

Table 1. Continued

S. NO.	Parameters of Mobile Learning	Sources	Behaviorism	Cognitivism	Constructivism	Connectivism
12.	Ubiquitous access to learning resources owing to Wi-Fi connectivity	Wong (2012); Dahlstrom et al. (2012)			X	X
13.	Social Interactivity To Promote Learning	Klopfer et al. (2002); Nouri & Pargman (2016)			X	X
14.	Context-Sensitive Learning	·Klopfer et al. (2002); Benamar et al. (2015); Nouri & Pargman (2016)			X	X
15.	Ability to construct and traverse the networks of knowledge which are diverse, autonomous and have open structure	Downes (2008)				X
16.	Multi-Modal (Audio, Visual, Text) Communication With Peers, Teachers And Experts	Kearney et al. (2012)			X	X
17.	Accessing New Information By Students	Traxler (2007)			X	X
18.	Motivating Students' Engagement	Nortcliffe (2010); Nouri & Pargman (2016)	X	X	X	X
19.	Formative Assessment And Provision Of Feedback	Nouri & Pargman (2016)	X	X	X	X

continued on following page

Table 1. Continued

S. NO.	Parameters of Mobile Learning	Sources	Behaviorism	Cognitivism	Constructivism	Connectivism
20.	Foster Students' Creativity And Collaboration	Nouri et al. (2011); Jeong & Hmelo-Silver (2016)			X	X
	Total no. of parameters supported		3	4	18	20

guided by behavioristic principles and therefore cannot fulfill the requirements of new-age, 'always-on' learners. In the present digital era, to keep pace with evolving learning goals behavioristic learning theory has to be supported with cognitivism theory which in turn has to be supplemented with constructivism and connectivism.

In their article in Wikibook the authors, Caron & Brennaman (2009) state that as the new technologies continue to evolve, the previously applied learning theories will either adapt themselves to the new paradigm or a new theory will be born and this cycle of evolution will continue. The choice of the learning theory depends upon the instructional objectives set out by the teacher at the beginning of the teaching session. And how to incorporate the learning theory is the decision of the teacher. There are six levels of cognitive domain (Bloom, 1956) the lowest level is *Knowledge* followed by *Comprehension, Application, Analysis, Synthesis* and the highest level is *Evaluation* level (see Figure 2). These levels are accumulative in nature i.e., knowledge is a prerequisite for comprehension, which is prerequisite for application level objective and so on. Different learning theories can be applied to achieve different learning objectives (see Figure 2). There appears to be a theoretical shift from behaviorism to constructivism because of increased connectivity and new platforms (like social networking sites, online communities of practice and learning, collaboration tools) that support constructivism. This does not lend behaviorism as redundant theory of learning. In fact, as the instructional objectives move from simple (e.g., knowledge) to complex (e.g., evaluation) domain, the theoretical perspective also moves from behaviorism to connectivism paradigm. So we surmise that a blend of learning theories is the mainstay of desired learning outcomes. Behaviorism can be used to achieve lower level cognitive objectives and cognitivism and constructivism can be used to achieve middle and higher level objectives. Connectivism is best suited for new age learning. Connectivist theory helps in sustaining online learning communities. The collaborative nature of mobile learning will help in transcending the boundaries between nations and promote global education.

Figure 2. Increasing level of cognition and learning theories continuum

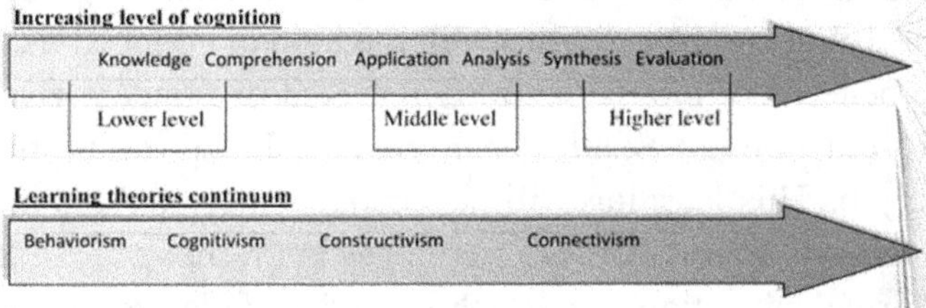

Commented [PUB-361]: Pict Element 2
Commented [PUB-332]: Anchored Object 19
Commented [PUB-203]: Anchored Object 6
Commented [PUB-194]: Anchored Object 5
Commented [PUB-35]: Image 3
Commented [PUB-376]: Pict Element 3
Commented [PUB-217]: Anchored Object 7
Commented [PUB-48]: Image 4
Commented [PUB-389]: Pict Element 4
Commented [PUB-2210]: Anchored Object 8
Commented [PUB-511]: Image 5
Commented [PUB-3912]: Pict Element 5
Commented [PUB-2313]: Anchored Object 9
Commented [PUB-614]: Image 6
Commented [PUB-4015]: Pict Element 6
Commented [PUB-2416]: Anchored Object 10
Commented [PUB-717]: Image 7
Commented [PUB-4118]: Pict Element 7
Commented [PUB-2519]: Anchored Object 11
Commented [PUB-820]: Image 8
Commented [PUB-4221]: Pict Element 8
Commented [PUB-2622]: Anchored Object 12
Commented [PUB-923]: Image 9
Commented [PUB-4324]: Pict Element 9
Commented [PUB-2725]: Anchored Object 13
Commented [PUB-1026]: Image 10
Commented [PUB-4427]: Pict Element 10
Commented [PUB-2828]: Anchored Object 14
Commented [PUB-1129]: Image 11
Commented [PUB-4530]: Pict Element 11
Commented [PUB-2931]: Anchored Object 15
Commented [PUB-1232]: Image 12
Commented [PUB-4633]: Pict Element 12
Commented [PUB-3434]: Anchored Object 20
Commented [PUB-3135]: Anchored Object 17
Commented [PUB-3036]: Anchored Object 16
Commented [PUB-1337]: Image 13
Commented [fig-238]: Figure Caption: text Figure 2:

CONCLUSIONS

Chris Dede (West, 2013) has aptly remarked, "Teaching is like an orchestra. There are many different instruments, and to reach everyone you need to put a symphony of different kinds of pedagogy together. Learning technologies provide a set of instruments teachers can use to achieve that range of instructional strategies. Effective teaching requires that we determine the best theoretical perspectives for the types of learning we deal with and draw on the implications of those perspectives for teaching". Carlile and Jordan (2005) also suggested that there is '*no agreed theory of learning'* only a range of theories to choose from. Therefore it is proposed that connectivism has the potential to meet the demand of new age learners. Connectivism is representation of how the learning paradigms can be incorporated in teaching-learning with an added dimension of networking. The goal of mass education, global education and work-based learning can be achieved with the help of connectivism based mobile learning. The benefits of mobile learning powered by connectivism include check on high drop-out rates in South Asian nations. It will allow the youth to learn while on the job. This learning will not be disconnected from the formal education that they receive in universities or colleges but rather a flexible mode of learning where in formal education leaps the boundaries of classroom and empower the learner to learn at his own pace. His social presence in the classroom is maintained through his involvement in group discussions and regular postings both from the teachers, peers and from his side. This may not only increase learner engagement and motivation to learn but also help in alleviating socio-economic problems that the learner faces.

REFERENCES

Alexander, P., Schallert, D., & Reynolds, R. (2009). What is learning anyway? A topographical perspective considered. *Educational Psychologist, 44*(3), 176–192. doi:10.1080/00461520903029006

Ally, M., & Prieto-Blázquez, J. (2014). What is the future of mobile learning in education? *Revista de Universidad y Sociedad del Conocimiento, 11*(1), 142–151. doi:10.7238/rusc.v11i1.2033

Barak, M., & Levenberg, A. (2016). Flexible thinking in learning: An individual differences measure for learning in technology-enhanced environments. *Computers & Education, 99*, 39–52. doi:10.1016/j.compedu.2016.04.003

Barker, A., Krull, G., & Mallinson, B. (2009). A proposed theoretical model for m-learning adoption in developing countries. In mLearn 2005-4th World conference on mLearning, Cape Town. In M. Pagani (Ed.), *Mobile and wireless systems beyond 3G: Managing new business opportunities*. Hershey, PA: IGI Global.

Benamar, A., Belkhatir, N., & Bendimerad, F. (2013). Adaptive and context-aware scenarios for pervasive technology-enhanced learning system. *Int. Arab J. e-Technol., 3*(1), pp. 58-67.

Boghossian, P. (2006). Behaviorism, constructivism, and Socratic pedagogy. *Educational Philosophy and Theory, 38*(6), 713–722. doi:10.1111/j.1469-5812.2006.00226.x

Bullock, D. H. (1982). Behaviorism and NSPI: The erratically applied discipline. *Performance & Instruction*, *21*(3), 4–11. doi:10.1002/pfi.4170210306

Carlile, O., & Jordan, A. 2005. It works in practice but will it work in theory? The theoretical underpinnings of pedagogy. *Emerging issues in the practice of university learning and teaching, 1*, pp. 11-26. Retrieved from http://www.aishe.org/readings/2005-1/

Caron, J., & Brennaman, K. (2009). *Symbiosis: co-evolution of emerging technology, learning theory, and instructional design.* Retrieved from https://sites.google.com/a/boisestate.edu/edtechtheories/caron_brennaman

Cheng, T. L. (2013). Applying networked learning to improve learner interactions: A new paradigm of teaching and learning in ODL. *Asian Association of Open Universities Journal*, *8*(2), 67–85. doi:10.1108/AAOUJ-08-02-2013-B006

Dahlstrom, E., Grunwald, P., de Boor, T., & Vockley, M. (2011). ECAR national study of students and information technology in higher education. *EDUCAUSE Center for Applied Research.* Retrieved from http://www. educause. edu

Downes, S. (2007). What connectivism is [Web log post]. Retrieved from http://halfanhour.blogspot. co.uk/2007/02/what-connectivism-is.html.

Fernández-López, Á., Rodríguez-Fórtiz, M. J., Rodríguez-Almendros, M. L., & Martínez-Segura, M. J. (2013). Mobile learning technology based on iOS devices to support students with special education needs. *Computers & Education*, *61*, 77–90. doi:10.1016/j.compedu.2012.09.014

Garcia, L., & Ferreira, M. J. (2014). The impact of chaos and connectivism in the collaborative/cooperative learning. [RJOPES]. *Research Journal in Organizational Psychology and Educational Studies*, *3*(2), 76.

Garrison, D. R., & Kanuka, H. (2004). Blended learning: Uncovering its transformative potential in higher education. *The Internet and Higher Education*, *7*(2), 95–105. doi:10.1016/j.iheduc.2004.02.001

Hassan, O. A. B. (2011). Learning theories and assessment methodologies – an engineering educational perspective. *European Journal of Engineering Education*, *36*(4), 327–339. doi:10.1080/03043797.2011.591486

http://www.economist.com/node/10650775

http://www.gsma.com/publicpolicy/wp-content/uploads/2012/11/gsma-deloitte-impact-mobile-telephony-economic-growth.pdf

Huang, Y. M., Huang, Y. M., Huang, S. H., & Lin, Y. T. (2012). A ubiquitous English vocabulary learning system: Evidence of active/passive attitudes vs. usefulness/ease-of-use. *Computers & Education*, *58*(1), 273–282. doi:10.1016/j.compedu.2011.08.008

Hwang, G. J., & Wu, P. H. (2014). Applications, impacts, and trends of mobile technology-enhanced learning: A review of 2008–2012 publications in selected SSCI journals. *International Journal of Mobile Learning and Organisation*, *8*(2), 83–95. doi:10.1504/IJMLO.2014.062346

Islam, Y. M., Ashraf, M., Rahman, Z., & Rahman, M. (2005). *Mobile telephone technology as a distance learning tool* (pp. 226–232). ICEIS.

Jeong, H., & Hmelo-Silver, C. E. (2016). Seven affordances of computer-supported collaborative learning: how to support collaborative learning? How can technologies help? *Educational Psychologist*, *51*(2), 247–265. doi:10.1080/00461520.2016.1158654

Jeong, H., & Hmelo-Silver, C. E. (2016). Seven affordances of computer-supported collaborative learning: how to support collaborative learning? How can technologies help? *Educational Psychologist*, *51*(2), 247–265. doi:10.1080/00461520.2016.11 58654

Jonassen, D. H. (1991). Objectivism versus constructivism: Do we need a new philosophical paradigm? *Educational Technology Research and Development*, *39*(3), 5–14. doi:10.1007/BF02296434

Kam, M., Kumar, A., Jain, S., Mathur, A., & Canny, J. (2009, April). Improving literacy in rural India: Cellphone games in an after-school program. In *2009 International Conference on Information and Communication Technologies and Development (ICTD),* (pp. 139-149). IEEE.

Kearney, M., Schuck, S., Burden, K., & Aubusson, P. (2012). Viewing mobile learning from a pedagogical perspective. *Research in Learning Technology*, 20.

Keskin, N. O., & Metcalf, D. (2011). The current perspectives, theories, and practices of mobile learning. *TOJET: The Turkish Online Journal of Educational Technology, 10*(2).

Klopfer, E., Squire, K., & Jenkins, H. (2002). Environmental detectives: PDAs as a window into a virtual simulated world. In *International Workshop on Wireless and Mobile Technologies in Education, 2002. Proceedings. IEEE* (pp. 95-98). IEEE.

Kurti, A., Spikol, D., & Milrad, M. (2008). Bridging outdoors and indoors educational activities in schools with the support of mobile and positioning technologies. *International Journal of Mobile Learning and Organisation*, *2*(2), 166–186. doi:10.1504/IJMLO.2008.019767

Lan, Y. F., Tsai, P. W., Yang, S. H., & Hung, C. L. (2012). Comparing the social knowledge construction behavioral patterns of problem-based online asynchronous discussion in e/m-learning environments. *Computers & Education*, *59*(4), 1122–1135. doi:10.1016/j.compedu.2012.05.004

Lin, T. J., Duh, H. B. L., Li, N., Wang, H. Y., & Tsai, C. C. (2013). An investigation of learners' collaborative knowledge construction performances and behavior patterns in an augmented reality simulation system. *Computers & Education*, *68*, 314–321. doi:10.1016/j.compedu.2013.05.011

Lock, J. V., & Johnson, C. (2018). Playing together: designing online music courses using a social constructivist framework. In Pedagogy development for teaching online music (pp. 183-201). Hershey, PA: IGI Global.

Marais, N. (2010). Connectivism as learning theory: The force behind changed teaching practice in higher education. *Education, Knowledge & Economy*, *4*(3), 173–182.

Meeker, M. (2014). Internet trends 2014–code conference.

Motlik, S. (2008). Mobile learning in developing nations. *The International Review of Research in Open and Distributed Learning*, *9*(2). doi:10.19173/irrodl.v9i2.564

Naismith, L., Lonsdale, P., Vavoula, G., & Sharples, M. (2004). NESTA Futurelab Report 11: Literature review in mobile technologies and learning. Bristol, UK: NESTA Futurelab. Retrieved from http://www.nestafuturelab.org/research/reviews/reviews_11_and12/11_01.htm

Ng'ambi, D. (2013). Effective and ineffective uses of emerging technologies: Towards a transformative pedagogical model. *British Journal of Educational Technology*, *44*(4), 652–661. doi:10.1111/bjet.12053

Nortcliffe, A., & Middleton, A. (2013). The innovative use of personal smart devices by students to support their learning. Increasing student engagement and retention using mobile applications: Smartphones, Skype, and texting technologies, pp. 175-208.

Nouri, J., & Pargman, T. C. (2016, September). When teaching practices meet tablets' affordances. insights on the materiality of learning. In *European Conference on Technology Enhanced Learning* (pp. 179-192). Springer International Publishing. 10.1007/978-3-319-45153-4_14

Pegrum, M. (2014). *Mobile learning: Languages, literacies and cultures* (p. 5). Springer. doi:10.1057/9781137309815

Pouezevara, S. L., & Khan, R. (2007). Learning communities enabled by mobile technology: A case study of school-based, in-service secondary teacher training in rural Bangladesh. *Innovative information and communication technology in education and its potential for reducing poverty in the Asia and Pacific region.*

Salmon, G. (2001). Changing Learning Environments. *Association of Learning Technology (ALT) Conference, 2001.* Retrieved from https://www.alt.ac.uk/search?s=salmon%20changing%20learning%20environ%2Cents

Samarajiva, R., & Zainudeen, A. (2008). *ICT infrastructure in emerging Asia: Policy and regulatory roadblocks.* IDRC.

Sener, J. (1997, March). Constructivism: Asynchronous learning networks. *ALN Magazine, 1*, 1.

Sharples, M. (2007). *Big issues: Report of a workshop by the Kaleidoscope Network of Excellence.* University of Nottingham.

Sharples, M., Taylor, J., & Vavoula, G. (2005, October). Towards a theory of mobile learning. In Proceedings of mLearn (Vol. 1, No. 1, pp. 1-9).

Siemens, G. (2004). *Connectivism. A learning theory for the digital age.* Retrieved from http://www. elearnspace. org/Articles/connectivism. htm

Siemens, G. (2005, Jan. 1). *Connectivism: A learning theory for the digital age. International Journal of Instructional Technology and Distance Learning (ITDL).* Retrieved from http://er.dut.ac.za/bitstream/handle/123456789/69/Siemens_2005_Connectivism_A_learning_theory_for_the_digital_age.pdf?sequence=1

Siemens, G. (2005). Connectivism: A learning theory for the digital age. *International Journal of Instructional Technology and Distance Learning, 2*(1), 3–10.

Skinner, B. F. (1966). *BF Skinner.* Penn State Audio-Visual Services.

Traxler, J. (2007). Defining, discussing and evaluating mobile learning: The moving finger writes and having writ..... *The International Review of Research in Open and Distributed Learning, 8*(2). doi:10.19173/irrodl.v8i2.346

Traxler, J., & Dearden, P. (2005, September). The potential for using SMS to support learning and organisation in sub-Saharan Africa. In *Proceedings of Development Studies Association Conference*, Milton Keynes.

Vaill, P. B. (1996). *Learning as a way of being: Strategies for survival in a world of permanent white water* (Vol. 216, p. 42). Jossey-Bass.

Valk, J. H., Rashid, A. T., & Elder, L. (2010). Using mobile phones to improve educational outcomes: An analysis of evidence from Asia. *The International Review of Research in Open and Distributed Learning, 11*(1), 117–140. doi:10.19173/irrodl.v11i1.794

Wang, Z., Chen, L., & Anderson, T. (2014). A framework for interaction and cognitive engagement in connectivist learning contexts. *The International Review of Research in Open and Distributed Learning, 15*(2). doi:10.19173/irrodl.v15i2.1709

Webb, P. K. (1980). Piaget: Implications for teaching. *Theory into Practice, 19*(2), 93–97. doi:10.1080/00405848009542880

Wenger, E. (1998). *Communities of practice: Learning, meaning, and identity.* Cambridge University Press. doi:10.1017/CBO9780511803932

Wenger, E., McDermott, R. A., & Snyder, W. (2002). *Cultivating communities of practice: A guide to managing knowledge.* Harvard Business Press.

West, D. M. (2013). Mobile learning: Transforming education, engaging students, and improving outcomes. *Brookings Policy Report.*

Wong, L. H. (2012). A learner-centric view of mobile seamless learning. *British Journal of Educational Technology, 43*(1), E19–E23. doi:10.1111/j.1467-8535.2011.01245.x

Wong, L. H., & Looi, C. K. (2011). What seams do we remove in mobile-assisted seamless learning? A critical review of the literature. *Computers & Education, 57*(4), 2364–2381. doi:10.1016/j.compedu.2011.06.007

Zurita, G., & Nussbaum, M. (2004). Computer supported collaborative learning using wirelessly interconnected hand-held computers. *Computers & Education, 42*(3), 289–314. doi:10.1016/j.compedu.2003.08.005

KEY TERMS AND DEFINITIONS

Behaviorism: Behaviorism is actually a stimulus-response theory of learning and behavioristic school of thought considers knowledge as arising from stimulus-response repertoire where any learning that takes place occurs outside the individual and the cognitive function of an individual does not play any role.

Cognitivism: Cognitivism gained momentum in the late 1950s as a counter attack towards behaviorism, which relied upon overt or observable behavior as the determinant of human learning. The cognitivists emphasized the role of internal mental processes and how mind works during the process of learning.

Connectivism: Connectivism can be aptly described as the learning theory for the digital age. In the advancing technology era the knowledge is being constantly generated and is stored in the cyber space. The learner can derive this knowledge through specialized connections within a community

Constructivism: It is the confluence of cognitivism and social aspects of learning. The constructivists emphasize the role of conversation in learning apart from knowing how the mind works or processes the information.

Mobile Learning: Sharples et al. (2005c) have drawn a line between learning and mobile learning, According to them in mobile learning "It is the learner that is mobile, rather than the technology; Learning is interwoven with other activities as part of everyday life; Learning can generate as well as satisfy goals; The control and management of learning can be distributed; Context is constructed by learners through interaction; Mobile learning can both complement and conflict with formal education; Mobile learning raises deep ethical issues of privacy and ownership".

Theories of Learning: Various theories of learning have been advanced to explain the nature of learning process add reference. The theories can be broadly grouped under three broad categories: Behaviorism, Cognitivism and Constructivism.

Chapter 2
Promotion of Tourism Using Social Media

Vandana Ahuja
Amity Business School, Amity University, Noida, India

ABSTRACT

The tourism industry in India represents a booming sector. This is because of the advent of a large number of foreign tourists every year as well as the demographic dividend of India's population, which is increasingly adopting tourism as a lifestyle constituent. Additionally, the revenue generated by this sector makes it very important for India. Studies from the World Travel and Tourism Council show that tourism contributed 9.4% to India's GDP in 2017 and is expected to show a significant growth rate. This chapter traces the changing landscape of the tourism sector and the emergent role of social media, identifies the pillars of social media for the tourism industry and delineates the various social media platforms, tools, and communities relevant to the travel and tourism industry.

INTRODUCTION

While the Ministry of Tourism has a well-designed program for promotion of Tourism, the virtual world is giving considerable impetus to this sector. The widespread reach of social media and concerted efforts by the national and state tourism organisations, private stakeholders in the tourism sector, and travel and tourism communities has made this media a viable instrument for the promotion of tourism globally. Social media is transforming the way travellers search for, and share information, about travel destinations on Facebook, you tube and other SNSs.

DOI: 10.4018/978-1-7998-2185-4.ch002

BACKGROUND

India is popular globally, as a tourism destination, as also for niche avenues like adventure tourism, medical tourism, sports tourism, eco-tourism, rural tourism, cruise tourisms and spiritual tourism etc. Tamil Nadu, Maharashtra and Uttar Pradesh are the most popular states and Delhi, Mumbai, Chennai, Agra and Jaipur are the most popular cities. Compared to the global scenario, India is a reasonably priced destination and is therefore a popular choice amongst global tourists. Further, the good air transport opportunities and adequate infrastructure makes India an attractive destination. In addition to global tourism, India is witnessing a major boost to domestic travel. This makes tourism an important sector with regard to generation of revenue. Rising family incomes and a shift in the cultural mindset has encouraged more and more people to open their eyes and minds to new cultures and experiences to enjoy their lives and domestic tourism provides a significant opportunity. Contemporary times are witnessing the growth of the informed travellers who completes his research about a tourism destination before setting out on his journey.

CHANGING LANDSCAPE OF TOURISM MARKETING

New Opportunities in a Social Media World

Changing customer habits and expectations (Fig. 1) and the increasing adoption of technology have brought about a change in the landscape of tourism marketing. The

Figure 1. Changing landscape of tourism marketing

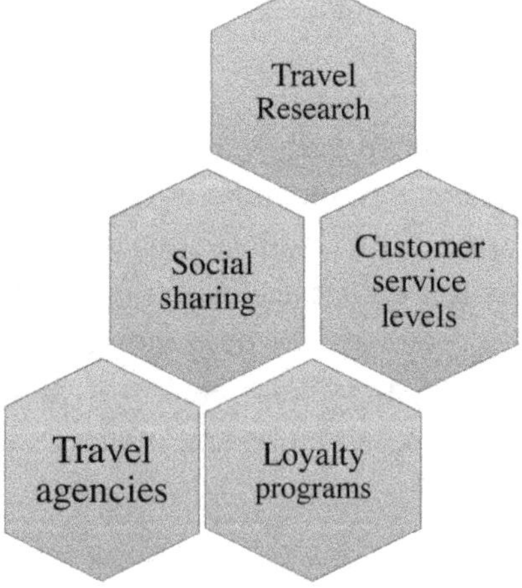

advent and growth of social media has created new opportunities for the tourism sector.

Transformation of Travel Research (Wang et al., 2013)

Travellers venture online to look for information, visualise the destinations, communicate with other travellers across informal communication channels, and consume content ie. reviews generated by other travellers. Social media has an important role to play here. There are well established tourism communities in the virtual world, which help people look for specific information. Sites like *Trip Advisor* compile reviews pertaining to various aspects of a travel excursion. An early adopter of social media, *Trip Advisor* also includes interactive travel forums.

Rise of Social Sharing (Kang et al., 2013)

Society is going through a transformation where sharing pieces of an individual's personal life for consumption by others is no longer taboo. The need for self-gratification and recognition in addition to garnering social attention is driving more and more people to indulge in social sharing. This has given an additional nudge to the social media craze. An example of the above, is Atameo.

Atameo is a virtual travel community formed around the belief that 'Travelling can have a sustained positive impact on the world'. This community is utilising the social sharing trend to create a virtual repository where breath-taking individual travel experiences can be documented. Interestingly, this documentation is being done by the travellers themselves, as they like to create their own stories, with photographs, maps, music, videos and all. This community of travellers, wanderers and explorers classifies tourists into tribes-action junkies, adventurers, backpackers, bikepackers, budget wizards, cultural buffs, family travellers, female solo travellers, foodies, green travellers, Jet setters, LGBTQ, Luxury travellers, nightlife aficionados, nomads, outdoor addicts, overlanders, photographers, riders, romantics, spiritual explorers, romantics, travel bloggers, wellness lovers and encourages them to generate beautiful travel memories, plain their next adventures and create inspiring trip compilations.

Customer Service (Bennett, 1993)

The world of tourism is all about the customer experience and good customer service can augment the quality of this experience. Brands in the tourism industry can use social media to communicate how their excellent customer service initiatives can help conjure delightful experiences for travellers.

Extensive Use of Travel Agencies (Law et al., 2004)

Research has shown that over 75% leisure travellers make use of an online travel agency because of a higher perceived credibility of the same. Sales teams, customer service and key account managers in the Travel and Tourism industry are making use of social media as a platform to help their relationships with their customers thrive. Maintaining good online reputations will help these travel organisations show their expertise and entice travellers to avail their services. The tourism and travel industry is getting very competitive as travellers can access user generated content pertaining to user experiences, compare prices and best deals and offers. Personalisation and customer centricity now serve as key differentiators between organisations in this sector. The opportunities for destination marketers are humongous and social media can be used to reach out to target consumer segments. The following section discusses pertinent issues which the Travel and Tourism industry should focus on, so that they can effectively leverage social media for their benefit.

Loyalty Programs

A faithful customer is an organisational asset. The travel industry has appreciated the benefits of customer loyalty and keeps on innovating the offerings to ensure superior benefits to loyal customers to be able to compete effectively in the wake of a large number of players entering the tourism industry. Tiering of services to offer different value propositions to different customers, multi-currency programs, customised redemption policies etc. are resulting in higher occupancy rates, higher operating margins and profitability for the tourism sector. Travel loyalty programs can be launched on social media platforms or mobile apps and shape the decisions of consumers.

Needs of Consumers in the Travel and Tourism Domain

A typical traveller needs help with regard to the following issues:

- Identification of tourism destinations based on specific needs ranging from family holidays to spiritual retreats or adventure tourism.
- Comparison of a set of destinations and finalisation of choice.
- Creation of a travel itinerary after adequate research pertaining to opportunities available for exploring cultural heritage, special events, carnivals, cruises and festivals, nature walks and retreats, wildlife safaris or beach getaways, ayurvedic treatment and culinary opportunities etc.
- Booking of tickets by air or train.

- Booking of appropriate hotels and resorts after relevant comparisons and finalisation of needs and requirements.

Consumers need the most price effective deals (Niininen, et al., 2007) for all the above. Additionally, they need information pertaining to availability of taxi/cab, best time to visit, how to reach a destination, activities available and so on.

The rise of the era of social travel platforms like Tripoto is taking care of the above consumer needs.

Tripoto is a social travel platform which is very popular in India. The online domain encourages people to share and discover travel experiences, details of their holidays and weekend getaways, their experiences and stories.

Tripoto has been successful in using the concept of storytelling. This concept propagates the sharing of stories, with improvisation, theatrics or embellishment, with the purpose of sharing information and instilling a belief or desire in the minds of the readers. This works, because, the consumers of today, are influenced by visual content, specially if the creator of the content is another individual like them. User generated content has the maximum impact on the peers.

Travel forums on Tripoto are a rich repository of explicit consumer experiences, visible through vivid videos-snorkelling, scuba diving, picturesque valleys and scenic meadows, all aimed at inspiring people to travel. The travel forums have a diverse set of stories ranging from experiences on beaches (destinations and resorts), mountains (beautiful destinations, treks and backpacking opportunities), stories of the rich cultural heritage of India (forts, palaces, temples, buddhist monasteries), weekend guides, wildlife tourism (safaris, birdwatching and wildlife parks).

Tripoto uses a robust social media presence to popularise travelling. Its posts like '*5 places to view the super moon in India*', and '*10 fun things to do in Bangalore*' use informative content to bring people onto the platform. By posting interactive content like-'*if you had to choose one friend who you'll go on a road trip with, to Ladakh who will it be?*' and '*Do you want your stories to be featured?*', Tripoto has generated conversations around content and has successfully built consumer engagement.

By hosting contributions by *Tripoto wanderers*, who are the members of the community, Tripoto is letting them get the recognition they deserve.

Tripoto shares information pertaining to travel itineraries of travellers and encourages others to book similar trips. Additionally, the platform helps consumers to book flights, search trending tour packages, search and book hotels online, allow people to post questions online, so that their peers can respond to the questions and create wishlists. The emergence of tourism portals like Tourism breaking news. com that offer live updates, valuable insights and opinions of relevance to the tourism industry and customised travel service providers like Tripraja.com is further

Figure 2. Pillars of social media

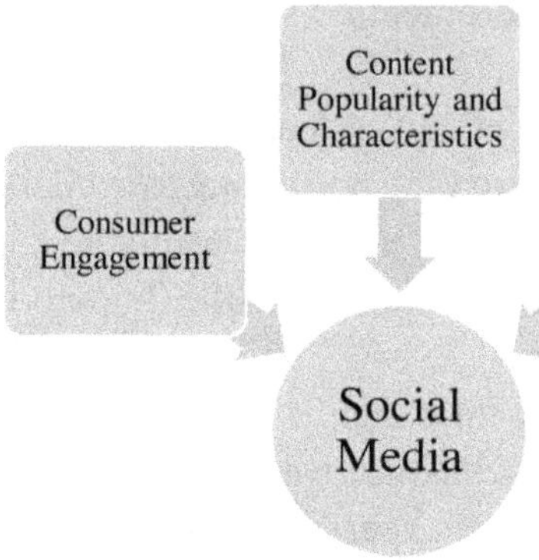

enriching the role of the virtual ecosystem in impacting and shaping the growth of tourism in India.

The Pillars of Social Media for the Tourism Sector

The above discussion clearly shows that the tourism sector needs to wake up to the need of well-planned strategies to ensure highest possible returns from its social media presence. The objective of organisations in this sector, is to ensure that their social media presence creates a social currency which can be transformed into revenue. Research shows that the three pillars of social media (Fig. 2) for the tourism sector are:

- Ability of social media content to generate consumer engagement (Djikman et al., 2015).
- Popularity and characteristics of social media content.
- Credibility of information on the social platforms.

Generation of Consumer Engagement

What drives consumer engagement (Fig. 2) on social platforms? Consumers use social media for the following purposes:

- **Entertainment**

Satisfaction of hedonic motivations is one of the biggest reasons why individuals venture online. Desire for gratification and enjoyment and a pleasurable experience, make them log onto a social media platform and engage in a conversation with a brand online.

- **Quest for Information**

Customers come online to look for information and are willing to participate in an online activity to satisfy this need.

- **Social Interaction**

Openness to experiences and extroversion are dimensions of an individual's personality which drive them to engage in peer to peer interactions in the virtual world. These interactions eventually lead to engagement and involvement with entities in the online world. Sometimes individuals also participate online, for compensatory self enhancement, to show that they are knowledgeable about certain matters, thereby gaining recognition in an online community.

- **Incentives or Benefits**

A customer's engagement intentions are significantly impacted by the social, hedonic and cognitive benefits that accrue from his presence and participation in a virtual space.

Research (Ozguven & Mucan, 2013) has shown that social media is used more by the people who are conscientious, are open to experiences, and the ones who are more satisfied with their lives. Brands can benefit by getting people to engage in conversations with them, participate in the online communities, engage in peer to peer dialogues etc. Consumers can feel engrossed in the discussions

Figure 3. Drivers of consumer engagement on social media

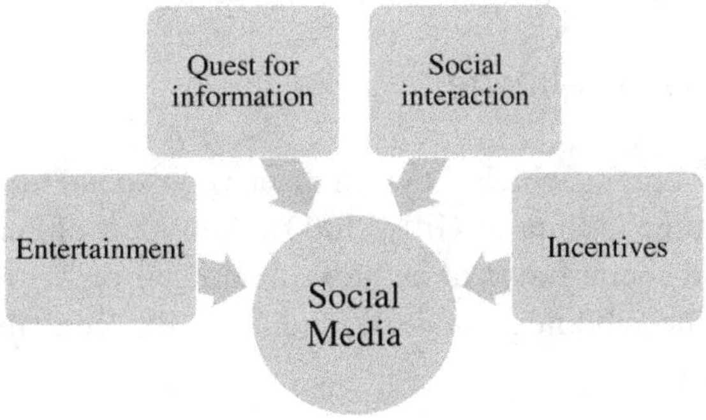

that are happening in an online community only if they respect and like the brand or community, the discussion is of some relevance to them and fulfils one of the four objectives as detailed above. When consumers are slightly engaged with a brand, they do not hesitate to *like* the content hosted by the brand. As this level of engagement grows, consumers may start participating passively or actively. Passive consumers may be silently consuming the content, whereas active consumers start *commenting* on the social media content posted by the brand and as engagement progresses to involvement, consumers start *sharing* the content posted by the brand. Sharing a brand's content is akin to endorsing the brand completely.

As per the lifecycle viewpoint of customer engagement (Shao & Ross, 2015), initially a customer joins a community on social media, to interact with and meet people and gather information. However, entertainment becomes a major motivation as individuals grow familiar with the community. Later, engagement depends upon the need to know more about the brand and its various products.

Additionally, consumer engagement also depends on the characteristics of the customer. Individual personality traits and attachment to social media are significant contributors to customer engagement and develop a sense of belongingness with the online community. This kind of a sense of attachment and belongingness brings pleasing emotional experiences to customers which results in sharing of information in both online and offline settings (Kumar, Aksoy, Donkers, Venkatesan, Wiesel, & Tillmanns, 2010).

Primary customer characteristics that impact social media usage are:

Attitude Towards Content

Social media has two dimensions: *Interactive* and *Interpersonal.* Informational influences may be positive or negative depending on the engagement level of the consumer. Brands need to ensure that they are not showing only their commercial side online, but also their emotional persona, so that the consumer engagement to the emotional persona can positively impact his engagement with the brand.

Need for Positive Self-Image

Consumers prefer brands which they can discuss on social media sites to create a positive self-image (Schau & Gilly, 2003). Adoption of certain brands adds to the lifestyle and social status of an individual. Consumers like to flaunt their association with these brands on social media and this contributes to consumer engagement.

Need for Social Relationships

Consumers interact and communicate with brands with which they enjoy social relationships and overlapping identities as per the Self Expansion theory. Brands may get adversely affected if the customer feels that the brand image is not consistent with the customer's own identity and this is just a one-sided relationship (Huang & Mitchell, 2014).

Additionally, gender and educational background also have a significant impact on the social media usage levels. This is a function of how well specific content resonates with the customers in terms of tastes, preferences and intellectualism.

Content Popularity

Stakeholders of the tourism world are creating consistent volumes of content in the online domain. Tourism organisations are posting content about destinations and locations, culture and cuisine, picturesque locations and options for spirituality and healing. Travel organisations are posting content pertaining to reaching the destinations and opportunities for stay and recreation. The content posting objectives of these organisations are attracting consumer attention and content consumption. Past researches on social media highlight that customer activities on social media can be divided into liking the content, sharing of content (posting), usage of content (consumption) (Schlosser, 2005) or commenting on the content.

Research also indicates (Jones, Ravid, & Rafaeli, 2004) that most users of social media choose to be silent bystanders and consume the available information rather than posting on social media. As per Nielson Research's report, more than 50% of social media users follow a brand, and a lesser percent of users actively contribute content about the brand on social media, which is a function of the level of consumer engagement and involvement, as discussed above. It has also been seen that a small percent of social media users, post a larger share of the content (Bughin, Chui, & Manyika, 2010). This implies that organisations need to interact with these significant consumers separately and use them as brand evangelists. Research has also shown that over time, less active users also become significantly active on social media (Hanna, Rohm, & Crittenden, 2011), as the content is interesting and the associated organisational brands are able to capture their interest and move them up the engagement continuum.

Diverse content typologies can generate different levels of consumer interest. It will hence, be useful for organisations to identify the popular content typologies which help them increase their reach. Research shows that to increase the popularity of messages, companies should use brand names, emotional & functional appeals, and information search cues.Subsequently it is vital for organisations to identify and explore the psychological motivations thatlead to the participation of consumers on social media.

The following section examines the content that is being posted by the stakeholders of the tourism industry and draws conclusions with respect to appropriate content typologies which will elicit desired levels of consumer participation.

Stakeholders of the Tourism World

Tourism organisations include international and national players, state owned tourism bodies, travel and tourism companies in the private sector, and other non-government organisations working in the tourism sector. These organisations may be involved in the education and training pertaining to the tourism field, enforcing regulations and investment, environmental management, or socio-cultural programs.

For instance, the World Tourism Organisation is a United Nations body dedicated towards the promotion of responsible and sustainable tourism, directed towards economic growth, inclusive development and environmental sustainability. The body focusses on enhancing knowledge and policy formulation in this sector and is committed to promoting tourism to achieve the Sustainable Development Goals (SDGs) set by the United Nations.

Similarly, the World Travel and Tourism Council, Pacific Asia Travel Association and several National Tourism Organisations focus on promotion of tourism, research on the economic and social impact of the same and organisation of global and regional summits focused on associated issues.

The social media presence of the above organisations is crafted around their organisational missions, visions and objectives.

Additionally, the private tourism organisations are focussed on tourist experiences and satisfying consumer needs and expectations from their travel forays. These include all consumer needs from the Travel and Tourism sector, as discussed earlier, in this chapter. The social media presence of these organisations is directed towards enticing the consumer through picturesque locations, culture and cuisine etc. and additional information pertaining to hotel and flight bookings and promotional schemes available. Table 1 summarises the social media content typologies for players in the tourism sector.

Content Characteristics

In addition to content typology, it is the characteristics of the content that increases consumer interactivity and engagement. Content needs to be relevant, emotionally appealing, reliable, should resonate with the customers, should be interactive and experience centric. Table 2 summarises the content characteristics of the social

Table 1. Social media content typologies for the tourism sector

Content Typology	Implication
Knowledge	This includes all posts aimed at the dissemination of knowledge, information and data. Content includes information pertaining to specific webinars, research outcomes, information pertaining to tourism summits and forums, affiliate members, soliciting proposals against tenders, workshops, meetings of tourism experts, travel and trade fairs, regional projects etc.
Picturesque	Interestingness (Yoo, K.-H., &Gretzel, U., 2011) of content is what makes it popular.This content contains pictures of sunsets, boating options, scenic beauty, wildlife, architecture, botanical gardens, natural beauty of the places, the gifts of nature, village life experiences, the sun, the sand and the sea help in attracting the attention of tourists across the globe. Travellers across the globe are looking for experiences they can cherish, make memories and appreciate the treasures of natural flora and fauna.
Culture and cuisine	This content refers to pictures of local festivals, food and drinks, authentic recipes, museums, art endeavours, and other rituals help social media marketers use the element of respect for culture to build a resonance with the consumers. Gourmet cuisine attracts connoisseurs, food critics, food and culture bloggers and writers and a diverse set of global travellers. Literature festivals and poetry events as well as exotic rendezvous can aid the cultural immersion of the visitors.
Social endeavours	The stakeholders of the tourism industry can further attract attention of travellers by showcasing any social causes like support for the girl child, education and literacy etc. that they are promoting.
Spirituality	By highlighting the healing properties of nature, peaceful environments, pollution free locales, opportunities for yoga, meditation and access to spiritualism, temples, churches and mosques, the tourism industry can help travellers discover their own spirituality and aid their inner transformation by immersing them in tranquillity.
Cruise and sports	This content includes information pertaining to attractive cruise tourism with state-of-the-art infrastructural support can feed the luxury needs of travellers. Posts pertaining to adventure tourism like pictures of snorkelling, kayaking, rafting, exotic locations, challenging opportunities and other niche tourism aspects are included here. When a country is hosting a specific sports event which is popular all across the world, then, posts about the sports activity can be used to promote the tourism opportunities in that country.
Competition and contests	Research has shown that interactive content garners the maximum response from the users. Rich and interactive posts on a brand page boost consumer participation and responsiveness. Tourism stakeholders can upload content pertaining to any contests or competitions that they are organising and motivate consumers to participate in the events and popularise the associated content.
Promotional Content	Travel and tourism organisations can share information pertaining to specialised tourism packages, seasonal discounts, special offers etc., so that more and more customers can be motivates to purchase the offers and travel to specific destinations. This can also include any customised packages that the organisations are offering their travellers.

media content. The purpose and format of the content are vital elements here and interactive, multisensory content that stimulates the senses and is vividly visual, draws favourable consumer responses.

Table 2. Content characteristics of social media content

Content Characteristics	Implications
Relevance	Users end up making a purchase decision when the user generated posts they refer to, is relevant to them, is current, updated and credible(Owusu, R. A., Mutshinda, C. M., Antai, I., Dadzie, K. Q., & Winston, E. M., 2016).
Emotional Appeal	Using emotional sentiments in social media posts is an effective social media marketing strategy used by marketers(Swani, K., Milne, G., & P. Brown, B., 2013).
Perceived reliability	Consistency and dependability of content created by brands on social media makes people feel that the information being posted online is credible and they tend to believe, follow and consume the information. Reliability is a precursor to consumer loyalty.
Perceptual homophily	If members perceive *interpersonal similarity with other members in a social media or travel community, the expectations from their participation and interactivity go up. Primarily members feel a sense of belongingness and resonance if they feel that the other members are similar to them or may have comparable interests, likes or dislikes.*
Interactivity	Content which drives consumers to respond, like a question or request for feedback or a contest etc. is very effective on social media.
Experience centric content	Content comprising of consumer experiences draws a more favourableresponse from consumers when the content is organic as compared to promotional/paid content. When the content is paid, promotional content gives better results than experience centric content.

It is vital for social media marketers to evaluate the content characteristics (Fig. 4.) regularly to ensure greater content effectiveness. Social media content strategies are all about generating high reach and consumer engagement. A careful understanding of content typologies and characteristics can help organisations achieve their social media content marketing objectives with ease.

Double incomes in unit families has made weekend getaways popular and different consumer groups have different requirements. For some, an extremely stupendous

Figure 4. Social media content characteristics for the tourism sector

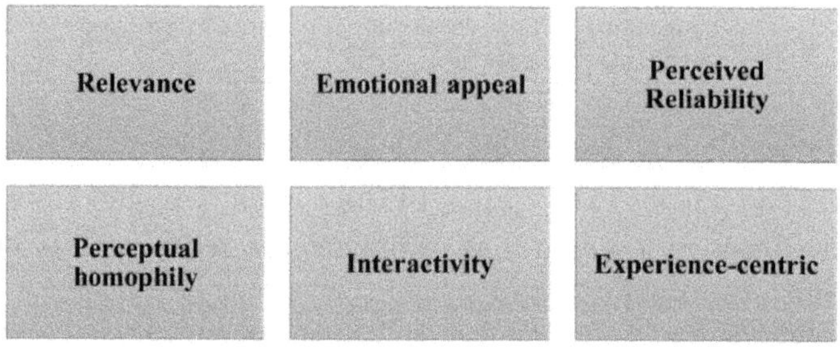

hotel ambience is significant, while for others, pricing is a valuable determinant. Consumer expectations from the travel experience are diverse. Hence, there is a need for customisation in the travel planning process. Subsequently, several new travel platforms have emerged. These platforms serve as useful information sources for consumers. Platforms like Trivago help visitors to locate appropriate hotels at a very fast pace, compare prices from different websites, simply by feeding in desired travel dates and helping in the search by filtering the process on the basis of price, distance from beach/airport, star categories, facilities etc. and throwing up responses ranging from budget hotels to luxury suites. Millions of aggregated hotel ratings and images allow travellers to complete their search after a thorough review.

Maintain Credibility of Information

Integrity of information is important to individuals when they are consuming content and engaging with it, in the online world. Relevance of information drives perceptions of credibility and trustworthiness. People make more effort to assess the credibility of a post when they are themselves involved in information search as compared to when creating content. Consumers depend on the websites of travel organisations, on reviews and testimonials written by other consumers and social media content generated by the organisations. It is important for social media marketers to appreciate the fact that the behavioural responses of consumers are the result of the degree of interestingness and trustworthiness of the social media content and the most informative content (Martínez-Navarro & Bigné, 2017) is perceived as the most credible information. If the source is considered as credible, consumer attitude is positively impacted. The consumer generated word of mouth is at times, more persuasive as compared to the firms' other more overt promotional tools on an online medium, because it is considered to be unprejudiced. Hence it plays an important role in shaping and influencing consumer behaviour.

Organisations in the tourism industry can vary the type of social media content that they are hosting on their online communities to elicit the desired responses from consumers. They can also study consumer characteristics, to find ways to segment consumers and target them separately, with different promotional strategies. Similarly, organisations can also work on enhancing perceived source credibility to induce favourable responses from the consumer communities.

Database Marketing-Big Data Analytics and the Tourism Industry

There is a rich pool of data that travellers post on travel communities, leading to the creation of vast amounts of data, on the cloud. This data can be analysed by organisations, to aid decision making and improving overall performance through an interconnection of scattered information available across the web. By using relevant data capture, extraction, visualisation and analytical tools, organisations can use the information for envisioning tourist demand. The digital traces being left by tourists, on the mobile and online world, can help tourism organisations in drawing inferences pertaining to individual behaviour and activity, interact with them across their tour, interact with potential guests to increase visitor statistics and even try to trigger consumer repurchase intent and get him to make future travel plans with the same tourism organisation. Organisations can use big data to support consumer experiences and use predictive analytics to plan for the future.

The tourism industry can make use of this data for the following 5 purposes:

1. **Managing and Enhancing Profitability:**
   This can be achieved by the travel and tourism industry to sell the products to the customers and better revenue management can help in identification of the marketing value propositions for the various customers. Data pertaining to room availability and pricing, costing of travel itineraries, information about flights etc. can enable demand prediction through better capacity planning. A more efficient utilisation of organisational resources can help enhance profitability of organisations in this sector.
2. **Managing Consumer Sentiment and Using Influencer Marketing:**
   Analysis of consumer comments on social media can help organisations identify whether they are happy or disappointed with organisations or experiences. Popular tourist destinations and travel packages can be identified. Their positive opinions can be used as testimonials and significant influencers can be identified and used by organisations for marketing. Additionally, this information can be used for training of consumers to ensure greater customer satisfaction in the future.
3. **Consumer Segmentation for Better Marketing Conversion:**
   The diversity of potential consumers makes it imperative for the marketing function in the travel industry to bifurcate consumers into homogeneous groups and subsequently develop targeting strategies for a planned marketing approach. Targeted promotional content enhances the productivity of marketing.
4. **Better Customer Experience Management:**
   Consumer data can be leveraged for an overall enhancement of all facets of the customer experience. This data can include everything from social media conversations and online reviews, to service usage data. This can give insights into consumer repurchase intent. This can also help in the

identification of well performing marketing resources, eventually aiding organisations in strategic decision making.

5. **Market Research:**
   Big data is a significant market research tool vis-à-vis a careful analysis of the consumer expectations form the tourism industry, the pricing models, the promotional strategies that work best in enticing customers, time-share plans, competitor analysis etc., both on collaborative online travel directories as well as websites of well established tour and travel organisations.

Case Study 4.1

Kerala Tourism: God's Own Country, Kerala

India is a land which boasts of a vast cultural heritage and diversity and is blessed with treasures which are now being used for tourism and eco-tourism endeavours. Situated on the Malabar coast in southwestern India, Kerala is one such natural bounty endowed on India. The state has used its tourism industry to contribute significantly to its economy.

Kerala Tourism Development Corporation is a state-owned tourism corporation, which is working aggressively towards the growth of the tourism industry in the state and has transformed Kerala into a niche holiday destination in India. The organisation practices responsible tourism marketing by focussing on the economic, social and environmental issues of the local community while promoting the state globally.

Primary objectives of the tourism body include:

- Promotion of Tourism in Kerala through well-crafted campaigns.
- Development of key tourist destinations through secondary support.
- Build credibility and popularity for the tourism industry in the state, by ensuring excellent quality of hospitality for the tourists.
- To serve as an information hub for national and international tourists.
- Contribute to the economy of the state through higher financial returns generated through tourism.
- Promote socially viable projects for the socio-economic well being of the local communities.

Kerala tourism actively uses social media to propagate brand Kerala and ensure high brand recall amongst current and potential tourists.

Research (Kietzmann, Silvestre, McCarthy, & Pitt, 2012) suggests seven building blocks against which marketers should try to develop their content. Customers today are not merely consuming online content, making online purchases and existing silently on the respective eplatforms, but are actively creating content, building interactions and sharing and endorsing the content. This opportunity can be tapped by marketers to lead the consumers towards evangelism. Identity, conversations, sharing, presence, relationships, reputation, and groups are the seven building blocks of social media which can be used by respective entities to augment the power of their social networks.

Kerala Tourism's presence across Facebook, Twitter and Instagram is well crafted. A brief look into the content brings up some interesting facts (Table 3).

Some additional strategies that Kerala Tourism can incorporate in their social media strategy are:

- Encourage the user base to share their photographs or experiences to create a web of peer to peer content.
- Invite stakeholders from the tourism industry-hotels, tourism operators etc. to share their content on the Kerala tourism Facebook page and subsequently establish synergistic relationships with other participants in the fraternity.
- Kerala tourism can also share content pertaining to Kerala, posted by other consumers. This can appeal to the self-gratification needs of consumers and can help Kerala tourism gain consumer evangelists by appealing to the emotional disposition of the individuals.

Benefits to organizations will accrue when companies understand the need to proceed with their social media policy, in a structured format. Companies need to appreciate the value associated with respecting the diverse pillars of the social media content strategy, the various types of content, and further the various dimensions of the social media strategy of an organization. By having the right components of the social media ecosystem in the right measure, organizations can harness the consumer participation thereby generated and enhance the productivity of their social media endeavours.

CONCLUSIONS

The tourism industry in India represents a booming sector. This is because of the advent of a large number of foreign tourists every year as well as the demographic dividend of India's population, which is increasingly adopting tourism as a lifestyle constituent. Additionally, the revenue generated by this sector makes it very important for India. Studies from the World Travel and Tourism Council show that tourism contributed 9.4% to India's GDP in 2017 and is expected to show a significant growth

Table 3. Examination of content typologies on the Kerala Tourism Facebook page, on the basis of content pillars (Kietzmann et al., 2011)

Content Pillars	Examination of the Kerala Tourism Page
Identity	The page has a lot of content highlighting the spiritualism of brand Kerala, the picturesque bounty that nature has bestowed on the state, the backwater lagoons, the sun and sand experiences, the exotic beaches, the sports opportunities offered by the state-surfing, rafting, rowing, etc. The visually attractive content being hosted has successfully captured the essence of the offerings provided by the state. Pictures of rippling waters and ayurvedic treatments has helped create a brand identity for Kerala as an enjoyable retreat which can help improve individual wellness and holistic rejuvenation. A significant volume of content focuses on the cuisines, the wildlife opportunities that Kerala has to offer, while also showcasing panoramic views of festival and culture and village life experiences, thereby creating a unique brand identity for Kerala Tourism.
Conversations	The Kietzmann model focused on peer to peer consumer communication which would eventually aid in the growth of the brand through positive word of mouth propagation. It also focused on consumers coming together for meet ups for sharing their ideas and collective exchanges. The Kerala Tourism page has been successfully able to engage the consumer and a distinct consumer-brand relationship exists. However, a peer to peer connection appears missing as of now. The brand can use their social media presence to enhance the peer to peer consumer communication. This can be done by organizing events where the consumer community can physically come together. This will benefit the brand in two ways-firstly, it will further strengthen the brand-consumer relationship as also build a peer to peer connect which is what formulates the base for creating long term relationships.
Sharing	The sharing dimension focuses on how consumers exchange, distribute and receive content. Kerala tourism has been highly successful with regard to motivating its consumer base in its endeavour to get consumers to share the content that it has posted, through a successful consumer engagement philosophy.
Presence	Kietzmann's model referred to presence as the extent to which others in the network know if others are available. In the case of Kerala tourism's Facebook page, as soon as an individual comments on a Facebook post, they are visible to others in the network and a kinship develops on the basis of the similar interest of being part of the same community.
Relationships	The mechanism of relationships pertains to how well users in a network relate to each other and works on the same line as presence. People associated with certain networks demonstrate a degree of homogeneity and tend to form informal relationships (based on perceived trustworthiness and mutual benefit). Once peer to peer consumer interaction starts proliferating, as conversations develop, there are significant opportunities for these relationships to develop. For instance, these Facebook pages can help groups of tourists and tourism operators to connect with each other and form a mutually benefit communication exchange.
Reputation	While Facebook pages of brands, as in the case of Kerala tourism, help the brand in developing a well defined reputation on the basis of content that is hosted, they do little for what Kietzmann defines reputation as a building block of content-the extent to which users know the social standing of others in an online network.
Groups	This can be measured by the extent to which users form communities. As of now, the users associated with the Facebook page of Kerala tourism, have a relationship with the brand, but do not seem to have entered into any significant relationship amongst themselves.

rate. While the Ministry of Tourism has a well-designed program for promotion of Tourism, the virtual world is giving considerable impetus to this sector. Changing customer habits and expectations and the increasing adoption of technology have brought about a change in the landscape of tourism marketing. The advent and growth of social media, transformation of travel research, rise of social sharing, rise of need for customer satisfaction, growth of travel agencies and competitive loyalty programs has created new opportunities for the tourism sector. The tourism sector needs to wake up to the need of well-planned strategies to ensure highest possible returns from its social media presence. The objective of organisations in this sector, is to ensure that their social media presence creates a social currency which can be transformed into revenue. The three pillars of social media for the tourism sector are-Ability of social media content to generate consumer engagement, Popularity and characteristics of social media content and Credibility of information on the social platforms. *Entertainment, Quest for information, social interaction and incentives* are the drivers of consumer engagement on social media. Most significant content typologies on social media in the tourism sector include content pertaining to knowledge dissemination, picturesque nature of content, content about culture and cuisine, social endeavours, spirituality, cruises and sports, competition and contests and promotional content. Significant content characteristics that drive effectiveness on social media include relevance, emotional appeal, perceived reliability, perceptual homophily, interactivity and experience centric nature of content.

REFERENCES

Bennett, M. M. (1993). Information technology and travel agency: A customer service perspective. *Tourism Management*, *14*(4), 259–266. doi:10.1016/0261-5177(93)90060-X

Bughin, J., Chui, M., & Manyika, J. (2010). Clouds, big data, and smart assets: Ten tech-enabled business trends to watch. *The McKinsey Quarterly*, *56*(1), 75–86.

Dijkmans, C., Kerkhof, P., & Beukeboom, C. J. (2015). A stage to engage: Social media use and corporate reputation. *Tourism Management*, *47*, 58–67. doi:10.1016/j.tourman.2014.09.005

Hanna, R., Rohm, A., & Crittenden, V. L. (2011). We're all connected: The power of the social media ecosystem. *Business Horizons*, *54*(3), 265–273. doi:10.1016/j.bushor.2011.01.007

Huang, H. H., & Mitchell, V. (2014). The role of imagination and brand personification in brand relationships. *Psychology and Marketing*, *31*(1), 38–47. doi:10.1002/mar.20673

Jones, Q., Ravid, G., & Rafaeli, S. (2004). Information overload and the message dynamics of online interaction spaces. *Information Systems Research*, *15*(2), 194–210. doi:10.1287/isre.1040.0023

Kang, M., & Schuett, M. A. (2013). Determinants of sharing travel experiences in social media. *Journal of Travel & Tourism Marketing*, *30*(1-2), 93–107. doi:10.1080/10548408.2013.751237

Kietzmann, J. H., Silvestre, B. S., McCarthy, I. P., & Pitt, L. F. (2012). Unpacking the social media phenomenon: Towards a research agenda. *Journal of Public Affairs*, *12*(2), 109–119. doi:10.1002/pa.1412

Kumar, V., Aksoy, L., Donkers, B., Venkatesan, R., Wiesel, T., & Tillmanns, S. (2010). Undervalued or overvalued customers: Capturing total customer engagement value. *Journal of Service Research*, *13*(3), 297–310. doi:10.1177/1094670510375602

Law, R., Leung, K., & Wong, R. (2004). The impact of the Internet on travel agencies. *International Journal of Contemporary Hospitality Management*, *16*(2), 100–107. doi:10.1108/09596110410519982

Martínez-Navarro, J., & Bigné, E. (2017). The value of marketer-generated content on social network sites: Media antecedents and behavioral responses. *Journal of Electronic Commerce Research*, *18*(1), 52.

Niininen, O., Buhalis, D., & March, R. (2007). Customer empowerment in tourism through consumer centric marketing (CCM). *Qualitative Market Research*, *10*(3), 265–281. doi:10.1108/13522750710754308

Owusu, R. A., Mutshinda, C. M., Antai, I., Dadzie, K. Q., & Winston, E. M. (2016). Which UGC features drive web purchase intent? A spike-and-slab Bayesian variable selection approach. *Internet Research*, *26*(1), 22–37. doi:10.1108/IntR-06-2014-0166

Ozguven, N., & Mucan, B. (2013). The relationship between personality traits and social media use. *Social Behavior and Personality*, *41*(3), 517–528. doi:10.2224bp.2013.41.3.517

Schau, H., & Gilly, M. (2003). We are what we post? Self-presentation in personal web space. *The Journal of Consumer Research*, *30*(3), 385–404. doi:10.1086/378616

Schlosser, A. E. (2005). Posting versus lurking: Communication in a multiple audience context. *The Journal of Consumer Research*, *32*(2), 260–265. doi:10.1086/432235

Shao, W., & Ross, M. (2015). Testing a conceptual model of Facebook brand page communities. *Journal of Research in Interactive Marketing*, *9*(3), 239–258. doi:10.1108/JRIM-05-2014-0027

Swani, K., Milne, G., & Brown, P., B. (. (2013). Spreading the word through likes on Facebook: Evaluating the message strategy effectiveness of Fortune 500 companies. *Journal of Research in Interactive Marketing*, *7*(4), 269–294. doi:10.1108/JRIM-05-2013-0026

Wang, D., & Fesenmaier, D. R. (2013). Transforming the travel experience: The use of smartphones for travel. In *Information and communication technologies in tourism 2013* (pp. 58–69). Berlin, Germany: Springer. doi:10.1007/978-3-642-36309-2_6

Yoo, K.-H., & Gretzel, U. (2011). Influence of personality on travel-related consumer-generated media creation. *Computers in Human Behavior*, *27*(2), 609–621. doi:10.1016/j.chb.2010.05.002

KEY TERMS AND DEFINITIONS

Content Typology: This refers to the type of content posted by an organisation or individual on social media. Content can be of organisational or brand building type, relationship building type or promotional type.

Database Marketing: This refers to the usage of consumer databases by marketers for analysis and extraction of actionable information. This serves as the basis of decision making in the field of marketing.

Social Media: This refers to media vehicles and platforms, websites and applications that permit individuals to create, consumer and share content in participatory environments. The concept of social media revolves around the content generated by individuals and organisations across social networking platforms. The nomenclature has been derived from the social nature of the content.

Virtual Communities: These are online platforms enabling the formation of virtual groups or cliques. These groups are thronged by individuals with some level of homogeneity.

Chapter 3
A Content Marketing Framework to Analyze Customer Engagement on Social Media

Sofia Balio
School of Economics and Management, University of Porto, Portugal

Beatriz Casais
https://orcid.org/0000-0002-7626-0509
School of Economics and Management, University of Minho, Portugal & IPAM Porto, Portugal

ABSTRACT

Factors influencing customer engagement on Facebook have been extensively analyzed but there are barely evidences if those factors also effect customer engagement on Instagram. A digital analysis was conducted including a content analysis of the post appeals and of the message interactivity as well as multiple linear regressions to explore the influence of the factors mentioned above on customer engagement. It was possible to conclude which factors can be used to increase customer engagement on social media, namely message interactivity and certain post appeals. Different conclusions are withdrawn when comparing Facebook to Instagram, proving empirically that different social networking sites have distinct influence on customer engagement. This chapter is relevant for content and social media strategies and helps brands increase their customer engagement.

DOI: 10.4018/978-1-7998-2185-4.ch003

INTRODUCTION

Social media has been increasing its presence in our daily lives and therefore it has introduced various opportunities to companies to exploit different ways of improving their business. As so, social media has also been increasing its importance in the business world (Ngai et al., 2015; Phua et al., 2017). The main advantage is the possibility of a two-way communication between companies and customers, encouraging the customer engagement on social media (Malthouse et al., 2016).

It is it vital for companies to understand how they can better interact with their online community and what factors influence the customer engagement. Academic research in this field, despite being common, does not capture the continuous development in terms of metrics, features of social networking sites and new platforms (Coelho et al., 2016; Dessart et al., 2016).

Both Facebook and Instagram are constantly changing and thus the academic field is also in a permanent need to renew its conclusions and results. As so, this study enters the wide range of papers that covered the social networking sites topics, but in a deeper and more concise sub-subject that lacks in terms of academic studies: the customer engagement on Facebook and Instagram.

This study aims to help managers and brands to better analyze their customer engagement, in particular, to understand the influence that certain factors have on the content that brands share with their customers.

Post type, time frame, message interactivity and post appeal were considered as the four types of factors influencing how customers express their engagement through the likes, reactions, comments and shares on Facebook and Instagram. Previous studies have only focused on likes and comments (De Vries et al., 2012; Sabate et al., 2014; Erkan, 2015; Coelho et al., 2016), and therefore, this study will contribute with more in-depth insights by adding the number of reactions and shares as metrics of customer engagement on social media. Additionally, this work will narrow the gap concerning the knowledge about how these factors influence customer engagement on social media platforms beyond Facebook, by extending the analysis to Instagram (Carah & Shaul, 2015).

In summary, this study aims to upgrade the past studies according to the evolution of the social networking sites and to answer the following question:

What factors should be taken into consideration and what is the impact of each one on the customer engagement on Facebook and Instagram?

BACKGROUND

Customer Engagement

One of the key factors of success for business nowadays is the ability to create and maintain long term relationships with customers. This has been a concern and a goal for managers and brands since a long time but the appearance of social media and the evolution of Web 2.0 highlighted the importance of establishing interactions with customers (Malthouse et al., 2016). Thus, customer engagement is a relevant topic for managers across all industries and companies.

Customer engagement presents several advantages for brands since it is seen as a factor that drives better organizational performance, increases sales, profitability and customer loyalty (Bowden, 2009). Gambetti and Graffigna (2010) also argue that customer engagement plays a key role in having a competitive advantage and that due to the change of customers' role in the buying process, companies have to adapt and respond to their new needs (the desire of co-create brand content, interact with other customers and have emotional experiences). Similarly, Verhoef et al. (2010) discuss that the role of customers has changed over the past few years as they have become more active and participate, not only in the buying process but also in activities provided by brands and/or initiated by themselves.

As pointed out by both van Doorn et al. (2010) and Sashi (2012), customer engagement goes beyond the simple act of purchase as customers now are deeply involved with brands. For instance, customers who are engaged and have a relationship with the brand are more likely to give good feedback about their experience with family and friends which generates word-of-mouth about the brand. Consequently, they could become brand advocates that generate value for the brand. Thus, customer engagement isn't static, but instead, is a process of interactions that goes beyond the moment of the purchase (Verhoef et al., 2010).

Nevertheless, customer engagement can also have a negative impact on brands. As stated before, if customers start sharing negative eWOM, for instance, brands will suffer negative publicity and potential customers could be pulled away. Thus, it is crucial for brands to properly manage customer engagement (Hollebeek et al., 2014).

As suggested by previous studies (Cvijikj & Michahelles, 2013; Sabate et al., 2014; Kim & Yang, 2017), users can engage on Facebook through three distinct behaviors: liking, commenting and sharing. Regarding Instagram, the main behaviors of engagement are liking and commenting (Erkan, 2015; Coelho et al., 2016).

Notwithstanding, it is proposed by Kim and Yang (2017) that these behaviors don't have the same weight and don't represent the same level of engagement. Neither for the customers nor for the algorithms of Facebook and Instagram. Consequently, it is relevant to include all of them when studying the costumer engagement on an environment such as social media.

Both social networking sites (SNSs) have an internal algorithm that is in charge of analyzing each post that is made. Based in that analysis, the algorithm then ranks them and decides which posts will appear in the News Feed or Timeline of users. This algorithm is constantly changing and always incorporating new variables, but one of the key criteria is the user interaction which is determined by the number of likes, comments and shares that a post receives. Furthermore, it is thought that a share is equivalent to 2 comments and that each comment is equivalent to 7 likes (Wagner et al., 2017).

In regard to the customer effort, Kim and Yang (2017) also propose that these three behaviors require a different amount of intensity. The like is the behavior that requires the lowest cognitive effort, once that it can be done through a simple click. On the contrary, a comment needs more commitment from the user, since he will have to express himself through words or *emojis*. Sharing represents the highest level of effort. On one hand, when a user shares a post, it will appear both on the News Feed and on his profile, while when someone comments a post, it will only appear in the News Feed and disappear after some time. On the other hand, as the shared post will appear on the profile of the user, it could indicate that it is part of the user's self-presentation. Online users tend to be very careful when it comes to their self-presentation. Therefore, it could indicate that a higher level of effort is required as it may be a strategic and thought behavior.

Reactions are a powerful measure and are a more precise indicator of how users feel about a given content. This is particularly important for brands, once they can get a deep knowledge on how their products are perceived online or how their community feels about their content strategy. This is an indication that indeed reactions are now part of the metrics that should be analyzed and that brands should pay attention to them. As it was suggested by Swani and Milne (2017) it would be interesting to investigate the effect of this new type of interaction on customer engagement on social media. Also, as there are more forms of engagement beyond likes and comments, it is crucial to include and analyze this matter more extensively. However, barely no literature was found on the thematic of establishing this relationship. Most the authors so far still only consider the number of likes and comments as their dependent variables (Sabate et al., 2014; Erkan, 2015; Coelho et al., 2016; Kim & Hull, 2017). More recently, authors such Wagner et al. (2017) and Wang et al. (2017) also incorporate into their conceptual framework the shares as a dependent variable, which, as explained above, is one of the behaviors that users have to engage on SNSs.

Determinants of Customer Engagement on Social Media

In the conceptual framework proposed by De Vries et al. (2012), the brand post popularity was measured through the number of likes and the number of comments. As determinants of it, they suggested that the vividness and interactivity of the brand post should be taken into consideration as well as the position of the post in the brand fan page. Additionally, they argued that the valence of comments could also have an impact on the brand post popularity, as a positive comment could improve the interest of a post. Finally, as the content of a post could be either informational or entertaining, the model also incorporated this dimension.

In respect to the results they found out that in order to increase the number of comments, managers should create highly interactive posts, such as posts with a question to encourage the response of users. However, it was also empirically proven that this type of posts are negatively related to the number of likes. This study made a crucial contribution to the academic field and contributed with important insights for managers but they also pointed out some limitations such as not incorporating other SNSs (De Vries et al., 2012). Sabate et al. (2014) even made a distinction between soft criterion and hard criterion. The first one takes into consideration semantic and interpretation aspect behind the message of the post. On the other hand, hard criterions are the ones that don't require a subjective interpretation and that can be quantified. A group of studies have focused only on soft criterions and have analyzed the effect of such post categories as advertising, fan, events, information and promotion (Coelho et al., 2016) or the post appeals as emotional and utilitarian (Wagner et al., 2017). Another group only analyzed hard criterion by studying the content richness taking into consideration if the post was an image, a video or a link and the time frame depending on the time of publication and the day of the week of publication (Sabate et al., 2014). Some who went deeper, developed their conceptual framework including both soft and hard criterion. For instance, Kim and Yang (2017) studied how different message features could impact the engagement on social media. They argued that both the form (text, photo, audio, video) and message interactivity defined as if the message was response-inviting or not, should be criterions in their framework, for example.

Post Type

Concerning post type, which is a hard criterion, it has been studied by a few authors. The results concerning its impact prove its relevance once that most of the studies show that this category is a significant predictor of the measures of customer engagement (Cvijikj & Michahelles, 2013; Sabate et al., 2014; Kim & Yang, 2017; Swani & Milne, 2017). However, when analyzing the results of these studies, it is also possible to see the variety of different conclusions. For instance, Kim and Yang (2017) showed that photos have a negative impact on the number of comments while Cvijikj and Michahelles (2013) showed the opposite. These specific studies had focus on different industries and companies as the object of study, which may explain the contrary conclusions, among other factors. Nevertheless, this indicates that this kind of study is relevant through the years and the academic research still needs different industries and countries incorporated in the analysis, in order to have more solid results.

In past studies, post type, have been related with the vividness of the posts. Academics argued that vividness represents the richness of the features of a post (De Vries et al., 2012). In other words, this richness is the breadth and depth of a message that stimulates different senses of the user. For instance, when a brand posts an image with contrasting colors or an interesting link to another website, the attractiveness of the post can increase. By stimulating different senses, the different post types can potentially condition the behavior towards the posts which consequently, affects customer engagement (Sabate et al., 2014).

De Vries et al. (2012) suggested that the vividness of each post should be divided into different levels. The low level of vividness was defined as a photo or image, the medium level was an event and the highest level was a video. One could argue that defining different levels of vividness can lead to potential subjective bias, because there is no certainty on how users will perceive it (Sabate et al., 2014).

Time Frame

Previous research has also studied the effect of time on customer engagement, as it is of extreme importance for brands to know when to post on SNSs, as pointed out by the literature (Cvijikj & Michahelles, 2013; Sabate et al., 2014). Academics have studied time frame through mainly, three different perspectives: the first one takes into account either the post is published on weekdays or during the weekend; the second one argues about the influence of the time of publication (hours) and finally, the third one considers the seasonality of the post through the analysis of the different months of the year.

Regardless the different views and results, the consensus among the authors is that, in an environment such Facebook or Instagram, where the News Feed or Timeline is always receiving new content, brands must take into consideration the influence of time on customer engagement (Cvijikj & Michahelles, 2013; Coelho et al., 2016).

The most frequent perspective is the contrast between weekdays and weekends. Wagner et al. (2017) and De Vries et al. (2012) included this as a control variable and Sabate et al. (2014) and Cvijikj and Michahelles (2013) studied it as one of the independent variables of their models. Some studies showed that this variable had no impact while others showed that posts during weekdays had more customer engagement. Moreover, although Sabate et al. (2014) had included both weekdays and time of publication, their model was only able to establish a connection between the time of publication and the number of comments. This indicates that, despite previous efforts, work on this field is still needed.

The second approach was implemented on the work of Sabate et al. (2014) and Cvijikj and Michahelles (2013) who suggested that users were more active on the Internet during peak hours (the period when users were more active on SNS). Contrary to what was expected, on the work of Cvijikj and Michahelles (2013), it was found that posts during peak hours have a negative effect on engagement. The authors state that this probably happens because during peak hours, users want to interact with their friends and not with brands. As a consequence, it is suggested that companies should post during the period with low activity (off peak hours) in order to increase customer engagement.

Coelho et al. (2016) applied the third perspective and studied the seasonality as a control variable. The work included months from January to August and showed that different months implied different behaviors, proving that customer engagement is influenced by the month a post is published. On Facebook, some months had a positive effect while others a negative one. In the case of the number of likes, months such as March, April, May and June had one of the most powerful increases and the number of comments also increased during February, March, April and July. The authors believe that these results could be explained by the existence of a national holidays and the vacation period of the country of the companies surveyed. On Instagram the impact, although not the same for every month, was all positive.

There is a massive amount of content on social media, but not all receive the same engagement. Another key factor is the perceived interactivity that a user have (Kim & Yang, 2017). In other words, the perception that an online user has on the communication that he or she can establish with the brand is decisive to create engagement. This communication should happen in a two-way dialogue, be responsive and controllable (Mollen & Wilson, 2010).

Interactivity

Interactivity has been a topic of interest for the past few years and a lot of definitions and categories were suggested and added to the discussion. Although there is no agreement on the definition, there is a consent about its importance in communication and in the maintenance of relationships (Kim & Yang, 2017). Ariel and Avidar (2015), show that there are three common perspectives about interactivity: it could be seen as a "perception-related variable", as a "process-related variable" or as a "medium characteristic". From their point of view, interactivity is part of the communication process. This is, as interactivity is "an attribute of the process of communication itself", it is present on traditional media as well as in new media platforms. It is acknowledged that new media can facilitate the interactivity but the main predictor of the degree of interactivity will rely on the "process of message transition and reciprocity". Go and Bortree (2017) also believe that social media enables message interactivity by providing several ways in which organizations can communicate with their audience.

In an environment as Facebook and Instagram, where all the organizations have the same opportunities in terms of technological aspects in order to influence interactivity (Kim & Yang, 2017), the perceived interactivity does not depend on technology but on the degree to which brands decide to take actions and use the tools available to engage in a two-way communication (Lee & Park, 2013).

Post Appeal

Post appeal have also received attention from the academic field and its relationship with customer engagement have been suggested as well as tested. The firsts authors trying to study how the message appeal can influence the way consumers are persuaded, focused on two main approaches, that although being different aren't mutually exclusive.

One of the approaches had its focus on the importance of factual information. The other approach had the emotions as the focus and in this case, the content could take advantage of emotions. Brands could try to provoke feelings or emotions associated to the product and people would adjust their buying behavior accordingly, either emotions were positive or negative (Bagozzi et al., 1999).

Academics continued to study and analyzing what kind of appeal, either rational or emotional would be the best, but the question remains controversial. Nevertheless, what has been proven is that, beyond the type, message appeal as a whole has an effect on message perception, which consequently results in an effective communication (Wagner et al., 2017).

Present studies, still utilize this categorization of functional and emotional appeals in order to contribute to the literature (Liu et al., 2017). However, as suggested by Swani et al. (2017) it would be beneficial to go further and to also analyze the categories of emotional and functional appeals such as humor, love, and so on and so forth. This was already attempted by some studies, but it is still at its early stage of analysis.

Wagner et al. (2017) was one of that studies. Through the proposed framework, it was also concluded that the main factor of success on communication is the "overall theme of a post", or as it was posited, the post appeal. As suggested by the authors, post appeal can affect the attitude of a user toward a post, once that every post has a theme and it is perceived by SNSs users. Consequently, depending on the attitude, an action such as liking, commenting or sharing can be generated. Thus, the post appeal constitutes an important factor on the study of customer engagement.

Results from the studies of Wang et al. (2017) and Liu et al. (2017) corroborate that post appeal have a significant effect on social media engagement. The first one only included likes and shares as the metrics of engagement and the second one incorporated likes, comments and shares.

In the work of Wang et al. (2017) the motivation arouse because there was a significant difference between the engagement of the posts. Notwithstanding, the relation of post appeals with engagement has barely been analyzed.

Both studies showed that some themes or topics have a positive effect while others have a negative effect. Additionally, some appeals have a more significant effect than others. What is curious is that, Wang also found out that the most frequent themes are not the ones which create more engagement. This could mean that brands are not defining their strategies taking this important information into consideration and this way they are missing out the full potential of SNSs and customer engagement.

Content Marketing

Nowadays, traditional marketing is not sufficient in order for brands to remain competitive, the paradigm has shifted and strategies must be adjusted. This era is known as the new digital era and content marketing is one of the key factors of success and one of the crucial tools of digital marketing. Consequently, is it important for companies to understand what is this concept about and how to incorporate it in their marketing efforts.

Although its relevance has been growing only in the past decade, the truth is that content marketing was already present in the early nineties. In fact, some business owners were developing their brands through this approach. For instance, André Michelin, launched the Michelin Guide which featured information about how to repair tires and a list of hotels and city maps. This magazine instead of being commercialized was given for free. Other examples exist and the common aspect about them is that, these businessmen were already building brand stories as a way of creating an emotional connection that hopefully would result in the sales of their product or service.

The difference between content marketing and advertising was also established. It is stated that advertising has its focus on sales and motivating purchase whereas content marketing is more about establishing relationships with the customer and using storytelling in order to fortify their brand messaging and positioning.

Moreover, content marketing serves several objectives such as increasing brand awareness, attracting news leads into the business, building relationships with the customer as well as enhancing customer loyalty, among others. Nevertheless, if these advantages for companies aren't trackable and measurable, they would never know when the goal is fulfilled. As a consequence, some metrics are required in order to validate the approach of content marketing. There are four different types of metrics that could be used, namely consumption metrics, sharing metrics (likes, shares, among others), lead and sales metrics (Holliman & Rowley, 2014). Ahmad et al. (2016) also pointed out that metrics such as liking, *hashtagging*, retweeting, commenting and sharing the content that brands post online are measures for analyzing the effectiveness of content marketing.

Additionally, Ahmad et al. (2016) also stated that social media platforms are useful tools for gathering such measures. If in traditional marketing it was sometimes difficult to measure the impacts of strategies, in the era of digital marketing it is easier to analyze results. It is thanks to the technology of Web 2.0 that brands can follow the outcomes of their marketing efforts, as it is the case of monitoring the customers' behavior through their engagement on social media.

Content plays a crucial role on the marketing world and as emphasized by some studies, having a valuable and relevant content can help driving engagement on social media. On the other hand, engagement itself also helps to increase the effectiveness of content marketing once it is easier to influence costumers' perceptions on a brand or product if they are indeed engaged and paying attention to the content. Otherwise, it is difficult to really accomplish objectives such as establishing relationships with customers and increasing brand awareness.

THE RESEARCH OBJECTIVE

The objective of this study is to provide insights about what should be taken into consideration and its impact when using Facebook and Instagram in order to understand customer engagement. For this purpose, four main categories were inducted: post type, time frame, message interactivity and post appeal to better explain the behaviors of customer engagement on Facebook and Instagram. Two conceptual frameworks are presented due to the differences between the two SNSs, Facebook and Instagram.

A content analysis of the post appeals and message interactivity and an empirical analysis were conducted. For each dependent variable and for each SNS, multiple OLS linear regressions were estimated. All the dependent variables were transformed using the natural logarithm in order to ensure a normal distribution of the residuals. Additionally, outliers were eliminated if the studentized residual exceeded -3 or +3. Moreover, in order to improve the explanatory power of the variable *Length of the post caption*, it was transformed by using the natural logarithm. Thus, this study tested

Figure 1. Framework to analyze customer engagement on Instagram

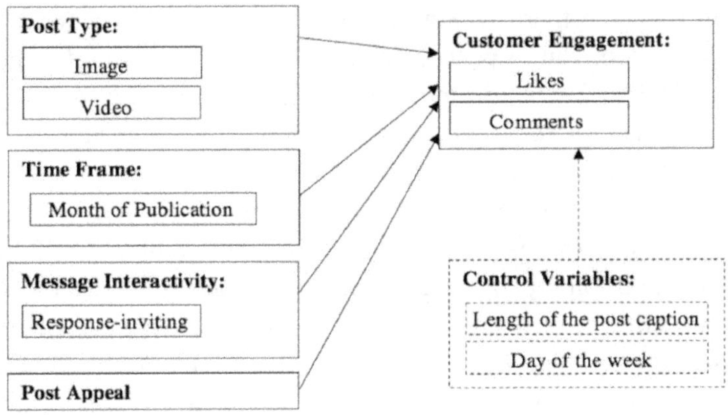

six models, four concerning Facebook, namely *LN (Likes +1), LN (Reactions +1), LN (Comments +1)* and *LN (Shares +1)*, and two regarding Instagram, respectively *LN (Likes +1)* and *LN (Comments +1).*

After the data collection of posts from Instagram and Facebook of a company, posts were treated and coded for post type, time frame, message interactivity and post appeal. The first two correspond to hard criterion and enable a pragmatic

Figure 2. Framework to analyze customer engagement on Facebook

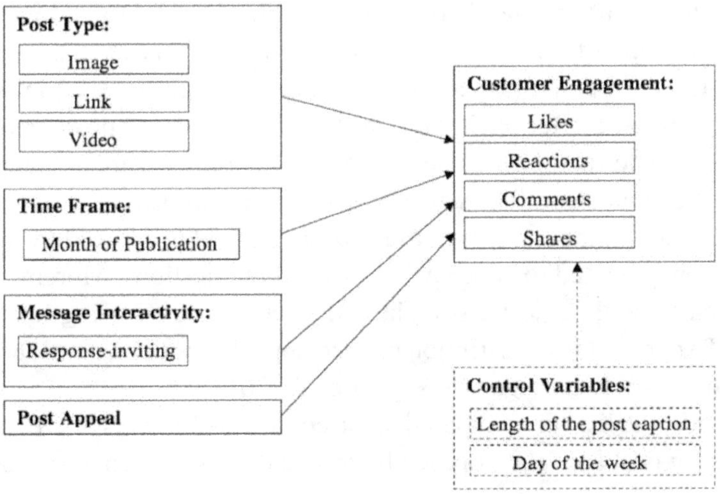

coding procedure while the other ones require a more subjective analysis as it is natural for soft criterion.

Regarding post type, there were three different and mutually exclusive possibilities: image, link and video. Thus, a post could only be one type and this differentiation was intuitive to code. For the time frame, the coding procedure was also immediate as it is possible to see in the screenshots the date of publication of the post. Consequently, the month of publication was coded for each post.

Message Interactivity investigates the response-inviting aspect of the message of the post. Any message that asks or encourages a response directly will be considered as interactive. Additionally, messages that include questions (excluding rhetorical questions) or actions verbs are examples of what can be considered response-inviting. As suggested by the coding scheme of Kim and Yang (2017), in order to the post be considered as interactive, the message needs to "solicit responses from the public directly".

The posts were also coded for its central appeal as performed on the work of Wagner et al. (2017) that, as stated before, created a coding instrument with twelve emotional appeals and twelve functional appeals. In their study, post appeals emerged from their coding instrument and their sample of posts didn't influence it. On the contrary, Wang et al. (2017), in order to define the coding instrument, firstly read their sample of posts and after developed eleven post appeals. Swani et al. (2017), although only distinguish between emotional and functional appeals, did suggest categories of both such as humor, romance and contest, among others. In this study, on both cases of Facebook and Instagram, a mix approach was used. A reading of the whole sample was performed before developing the appeals, but the processing of the appeals also followed the procedures suggested by the literature when generating a coding instrument.

In order to construct a valid coding instrument, it is desirable that the appeals represent wide topics because otherwise it would be difficult to distinguish clearly the categories. As a consequence, while reading through the sample this concern was already present. After having the initial list of potential post appeals, a more detailed analysis to that list was performed to secure that similar categories were grouped. As a final step all categories that weren't immediately perceived, were eliminated. This is important because during the coding procedure it should be easy to comprehend and to code each post without questions. Moreover, the name of the appeals should also be straightforward and created using understandable language. To complete, a description of each appeal should be developed to ensure the minimum level of ambiguity (Wagner et al., 2017).

Afterwards, the list was compared to the coding instruments of previous studies. From the eight post appeals proposed by this study, six of them correspond to post appeals previously used by Wang et al. (2017), Wagner et al. (2017) and Swani et al. (2017).

The control variables, day of the week and length of the caption of the post, were also coded. Each post was coded as "1 = weekday" if they corresponded to days from Monday to Friday and "0 = weekend" if Saturday and Sunday were the day of publication. Regarding the length of the caption an Excel function was used (LEN) in order to facilitate the process and to ensure the accuracy of this variable. Every caption was copied to an Excel file and then the function was executed.

The number of likes, reactions, comments and shares were documented by reading the information provided on the screenshots.

From a total of 382 posts from Facebook, it was concluded that some had to be excluded. Three of them were milestones, which don't fall into neither of the post types in this study and therefore were excluded. Another three were GIFs, and for the same reason were also excluded. One of the posts, for an unknown reason, didn't had an available URL. As a content analysis will be performed, this post was also excluded, once it is not possible to perform a rigorous content analysis in order to identify the post appeal. Concerning Instagram, only one post was eliminated as it didn't fall into any post appeal. Additionally, only brand posts were considered on both SNSs.

To conclude, the sample is composed of 375 posts from Facebook and 52 from Instagram.

SOLUTIONS AND RECOMMENDATIONS

In this study, factors such as post type, time frame, message interactivity and post appeal were analyzed in order to investigate its effect on customer engagement through social media.

The first factor proposed by the framework of this study was post type and the goal was to identify which post type had more influence on customer engagement. This is an important issue, since each post type requires significantly different amount of time in order to be created. As time is a valuable asset, it is relevant for brands to know which is the best post type in terms of customer engagement. On Facebook, video was significantly and positively related to all of the metrics whereas images were only significant on the number of likes, reactions and comments. In addition, images were negatively related to the number of comments. Furthermore, it is noteworthy that video was the most important variable in every model except in the comments one, showing its relevance. The model for the number of likes is significant as a whole (F-value = 4.907, p-value <0.05) and has an explanatory power of 18% ($R^2 = 22.6\%$, adj. $R^2 = 18\%$).

Concerning post type, both image and video are significantly related with the number of likes. Image posts have a positive effect ($\beta = 0.462$, p-value < 0.05) as well as videos ($\beta = 1.234$, p-value < 0.05). However, attention should be paid to the greater impact of videos when comparing to images. Although both of them have a positive effect, video exert a more powerful effect.

The message interactivity is also significantly and positively related with the number of likes ($\beta = 0.313$, p-value < 0.05). Consequently, from these findings, it is suggested that video is the post type that has more influence on customer engagement on social media, followed by images.

On Instagram, results were different since video had a negative impact on the number of likes. Concerning post type, video ($\beta = -0.217$, p-value < 0.10) showed to be significantly and negatively related to the number of likes on Instagram. This could be considered a normal result since Instagram is mostly known by the share of images. Videos are also a post type possible, but not the most commonly used by users. Nevertheless, the platform has already updated the video features. In the beginning only 15 second were allowed and currently videos can be uploaded up to 60 seconds. This could be an improvement from the brand in order to promote the use of videos among users. However, from the results of this work, it is suggested that images are preferred over videos on Instagram.

Regarding time frame, results were very surprising. The aim of this study was to analyze which months had a positive effect on customer engagement but instead, findings only contemplate months with a negative impact. On Instagram, it wasn't possible to analyze this issue once none of the months was a significant variable. Concerning Facebook, December was negatively related with likes and comments, August with reactions and October with the number of reactions and comments. Although on the work of Coelho et al. (2016), the positive impact of some months were justified by the presence of national holidays, it is believe in this study, that the activity of users on social media is increased during work hours as showed by some studies. As a consequence, on periods of holidays and vacations as the case of December and August, it would be normal for the metrics of customer engagement to decrease.

With respect to message interactivity, the results of this study suggest different conclusions regarding the nature of the SNS. was expected that the number of comments would be increased by the response-inviting characteristic and this was empirically proved. Additionally, it was expected that the other variables (likes, reactions and shares) would be negatively impacted by the interactivity. However, the contrary was observed. Both likes and reactions were positively related to message interactivity. It can be concluded that brands have a crucial role when creating their content because this independent variable has an effect on the majority of the metrics of customer engagement.

These findings are partially in accordance with the previous work of Kim and Yang (2017) since in their study, the positive effect was only on the number of comments. Additionally, both this study and past studies confirm that having posts encouraging the response from users can increase the number of comments which is an expected result since it is the action the post aims for. Nevertheless, through the work of the present study it was proven that the number of likes and reactions were also positively affected by the response-inviting aspect of the message. This could mean that users also feel more encouraging to demonstrate their feelings about a post when the brand asks for their opinion. It is visible that it was very frequently that the brand simply asks if the users agreed with the message on the post. Consequently, as it could be only a yes or no answer, the yes could be demonstrated simply by a like on the post, leading to the increased of the number of likes and reactions.

On Instagram, message interactivity had no influence on the number of likes and as the model for the number of comments wasn't significant as a whole.

Regarding the study of post appeals, interesting findings were observed. On Facebook, both challenge and family were significant for all customer engagement metrics on social media.

Challenge was only positively related to the number of comments which is an understandable result. It was expected that, as the behavior stimulated by the response-inviting aspect is commenting, this variable would be the only one positively influenced as the other ones would be cannibalized. This wasn't what happened to interactivity. However, it happened for the challenge appeal. The difference, as discussed above is that the response-inviting aspect can indeed encourage different types of responses from the users. In the case of challenges, as the only way of participating is through comments, it is natural that this behavior is increased while others are decreased.

Family, on the other hand, was a positive influence in every metric, proving that it is an important and crucial appeal. The explanation behind this result could be related to the fact of relatability and identification. It is easy to establish connections with users through the thematic of family, once it is one of the most powerful memories and it is a big part of one's life. The great majority of the fans are women between the age of 35 to 44 that, most probably, are moms interested in the education of their children. Consequently, the topic of family is also of their interest and it is close to their hearts.

The metric that was influenced by more appeals were the reactions. Challenge, family, humor, pride and sad were those appeals and in exception from challenge, all the remaining ones had a positive influence on the number of reactions. Interestingly, these appeals can be easily related to the options for reactions on Facebook. For instance, humor is translated as the *Haha* reaction and sad by the *Sad* one. In addition, family and pride can both be associated to the love feeling represented by the *Love*

Table 1. The impact of each post appeal on the dependent variables

	Facebook				Instagram
	Likes	Reactions	Comments	Shares	Likes
Challenge	(-)	(-)	(+)	(-)	-
Family	(+)	(+)	(+)	(+)	(+)
Humor	-	(+)	-	-	-
Pride	-	(+)	-	-	-
Sad	-	(+)	-	-	-
Parenting	-	-	(-)	-	-

(-) post appeals with a negative effect; (+) post appeals with a positive affect

reaction, which through the reading of the sample from Facebook, was one of the most frequent reaction. These results also prove that, in fact, users perceive the main appeal of the post as they have associated them to corresponding reactions as suggested by the framework of Wagner et al. (2017).

Parenting was only significant on the comments model and had a negative influence on this variable.

In summary and in response to the third research question, the post appeals that have a positive effect on customer engagement can be seen on Table 1.

A frequency analysis was performed in order to analyze if the post appeals with a positive effect on customer engagement were the most frequently used as formulated on the fourth research question. This study reports mixed results depending on the type of SNS. On Facebook, more than half of the post are only about two topics: education and parenting. As stated previously, the second one is related to the decrease on the number of comments. Additionally, family, which the only appeal that impacts positively all customer engagement metrics, is solely used 9.6% of the times, which is reasonably low. Humor and pride are also seldom used. Sad, which accounts for less than 1% also proved to be positively related with the number of reactions. It could be though by brands that using sad emotions is prejudicial for customer engagement, however, when used properly, it can have a positive impact. Additionally, the challenge appeal which is the most important variable in the comments model, meaning that it is the most powerful factor, is barely used. Towards these findings, it could be argued that brands could be more data driven and should include the study of post appeal on their analysis. Moreover, making use of the appeals that are similar to reactions is also a behavior that could be beneficial to improve customer engagement on social media.

On Instagram, humor showed to be a positive influence on the number of likes and it is, in fact, the most used appeal. The appeals used on each SNS aren't the same, however, the one they have in common, humor, when significant, has a positive effect on both Facebook and Instagram. Thus, attention should be paid to this appeal by brands.

In terms of managerial implications, it is advised for brands and their managers to consider each SNS as independent. This is, while it is true that having presence in multiple platforms is beneficial (depending off course on the type of company and its goals), it is necessary to recognize that the same strategies or the same content won't have the same results on both platforms. For instance, if on Facebook users potentially prefer videos, on Instagram, the best way to reach the audience is through images. While on Facebook, response-inviting content seems to be relevant and have a positive impact on customer engagement, on Instagram this aspect doesn't appear to be significant. In fact, on Facebook, response-inviting was relevant for both the number of likes, reactions and comments which turns this factor into one of the most important of the framework presented in this work. For brands, this is important, once they can really focus on developing the ability of establishing a of and it will have a positive impact on most of the metrics of customer engagement on social media.

The framework proposed by this study also contributes for the literature and future research as it showed to be relevant and therefore can be applied to different situations. Additionally, it incorporates both soft and hard criterion which is an important contribution since both types of factors should be taken into consideration when studying customer engagement on social media.

CONCLUSIONS

The findings of this study suggest that all four factors, namely post type, time frame, message interactivity and post appeal have influence on customer engagement.

Through the results from the message interactive factor, it is important to notice that brands play a crucial role in setting the tone and the type of communication that is establish with users. This was a factor that had an influence on 3 out of 4 metrics of customer engagement on Facebook, proving its relevance. Not only brands encourage comments by posting response-inviting content but also encourage likes and reactions from users. This proves that brands should promote an open dialogue between them and customers (Mollen & Wilson, 2010) and that they should be the first showing they are open and interested in having a dialogue and caring about the opinions of customers.

Post appeal also proved to be of extreme importance. Users want to be involved and connected with brands and they want to have unique experiences. Creating such a feeling and a connection is not easy, and thus, understanding what post appeals work best in terms of customer engagement is important. From the results of this study, it is possible to conclude that family and challenge are the most salient appeals regarding Facebook. This is interesting because the challenge appeal is related to the message interactivity. In other words, it could be argued that users, indeed, like and have a positive response to content that requires their active participation. This is also in agreement with what is thought about the new role of customers as they seek for a more active role in the buying process and their desire to co-create value with the brand (Gambetti & Graffigna, 2010). Consequently, brands should definitely take these results into account and try to incorporate message interactivity in their content and make customers feel that their opinion is valued. Regarding Instagram, humor proved to be a positive influence on the number of likes which also impacted positively the number of reactions on Facebook. Thus, when significant, this appeal also stood out by being a positive influence on customer engagement. It is also important to notice, that this work contributes to enrich literature about post appeals. Traditionally, the majority of studies only distinguished between emotional or functional appeals, without incorporating the different cues within each category. This work confirms some results proposed by Wagner et al. (2017) and Wang et al. (2017) and proposes new cues that haven't been studied yet, such as parenting, motivation and sad.

Furthermore, this work showed that depending on the SNS, factors have a different impact on customer engagement, and so, the conclusions withdrawn for Facebook aren't the same for Instagram. Coelho et al. (2016) has already pointed out the potential mediating role that distinct SNSs could have on results and with the findings of this study, it is possible to corroborate its suspicion and contribute to the literature on this topic. Although every SNS such as Facebook, Instagram, Twitter and LinkedIn have a common base, the goals, the audience that brands can reach and the features within the platforms are different. Therefore, due to these aspects it is possible that the impact of certain factors can differ. Thus, this is also a managerial implication since it is important for managers and brands to understand that their strategies must be adapted for each social media or that, even having the same content on multiple platforms, it would be normal not to have the same results in terms of customer engagement.

Regarding post type, as stated before, the existent literature reports mixed results. In this study, it can be inferred that on Facebook, video is always more significant than images and thus it is recommended for brands to make use of videos. This is a conclusion that agrees with the most recent studies, which could signal that through time, videos have gained more relevance and importance within Facebook and its users. On Instagram, the implication isn't the same as the impact of video on the number of likes is negative. Thus, in order to increase customer engagement on Instagram it is recommended to brands to use images.

With respect to the time frame, the goal of this study was to identify which months had a positive effect on customer engagement. On the contrary, only months with a negative influence were identified. Given that those months were August and December, which are characterized by being a period of vacations and holidays, it could be argued that users have more online presence and activity during the work period.

Attention should be paid to the importance of the reactions as they are gaining relevance and use among users. As stated before, it can be a powerful measure for brands, as they can better understand how their customers feel and how they react towards their content and products. Additionally, as showed by this study, it was one of the metrics of customer engagement that suffered more impact from the factors included in the framework, specially by post appeals. This emphasizes its relevance as a powerful data that should be analyzed by brands. For the academic research this is also an interesting contribution since, at the time, there is barely any literature that considers the number of reactions as a metric of customer engagement on social media.

To summarize, in order for brands to increase their customer engagement, it is suggested that, on Facebook, they make use of videos, response-inviting content and utilize both family and challenge appeal. On Instagram, images should be the first option combined with the humor appeal.

FUTURE RESEARCH DIRECTIONS

This study showed that results were different between Facebook and Instagram which opens the way for questioning if other social networking sites would also have different results or if they would have a similar behavior to one of these. Thus, it is also encouraged, that future researchers study other social networking sites such as LinkedIn or Pinterest. Additionally, more evidences are needed regarding Instagram, once that there are few studies concerning customer engagement on this platform. Consequently, future work could apply the framework presented in this study to other companies on Instagram and compare the results obtained.

REFERENCES

Ahmad, N. S., Musa, R., & Harun, M. H. M. (2016). The impact of social media content marketing (SMCM) towards brand health. *Procedia Economics and Finance*, *37*, 331–336. doi:10.1016/S2212-5671(16)30133-2

Ariel, Y., & Avidar, R. (2015). *Information, Interactivity, and Social Media.*, *23*, 19.

Bagozzi, R. P., Gopinath, M., & Nyer, P. U. (1999). The role of emotions in marketing. *Journal of the Academy of Marketing Science*, *27*(2), 184–206. doi:10.1177/0092070399272005

Bowden, J. L.-H. (2009). The process of customer engagement: a conceptual framework. *Journal of Marketing Theory and Practice*, *17*(1), 63–74. doi:10.2753/MTP1069-6679170105

Carah, N., & Shaul, M. (2015). Brands and Instagram: Point, tap, swipe, glance. *Mobile Media & Communication*, *4*(1), 69–84. doi:10.1177/2050157915598180

Coelho, R. L. F., Oliveira, D. S. D., & Almeida, M. I. S. D. (2016). Does social media matter for post typology? Impact of post content on Facebook and Instagram metrics. *Online Information Review*, *40*(4), 458–471. doi:10.1108/OIR-06-2015-0176

Cvijikj, I. P., & Michahelles, F. (2013). Online engagement factors on Facebook brand pages. *Social Network Analysis and Mining*, *3*(4), 843–861. doi:10.100713278-013-0098-8

De Vries, L., Gensler, S., & Leeflang, P. S. H. (2012). Popularity of brand posts on brand fan pages: an investigation of the effects of social media marketing. *Journal of Interactive Marketing*, *26*(2), 83–91. doi:10.1016/j.intmar.2012.01.003

Dessart, L., Veloutsou, C., & Morgan-Thomas, A. (2016). Capturing consumer engagement: Duality, dimensionality and measurement. *Journal of Marketing Management*, *32*(5-6), 399–426. doi:10.1080/0267257X.2015.1130738

Erkan, I. (2015). Electronic word of mouth on Instagram: Customers' Engagements with Brands in Different Sectors. *International Journal of Management, Accounting, and Economics*, *2*(12), 1435–1444.

Gambetti, R., & Grafigna, G. (2010). The concept of engagement: A systematic analysis of the ongoing marketing debate. *International Journal of Market Research*, *52*(6), 801–826. doi:10.2501/S147078531020166

Go, E., & Bortree, D. S. (2017). What and how to communicate CSR? The role of CSR fit, modality interactivity, and message interactivity on social networking sites. *Journal of Promotion Management*, 1–21.

Hollebeek, L. D., Glynn, M. S., & Brodie, R. J. (2014). Consumer brand engagement in social media: conceptualization, scale development and validation. *Journal of Interactive Marketing*, *28*(2), 149–165. doi:10.1016/j.intmar.2013.12.002

Holliman, G., & Rowley, J. (2014). Business to business digital content marketing: Marketers' perceptions of best practice. *Journal of Research in Interactive Marketing*, *8*(4), 269–293. doi:10.1108/JRIM-02-2014-0013

Kim, C., & Yang, S.-U. (2017). Like, comment, and share on Facebook: How each behavior differs from the other. *Public Relations Review*, *43*(2), 441–449. doi:10.1016/j.pubrev.2017.02.006

Kim, J. K., & Hull, K. (2017). How fans are engaging with baseball teams demonstrating multiple objectives on Instagram. *Sport, Business, and Management International Journal (Toronto, Ont.)*, *7*, 216–232.

Lee, H., & Park, H. (2013). Testing the impact of message interactivity on relationship management and organizational reputation. *Journal of Public Relations Research*, *25*(2), 188–206. doi:10.1080/1062726X.2013.739103

Liu, J., Li, C., Ji, Y. G., North, M., & Yang, F. (2017). Like it or not: The Fortune 500's Facebook strategies to generate users' electronic word-of-mouth. *Computers in Human Behavior*, *73*, 605–613. doi:10.1016/j.chb.2017.03.068

Malthouse, E. C., Calder, B. J., Kim, S. J., & Vandenbosch, M. (2016). Evidence that user-generated content that produces engagement increases purchase behaviours. *Journal of Marketing Management*, *32*(5-6), 427–444. doi:10.1080/0267257X.2016.1148066

Mollen, A., & Wilson, H. (2010). Engagement, telepresence and interactivity in online consumer experience: Reconciling scholastic and managerial perspectives. *Journal of Business Research*, *63*(9-10), 919–925. doi:10.1016/j.jbusres.2009.05.014

Ngai, E. W. T., Tao, S. S. C., & Moon, K. K. L. (2015). Social media research: Theories, constructs, and conceptual frameworks. *International Journal of Information Management*, *35*(1), 33–44. doi:10.1016/j.ijinfomgt.2014.09.004

Phua, J., Jin, S. V., & Kim, J. (2017). Gratifications of using Facebook, Twitter, Instagram, or Snapchat to follow brands: The moderating effect of social comparison, trust, tie strength, and network homophily on brand identification, brand engagement, brand commitment, and membership intention. *Telematics and Informatics*, *34*(1), 412–424. doi:10.1016/j.tele.2016.06.004

Sabate, F., Berbegal-Mirabent, J., Cañabate, A., & Lebherz, P. R. (2014). Factors influencing popularity of branded content in Facebook fan pages. *European Management Journal*, *32*(6), 1001–1011. doi:10.1016/j.emj.2014.05.001

Sashi, C. M. (2012). Customer engagement, buyer-seller relationships, and social media. *Management Decision*, *50*(2), 253–272. doi:10.1108/00251741211203551

Swani, K., & Milne, G. R. (2017). Evaluating Facebook brand content popularity for service versus goods offerings. *Journal of Business Research*, *79*, 123–133. doi:10.1016/j.jbusres.2017.06.003

Swani, K., Milne, G. R., Brown, B. P., Assaf, A. G., & Donthu, N. (2017). What messages to post? Evaluating the popularity of social media communications in business versus consumer markets. *Industrial Marketing Management*, *62*, 77–87. doi:10.1016/j.indmarman.2016.07.006

Van Doorne, J., N. Lemon, K., Mittal, V., Nass, S., Pick, D., Pirner, P., & Verhoef, P. (2010). *Customer engagement behavior: theoretical foundations and research directions.*

Verhoef, P. C., Reinartz, W. J., & Krafft, M. (2010). Customer engagement as a new perspective in customer management. *Journal of Service Research*, *13*(3), 247–252. doi:10.1177/1094670510375461

Wagner, T. F., Baccarella, C. V., & Voigt, K.-I. (2017). Framing social media communication: Investigating the effects of brand post appeals on user interaction. *European Management Journal*, *35*(5), 606–616. doi:10.1016/j.emj.2017.05.002

Wang, R., Kim, J., Xiao, A., & Jung, Y. J. (2017). Networked narratives on Humans of New York: A content analysis of social media engagement on Facebook. *Computers in Human Behavior*, *66*, 149–153. doi:10.1016/j.chb.2016.09.042

KEY TERMS AND DEFINITIONS

Content Marketing: It is used to attract, acquire and engage with a well-defined public through the distribution of relevant content. The final goal is to lead to a desirable customer action which could be seen as the purchase of the product of service of the brand that employed the content marketing strategy.

Customer Engagement: Emotions and relationships customers have with brands, representing loyalty.

Post Types: Image, link and video.

Chapter 4
A Literature Review of Social Media for Marketing:
Social Media Use in B2C and B2B Contexts

Bahtışen Kavak
https://orcid.org/0000-0002-5252-5410
Hacettepe University, Turkey

Neslişah Özdemir
https://orcid.org/0000-0003-2380-6149
Kastamonu University, Turkey

Gülay Erol-Boyacı
https://orcid.org/0000-0002-8123-3011
Başkent University, Turkey

ABSTRACT

Digital economy has become a priority for companies and countries since consumer profile and consumption habits have greatly changed. Companies have begun to transfer the services they offer to the Internet. Also, a digital economy creates networks amongst individuals, communities, companies, and markets. With digitalization, not only have consumers' profiles changed, but marketing tools have changed as well. Social media marketing (SMM) is the product of this trend and is marketing through social media channels (SMCs). Therefore, this chapter examines social media use within business-to-consumer (B2C) and business-to-business (B2B) contexts. Moreover, the authors focus on the differences of SMCs adoption in B2C and B2B contexts.

DOI: 10.4018/978-1-7998-2185-4.ch004

INTRODUCTION

The use of social media has expanded in recent years. Social media is a term that academics and professionals use to describe this media. One of the basic definitions of social media is "sites where users actively participate to determine what is popular" ("SEMPO," 2017), and another definition is "a platform for interaction and networking" (Eisenberg, 2008). Social media is beginning to be considered as an important marketing tool in digital economies for companies. The use of social media is assumed to make changes in the ways *business-to-consumer* (B2C) and *business-to-business* (B2B) marketers communicate, interact, consume, and create within and outside the company (Vize & Sherrett, 2017, p. 46).

This chapter aims to provide a literature review of social media for marketing. The main objective of marketing is to reach consumers and influence their purchasing behaviors. As social media is an effective tool to reach audiences and promote products or services, companies give value to Social Media Marketing (SMM). SMM is used for the purpose of brand awareness, developing brand image, increasing communication efficiency, improving customer relationships, and to stimulate sales. However, the purposes of SMM have to be evaluated in terms of the customer life cycle process.

The social media literature gives special emphasis to consumers in the B2C context (Michaelidou, Siamagka, & Christodoulides, 2011). In other words, researchers have focused more on the user side rather than on the companies' views (Jussila, 2015, p. 3). B2C companies are aware of the importance of social media and desire to reach consumers by using social media channels (SMCs). They use social media to attract new customers, develop relationships, and increase awareness. Moreover, they enhance interaction with consumers through SMCs. In contrast, until recently, B2B organizations believed that social media use was only beneficial in a B2C context (Jussila, Kärkkäinen, & Aramo-Immonen, 2014) and perceived SMCs to be inadequate for their industry. Nevertheless, B2B has begun to realize the importance of social media in today's marketing environment. For instance, the Content Marketing Institute (CMI, 2018) put forth that 92% of B2B marketers support using SMCs (e.g., LinkedIn, Twitter, etc.) more than using traditional tools such as trade shows, direct mail, and catalogues.

While trying to adopt social media, B2B companies have different purposes. First, companies desire to scan market trends and evaluate changing customer attitudes. Moreover, demonstrating products and providing training to business partners via social media are important to them. In addition to this, employee recruitment and retention are the leading motives for using SMCs (Vize & Sherrett, 2017, p. 50). Therefore, the use of SMCs as marketing tools has increased. Some B2B brands have their own original content and others have YouTube pages. They publish special content for SMCs on sites such as Facebook, Twitter, and LinkedIn, and share the videos produced via YouTube with users.

Since market characteristics are different from one another, the usage of SMCs also differs within B2C and B2B contexts. While some empirical studies do explore the differences in SMC usage between B2C and B2B contexts, this topic is limited in much of the literature (Moore, Hopkins, & Raymond, 2013; Swani, Brown, & Milne, 2014; Iankova, Davies, Archer-Brown, Marder, & Yau, 2018).

This chapter, therefore, aims to focus on the differences between SMC usage within B2B and B2C contexts. For this reason, this chapter includes background information, definitions and classification of social media, a definition and the purposes of SMM, and social media usage in B2C and B2B environments. Finally, solutions and recommendations, future research directions, and conclusion are also provided.

BACKGROUND

The concept of social media is one of the biggest changes since the industrial revolution (Smith & Zook, 2011, p. 9). The foundation of social media today is based on many of the popular social media sites introduced in the 1990s (Figure 1).

To have a better understanding of the modern communication environment, evolution of social media history is significant. In this regard, Figure 1 demonstrates examples for the timeline of SMCs in chronological order. In the 1990s, the earliest form of SMCs, such as Craigslist, Black Planet, and Blogger, were developed (Flanigan & Obermier, 2016) to provide online services based on sharing information and stories. After 2000, SMCs were advanced and Wikipedia, LinkedIn, MySpace, Facebook, YouTube, and so on were born (Funk, 2011, p. 8). These new channels enabled people to not only share stories or ideas, but also to meet and contact one another. Today, multiple users can communicate in real time, share pictures, videos, and any kind of document through SMCs.

Table 1 shows some statistical indicators about active social media user rates in five regions. As it is shown in Table 1, during the 2016, the total number of Internet users has increased 10% (354 Million); meanwhile the total number of active social media users has increased 21% (482 Million). When it is examined, the regional data, in all the five regions (Africa, Americas, Asia-Pacific, Europe, Middle East), both the Internet and social media user rates have increased.

Social media, one of the basic tools of digital marketing, brings innovations in terms of the relationship between businesses and customers. While customers are the same, their buying behaviors and opportunities have changed as traditional advertising channels, such as TV commercials, billboards, and radio (Smedescu, 2013) have

Figure 1. Examples for timeline of SMCs
Source: (Funk, 2011, p. 9; Flanigan & Obermier, 2016)

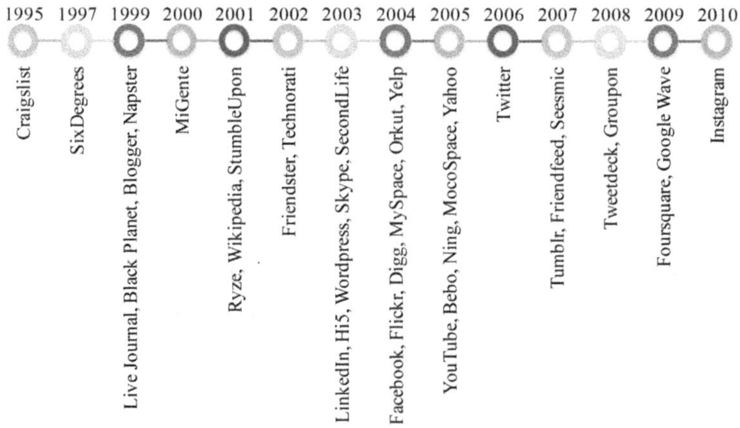

Table 1. A few statistical indicators of Internet and active social media users for different regions

	Population	Internet Users*	Active Social Media Users*
Total	7.476 Billion	3.773 Billion *(+10%)* *(+354 Million)*	2.789 Billion *(+21%)* *(+482 Million)*
Africa	1.231 Million	362 Million *(+4%)* *(+13 Million)*	170 Million *(+32%)* *(+42 Million)*
America	1.006 Million	718 Million *(+8%)* *(+53 Million)*	599 Million *(+17%)* *(+88 Million)*
Asia Pacific	4.153 Billion	1.909 Billion *(+15%)* *(+247 Million)*	1.514 Billion *(+25%)* *(+303 Million)*
Europe	839 Million	637 Million *(+3%)* *(+21 Million)*	412 Million *(+ 5%)* *(+ 20 Million)*
Middle East	246 Million	147 Million *(+15%)* *(+19 Million)*	93 Million *(+47%)* *(+30 Million)*

*Data shown in parentheses are based on annual change between 01.01.2016 and 01.01.2017.

**Note: Data was retrieved from "We Are Social January Report" (2017).

been expanded through the availability of new informational and shopping sites on the Internet. There is less dependence on traditional communication channels in this era. Hence, businesses use social media and shape the marketplace in terms of new communication approaches (Constantinides, 2014).

The use of social media within marketing contexts contributes to businesses in various ways. First, social media contributes to companies engaged in market research. Automated data collection and evaluation of profiles, links, and shares in social media provide market researchers with the opportunity to evaluate market segmentation, monitor consumer behavior, market positions of products, and offer new product development information. Furthermore, social media provides more personalized resolutions to their customers with regard to any problems or concerns with products (Al Khalili, 2018). In addition to this, through the mutual communication provided in SMCs, customers, or potential customers, obtain information about the culture and products of companies, and as a result of this communication, companies obtain feedback by learning the expectations of their customers and their thoughts about the company or their products (Hacıhasanoglu, 2017).

Social media utilization in digital economies is a contemporary issue. In order to determine social media use in digital economies, the organizations classify their markets, such as B2C and B2B. In B2C, customers are ordinary people who want to know other customer reviews and receive special treatment. However, in B2B, companies are seeking direct contact and special offers (AlSuwaidan & Ykhlef, 2016). When compared to B2C markets, there are fewer customers in B2B markets, and the social networks that exist between business partners are important in terms of providing strong cooperation. Therefore, social media use between B2C and B2B markets differ in terms of market features.

While studies on the usage of social media in B2C is widespread, studies focusing on the extent of social media adoption by B2B companies has been limited in the literature. Michaelidou, Siamagka, and Christodoulides (2011) are among the initial researchers who explored SMEs in B2B contexts, their social networking practices, and the measurement of effectiveness of social networking sites. They found that B2B SMEs used social networking sites to accomplish brand objectives and attract new customers. Brennan and Croft (2012) investigated B2B technology companies to determine their social media usage. They found that social media leaders in B2B markets used SMCs to position themselves as opinion leaders, to ensure a market-driven role, and to maintain relationship with third parties.

Research that focuses on the differences between usage of social media between B2C and B2B is limited. Moore, Hopkins, and Raymond (2013) and Swani, Brown, and Milne (2014) investigated the usage differences between these two contexts, but only for social media posts, especially on Twitter and Facebook. Moreover, Iankova, Davies, Archer-Brown, Marder, and Yau (2018) examined the differences in the ways that B2B and B2C businesses used social media, as well as mixed B2B/ B2C and B2B2C business models, and perceived significant differences. Therefore, this chapter highlights social media usage in B2C and B2B contexts, especially in terms of differences of trends in usage.

SOCIAL MEDIA

In this next section, the authors have examined social media in terms of two titles: definition of social media and classification of SMCs.

Definition of Social Media

In a broad perspective, social media is "any web presence where users can add their own content, but do not have control over the website in the same way as they would their own website" (Charlesworth, 2015, p. 150). From a similar point of view, social media is defined as, "The production, consumption, and exchange of information through online social interactions and platforms" ("MARKETO," 2010, p. 5).

Moreover, social media is also referred as Web 2.0, which is based on word-of-mouth and information sharing (Barefoot & Szabo, 2010, p. 4). There are different definitions from this perspective:

• Social media is a group of internet-based applications that build on the ideological and technological foundations of Web 2.0 and that allow the creation and exchange of user-generated content (Kaplan & Haenlein, 2010).

• Web 2.0 presents businesses with new challenges, but also new opportunities for getting and staying in touch with their markets, learning about the needs and opinions of their customers, as well as interacting with customers in a direct and personalized way (Tapscott & Williams, 2008, p. 20).

Table 2. Differences between web 1.0 and web 2.0

Web 1.0 was about...	Web 2.0 is about...
• Reading • Advertising • Lectures • Websites • Professionals • Companies • Owning	• Writing • Word-of-Mouth • Conversations • Web Services • Amateurs • Communities • Sharing

Source: (Barefoot & Szabo, 2010, p. 4)

Some academics and professionals use the term "Web 2.0" to define social media. Based on the Web 2.0 definitions, Table 2 provides details that show what Web 2.0 is and how it is different from Web 1.0.

As seen in Table 2, Web 1.0 offers one-way communications, whereas Web 2.0 offers two-way communications. In Web 1.0, people can only read the contents and cannot share their opinions or feelings. However, in Web 2.0, it is possible to write and share opinions. So, Web 2.0 allows people to have conversations via the Internet from wherever they are.

Therefore, social media could be described as Internet-based applications that enable sharing and exchange of information, ideas, interests, and creation of virtual networks and communities. Social media is a new way of sharing and accessing user-generated information in a simple, instant, and bilateral way. It provides users with personal information, videos, photos, and other contents easily transmitted through the virtual environment.

In general, people primarily use social media for searching for entertainment, travel, food, and shopping, or for obtaining information about products and brands ("MARKETO," 2016, p. 10). Charlesworth (2015, p. 155) suggested that social media users are driven by the following:

- The need to socialize is one of the main reasons. People want to be in touch with their friends and have a social network.
- There is a need for self-expression. Expression of personality, emotions, or ideas, through SMCs is easier today when compared to the past.
- People want to find others who have similar tastes and interests. Some SMCs are designed to build networks.
- Contrary to the traditional word-of-mouth, SMCs provide access to unlimited information about any brand or product.
- The desire to search for a job, to find cheaper goods or services, and to find free software products are examples of some of the financial advantages served by social media.

It can be concluded that people have a variety of motives that include socialization, self-expression, networking, accessing information, and utilizing financial advantages while using social media.

Classification of Social Media Channels (SMCs)

SMCs are user-friendly, cost effective, scalable Internet and mobile-based technologies. With these technologies it is possible to share user-generated contents (Fischer & Reuber, 2011). In the literature, there are different classifications for SMCs. One of the classifications made by Kaplan and Haenlein (2010) is based on social presence and media richness (low, medium, high) and self-presentation

Figure 2. Classification of SMCs
Source: (Zimmerman & Ng, 2017, p. 25)

Social Content-Sharing	Social-Networking	Social-Bookmarking	Social Geolocations and Meetings	Community Building	Social News
• Blogs and content-posting sites • Images • Video • Audio	• Full networks • Short message networks • Professional networks • Specialty networks	• Recommendation services • Social-shopping services • Other bookmarking services.	• Foursquare • Meetups • Other GPS (Global Positioning System) applications	• Community-Building sites • Wikis • Review sites	• Digg • Reddit • Other news sites

and self-disclosure (low, high). According to Kaplan and Haenlein (2010), there are six different social media classes: 1). Collaborative projects (e.g., Wikipedia); 2). Content communities (e.g., YouTube); 3). Virtual game worlds (e.g., World of Warcraft); 4). Blogs; 5). Social networking sites (e.g., Facebook); and 6). Virtual social worlds (e.g., Second Life).

When SMCs are evaluated in terms of social presence and media richness, blogs and collaborative projects have the lowest scores. Because they are text based, they include simple exchanges. Social networking sites and content communities are in the medium part, according to social presence and media richness since they often provide visual and video sharing. The highest part consists of virtual social worlds and virtual game worlds that provide to users with face-to-face interaction in a visual environment.

On the other hand, those SMCs can be classified with regards to self-presentation and self-disclosure. Since collaborative projects concentrate on particular content, blogs provide higher self-presentation and self-disclosure. Social networking sites score higher than content communities in terms of self-presentation and self-disclosure, as content communities focus on specific content. Virtual social worlds allow for more self-disclosure and self-presentation than virtual game worlds that have hard rules that push users to act in a precise way (Kaplan & Haenlein, 2010). Furthermore, Zimmerman and Ng (2017, p. 25) categorizes SMCs into six types (Figure 2).

As shown in Figure 2, SMCs consist of social content sharing, social networking, social-bookmarking, social geolocations and meetings, community building, and social news channels (Zimmerman & Ng, 2017, p. 25).

- **Social Content-sharing Channels:** These services provide posting and commenting on text, videos, photos, and podcasts. They include blogs and content-posting sites (e.g. WordPress, Blogger, Medium, and Tumblr); video (e.g. YouTube, Vimeo, Vine.co); images (e.g. Flickr, Instagram, Snapchat, SlideShare, Pinterest); and podcasts (e.g. Podbean, BlogTalkRadio).

- **Social-networking Channels:** These channels facilitate the exchange of personal information such as messages, photos to friends and family, and also offer services in terms of business. Social-networking channels consist of full networks (e.g. Facebook, Google Plus); short message networks (e.g. Twitter); professional networks (e.g. LinkedIn); and specialty networks (e.g. Q&A network Quora).
- **Social-bookmarking Channels:** These channels provide users with the opportunity to store, organize, and search Internet pages. Social-bookmarking channels include recommendation services (e.g. StumbleUpon, Delicious), social-shopping services (e.g. Wanelo, ThisNext), and other bookmarking services.
- **Social Geolocation and Meeting Channels:** These channels bring people together in actual space and include Foursquare, Meetups, and other GPS (Global Positioning System) applications.
- **Community-building Channels:** These channels include many comments and material sharing sites. Especially, forums and massage boards, which are good examples of these channels. They include community building sites (e.g. Ning); Wikis (e.g. Wikipedia) and review sites (e.g. TripAdvisor, Yelp).
- **Social News Channels:** A social news website involves user-posted stories. They include Digg, Reddit and other news sites.

While there are different classifications of SMCs, this chapter reviews SMCs in terms of social content sharing and social networking channels. Today, the top five social media networking platforms used by marketers in terms of unique monthly visitors are: Facebook, YouTube, Twitter, Instagram, and LinkedIn ("Most Popular Networking Sites," 2017). Therefore, those channels will be identified in detail.

Facebook is a social networking site launched in 2004. At first, Facebook was a social network for Harvard students. Today, it has more than 300 million active users from 170 countries (Reece, 2010, p. 246). People can get connected with their friends easily around the world thanks to Facebook. LinkedIn is the world's largest proficient network site with more than 175 million members worldwide (Funk, 2011, p. 48).

Twitter, launched in 2006, is based in San Francisco and can be immediately translated from English to 16 other languages. Thus, it can be easily used by people all over the world (Coles, 2015, p. 82). Twitter includes 140 characters and initially was created for college kids somewhat like Facebook, but its popularity is growing very fast.

Figure 3. Examples for commonly used channels
Note: Data was retrieved from "Social Media Marketing Industry Report (SCRIBD)," 2017.

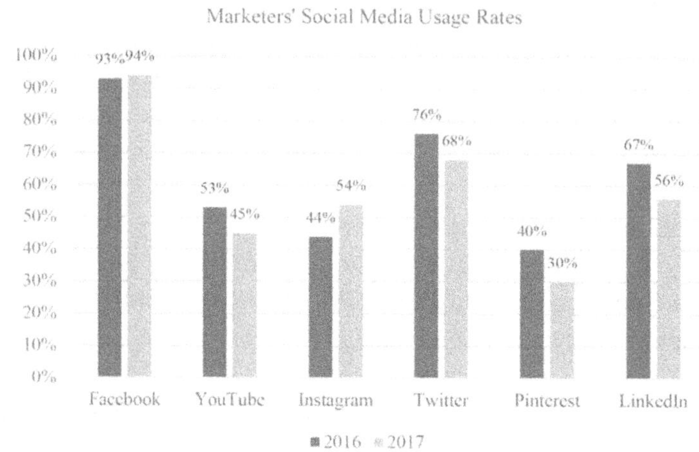

YouTube was born in 2005. It is a global video-sharing site owned by Google (Coles, 2015, p. 202). With over 600 videos being uploaded to YouTube every 60 seconds, this means that online videos have become much more popular (Odden, 2012, p. 144). People share videos on YouTube and it clicked and spread around the world in a very short while.

Instagram, with nearly 100 million users, provides people with the ability to share photos from their smartphones. It is the largest mobile, social network, and is owned by Facebook (Schaffer, 2013, p. 43). Moreover, it is one of the growing social networks focused on visual communications (Charlesworth, 2015, p. 193).

Popular SMCs used by marketers are important statistical indicator to differentiate the channels from each other. For instance, Figure 3 shows some of commonly used SMCs and changes of usage in over a two-year period (2016-2017) as a percentage.

According to Figure 3, in 2017, marketers' usage rates of Facebook rose from 93% to 94%, meanwhile Instagram jumped from 44% to 54%. The other four channels' usage rates declined in 2017. YouTube and Twitter dropped 8%. Pinterest and LinkedIn declined 10% and 11%, respectively. Each product, or even B2B propositions, would be provided over the Internet and retailers would find "creative ways to overcome customer expectations" (Falls & Deckers, 2012, p. 14). For this reason, marketing managers should decide which SMCs to use according to their business context (Funk, 2011, p. 50). For instance, Figure 4 shows some types of SMCs and their usage rates among Inc. 500 companies between 2013 and 2016. During the four-year period, Instagram usage rate rose tremendously while Facebook usage

Figure 4. Examples of SMCs usage rates among Inc. 500 companies in US
Note: Data was retrieved from Barnes & Daubitz, 2017.

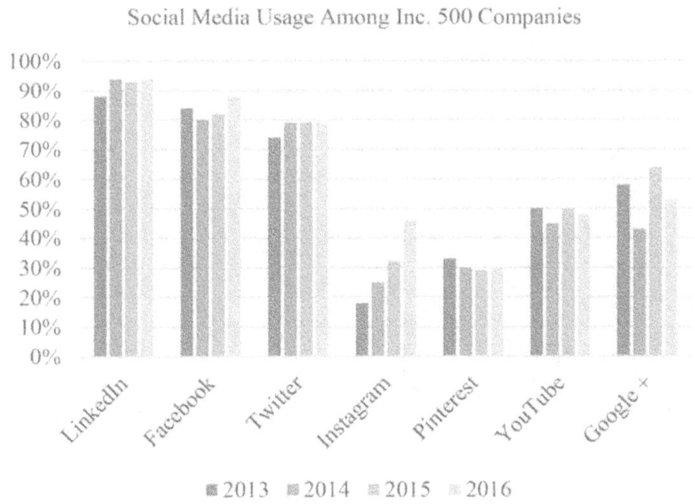

rate fluctuated negatively. This dramatic change may be interpreted as consumer's preferences having changed and marketers monitoring their movements to reach consumers through the best channel. LinkedIn and Twitter usage rates increased in 2014 compared to 2013, but it was nearly stable during the next two years. Another remarkable negative fluctuation is seen in the Google Plus usage rate. When it is examined, it is possible to say that the usage rates of Pinterest and YouTube have tended to decrease.

Total active social media user numbers show the importance of social media. Active users of some popular channels are changing over the years. For instance, Figure 5 shows some of the popular SMCs' active user numbers worldwide in 2017.

As seen in Figure 5, some SMCs are more popular than others, and Facebook was the leading SMC worldwide in 2017. That is the reason why marketers should examine which SMCs are more popular year by year.

SOCIAL MEDIA MARKETING (SMM)

Definition of SMM

SMM is considered marketing through SMCs (Smedescu, 2013). It is defined as the use of SMCs for promoting a company and its products. Since SMCs increase

Figure 5. An example of the number of active users (in millions) of some popular channels
Note: Data was retrieved from "We Are Social January Report" (2017).

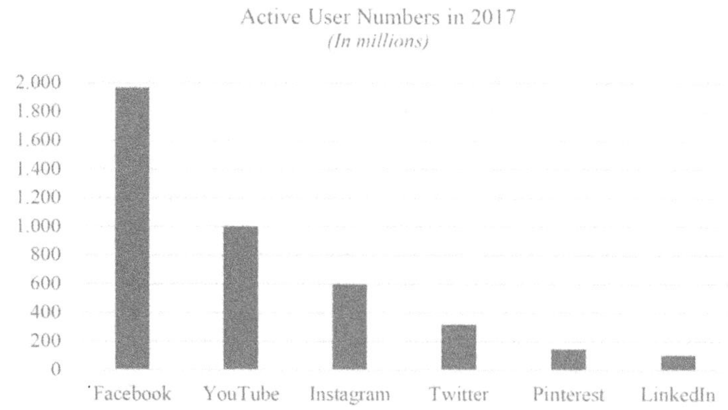

the viability on the digital platforms, SMM use these channels. SMM is a term that is related to relationship marketing in terms of giving importance to making connections with the consumers instead of selling (Cicek & Eren-Erdogmuş, 2013). It facilitates companies building communications channels with their customers, marketing their products, and enhancing customer loyalty. In order to manage communication with customers, it requires effort and attention (Saravanakumar & SuganthaLakshmi, 2012).

Therefore, SMM can be described as an accurate digital marketing method that promotes products of a company, increases brand awareness, customer loyalty, and creates potential customers through SMCs for the business.

SMM is assumed to be a set of combined tools and actions that an organization expects to not only accomplish its marketing goals, but also to satisfy the needs of its target market using SMCs (Ananda, Hernández-García & Lamberti, 2016). Companies tend to use SMM to provide information about their products and also interact with their consumers to establish relationships. Moreover, SMM are the marketing strategies adopted by companies to become part of the online networking of consumers (Deepa & Deshmukh, 2013). On the other hand, SMM as a marketing strategy should not be seen only as providing effective communication through SMCs. SMM itself is too complex to be managed. In this direction, Felix, Rauschnabel, and Hinsch (2017) assert a strategic framework for SMM and identify four dimensions of it. These dimensions are SMM scope, SMM culture, SMM structures, and SMM governance. SMM scope explores whether companies use SMM primarily as a real tool for communicating with one or more stakeholders or for extensive (both internal and external) cooperation.

SMM culture allocates between conservatism and modernism. Conservatism is determined in terms of a traditional approach to SMM. On the other hand, modernism is represented by an open and flexible SMM culture. SMM structures refer to the organization and departmentalization of SMM tasks. Hierarchies and networks are important terms for the SMM structure. According to hierarchic structure, there is a SMM assignee in contrast to networks, which show an organizational structure where all employees are accountable for SMM. The last strategic dimension of SMM is SMM governance. This dimension represents how the company sets rules and guidelines and how SMM responsibilities are reviewed within the company. In this way, identifying SMM strategies for businesses contributes to accomplishing SMM purposes. The authors evaluate these purposes in detail.

Purposes of SMM

The purposes of SMM include increasing sales and brand awareness, developing brand image, reducing marketing costs, and composing traffic to online platforms (Felix, Rauschnabel, & Hinsch, 2017). Of these, most marketers value social media most for branding (Ashley & Tuten, 2015). SMM has also a direct impact on product sales, brand recognition, and existing in the sector.

Both B2C and B2B companies use SMM to increase communication efficiency, improve customer relationships, build brands, and stimulate sales (Karjaluoto, Ulkuniemi, & Mustonen, 2015). SMM offers various advantages to companies through SMCs. For example attracting new customers and enhancing the customer interaction already established are one of the advantages (Pradiptarini, 2011). SMM is not only a product promotion area, but also an area where companies can show the sensitivity of their brands, the community view, the company philosophy, and customer sensitivity.

Channels that come to mind for SMM are Facebook, Twitter, Instagram, YouTube, Google Plus, Pinterest, and LinkedIn. Although active campaigns and advertising activities can be organized in all of these channels, it is undoubtedly important to choose the right channels appropriate to the nature of the products provided. For instance, Instagram is considered to be the suitable channel among photo sharing platforms. While it is more appropriate for a textile company to give more importance to this channel by taking advantage of Instagram's practical and photo-based feature, it is more accurately for a game company to focus on YouTube, which is much more preferred by children.

The role of social media in marketing should be explained with the customer's point of view in mind. Customers go through the customer life cycle process that consists of six stages (Figure 6).

Figure 6. Customer life cycle
Source: ("MARKETO," 2016, p. 17)

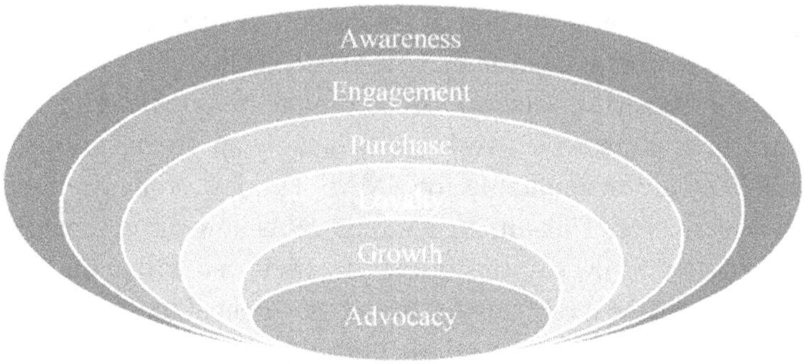

As it is observed in Figure 6, the first stage of the customer life cycle is awareness. The aim of this stage is to increase brand awareness, capture the interest of audiences, and ensure that they reach the right channels with relevant, personalized messages.

Engagement is the second stage. People, who are willing to buy, are interested in the company. In this stage, businesses listen to the potential customers and then engage them. Using beneficial context would be crucial to maintain a connection with audiences. In other words, this stage is for pushing audiences to purchase by using social media. According to the Global Web Index (2018), more than one-third of users are looking for brands in social media—they are already using them to engage with brands they like.

The third stage in the customer life cycle is purchase. In the purchasing stage, buyers are ready to purchase from the company. Monitoring the purchase process would be useful to understand and control buyers.

Loyalty/retention is the fourth stage. After the purchasing stage, businesses want to build long-term relationships with their customers by establishing trust. For businesses, it is possible only by using social media effectively to respond to customers for any problems and listening to their issues about services.

Growth is the next stage in customer life cycle. This stage shows that selling is not the end of marketing. Businesses must create value by understanding the current customer needs by segmenting them in terms of using different SMCs.

The last stage of customer life cycle is advocacy. The purpose of this stage is to encourage customers to become brand advocates and to provide an excellent customer experience to recommend the brand to friends and family. Since brand advocates are also the social media audiences of businesses, using SMCs, such as Twitter or Facebook, to provide connection with them is important.

Considering these six stages of the customer life cycle, it can be asserted that identifying purposes of each stage in the customer life cycle is crucial for businesses to ensure long-term relationships with their customers. That is why B2C and B2B organizations should decide which social media platforms to choose at every stage of the customer life cycle (Funk, 2011, p. 50).

Social media usage in the marketing context has been a crucial issue. Therefore, the authors also evaluated social media usage for B2B and B2C contexts.

Social Media for B2C

Social media is a tool for creating awareness, persuasion, and accomplishment of marketing objectives in B2C businesses. Many B2C organizations, such as Ford, KLM, ING, NS, and T-Mobile, are already actively using social media for their marketing strategies (Busscher, 2013). For instance, Ford's social media strategy includes using different SMCs such as Facebook, Twitter, and YouTube. Ford users are encouraged to share their experiences on these channels.

Social media usage as a marketing channel in B2C businesses has expanded because businesses can reach their customers to engage them for brand conversations. While SMCs are used in B2B contexts to target professionals, B2C practitioners use SMCs to connect with the general public (Iankova, Davies, Archer-Brown, Marder, & Yau, 2018). Moreover, they add value to the interaction with individual consumers, enabling businesses to engage in one-on-one dialogue with their customers (Moore, Hopkins, & Raymond, 2013). Social media provides B2C companies to contact consumers directly with much lower costs for interaction than traditional communication tools.

B2C companies use SMCs for increasing brand awareness, loyalty, and sales. Moreover, attracting new customers and cultivating relationships are also among their objectives for using SMCs (Swani, Brown, & Milne, 2014). Since consumers perceive the information obtained from social media as being more trustworthy than from other sources (Foux, 2006), B2C marketers desire to use SMCs.

From the B2C point of view, marketers are more focused on Facebook, YouTube, and Instagram (Stelzner, 2016). Thus, these channels need to be considered in terms of B2C marketing.

Facebook

Facebook proposes that marketers reach to highly segmented customers and provide a platform to actively engage with their customers (Charlesworth, 2015, p. 151). Building communities by users and advertising for customers by businesses contribute to Facebook's rapid growth. At first, new users had some hesitation about the site

Figure 7. Examples of product brands with the most Facebook fans as of April 2019 (in millions)
Source: ("STATISTA," 2019)

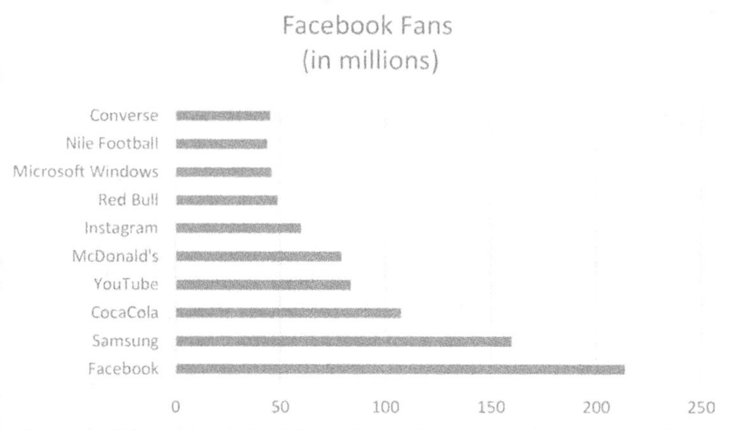

besides being too intrusive, but, in the long run, they became addicted to it (Funk, 2011, p. 48). The research completed by Saravanakumar and SuganthaLakshmi (2012), emphasized that 77% of consumers interacted with brands on Facebook by reading the messages and updates about them. In addition to this, 56% of consumers recommend a brand to their friends after becoming a fan of a brand on Facebook. It shows that Facebook is an influencing tool for customers. For instance, Table 4 supports the importance of Facebook for B2C marketing. It shows the most popular product brands on Facebook for April 2019 in terms of fans in millions.

According to data in Figure 7, Facebook for Every Phone is the most popular page on Facebook with 213 million fans. Coca-Cola and Samsung are the following popular pages on Facebook with respectively 159 million and 107 million fans. Other product brands are showed in order with respect to number of their fans. Since Facebook is a popular social network, it might be accepted as a crucial marketing tool to reach target audiences for marketers. Thus, companies should consider using Facebook when formulating their B2C marketing strategies as an effective tool to reach new and existing customers. With regard to a B2C perspective for using Facebook to reach customers, GENOGRAFİ provides a good example in Turkey (Figure 8).

GENOGRAFI is a personal genetic analysis service that allows you to get detailed information about your DNA and how it can affect your life. Genetic analysis is an interesting issue and it needs to be explained to people by using communication channels to elucidate. Therefore, GENOGRAFI tries to provide awareness to its target audience by using SMCs. Figure 8 shows the distribution of GENOGRAFI's

Figure 8. Distribution of GENOGRAFI's fans on Facebook
Note: Figure was retrieved from www.socialbakers.com based on GENOGRAFI's fans on June 1, 2017.

Facebook fans all over the world. Most of the company's Facebook followers are from Turkey. As a result of Facebook advertisements, the number of fans are increasing and expanding into new countries such as the United States, Sweden, Germany, and the United Kingdom.

YouTube

Another important tool for B2C marketing is YouTube. YouTube is becoming an important part among SMCs since as viral marketing is becoming more popular. YouTube is a blessing to visual brands, comprising big fashion, entertainment, music, sports, and lifestyle brands (Funk, 2011, p. 50). From B2B to B2C, whether a small business or large, videos in YouTube are effective for all markets and types of customers (Odden, 2012, p. 144). The cost of making a YouTube video is low. Thus, businesses can use YouTube to create greater brand awareness, product advertising, retail promotion, product support, and direct sales (Miller, 2011, p. 11). For instance, they can display advertisements or provide information about a company's products or services for their target customers.

When businesses use YouTube to share video that has customer centric titles, customers can easily find the business content. Subscribers and views are the terms used to determine the impacts of business. For instance, number of views can show the impact of a brand. Companies can use YouTube for giving information or advice about using their products.

Instagram

From the B2C perspective, consumer brands use Instagram to showcase their products and provide a connection with audiences in terms of posts, contests, and giveaways ("MARKETO," 2016, p. 9). Businesses can use Instagram by putting pictures of their brand's products. For instance, customers can follow the brand Instagram page and obtain information about product features and price. Moreover, they can also order the product of the brand. Besides being a platform to reach the target market in terms of brands, events can use Instagram to reach their audiences. For instance, events, such as weddings or birthdays, can share photos on Instagram to promote the company.

Instagram offers an advantage for businesses in terms of creating advertising to reach only the targeted market. By collaborating with Facebook (a database of Facebook contains user's interests), consumers are well known, and with this method, accurate and relevant messages are communicated to the users.

Beyond any doubt, Instagram is the most visual SMC. Companies can create images depending on their industry. For instance, a clothing brand can share images of various styles with their prices. They can also use celebrities to post their images. To conclude, Instagram can be used not only as part of content marketing, but also as a social media strategy to reach specific audiences. Using relevant content that is attractive, informative, and memorable, along with a company's products or services will gain the attention of a large audience.

Social Media for B2B

Using social media for B2B marketing strategies provides companies with a way to create content on SMCs to find, attract, and inform potential customers and suppliers (Batum & Ersoy, 2016). Since companies place special emphasis on the value of relationship networks' for buyers and sellers, they adopt social media to increase buyer engagement and develop customer relationships (Swani, Brown, & Milne, 2014).

B2B organizations also utilize social media to identify new business opportunities and for product development, to enhance relationships with customers, and to improve collaboration, both inside and between organizations (Jussila, Kärkkäinen & Aramo-Immonen, 2014). What is more, social media for B2B provides a variety of marketing applications, such as content marketing, market research, and business networking. For instance, thanks to content marketing, B2B companies can deliver business-related content to customers via social media to be an effective center in the network (Brennan & Croft, 2012). Employee recruitment and retention also constitutes their usage purposes. Moreover, B2B companies adopt SMCs to demonstrate products and provide training to business partners (Vize & Sherrett, 2017, p. 50).

According to Kho (2008), in contrast to B2C users, better-designed social media tools can provide more benefits for B2B users. It is proven that SMCs that facilitate more personalized interactions between buyers and suppliers can improve corporate credibility and build better relationship between both. SMCs can be used for communication with suppliers and customers within a B2B context (Busscher, 2013). The top five SMCs, analyzed in terms of B2B usage are: LinkedIn, Facebook, Twitter, Instagram, and YouTube.

LinkedIn

The purpose of using LinkedIn is to create networks, establish new business connections, and to become aware of innovations. People can learn about a company by following its profile on LinkedIn. Besides this, business experts, communities, associations, and companies can successfully use LinkedIn to obtain information (Reece, 2010, p. 245). LinkedIn also ensures a form of self-promotion and career networking (Tuten, 2008, p. 24). It means people who are interested in a company have a chance to learn more about it by following its LinkedIn page, which will also show any job positions available with the company. Moreover, it is a professional platform that employees can use not only for promoting their company brand, but also to promote their personal brand.

Building relationships with suppliers and customers is an important issue in B2B marketing. Businesses aim to provide trustworthy relations with their partners. According to Shih (2009, p. 124), B2B companies can use LinkedIn to communicate with their customers and suppliers, and to build relationships and trust. Moreover, they can easily define possible partners with regards to B2B selling.

Despite Facebook and MySpace being favored and having bigger networks, LinkedIn is more suitable for businesses to use as a platform for their marketing (Reece, 2010, p. 245; Zahay, 2015, p. 80). Thus, when marketing to businesses, a company or individual should choose LinkedIn as a platform.

In Turkey, GENOMİZE uses LinkedIn to inform its audiences about the company, declares new job opportunities and views how you are connected with employees. Moreover, GENOMİZE identifies its profession such as Biotechnology, Genomics, Software, RNA-seq, DNA-Seq, Data Management to connect with other businesses in terms of B2B.

Facebook

Facebook is as a viable option for SMM for B2B. Companies can reach current and future customers and potential employees thanks to using Facebook. Therefore, there are some ways for B2B companies to use Facebook efficiently. First of all, companies can use images on their Facebook page to create attention in their news feed. They can share company news, such as showing the company's success. Moreover, if a company shares pictures of employees enjoying their work, it will provide insight to other people about the company's culture and business relations. Companies also share interesting images or inspiring content to attract audiences. Facebook also enables businesses to communicate with their fans through videos. For example, if a company wants to provide training programs for business owners, it can promote this on Facebook through videos. Sharing the company's story is another way in terms of a B2B perspective. "ThrowbackThursday" is a popular word in social media jargon, so companies share their history by telling stories and posting images. Thanks to this, audiences can adopt and feel more connected to a company.

Advertising on Facebook is another way for B2B companies to use this SMC. Companies can easily reach business owners needing their product thanks to Facebook advertisements. To conclude, companies can reach their target audiences using these popular SMCs. They can also identify which media provides them with the best responses from their fans and followers.

From the B2B perspective, in Turkey, GENOMİZE, a young, dynamic, biotechnology initiative that is academically rooted that specializes in the production and analysis of genomic data uses Facebook actively to reach customers and businesses. Initially, customers obtain information about the company thanks to Facebook following its main page about health issues in terms of genomic data. GENOMİZE declares that if you are a business that provides genetic diagnosis, you can use SEQ. Moreover, if you want to apply genome analysis to yourself, GENOMİZE suggests taking a more detailed look at GENOGRAFI. For GENOMİZE, Facebook is an efficient channel to reach targeted audiences and provide awareness in terms of B2B marketing.

Twitter

People prefer using Twitter for answering the question, "What are you doing?" (Reece, 2010, p. 247) or "What is happening?" (Coles, 2015, p. 82). It can be about a person's action, such as eating something, or business news. By using this platform, people share information about whatever they want, such as other people, companies, or products. Moreover, since Twitter is an effective marketing tool, marketers use its short message format to communicate with their target market (Charlesworth, 2015, p. 167). You can send messages to your followers directly. By following conversations of Twitter, hash tags, or tendency to your keywords, you can easily describe potent people in your industry or market. Thus, it is deduced that Twitter is an effective marketing channel—especially for B2B—for introducing your industry and building brand and customer loyalty. It provides companies with the ability to connect to potential dealers and future customers.

Since Twitter is an essential tool for B2B companies, there are some techniques for Twitter suitably use. First, employees of the company can use Twitter to stay up-to-date and follow the news about an industry. Moreover, companies post links to their latest acquisitions and product news on Twitter. Therefore, other companies interested in the company products can obtain information by following Twitter's news feeds. Companies can also read comments about their products and see competitor's opinions. The most important thing for companies is to optimize their business page with the right brand awareness creation and messaging.

Instagram

Instagram is a notable channel for B2B. Businesses can use Instagram to share attractive offers and funny visuals. Moreover, photographs of events and offices take part in Instagram to give information about businesses. Hashtags special for a company brand or industry are keywords of the business. Using hash tags on company posts provides the ability to reach the target market. For instance, a company can highlight what their products do by creating stunning visuals. Moreover, a company can combine videos and images to make its content interesting on Instagram.

Instagram has two strengths in terms of B2B. These are brand awareness and community. After providing brand awareness, companies build community. By building communities, companies can reach their target market. Instagram also has a story feature. Companies use this feature to take advantage of people's influence in marketing. Moreover, a company can use its leader's message on Instagram, such as building relationships and being the easiest company to do business with. What is more, Instagram can be used to showcase a company's culture. Companies can also display their creativity and expertise. For instance, a company in a creative industry can use Instagram's attractive visuals to gain clients.

YouTube

YouTube is an efficient channel for B2B in terms of sharing videos and providing a channel for companies to reach their target audiences. For instance, a company can create a business channel on YouTube and it would be a free advertising. On YouTube's business channel page is also the home page of the business. Therefore, it is essential to customize the page in terms of design and business content to be suitable as a marketing strategy. Businesses can reach this home page and online videos to obtain information about the business content.

There are some crucial points for B2B companies to know to be able to use YouTube successfully. First of all, videos on the business channel page should be relevant and beneficial for target customers. For this reason, companies should be clear on their purpose for using YouTube. It can be to gain more followers or customers. On the other hand, making the company visible in the search engines or providing customer loyalty might be a company's goals.

Another point regarding YouTube in terms of B2B companies is product demonstrations, conferences, events, and expert advice. Actually, companies should explain the reasons why other companies are doing business with them. Moreover, promoting videos on YouTube is an important point. Using the right description and tags for their videos will make them more accessible. Companies can also use YouTube Analytics to monitor the performance of their channel and videos. Thanks to this, they obtain information about the demographics of their followers and number of views. By using this data, they can formulate marketing strategies to reach their target audiences.

SOLUTIONS AND RECOMMENDATIONS

Usage of social media has become an indispensable part of everyday life. In today's business world, companies consider social media an important component to gain competitive advantage and high performance (Siamagka, Christodoulides, Michaelidou, & Valvi, 2015). Therefore, whether for B2B or B2C marketers, using SMCs becomes an important part for their marketing strategies.

There are some recommendations for B2C and B2B companies in terms of using social media. Defining the goal of using social media is important. Moreover, companies have to analyze their target markets well to understand the needs and interests of potential customers.

As previously mentioned, according to statistical indicators of some years, the total number of Internet users has increased 10% (354 million), meanwhile the total number of active social media users has increased 21% in one year. In other words, marketing practitioners who have not begun to use social media effectively will be left behind in the competition.

Due to the differences in peoples' reasons for participating in social media, SMC variations are designed to answer those different needs. This is one of the reasons that some SMCs become more popular than others. However, being a phenomenon for SMC does not last forever. Year after year, the number of individuals and businesses that use SMCs varies. Therefore, marketing managers should monitor their targeted consumer's online behaviors.

FUTURE RESEARCH DIRECTIONS

This chapter highlights that both B2C and B2B marketers are aware of the power of social media in the framework of their marketing strategy in the digital economy. The digital economy has transformed the marketing strategies of companies. Despite B2C companies often using SMCs as a part of their marketing tactics, adopting social media for B2B companies is a new issue. B2B companies have some hesitations regarding using social media. Actually, they do not know how to use SMCs efficiently. Therefore, researchers might provide guidelines to B2B marketers, so they might be able to begin to include SMCs in their marketing plans and implement their marketing strategies on behalf of social media.

Future studies might also focus on SMM barriers within B2B contexts. In other words, the literature could more clearly explore and define the difficulties for B2B marketers face in using SMCs in their integrated communication strategies, and also how B2B marketers might overcome these barriers.

CONCLUSION

This chapter shows that social media has become an important component when formulating marketing strategies in today's digital economy. Since statistical indicators based on the Internet user rates and active social media user rates all over the world show that traditional marketing communication tools are not enough to reach the consumers, marketers begin to give more importance to SMM, thus traditional marketing tools are being replaced by SMCs.

SMM can be described as an accurate, digital marketing method that promotes the products or services of a company, increases brand awareness, and creates customer loyalty. Because of social media's significant role in marketing, SMM has become a crucial marketing strategy for businesses. As a marketing strategy, SMM itself includes four different dimensions. These four dimensions are: 1). SMM scope; 2). SMM culture; 3). SMM structures; and 4). SMM governance (Felix, Rauschnabel, & Hinsch, 2017). To achieve the purposes of SMM, these four dimensions have to be taken in consideration. The purpose of SMM consists of developing brand awareness and brand image, reducing marketing costs, and inspiring users to post or share contents.

SMM is expressed as the whole of marketing efforts in order to not leave the customer alone during the customer life cycle stages through the use of SMCs. SMCs provide support to the customer's decision journey and aim to increase the number of customers that will progress to additional stages. For instance, in a B2B context, people who are interested in a company have a chance to learn about that company by following its LinkedIn pages, which enables the user to gain an awareness of the field of the business and the products of this company. Using LinkedIn captures the interest of audiences and results in greater awareness. After providing usable content to maintain a connection with audiences in the engagement stage, buyers become ready to purchase from the company. In this stage, using another SMC, such as YouTube to demonstrate and give detailed information about products of the company in which customers are interested, it pushes the customers to purchase the service or product. After the purchasing stage, companies want to cultivate long-term relationships with their customers to achieve loyalty. Their aim is to instantly respond to positive and negative comments through SMCs, such as Twitter and Facebook. During the last stage, advocacy, customers are expected to recommend the company to others. The usage of Twitter and Facebook to maintain the communication is important during this stage. To conclude, the customer life cycle provides a significant framework for B2B and B2C marketers to identify which SMCs are most effective for their specific business.

Social media is the output of the increased usage of the Internet for marketing practices and it had become more interesting for the marketing activities of both B2C and B2B contexts (Constantinides & Fountain, 2008). Due to the different structures of B2B and B2C markets, social media usage in these markets is dissimilar (Iankova, Davies, Archer-Brown, Marder, & Yau, 2018). B2B companies prefer using social media to create demand and build networks through their business partners. In other words, B2B social media interactions are heavily focused on relationships, which should be beneficial for all parties. On the other hand, B2C companies aim to provide interaction with existing and potential customers, share their content, marketing, and advertising campaigns through SMCs.

SMCs provide important opportunities for businesses to conduct marketing communication activities. It is revealed that SMCs are different from one another in terms of their forms of communication. To begin with, Facebook is good at building customer relationships. Secondly, Twitter has an ability to spread messages about a brand or a company to the target customers. Furthermore, Instagram is a channel that enables the sharing of images. In addition, YouTube is known for its ability to share videos. Lastly, LinkedIn is a means of networking with business partners all over the world. According to Charlesworth (2015, p. 195), Facebook and LinkedIn are considered to be social networking sites, while YouTube, Twitter, and Instagram are seen as social sharing sites.

This chapter also considers that SMCs usages are different in B2C and B2B contexts. According to the literature review, which includes trends in usage, B2C marketers are mostly focused on Facebook, YouTube, and Instagram, while LinkedIn is more preferred by B2B marketers (Reece, 2010, p. 245; Zahay, 2015, p. 80). The reason behind the difference is the goal of LinkedIn. LinkedIn is a professional social networking platform, enabling people in the business world to communicate and exchange information with others and wherein one can engage with business decision makers (Schaffer, 2013, p. 43). In the light of all this information, it can be concluded that the purpose of using social media and the adoption of SMCs differ in terms of B2C and B2B businesses.

REFERENCES

Al Khalili, M. (2018). *Barriers impacting social media marketing in industrial B2B* (Unpublished doctoral dissertation, Robert Morris University, Pennsylvania).

AlSuwaidan, L., & Ykhlef, M. (2016). Toward information diffusion model for viral marketing in business. *Int. J. Adv. Comput. Sci. Appl*, *7*(2), 637–646.

Ananda, A. S., Hernández-García, Á., & Lamberti, L. (2016). N-REL: A comprehensive framework of social media marketing strategic actions for marketing organizations. *Journal of Innovation & Knowledge*, *1*(3), 170–180. doi:10.1016/j.jik.2016.01.003

Ashley, C., & Tuten, T. (2015). Creative strategies in social media marketing: An exploratory study of branded social content and consumer engagement. *Psychology and Marketing*, *32*(1), 15–27. doi:10.1002/mar.20761

Barefoot, D., & Szabo, J. (2010). *Friends with benefits: A social media marketing handbook*. San Francisco, CA: No Starch Press.

Barnes, N. G., & Daubitz, C. (2017, February). *The 2017 Inc 500 and social media: time for reevaluation?* University of Massachusetts Dartmouth Center for Marketing Research. Retrieved from http://www.umassd.edu/cmr/

Batum, T., & Ersoy, N. (2016). The use of social media in B2B marketing communications: An explatory study on Turkish companies. *Afyon Kocatepe Üniversitesi İktisadi ve İdari Bilimler Fakültesi Dergisi*, *18*(2), 139–151.

Brennan, R., & Croft, R. (2012). The use of social media in B2B marketing and branding: An exploratory study. *Journal of Customer Behaviour*, *11*(2), 101–115. doi:10.1362/147539212X13420906144552

Busscher, N. M. (2013). *Social media: Their role as marketing tools in B2B marketing* (Bachelor's Thesis, University of Twente).

Charlesworth, A. (2015). *An introduction to social media marketing*. New York, NY: Routledge.

Cicek, M., & Eren-Erdogmus, I. (2013). Social media marketing: Exploring the user typology in Turkey. *International Journal of Technology Marketing*, *8*(3), 254–271. doi:10.1504/IJTMKT.2013.055343

Coles, L. (2015). *Marketing with social media: 10 easy steps to success for business*. Australia: John Wiley & Sons.

Constantinides, E. (2014). Foundations of social media marketing. *Procedia: Social and Behavioral Sciences*, *148*, 40–57. doi:10.1016/j.sbspro.2014.07.016

Constantinides, E. & Fountain, S. J. (2008). Web 2.0: Conceptual foundations and marketing issues. *Journal of direct, data and digital marketing practice*, *9*(3), 231-244.

Content Marketing Institute (CMI). (2018). *Benchmarks, budgets, and trends: North America*. Retrieved from https://contentmarketinginstitute.com/wpcontent/uploads/2017/09/2018

Deepa, N., & Deshmukh, S. (2013). Social media marketing: The next generation of business engagement. *International Journal of Management Research and Reviews*, *3*(2), 2461.

Eisenberg, B. (2008, Nov. 7). *Understanding and aligning the value of social media*. Retrieved from www.clickz.com

Falls, J., & Deckers, E. (2012). *No bullshit social media: The all-business, no-hype guide to social media marketing*. United States of America: Pearson Education.

Felix, R., Rauschnabel, P. A., & Hinsch, C. (2017). Elements of strategic social media marketing: A holistic framework. *Journal of Business Research*, *70*, 118–126. doi:10.1016/j.jbusres.2016.05.001

Fischer, E., & Reuber, A. R. (2011). Social interaction via new social media: (How) can interactions on Twitter affect effectual thinking and behavior? *Journal of Business Venturing*, *26*(1), 1–18. doi:10.1016/j.jbusvent.2010.09.002

Flanigan, R. L., & Obermier, T. R. (2016). An assessment of the use of social media in the industrial distribution business-to-business market sector. *The Journal of Technology Studies*, *42*(1), 18–28. doi:10.21061/jots.v42i1.a.2

Foux, G. (2006). Consumer-generated media: Get your customers involved. *Brand Strategy*, *8*(202), 38–39.

Funk, T. (2011). *Social media playbook for business: Reaching your online community with Twitter, Facebook, LinkedIn, and more:* Santa Barbara, CA*:* ABC- *Clio*, LLC.

Global Web Index. (2018). *Global web index's flagship report on the latest trends in social media*. Retrieved from https://www.globalwebindex.com/hubfs/Downloads/Social-H2-2018-report.pdf

Hacıhasanoglu, B. (2017). *Sosyal Medyada Pazarlama Stratejilerinin Oluşturulması ve Telekomünikasyon Sektörüne İlişkin Bir Uygulama* (Unpublished Master's Thesis, Istanbul Commerce University, Turkey).

Iankova, S., Davies, I., Archer-Brown, C., Marder, B., & Yau, A. (2018). A comparison of social media marketing between B2B, B2C and mixed business models. *Industrial Marketing Management*. doi:10.1016/j.indmarman.2018.01.001

Jussila, J. (2015). *Social media in business-to-business companies' innovation*. Tampere, Finland: Tampere University of Technology.

Jussila, J. J., Kärkkäinen, H., & Aramo-Immonen, H. (2014). Social media utilization in business-to-business relationships of technology industry firms. *Computers in Human Behavior*, *30*, 606–613. doi:10.1016/j.chb.2013.07.047

Kaplan, A. M., & Haenlein, M. (2010). Users of the world, unite! The challenges and opportunities of social media. *Business Horizons*, *53*(1), 59–68. doi:10.1016/j.bushor.2009.09.003

Karjaluoto, H., Ulkuniemi, P., & Mustonen, N. (2015). The role of digital channels in industrial marketing communications. *Journal of Business and Industrial Marketing*, *30*(6), 703–710. doi:10.1108/JBIM-04-2013-0092

Kho, N. D. (2008). B2B gets social media. *EContent (Wilton, Conn.)*, *31*(3), 26–30.

MARKETO. (2010). *The definitive guide to B2B social media*. Retrieved from http://designdamage.com/wp-content/uploads/2009/04/The-Definitive-Guide-to-B2B-SM.pdf

MARKETO. (2016). *The definitive guide to social media marketing*. Retrieved from http://www.workforcelink.com/library/The-Definitive-Guide-to-Social-Media-Marketing-Marketo.pdf

Michaelidou, N., Siamagka, N. T., & Christodoulides, G. (2011). Usage, barriers and measurement of social media marketing: An exploratory investigation of small and medium B2B brands. *Industrial Marketing Management*, *40*(7), 1153–1159. doi:10.1016/j.indmarman.2011.09.009

Miller, M. R. (2011). *YouTube for business: Online video marketing for any business*. USA: Que Publishing.

Moore, J. N., Hopkins, C. D., & Raymond, M. A. (2013). Utilization of relationship-oriented social media in the selling process: A comparison of consumer (B2C) and industrial (B2B) salespeople. *Journal of Internet Commerce*, *12*(1), 48–75. doi:10 .1080/15332861.2013.763694

Most Popular Social Networking Sites. Top 15 Rank Report (2017). Retrieved from http://www.ebizmba.com/articles/social-networking-websites

Odden, L. (2012). *Optimize: How to attract and engage more customers by integrating SEO, social media, and content marketing*. Hoboken, NJ: John Wiley & Sons.

Pradiptarini, C. (2011). Social media marketing: Measuring its effectiveness and identifying the target market. *UW-L Journal of Undergraduate Research*, *14*, 45–76.

Reece, M. (2010). *Real-time marketing for business growth: How to use social media, measure marketing, and create a culture of execution*. Upper Saddle River, NJ: Pearson Education.

ReportW. A. S. J. (2017). Retrieved from https://wearesocial.com/special-reports/ digital-in-2017-global-overview

Saravanakumar, M., & Sugantha Lakshmi, T. (2012). Social media marketing. *Life Science Journal*, *9*(4), 4444–4451.

Schaffer, N. (2013). *Maximize your social: A one-stop guide to building a social media strategy for marketing and business success*. Hoboken, NJ: John Wiley & Sons.

SEMPO. (2017, May 26). *Search engine marketing professional organization glossary*. Retrieved from http://www.sempo.org/ ?page=glossary

Shih, C. (2009). *The Facebook era: Tapping online social networks to build better products, reach new audiences, and well more stuff*. Boston, MA: Pearson Education.

Siamagka, N. T., Christodoulides, G., Michaelidou, N., & Valvi, A. (2015). Determinants of social media adoption by B2B organizations. *Industrial Marketing Management*, *51*, 89–99. doi:10.1016/j.indmarman.2015.05.005

Smedescu, D. A. (2013). Social media marketing tools. *Romanian Journal of Marketing*, *4*, 23–30.

Smith, P. R., & Zook, Z. (2011). *Marketing communications: Integrating offline and online with social media*. London, UK: Kogan Page Ltd.

Social Media Marketing Industry Report (SCRIBD). (2017). Retrieved from https:// tr.scribd.com/=document/348447903/2017-Social-Media-Marketing-IndustryReport? secret_password=kpsZVgcHwVfmvTHez7rH#download&from_embed

STATISTA. (2019). Product brands with the most Facebook fans as of April 2019 (in millions). Retrieved from https://www.statista.com/statistics/265657/leading-product-brands-with-the-most-fans-on-facebook/

Stelzner, M. A. (2016). *Social media marketing industry report: How marketers are using social media to grow their businesses, online social media examiner*. Retrieved from SocialMediaMarketing Industry Report2016.pdf.

Swani, K., Brown, B. P., & Milne, G. R. (2014). Should tweets differ for B2B and B2C? An analysis of fortune 500 companies' Twitter communications. *Industrial Marketing Management*, *43*(5), 873–881. doi:10.1016/j.indmarman.2014.04.012

Tapscott, D., & Williams, A. D. (2008). *WIKINOMICS: How mass collaboration changes everything*. New York, NY: Penguin Group.

Tuten, T. L. (2008). *Advertising 2.0: Social media marketing in a Web 2.0 world: Social media marketing in a Web 2.0 world*. United States of America: Praeger Publishers.

Vize, R., & Sherrett, M. (2017). Social media marketing for B2B: From information to decision to retention. In B. Rishi, & S. Bandyopadhyay (Eds.), *Contemporary issues in social media marketing* (pp. 46–59). New York: Routledge. doi:10.4324/9781315563312-4

Zahay, D. (2015). *Digital marketing management: A handbook for the current (or Future) CEO*. New York: Business Expert Press.

Zimmerman, J., & Ng, D. (2017). *Social media marketing all-in-one for dummies*. Hoboken, NJ: John Wiley & Sons.

ADDITIONAL READING

Agnihotri, R., Dingus, R., Hu, M. Y., & Krush, M. T. (2016). Social media: Influencing customer satisfaction in B2B sales. *Industrial Marketing Management*, *53*, 172–180. doi:10.1016/j.indmarman.2015.09.003

Bailyn, E. (2012). *Outsmarting social media*. Indianapolis, Indiana: Que Publishing.

Baird, C. H., & Parasnis, G. (2011). From social media to social CRM: Reinventing the customer relationship. *Strategy and Leadership*, *39*(6), 27–34. doi:10.1108/10878571111176600

Funk, T. (2013). *Advanced social media marketing: How to lead, launch, and manage a successful social media program*. New York: Apress. doi:10.1007/978-1-4302-4408-0

Järvinen, J., Tollinen, A., Karjaluoto, H., & Jayawardhena, C. (2012). Digital and social media marketing usage in B2B industrial section. *Marketing Management Journal, 22*(2), 102–117.

Kim, A. J., & Ko, E. (2012). Do social media marketing activities enhance customer equity? An empirical study of luxury fashion brand. *Journal of Business Research, 65*(10), 1480–1486. doi:10.1016/j.jbusres.2011.10.014

Mangold, W. G., & Faulds, D. J. (2009). Social media: The new hybrid element of the promotion mix. *Business Horizons, 52*(4), 357–365. doi:10.1016/j.bushor.2009.03.002

Wang, W. Y., Pauleen, D. J., & Zhang, T. (2016). How social media applications affect B2B communication and improve business performance in SMEs. *Industrial Marketing Management, 54*, 4–14. doi:10.1016/j.indmarman.2015.12.004

KEY TERMS AND DEFINITIONS

Business to Business (B2B): A concept where business is handled between companies rather than companies and individual customers.

Business to Consumer (B2C): A concept describes the commercial relationship conducted by companies directly with consumers.

Customer Lifecycle: A term used to determine the process a customer goes through when considering, buying, using, and maintaining loyalty to a product or service.

Social Media: Websites and applications consist of platforms where individuals or organizations can create, share, and exchange information with people and build online relationships, and communities.

Social Media Channel (SMC): A platform is classified according to the social presence or media richness and answers some kind of consumer needs.

Social Media Marketing (SMM): Part of Internet marketing that is marketing through SMCs.

Web 1.0: The first stage in the WWW, which only offers people one-way communication such as reading the contents.

Web 2.0: The second stage in the WWW, which offers people two-way communication such as showing their opinions or feelings.

Chapter 5
How Does Firm- and User-Generated Content Benefit Firms and Affect Consumers?
A Literature Review

Niray Tunçel
https://orcid.org/0000-0002-4299-6462
Hacettepe University, Turkey

Nihan Yılmaz
Hacettepe University, Turkey

ABSTRACT

Social media marketing is a new form of communication between firms and consumers. The interactive nature of social media platforms enables consumers to share their perceptions about firms by creating their own content in various forms. Besides, firms are able to attract and engage with consumers through creating effective content on their social media channels. Both user-generated content (UGC) and firm-generated content (FGC) have a significant role in firm performance and consumer behavior. However, the previous studies have mostly focused on the effects of UGC and addressed the issue from the consumer side. Therefore, as distinct from existing studies, the study at hand addresses the specific effects and benefits of UGC and FGC from both the firm and consumer sides, within a theoretical framework. In addition, based on the findings of the reviewed studies, the chapter presents some practical implications for business.

DOI: 10.4018/978-1-7998-2185-4.ch005

INTRODUCTION

Recently, social media has become a significant channel for social networking and content sharing. Since it is reliable, consistent, and prompt, it opens a new door for firms to create a new type of online marketing strategy (Nadaraja & Yazdanifard, 2013). As the Internet has revolutionized the ways people communicate, the current generation of technology users prefers to interact with each other online versus to face-to-face. Thus, for promoting their product and services, companies should reach consumers on online platforms, specifically on social media, where consumers spend a lot of time. This is because currently people do not meet in person to talk about what their friends think of the new TV they recently bought; instead they see their posts about the new product and leave their comments on Facebook (Cohen, 2014). Besides, new social media platforms let demographic groups cluster themselves into the ideal target markets for the companies presenting their common interests and brand choices, which in turn closes the gap between businesses and consumers. Thus, the businesses are able to utilize target groups more effectively and take more appropriate marketing and business decisions (Wu, Chen & Chung, 2010).

It is a well-known fact that fact-branded social campaigns allow extra touchpoints to boost continuing interaction between brands and consumers at any time possible, which enable brands to extend relationships with consumers, discover common themes in consumer feedback, and foster consumer engagement toward online content (Murdough, 2009). Any tangible and intangible stimuli from these touchpoints generate a range of associations about the brand in consumer memory (Keller, 2009). Companies also have various options on social media for branding; one of which is sharing branded content, which is also known as content marketing (Tuten & Solomon, 2013). The term "content marketing," invented by Pulizzi (2010), from the Content Marketing Institute (CMI), is not new, but still being developed. To define content marketing is difficult since its meaning differs based on the context. Marketers currently prefer content marketing more than they do interruptive advertising because content marketing is more effective on taking attention from consumers (Du Plessis, 2015; Zahay, 2014). Content marketing is ideal since it uses modest pulling, not pushing, techniques for inviting consumers to branded content (Liu & Huang, 2015). It applies integrated marketing communication and relationship marketing as well (Cronin, 2016). However, content marketing is not promoting a product or a service; rather, it is a branding process that generates and spreads valuable and appropriate brand content in order to attract and involve the target audience. Thus, the brands create and share their stories on online platforms to generate brand familiarity of the target audience (Brieger, 2013). In this manner, content marketing usually resembles publishing, native advertising, inbound marketing, and storytelling (Du Plessis, 2015; Holliman & Rowley, 2014).

Content marketing is a part of the branding function, as creating content for communicating and marketing to audiences can strengthen a brand's image. Utilizing social media platforms and content marketing opportunities is a part of a brand's overall strategy. Now that organizations have an online presence, it is important for brands to develop content marketing strategies and tactics that not only help strengthen overall brand image, but also help build trust (Ariganello, 2016). Besides brands or firms, consumers also can create and share their own brand-related content in any form they would like. This content is as important as firms' content since it spreads very quickly and easily among consumers. Thus, consumers and firms are exposed to each other's content through various social media channels. Not surprisingly, these two types of content together influence and benefit both consumers and firms.

Based on this reasoning, the current paper aims to reveal the effects and benefits of user-generated content (UGC) and firm-generated content (FGC) from the consumer and the firm aspects. In this regard, a literature review is conducted and the findings of investigated studies are presented in a theoretical framework. Previous studies mostly focused on UGC and a majority of them addressed its effects from the consumer side, not from the firm side. Likewise, FGC and its impact on firms and consumers are also missing. Hence, this study aims to fill these gaps in a theoretical context.

The structure of the paper is as follows: First, social media marketing is introduced; second, UGC and FGC are presented. Then, the literature review of the investigated studies is given. Following the conclusion, the paper finalizes with future research directions and implications for business.

BACKGROUND

Social Media Marketing

Social media marketing (SMM) has expanded throughout the world, and this expansion is unprecedented. SMM is a new way for businesses to access their targeted consumers easily. Barefoot and Szabo (2010) define SMM as using social media channels to promote a company and its products and services. In the age of e-communication, the traditional way of branding and marketing became outdated. Before social media, advertising and branding methods were restricted to advertising via conventional mass media channels and direct marketing (Scott, 2007). This type of communication included an untargeted audience, was one-way, and was not personalized. However, SMM offers interactive, innovative, and dynamic communication processes for organizations and consumers. Through various social media platforms, consumers can interact with companies and with each other, and affect and be affected through posting comments and product reviews (Alameddine,

2013). Using social media enables online users to communicate with thousands of others, regardless of where they are. People can generate, share, and bookmark content, and network with crowds, since social media is one of the most convenient platforms to present oneself and one's products to dynamic communities that may be interested (Roberts & Kraynak, 2008).

As the number of people using Facebook and Twitter, etc., grows, it is not surprising that the number of companies joining social media has shown an exponential increase as well (Wendlandt, 2012). Since it is easy to use and access, social media has become the trendsetter in topics, which can be from environment to entertainment, and its viral quality makes it a more attractive tool to businesses (Xiang & Gretzel, 2010). Besides, what SMM has over traditional marketing is that it is cost effective since it enables companies to interact with a large audience in an easy and inexpensive way (Curran, O'Brien & O'Hara, 2011; Saxton & Wang, 2013; Witman, 2013). The cost of SMM is much lower than any other marketing communication opportunities. Besides, SMM offers a chance to reach consumers that would not be accessible because of physical limitations related to the nature of traditional communication channels (Sheth & Sharma, 2005; Watson, Leyland, Berthon & Zinkham, 2002).

Due to social media's abovementioned benefits, marketers are beginning to comprehend the significance of using it in their marketing strategies to approach their customers (Nadaraja & Yazdanifard, 2013). According to a study by Stelzner (2015), "at least 91% of marketers want to know the most effective social tactics and the best ways to engage their audience with social media" (p. 5). Therefore, it is essential for researchers to investigate the current SMM campaigns of firms to come up with practical recommendations about which content type is the most appropriate to enhance the future image of organizations (Whiting & Deshpande, 2014). In addition, SMM also has the potential to increase the profit of a company, if the companies manage it effectively. However, if they cannot succeed at SMM, the results of it may be harmful to the companies. For instance, offensive and destructive content coming from unhappy consumers or competitors cannot be prevented (Cheung, Lee & Thadani, 2009), but companies can directly respond and neutralize them (Hennig-Thurau, Gwinner, Walsh & Gremler, 2004), so they can at least avoid undesirable outcomes.

When it comes to consumers, SMM has also changed their expectations of companies. According to research by Vlasic and Kesic (2007), consumers prefer companies provide interactive communications since they believe that to receive information they need from these organizations would be easy. The same study also revealed that consumers are expecting more customized offerings and think that interactivity is one of the key characteristics of a modern company. In addition, other research revealed that consumers view social media as a more reliable and trustworthy source regarding information about products and services than any other communication channels provided by an organization (Smith, Berry & Pulford, 1999). Besides, consumers use social media predominantly for sharing their experiences (i.e., their holidays) (Fotis, Buhalis & Rossides, 2011). Thus, it appears that using social media is not an option for companies anymore; rather, it is an inevitable tool to utilize as a marketing platform, to encourage interactivity and consumer engagement, to provide all requested information so it will serve for enhancing a brand, and to gives them a unique place in the marketplace (Kemmerer, 2013).

Thus, social media has evolved the relationship between firms and consumers more than any other marketing tools. Due to the interactive nature of social media communication, both parties are able to direct and determine each other's responses. Consumers accomplish it through their firm-related content and firms accomplish it through their social content; both of which are the focus of following section.

User-Generated Content

The rise of Web 2.0 technologies has enabled users to interact and collaborate with each other through social media. Users voluntarily share data, information, and media on online platforms by using self-created content, which can take many forms, such as reviews, ratings, videos, images, audio, and others. All types of content formed by the users are considered user-generated content (UGC) or, alternatively, user-created content (UCC). Although there is a lack of a broadly accepted definition, UGC is defined as "i) content made publicly available over the Internet, ii) which reflects certain amount of creative effort, and iii) which is created outside of professional routines and practices" (Vickery & Wunsch-Vincent, 2007, p. 4).

UGC has its benefits for content suppliers, consumers, and firms (Krumm, Davies & Narayanaswami, 2008). For instance, from the firm side, UGC is fairly less costly to gather since users share it for no charge. For the content suppliers, it can be rewarding because they can gain recognition for their contributions. On the other hand, from the consumer side, in addition to being informative and entertaining, UGC enables consumers to get a glimpse of real data from others not expurgated by regular media institutions. Thus, UGC broke the dominance of conventional content generators as the main source of legitimate information (Dhar & Chang, 2009). Furthermore, a recent study[1] conducted in the United States, the UK, and Australia showed that 79% of participants say UGC highly affects their purchasing decisions. Consumers find UGC approximately 10 times more effective than influencer content while making purchasing decisions. In addition, consumers are more likely (2.4x) to tell UGC is authentic compared to brand-generated content. Moreover, 51% of the consumers say they would be more likely to engage with and/or prefer a brand if it shares their photos, videos, or posts on its marketing channels. Lastly, from the firm side, UGC enables firms to demand higher prices for their products or services since consumers are more likely to spend approximately 31% more on products or services from the firms that have superior reviews.[2] Thus, positive UGC brings greater revenue and profit to the firms. In contrast, negative reviews do harm firms since every star a firm loses means a decrease in its revenue, from 5% to 9%, and a single negative review can cost a firm around 30 customers.[3] Besides, UGC helps firms communicate their values, perk up search engine optimization (SEO), boost social media metrics, and increase e-commerce sales.[4]

The previous studies (e.g., Goh, Heng & Lin, 2013; Schivinski & Dabrowski, 2016; Xun & Guo, 2017) have examined the effects of UGC, and the results of these studies showed that UGC has an impact on both consumers and firms, which or whose products or services are the subjects of this content. Thus, it is strongly believed that focusing on the particular effects of UGC will help the firms to understand its importance and benefit them in terms of creating appropriate strategies.

Firm-Generated Content

The growth in social media has changed the way of interaction between consumers and firms. It is one of the direct marketing channels through which firms are able to communicate with their current and potential customers. Firms can build, sustain, and reinforce their relationships with their target consumers by creating their own content (i.e. firm-generated content [FGC]) through social media (Poulis, Rizomyliotis & Konstantoulaki, 2019). FGC, which is described as "firm-initiated marketing communication in its official social media pages" (Kumar, Bezawada, Rishika, Janakiraman & Kannan, 2016, p. 7) is organized under the control of a brand (Coulter, Bruhn, Schoenmueller & Schäfer, 2012) and can be in any form (Daiya & Roy, 2016). Brands use FGC for several purposes. For instance, they present products on digital marketing channels to enhance brand visibility (Akar & Topçu, 2011). Besides, FGC aims to open a door for potential customers and propose topics for conversation that may create relationships between the brand and its potential customers and among the potential customers as well (Ceballos, Crespo & Cousté, 2016).

Previous market research has presented some practical facts about FGC. For instance, a research study showed that 72% of marketers think FGC is more influential than advertising in a magazine, 62% say FGC is more effective than TV advertising, and 69% indicate it is superior to both direct mail and public relations.[5] In addition, another study confirmed that 43% of people wish to be exposed to more video content from marketers.[6] In fact, Tubular Insights (2017) indicated that 32% of consumers engage with branded video on YouTube.[7] In addition, people share visual content on social media 40 times more than they do other types of content[8].

Moreover, FGC on social media has been the subject of interest in academic studies as well. For instance, it is confirmed that FGC has a significant and positive effect on consumer behavior (Kumar et al., 2016), dimensions of brand equity (Bashir, Ayub & Jalees, 2017), and brand loyalty (Godey et al., 2016). However, despite its significance for firms, FGC has not received enough attention from researchers since studies in social media marketing have mainly focused on UGC (Kumar et al., 2016). Therefore, together with UGC, this study also aims to reveal how FGC influences consumer behavior and benefits firms. The following section gives the results of studies that have examined UGC, FGC, and both.

LITERATURE REVIEW

Effects and Benefits of UGC

Firm Performance

Prior studies have revealed the effects of UGC in several areas. For instance, some research has focused on the effect of UGC on firm performance. Tirunillai and Tellis (2012) examined whether user-generated content (UGC) relates to stock market performance and confirmed that volume of chatter has a positive impact on abnormal returns and trading volume. In addition, negative UGC has a negative impact on abnormal returns, whereas positive UGC has no effect. Moreover, negative UGC raises the company risk but positive UGC does not have much influence. Xun and Guo (2017) investigated the relationship between UGC and company value and revealed that UGC about a firm positively associates with stock return but negatively associates with stock volatility. Besides, when the negative valence of a customer's UGC rises, the positive effect of UGC on a firm's stock return declines. Another study (Luo & Zhang, 2013) confirmed that a firm's stock performance is not only related to the consumer buzz in the form of user-generated reviews, recommendations, and blogs about the firm, but also related to the consumer buzz about its competitors.

Ye, Law, Gu and Chen (2011) conducted an empirical study to reveal the effect of online, user-generated reviews on sales, and the findings showed that traveler reviews have a significant positive impact on online sales. A 10% rise in traveler review ratings expands the online bookings by more than 5%. However, Cui, Lui and Guo (2012) confirmed that the percentage of negative reviews has a higher impact on new product sales than that of positive reviews, which confirms negativity bias. More specifically, the negative effect of negative reviews on sales is greater than the positive effect of positive reviews on sales. Besides, in their study, Tang, Fang and Wang (2014) analyzed the effect of different types of UGC on product sales as well. They showed that positive effect of positive UGC and negative effect of negative UGC on product sales become stronger when there is more mixed-neutral UGC (an equal amount of positive and negative claims). In contrast, indifferent-neutral UGC (includes neither positive nor negative claims) weakens the effects of both positive and negative UGC on product sales. Lastly, mixed-neutral UGC has a positive significant effect on product sales; however, indifferent-neutral UGC does not. Another study (Liang, Li, Yang & Wang, 2015) analyzing the effect of consumer reviews on product sales confirmed that negative comments about service quality hurt mobile app sales more than negative comments about product quality do.

Moreover, Kim, Lim and Brymer (2015) found that a better overall ratings and a higher response rate to negative comments in online reviews lead to a greater hotel performance. Similar research (Öğüt & Taş, 2012) also confirmed that higher customer ratings results in higher sales and additionally higher pricing of hotel rooms. Another study (Phillips, Barnes, Zigan & Schegg, 2017) in the tourism sector indicated that online reviews about hotel attributes (i.e., the quality of rooms, Internet provision, and the building) demonstrate the strongest impact on hotel performance, and positive comments have the highest effect on customer demand, which leads to higher revenue. In addition, Xie, Zhang and Zhang (2014) affirmed that overall rating, review variation, and review volume positively relate to hotel performance. Besides, variation and volume of consumer reviews moderate the link between overall rating and hotel performance. Together with variation and volume of consumer reviews, management responses moderate the link between certain attribute ratings and hotel performance. Another study (Nieto et al., 2014) found that ratings and number of reviews have positive impacts on business performance (establishment owner's satisfaction, profitability, and establishment owner's market perception). It also showed that the number of positive reviews is more significant.

Based on the findings of the aforementioned studies, it can be stated that UGC has a strong impact and benefit on a firm's performance in terms of stock returns, sales, demand, revenue, profit, and pricing. In addition, online ratings seem to be one of the most effective types of UGC that directly influence firm performance. Moreover, valence and volume of UGC are revealed to be the factors determining its effect. Direction and magnitude of the effects of positive, negative, and neutral UGC on firm performance differ.

Consumer Perception and Behavior

UGC is broadly considered to be one of the most influential factors that influences consumers. Previous studies have examined the influence of UGC on consumers' purchase intention, attitude, and decision-making. In addition, the impact of consumers' perceptions of UGC on their intentions and attitudes has also been a topic of interest. For instance, Ladhari and Michaud (2015), in an experimental study, analyzed the impact of comments written by Facebook friends on the intentions of booking a hotel, the trust in the hotel, the attitude toward the hotel, and the perception of its website. The results confirmed that respondents exposed to positive feedback have higher booking intentions, more positive attitudes toward the hotel, higher trust in the hotel, and more positive perceptions of its website, compared to the respondents exposed to negative feedback. In addition, trust in the comments moderates these effects. With a low trust level, the effect of feedback becomes insignificant in most cases; with a high trust level, the effect of feedback on the variables is significant.

Another experimental study (Gavilan, Avello & Martinez-Navarro, 2018) examined the effect of rating (good or bad) on the product/service consideration with the mediating role of trustworthiness. Besides, it also analyzed whether the number of reviews (high or low) moderates the link between rating and trustworthiness. The results showed that rating has a significant negative impact on trustworthiness and respondents exposed to the good rating have a lower trustworthiness score than respondents exposed to the bad rating. In addition, trust in the rating leads respondents to consider the product/service more. The interaction between the rating and the number of reviews is also confirmed. When there is a good rating supported by a high number of reviews, respondents' consideration for the offer strengthens. For a bad rating, the conditional indirect effect becomes insignificant.

In addition, Tsao, Hsieh, Shih & Lin (2015) determined the influence of review valence and quantity and interaction effects on booking intentions of two different consumer groups: conformist and non-conformist. The findings revealed that positive reviews have a stronger effect on booking intentions of conformist individuals. In addition, a greater number of reviews are more persuasive for individuals with a low degree of conformity. Lastly, it is revealed that a larger number of negative reviews are more harmful to the booking intentions of conformist individuals whereas a higher number of positive reviews have a higher impact on non-conformists. Another study (Daugherty & Hoffman, 2014) confirmed that people are more likely to pay attention to negative UGC and UGC about non-luxury brands. Besides, the interaction of valence and brand type has a stronger influence on consumer attention for non-luxury brands than luxury brands. Similarly, Park and Lee (2009) demonstrated that the effect of UGC on consumers is greater for negative UGC than for positive UGC. In addition, the effect of negative UGC becomes even stronger depending on the product type. The impact of negative UGC on the UGC effect on consumers is greater for experience goods than for search goods. Another research study (Lee & Youn, 2009) examining the impact of electronic word of mouth (eWOM) platforms on consumer judgment indicated that the effect of the eWOM platforms on consumer intention to suggest the product to friends was found only if the review was positive. However, when the review was negative, consumers did not want to suggest the product to their friends irrespective of the eWOM platform. Thus, the results of these studies show that the impact of negative UGC could be stronger than the one of positive UGC.

Furthermore, Ayeh, Au and Law (2013) analyzed the effect of source credibility (i.e., trustworthiness and expertise) of UGC on the attitude and intention of travelers to use UGC. The study confirmed that the trustworthiness of UGC has a positive impact on both attitude and intention, whereas the expertise of UGC has a positive influence only on attitude, and attitude has a positive effect on intention. These findings imply that online travelers are more likely to use UGC for travel planning if they if they believe that UGC is from credible travelers. Erkan and Evans (2016) confirmed that UGC quality, credibility, and usefulness; adoption of information; need for information; and attitude toward information are the key factors of UGC that affect the purchase intention of consumers. Another study (Wang, Cunningham & Eastin, 2015) investigated the impact of information type on message recall and the effect of information type and valence on attitude toward the review and product, credibility, and purchase intention. Results indicated that an attribute-centric message creates higher source credibility than a benefit-centric one does. In addition, when the message is benefit-centric, a positive message produces a greater attitude score toward the product. A positive review with benefit-centric information has the strongest positive effect on the product attitude and purchase intention of consumers. In addition, benefit-centric-reviews lead to greater recall than attribute-centric reviews.

In addition, some studies have showed that consumer engagement plays a significant role on the effect of UGC. For instance, Cheung, Xiao and Liu (2014) revealed that as consumers become more actively involved with a brand community, they are more likely to be influenced by peer consumer reviews when they make a purchase decision. Another study (Amaral, Tiago & Tiago, 2014) examined the influence of TripAdvisor engagement on tourists' choice of tourism service providers (i.e. restaurants). It confirmed that there are three consumer clusters, namely newbies, beginners, and specialists, according to their number of posts, expertise level, and votes. Newbies more frequently attend the restaurants with greater recommendation rates, while specialists go more to restaurants with the smallest percentage of recommendations. That is, users' responses to UGC differ according to their engagement levels. Furthermore, Lopez and Sicilia (2014) confirmed that consumer engagement increases perceived source trustworthiness and the influence of UGC on decision-making.

Moreover, prior studies have shown that UGC has an impact on consumer perceptions of brands. For instance, Schivinski and Dabrowski (2016) affirmed that UGC has a positive influence on brand equity and brand attitude. In their previous study, Schivinski and Dabrowski (2013) found that user-generated social media communication has a positive impact on brand loyalty and perceived quality of brand. A similar research by Bashir et al. (2017) also revealed that UGC influences perceived quality of brand, brand awareness, and brand association. Additionally, Christodoulides, Jevons and Bonhomme (2012) found evidence for the positive effect of UGC involvement on consumer-based brand equity.

After all, the findings of the abovementioned studies show that UGC has an effect on consumers in various aspects, and this effect varies depending on the valence, quantity, message type, perception of the consumers about UGC, and consumer engagement. Valence produces the asymmetrical results that positive UGC does not always lead to positive outcomes, as negative UGC does not always lead to negative outcomes. Likely, a higher quantity of UGC may not always be attractive to the consumers. In addition, the interaction of valence and quantity plays a significant role on the impact of UGC. Consumers' attitudes or intentions differ according to the message type (e.g., benefit- or attribute-centric), and if consumers believe that UGC is trustworthy and credible, they tend to hold a positive attitude and have a purchase intention. Another factor that leads consumers to purchase intention is their engagement level with UGC. The more they participate, the more they are influenced by UGC while making purchasing decisions. Lastly, UGC has a positive impact on consumer-based brand equity dimensions, which in turn creates a long-term benefit for the firm.

Effects and Benefits of FGC

Firm Performance

Like UGC, FGC is an important tool for firm performance. Paniagua and Sapena (2014) revealed that followers and likes resulting from FGC positively influence share value after the firm gains a critical bulk of followers. Another study (Lin & Goh, 2011) found support for the positive relationship between the FGC information richness and total sales. Other research (Wan & Ren, 2017) examined the link between FGC and product sales and confirmed that FGC has a positive impact on overall sales. Specifically, FGC marketing results in an average 51.47% increase in product sales. This effect differs according to the content (i.e., informative, persuasive, and promotional) and product type (i.e., high and low involvement). That is, informative FGC is stronger in triggering the sales of high involvement products than persuasive and promotional content. However, for low involvement products, persuasive and promotional content has more effect on sales. Besides, FGC is confirmed to affect supply chain performance as well. Swain and Cao (2014) revealed that if supply chain partners discuss information sharing and collaboration in a positive way on social media, supply chain performance enhances.

Consequently, the findings of these studies indicate that FGC has a positive impact on firm performance regarding share value, sales, and supply chain performance. Additionally, content and product type reveals to be two factors that shape the effect of FGC. Studies on this subject area are scarce, so further examination of FGC's effects on firm performance is important for a deeper understanding of the issue.

Consumer Perception and Behavior

Marketers use FGC to attract and engage with consumers. An effective FGC has several positive effects on consumers. For instance, Kumar et al. (2016) confirmed that FGC has a significant positive impact on customer spending and cross-buying behavior. This effect of FGC becomes stronger for more experienced, tech-savvy, and social media–prone customers. In addition, the authors reveal that all three characteristics (valence, receptivity, and customer susceptibility) of FGC have a positive impact, but the factor of FGC receptivity has the highest. Another study (Goh et al., 2013) examining the effect of FGC on consumer purchase behavior demonstrated that FGC valence has a positive impact on consumer demand, whereas FGC information richness does not. Contrary to these findings, Schivinski and Dabrowski (2013) did not find any support for the direct influence of FGC on purchase intention. Additionally, Ashley and Tuten (2015) addressed the relationship between the appeal of brand-generated social content and consumer engagement. The authors reveal that experiential appeals increases consumer engagement, while emotional appeals decreases it. In addition, FGC that includes incentives for consumer participation also enhances consumer engagement. Another study (Ding, Phang, Lu, Tan & Sutanto, 2014) revealed that regardless of its nature (i.e., product or social related), FGC simulates UGC, and social-related FGC promotes the growth of brand communities.

The prior studies have also analyzed the impact of UGC on consumers' brand perception. Bashir et al. (2017) demonstrated that FGC has a positive significant effect on perceived quality, brand awareness, and brand association. However, Schivinski and Dabrowski (2013) did not find any support for FGC's effect on brand awareness/association, perceived quality, and brand loyalty. However, in a later study, Schivinski and Dabrowski (2016) revealed that FGC positively influences brand attitude. In addition, Coulter et al. (2012) proved that FGC has a significant impact on functional brand image. Another study (Godey et al., 2016) found that for luxury brands, FGC has a positive impact on brand equity (brand awareness and brand image); brand preference; brand loyalty; and willingness to pay premium prices for Chinese, French, Indian, and Italian consumers.

The abovementioned studies show that FGC has an impact on consumers' purchase intention, consumer engagement, and consumers' brand perception. However, the effect of FGC on consumers' purchase intention and brand perception is conflicting. Even though there is evidence for the positive impact of FGC on purchase intention and brand perception, this effect was revealed to be insignificant in some studies. Thus, these contradictory results require further examination of FGC regarding its effect on purchase intention and brand perception.

CONCLUSION

It is a fact that UGC and FGC are two powerful factors affecting both firms and consumers. This theoretical paper addresses these specific effects based on a literature review. From the firm side, UGC appears to be a significant factor for stock returns, sales, demand, revenue, profit, and pricing. One of the most impactful factors of UGC on firm performance is online ratings. Besides these, valence and volume are the determinants for the magnitude and direction of UGC's effect. From the consumer side, UGC is revealed to be an important factor on purchase intention, decision-making, and brand perception. Valence, volume, message type, perception of the consumers about UGC, and engagement level determine UGC's effect on consumers.

Like UGC, FGC has its effects and benefits for both firms and consumers. However, although UGC has been a popular issue for researchers, FGC appears to be an overlooked subject. From the firm side, FGC has a positive impact on share value, sales, and supply chain performance. Its effect differs regarding the content and product type. From the consumer side, FGC is effective on consumers' purchase intention, consumer engagement, and consumers' brand perception. However, its effect on purchase intention and brand perception is not clear since these impacts are revealed to be both significant and insignificant. Hence, this issue necessitates further consideration. After all, both UGC and FGC are useful tools to improve firm performance and affect consumers in a positive manner, so the integration and management of these tools together is crucial. Firms should work hard on creating effective FGC, which stimulates consumers to create and spread positive firm-related UGC. Thus, they should come up with creative message appeals to motivate consumers to share UGC and create consumer engagement on social platforms. Then, by evaluating UGC, firms can understand better what type of FGC is effective. Besides, interactivity is an important factor that motivates consumers to present their firm-related content, so firms should take them seriously and respond to both negative and positive UGC coming from consumers.

FUTURE RESEARCH DIRECTIONS

The current study presents the effects and benefits of UGC and FGC within a theoretical framework. Based on the reviewed studies, the authors suggest that FGC needs more focus from the researchers since most of the studies have examined the effects and benefits of UGC. Thus, the authors believe that future empirical studies would shed a light on the undiscovered potential of FGC for both firms and consumers. In addition, consumer perspective currently dominates the subject of interest in the majority of the research. Thus, there is huge potential for the research area of UGC and FGC focalizing on the firm side. Also, the number of comparative studies (e.g., Bashir et al., 2017; Godey et al., 2016; Goh et al., 2013) regarding the effects of UGC and FGC is very limited. In addition, these studies commonly address the issue from the consumers' aspect as well. Therefore, assessing the comparative effects of UGC and FGC on firms would fill this gap in the literature. Another suggestion is that since the results of the studies about the effects of FGC on consumers are conflicting, further studies can address and focus on the reasons for the contradictory findings. Last, the effect of UGC and FGC differs according to some factors such as valence, quantity, and type of the content, so further research can focus on the other factors, which may determine the effect of UGC and FGC.

IMPLICATIONS FOR BUSINESS

UGC and FGC do have their own particular effects both on firms and on consumers. Although firms have total control over FGC, they do not have this opportunity when it comes to UGC. However, firms always have a chance to build appropriate strategies to manage UGC. One important point is that the valence of UGC is revealed to be very effective on firms in terms of its performance and product sales. Negative reviews seem to have greater impact than positive reviews do. Thus, firms should first focus on the negative customer reviews and try to unveil what these negative reviews tell about the firm and its products and services. Then, they should determine the most frequently mentioned subjects of these negative reviews and take actions to fix these issues if it is possible. If not, they should respond to the suppliers of these reviews in an empathetic manner since firm responses, especially to the negative reviews, leads to a greater firm performance. On the other hand, the magnitude and direction of UGC's effect are contradictory; that is to say, negative comments do not always lead to negative outcomes, as positive comments do not always lead to positive outcomes, or negative reviews may be more effective than positive ones in some cases and vice versa in other cases. Since the effects of UGC are sensitive to some factors such as product type and consumer type, firms should determine those factors for the effective management of both negative and positive UGC.

In addition, UGC volume appears to be another significant factor since a high volume of UGC has potential to lead some consumers to purchase a firm's products or services. Thus, it is essential to motivate customers to share their ideas and opinions about the products or services they have experienced. Firms may use promotional tools to succeed at this. For instance, they could offer discounts or coupons to initiate their customers to share their experiences on online social platforms. In addition, source credibility and trustworthiness of UGC are effective to catch consumers as well. A trustful review coming from a credible source would convert potential buyers into actual ones. Thus, firms should identify the credible reviewers and work with them to attract new customers.

Furthermore, consumer engagement plays a significant role on the effect of UGC. The more consumers engage with a social community, the more they trust the shared content on that platform and are affected by it. Hence, for their social platforms, firms should generate content that creates consumer engagement. For this, a better understanding of consumer expectation is crucial. Firms should find answers for some questions such as "What type of content do consumers prefer?," "Which message appeals attract and motivate consumers to engage?," and "What type content is appropriate for different types of products or services?"

Eventually, the management of UGC is a tougher path for the firms since they do not have control over creating and sharing it as they do with FGC. However, FGC is one powerful tool to generate UGC so an effective management of both benefits firms in the long term.

This research received no specific grant from any funding agency in the public, commercial, or not-for-profit sectors.

REFERENCES

Akar, E., & Topçu, B. (2011). An examination of the factors influencing consumers' attitudes toward social media marketing. *Journal of Internet Commerce*, *10*(1), 35–67. doi:10.1080/15332861.2011.558456

Alameddine, A. (2013). *Perceptions of executives from seven selected companies of the use of social media in marketing practices* (Doctoral dissertation, Pepperdine University, California).

Amaral, F., Tiago, T., & Tiago, F. (2014). User-generated content: Tourists' profiles on Tripadvisor. *International Journal of Strategic Innovative Marketing*, *1*(3), 137–145.

Ariganello, M. (2016). *Creating the brands we trust: How organizations in the lifestyle category build consumer trust through effective branding and content marketing in the 21st century* (Master's thesis, University of Southern California, California).

Ashley, C., & Tuten, T. (2015). Creative strategies in social media marketing: An exploratory study of branded social content and consumer engagement. *Psychology and Marketing*, *32*(1), 15–27. doi:10.1002/mar.20761

Ayeh, J. K., Au, N., & Law, R. (2013). "Do we believe in TripAdvisor?" Examining credibility perceptions and online travelers' attitude toward using user-generated content. *Journal of Travel Research*, *52*(4), 437–452. doi:10.1177/0047287512475217

Barefoot, D., & Szabo, J. (2010). *Friends with benefits: A social media-marketing handbook*. San Francisco, CA: No Starch Press.

Bashir, M. A., Ayub, N., & Jalees, T. (2017). The impact of the firm generated contents and the user generated contents through social media on brand equity elements. *Pakistan Business Review*, *19*(3), 744–760.

Brieger, C. (2013). *Exploring new communication strategies for a global brand – Transmedia storytelling and gamification* (Master's thesis, Norwegian School of Economics, Norway).

Ceballos, M., Crespo, Á. G., & Cousté, N. L. (2016). Impact of firm-created content on user-generated content: Using a new social media monitoring tool to explore Twitter. In *Proceedings 2015 Academy of Marketing Science (AMS) World Marketing Congress Rediscovering the Essentiality of Marketing* (pp. 303-306). Cham, Switzerland: Springer. 10.1007/978-3-319-29877-1_61

Cheung, C., Xiao, B., & Liu, I. (2014). Do actions speak louder than voices? The signaling role of social information cues in influencing consumer purchase decisions. *Decision Support Systems*, *65*, 50–58. doi:10.1016/j.dss.2014.05.002

Cheung, C. M. K., Lee, M. K. O., & Thadani, D. R. (2009). The impact of positive electronic word-of-mouth on consumer online purchasing decision. In *Proceedings Visioning and Engineering the Knowledge Society. A Web Science Perspective. WSKS 2009* (pp. 501-510). Berlin, Germany: Springer. 10.1007/978-3-642-04754-1_51

Christodoulides, G., Jevons, C., & Bonhomme, J. (2012). Memo to marketers: Quantitative evidence for change: How user-generated content really affects brands. *Journal of Advertising Research*, *52*(1), 53–64. doi:10.2501/JAR-52-1-053-064

Cohen, R. (2014). Social media marketing: Creating a successful commercial campaign targeting women in their '30-'40. (Master's thesis, Long Island University, New York).

Coulter, K. S., Bruhn, M., Schoenmueller, V., & Schäfer, D. B. (2012). Are social media replacing traditional media in terms of brand equity creation? *Management Research Review*, *35*(9), 770–790. doi:10.1108/01409171211255948

Cronin, J. (2016). Teach students to communicate a brand story with transmedia storytelling. *Journal of Research in Interactive Marketing*, *10*(2), 86–101. doi:10.1108/JRIM-01-2015-0004

Cui, G., Lui, H. K., & Guo, X. (2012). The effect of online consumer reviews on new product sales. *International Journal of Electronic Commerce*, *17*(1), 39–58. doi:10.2753/JEC1086-4415170102

Curran, K., O'Brien, S., & O'Hara, K. (2011). The role of Twitter in the world of business. *International Journal of Business Data Communications and Networking*, *7*(3), 14. doi:10.4018/jbdcn.2011070101

Daiya, A., & Roy, S. (2016). User and firm generated content on online social media: A review and research directions. [IJOM]. *International Journal of Online Marketing*, *6*(3), 34–49. doi:10.4018/IJOM.2016070103

Daugherty, T., & Hoffman, E. (2014). eWOM and the importance of capturing consumer attention within social media. *Journal of Marketing Communications*, *20*(1-2), 82–102. doi:10.1080/13527266.2013.797764

Dhar, V., & Chang, E. A. (2009). Does chatter matter? The impact of user-generated content on music sales. *Journal of Interactive Marketing*, *23*(4), 300–307. doi:10.1016/j.intmar.2009.07.004

Ding, Y., Phang, C. W., Lu, X., Tan, C. H., & Sutanto, J. (2014). The role of marketer-and user-generated content in sustaining the growth of a social media brand community. In *Proceedings 2014 47th Hawaii International Conference on System Sciences* (pp. 1785-1792). New York: IEEE. 10.1109/HICSS.2014.226

Du Plessis, C. (2015). *An exploratory analysis of essential elements of content marketing*. In *Proceedings ECSM 2015 2nd European Conference on Social Media*, (pp. 122-129). UK: Academic Conferences Publisher International.

Erkan, I., & Evans, C. (2016). The influence of eWOM in social media on consumers' purchase intentions: An extended approach to information adoption. *Computers in Human Behavior*, *61*, 47–55. doi:10.1016/j.chb.2016.03.003

Fotis, J., Buhalis, D., & Rossides, N. (2011). Social media impact on holiday travel planning: The case of the Russian and the FSU markets. [IJOM]. *International Journal of Online Marketing*, *1*(4), 1–19. doi:10.4018/ijom.2011100101

Gavilan, D., Avello, M., & Martinez-Navarro, G. (2018). The influence of online ratings and reviews on hotel booking consideration. *Tourism Management*, *66*, 53–61. doi:10.1016/j.tourman.2017.10.018

Godey, B., Manthiou, A., Pederzoli, D., Rokka, J., Aiello, G., Donvito, R., & Singh, R. (2016). Social media marketing efforts of luxury brands: Influence on brand equity and consumer behavior. *Journal of Business Research*, *69*(12), 5833–5841. doi:10.1016/j.jbusres.2016.04.181

Goh, K. Y., Heng, C. S., & Lin, Z. (2013). Social media brand community and consumer behavior: Quantifying the relative impact of user- and marketer-generated content. *Information Systems Research*, *24*(1), 88–107. doi:10.1287/isre.1120.0469

Hennig-Thurau, T., Gwinner, K. P., Walsh, G., & Gremler, D. D. (2004). Electronic word-of-mouth via consumer-opinion platforms: What motivates consumers to articulate themselves on the Internet? *Journal of Interactive Marketing*, *18*(1), 38–52. doi:10.1002/dir.10073

Holliman, G., & Rowley, J. (2014). Business to business digital content marketing: Marketers' perceptions of best practice. *Journal of Research in Interactive Marketing*, *8*(4), 269–293. doi:10.1108/JRIM-02-2014-0013

Keller, K. L. (2009). Building strong brands in a modern marketing communications environment. *Journal of Marketing Communications*, *15*(2-3), 139–155. doi:10.1080/13527260902757530

Kemmerer, K. (2013). *Unleashing the power of social media marketing within the non-profits, through the lens of social cognitive theory* (Master's thesis, Liberty University, Virginia).

Kim, W. G., Lim, H., & Brymer, R. A. (2015). The effectiveness of managing social media on hotel performance. *International Journal of Hospitality Management*, *44*, 165–171. doi:10.1016/j.ijhm.2014.10.014

Krumm, J., Davies, N., & Narayanaswami, C. (2008). User-generated content. *IEEE Pervasive Computing*, *7*(4), 10–11. doi:10.1109/MPRV.2008.85

Kumar, A., Bezawada, R., Rishika, R., Janakiraman, R., & Kannan, P. K. (2016). From social to sale: The effects of firm-generated content in social media on customer behavior. *Journal of Marketing*, *80*(1), 7–25. doi:10.1509/jm.14.0249

Ladhari, R., & Michaud, M. (2015). eWOM effects on hotel booking intentions, attitudes, trust, and website perceptions. *International Journal of Hospitality Management*, *46*, 36–45. doi:10.1016/j.ijhm.2015.01.010

Lee, M., & Youn, S. (2009). Electronic word of mouth (eWOM): How eWOM platforms influence consumer product judgement. *International Journal of Advertising*, *28*(3), 473–499. doi:10.2501/S0265048709200709

Liang, T. P., Li, X., Yang, C. T., & Wang, M. (2015). What in consumer reviews affects the sales of mobile apps: A multifacet sentiment analysis approach. *International Journal of Electronic Commerce*, *20*(2), 236–260. doi:10.1080/10864415.2016.1087823

Lin, Z., & Goh, K. Y. (2011). *Measuring the business value of online social media content for marketers*. Paper presented at Thirty Second International Conference on Information Systems, Shanghai (1-13). Atlanta, GA: Association for Information Systems (AIS).

Liu, H. W., & Huang, H. C. (2015). Tradeoff between push and pull strategy: The moderating role of brand awareness. In H. Spotts (Ed.), *Marketing, technology and customer commitment in the new economy* (pp. 259–264). Cham, Switzerland: Springer. doi:10.1007/978-3-319-11779-9_98

Lopez, M., & Sicilia, M. (2014). eWOM as source of influence: The impact of participation in eWOM and perceived source trustworthiness on decision making. *Journal of Interactive Advertising*, *14*(2), 86–97. doi:10.1080/15252019.2014.944288

Luo, X., & Zhang, J. (2013). How do consumer buzz and traffic in social media marketing predict the value of the firm? *Journal of Management Information Systems*, *30*(2), 213–238. doi:10.2753/MIS0742-1222300208

Murdough, C. (2009). Social media measurement: It's not impossible. *Journal of Interactive Advertising*, *10*(1), 94–99. doi:10.1080/15252019.2009.10722165

Nadaraja, R., & Yazdanifard, R. (2013). Social media marketing: Advantages and disadvantages. *Social Media Marketing*, 1-10.

Nieto, J., Hernández-Maestro, R. M., & Muñoz-Gallego, P. A. (2014). Marketing decisions, customer reviews, and business performance: The use of the Toprural website by Spanish rural lodging establishments. *Tourism Management*, *45*, 115–123. doi:10.1016/j.tourman.2014.03.009

Öğüt, H., & Taş, B. (2012). The influence of internet customer reviews on the online sales and prices in hotel industry. *Service Industries Journal*, *32*(2), 197–214. doi:10.1080/02642069.2010.529436

Paniagua, J., & Sapena, J. (2014). Business performance and social media: Love or hate? *Business Horizons*, *57*(6), 719–728. doi:10.1016/j.bushor.2014.07.005

Park, C., & Lee, T. M. (2009). Information direction, website reputation and eWOM effect: A moderating role of product type. *Journal of Business Research*, *62*(1), 61–67. doi:10.1016/j.jbusres.2007.11.017

Phillips, P., Barnes, S., Zigan, K., & Schegg, R. (2017). Understanding the impact of online reviews on hotel performance: An empirical analysis. *Journal of Travel Research*, *56*(2), 235–249. doi:10.1177/0047287516636481

Poulis, A., Rizomyliotis, I., & Konstantoulaki, K. (2019). Do firms still need to be social? Firm generated content in social media. *Information Technology & People*, *32*(2), 387–404. doi:10.1108/ITP-03-2018-0134

Pulizzi, J. (2010). *New research: B2B content marketing: benchmarks, trends and budgets*. Content Marketing Research, Content Marketing Institute. Retrieved from https://contentmarketinginstitute.com/wp-content/uploads/2010/09/B2B_Trends_2010.pdf

Roberts, R. R., & Kraynak, J. (2008). *Walk like a giant, sell like a madman*. Hoboken, NJ: Wiley.

Saxton, G. D., & Wang, L. (2013). The social network effect: The determinants of giving through social media. *Nonprofit and Voluntary Sector Quarterly*, 1–19.

Schivinski, B., & Dąbrowski, D. (2013). The impact of brand communication on brand equity dimensions and brand purchase intention through Facebook. Gdansk (Poland): Gdansk University of Technology, Faculty of Management and Economics, 4(4), 1-24.

Schivinski, B., & Dabrowski, D. (2016). The effect of social media communication on consumer perceptions of brands. *Journal of Marketing Communications*, *22*(2), 189–214. doi:10.1080/13527266.2013.871323

Scott, D. (2007). *The new rules of marketing and PR*. Hoboken, NJ: John Wiley & Sons.

Sheth, J. N., & Sharma, A. (2005). International e-marketing: Opportunities and issues. *International Marketing Review*, *22*(6), 611–622. doi:10.1108/02651330510630249

Smith, P. R., Berry, C., & Pulford, A. (1999). *Strategic marketing communications*. London, UK: Kogan Page.

Stelzner, M. A. (2015). *2015 Social media marketing industry report*. Retrieved from http://www.socialmediaexaminer.com/report/

Swain, A., & Cao, Q. (2014). Impact of online firm generated content (FGC) on supply chain performance: An empirical analysis. In *Proceedings 2014 47th Hawaii International Conference on System Sciences* (pp. 561-573). New Jersey: IEEE.

Tang, T., Fang, E., & Wang, F. (2014). Is neutral really neutral? The effects of neutral user-generated content on product sales. *Journal of Marketing*, *78*(4), 41–58. doi:10.1509/jm.13.0301

Tirunillai, S., & Tellis, G. J. (2012). Does chatter really matter? Dynamics of user-generated content and stock performance. *Marketing Science*, *31*(2), 198–215. doi:10.1287/mksc.1110.0682

Tsao, W. C., Hsieh, M. T., Shih, L. W., & Lin, T. M. (2015). Compliance with eWOM: The influence of hotel reviews on booking intention from the perspective of consumer conformity. *International Journal of Hospitality Management*, *46*, 99–111. doi:10.1016/j.ijhm.2015.01.008

Tuten, T., & Solomon, M. (2013). *Social media marketing*. Upper Saddle River, NJ: Pearson.

Vickery, G., & Wunsch-Vincent, S. (2007). *Participative web and user-created content: Web 2.0 wikis and social networking*. Paris, France: Organisation for Economic Cooperation and Development.

Vlasic, G., & Kesic, T. (2007). Analysis of consumers' attitudes toward interactivity and relationship personalization as contemporary developments in interactive marketing communication. *Journal of Marketing Communications*, *13*(2), 109–129. doi:10.1080/13527260601070417

Wan, F., & Ren, F. (2017). The effect of firm marketing content on product sales: Evidence from a mobile social media platform. *Journal of Electronic Commerce Research*, *18*(4), 288–302.

Wang, S., Cunningham, N. R., & Eastin, M. S. (2015). The impact of eWOM message characteristics on the perceived effectiveness of online consumer reviews. *Journal of Interactive Advertising*, *15*(2), 151–159. doi:10.1080/15252019.2015.1091755

Watson, R. P., Leyland, F. P., Berthon, P., & Zinkham, G. (2002). U-commerce: Expanding the universe of marketing. *Journal of the Academy of Marketing Science*, *30*(4), 333–347. doi:10.1177/009207002236909

Wendlandt, L. B. (2012). *Return on investment concerns in social media marketing: An examination of recent cases* (Master's thesis, The College of St. Scholastica, Minnesota).

Whiting, A., & Deshpande, A. (2014). Social media marketing: A myth or a necessity. *Journal of Applied Business & Economics, 16*(5), 74–81.

Witman, P. (2013). Social media for social value. *Computer, 46*(7), 82–85. doi:10.1109/MC.2013.247

Wu, J. J., Chen, Y. H., & Chung, Y. S. (2010). Trust factors influencing virtual community members: A study of transaction communities. *Journal of Business Research, 63*(9), 1025–1032. doi:10.1016/j.jbusres.2009.03.022

Xiang, Z., & Gretzel, U. (2010). Role of social media in online travel information search. *Tourism Management, 31*(2), 179–188. doi:10.1016/j.tourman.2009.02.016

Xie, K. L., Zhang, Z., & Zhang, Z. (2014). The business value of online consumer reviews and management response to hotel performance. *International Journal of Hospitality Management, 43*, 1–12. doi:10.1016/j.ijhm.2014.07.007

Xun, J., & Guo, B. (2017). Twitter as customer's eWOM: An empirical study on their impact on firm financial performance. *Internet Research, 27*(5), 1014–1038. doi:10.1108/IntR-07-2016-0223

Ye, Q., Law, R., Gu, B., & Chen, W. (2011). The influence of user-generated content on traveler behavior: An empirical investigation on the effects of e-word-of-mouth to hotel online bookings. *Computers in Human Behavior, 27*(2), 634–639. doi:10.1016/j.chb.2010.04.014

Zahay, D. (2014). Beyond interactive marketing. *Journal of Research in Interactive Marketing, 8*(4), 32–46. doi:10.1108/JRIM-08-2014-0047

ADDITIONAL READING

Arrigo, E. (2014). Social media opportunities for market-driven firms. In W. Cellary & ... (Eds.), *Integrating social media into business practice, applications, management, and models* (pp. 180–199). Pennsylvania: IGI Global. doi:10.4018/978-1-4666-6182-0.ch010

Chen, Y., Liu, Y., & Zhang, J. (2012). When do third-party product reviews affect firm value and what can firms do? The case of media critics and professional movie reviews. *Journal of Marketing, 76*(2), 116–134. doi:10.1509/jm.09.0034

Cox, C., Burgess, S., Sellitto, C., & Buultjens, J. (2009). The role of user-generated content in tourists' travel planning behavior. *Journal of Hospitality Marketing & Management*, *18*(8), 743–764. doi:10.1080/19368620903235753

Daugherty, T., Eastin, M. S., & Bright, L. (2008). Exploring consumer motivations for creating user-generated content. *Journal of Interactive Advertising*, *8*(2), 16–25. doi:10.1080/15252019.2008.10722139

Nadda, V. K., Dadwal, S. S., & Firdous, A. (2015). Social media marketing. In N. Hajli (Ed.), *Handbook of research on integrating social media into strategic marketing* (pp. 359–379). Pennsylvania: IGI Global. doi:10.4018/978-1-4666-8353-2.ch021

Tajvidi, R., & Karami, A. (2017). The effect of social media on firm performance. *Computers in Human Behavior*, 1–10.

KEY TERMS AND DEFINITIONS

Brand Equity: Value of a brand based on consumer perception of and experiences with the brand.

Consumer Engagement: Connection between consumers and firms through various communication channels.

Content Appeal: Attractiveness and persuasiveness of the content for its target audience.

Content Marketing: Creating and sharing online content that motivates consumers to have interest in a firm's products or services.

Content Valence: Goodness (positive) or badness (negative) of the content; can be neutral as well.

Content Volume: The quantity of content.

FGC (Firm-Generated Content): All types of content created under the control of firms to be used in their own social media channels.

UGC (User-Generated Content): All types of online content created and published by users for non-professional purposes.

ENDNOTES

1 https://stackla.com/resources/reports/bridging-the-gap-consumer-marketing-perspectives-on-content-in-the-digital-age/

2 https://www.brightlocal.com/blog/the-impact-of-online-reviews/

3 https://www.brightlocal.com/blog/the-impact-of-online-reviews/

4 https://taggbox.com/blog/user-generated-content/

5 https://thecontentcouncil.org/files/galleries/spending_2011_final.pdf

6 https://wpforms.com/the-ultimate-list-of-online-business-statistics/

7 https://www.hubspot.com/marketing-statistics

8 https://medium.com/@tech4growthnet/important-2017-powerful-social-media-and-influencer-marketing- stats-and-facts-16a8c45c18bf

Chapter 6
Social Media and E-Commerce:
A Study on Motivations for Sharing Content From E-Commerce Websites

Tiago Da Costa
Faculty of Economics, University of Porto, Portugal

Beatriz Casais
https://orcid.org/0000-0002-7626-0509
School of Economics and Management, University of Minho, Portugal & IPAM Porto, Portugal

ABSTRACT

Several studies have approached the link between social media and e-commerce with different lenses, however, the study of motivations for sharing content specifically from e-commerce websites into social media has not been thoroughly approached and provides fertile ground for further exploration. This chapter uncovers which motivations serve as a background for individuals sharing intentions of e-commerce content. After a focus group with 7 individuals, results indicate participants focus more on intrinsic rewards than extrinsic ones when sharing, that self-interest is more predominant than reciprocity as a motivator for sharing, one-to-one exchanges are the preferential direction of exchange. Also, websites with cleaner designs and higher usability positively impact sharing intentions, experiences tend to be more likely shared than physical products, and participants are purposeful in their selection of sharing channels.

DOI: 10.4018/978-1-7998-2185-4.ch006

INTRODUCTION

Understanding the motivations for sharing content from e-commerce websites into social media networks is a field of knowledge that can be expanded and there are no studies about the motivations of users in a specific e-commerce context to share product and other information on social media channels. Therefore, we believe that going deeper and analyzing motivations in this very specific context should provide a new contribution to this field of study. On a more practical side, we believe that it is also in the best interest of companies operating e-commerce websites, to understand what consumers think and what drives them to share content in order to adapt their websites' content strategically, significantly improving the *shareability* of the content and efficiently using the users of social networks to spread the word about products or services promoted by the company.

BACKGROUND

E-Commerce and Social Media Sharing

Social media brings big challenges to companies as consumers have evolved from being passive recipients in business transactions (Zhao et al., 2013). With the empowerment given to consumers by social media these have been taking an increasingly active role in co-creating everything from product design to promotional messages. Customers want companies to listen, engage, and respond. However, when companies change their mentality from business-centered to consumer-centered thinking, they can see that social media bring them great opportunities for engaging consumers and listening to them for what they would like and need. As consumers spend more of their time on social media, purchase decisions have become highly influenced by interactions through these networks, a fact which has lead businesses to place more emphasis on marketing strategies which focus on two-way communication platforms to reach online consumers and take advantage of word-of-mouth (Song & Yoo, 2016). Internet-based social media are quickly merging into the domain of e-commerce as a wide range of applications has been adopted on e-commerce platforms because internet-based social media provide online retailers withgreat opportunities to build their brand, and to promote and sell their products (Qu, Wang, Wang, & Zhang, 2013). As a reflection of the growth of social media, commercial websites have shifted from a unidirectional information provider format, called web 1.0 to multidirectional collaborative web technologies, denominated web 2.0 (Aluri, Slevitch, & Larzelere, 2015).

Social media and the web 2.0 have provided a huge potential to transform e-commerce into a more organized environment. The impacts of web 2.0 on e-commerce encompass both business outcomes and social interaction between customers in the sense that, besides directly influencing business transactions, it can also provide opportunities to strengthen relationships with customers, increase traffic into company websites and also support product and brand development (Huang & Benyoucef, 2013). Within such an environment, customers have access to social knowledge and experiences which allow them to assess their online purchase purposes and help them in making more informed purchase decisions while, at the same time, businesses are given information on the customers' behaviors and shopping experiences, which can be used to enhance their business strategies. This practice can be considered as part the construct of *social embeddedness* which, as described by Hess, Lang and Xu (2011) refers to the extent to which organizations can be "*connected to other actors other actors via linkages of a social network or the extent to which human action of consumers (including their economic behavior) takes place within a web of social attachments such as friendship and kinship*." (p. 157).

Today it is fairly simple for website administrators to add several social sharing buttons on their web pages such as Facebook "Share" or Twitter "Tweet this". With hundreds of social networking sites all over the world currently and in order to facilitate the sharing of videos, news, information or online products with their friends via their preferred channels, several companies aggregate social sharing buttons and provide a simple widget for websites. These social sharing widgets always contain most popular social networking sites and traditional sharing media such as email for instance.

Cappel and Zhenyu (2017) reveal that companies whose websites contained e-commerce capabilities had both a significantly higher social media presence and social media followers and interactions than companies whose websites did not possess this capability.

The acknowledgment of such a reality leads us to try and understand how e-commerce websites use these embedded social media tools and, more specifically, how customers view these tools and what are the underlying motivations to share content from e-commerce websites on social media platforms. We understand sharing in the context of this work as described by Kietzmann, Hermkens, McCarthy and Silvestre (2011) as representing the "*extent to which users exchange, distribute and receive content*" (p. 245). Sharing is a way of interacting in social media but the impact of this activity on the users will to convert or even to build relationships with one another depends on the functional objective of the specific social media platform. Sharing on social networking sites can generate traffic back to the websites from where the sharing takes place, as when an individual shares a web page on Facebook, for instance, his or her friends can see this link and it is possible for them to follow the link directing to those web pages. In the e-commerce environment, the web 2.0 and social media shift market power from companies to customers, who are looking for more social and interactive ways to stimulate engagement, and provides them with new approaches to interact with both marketers and communities of peers at the same time (Huang & Benyoucef, 2013).

Existing knowledge states that the website quality and emotional social support are antecedents of social commerce interactions (Molinillo, Liébana-Cabanillas & Anaya-Sánchez, 2018). In the present study, we intend to delve into the motivations of users to share content from e-commerce websites onto social media platforms. We assume that the sharing action is rooted in the volition of the users to do so. Also, of interest for the present study, we have previously established the patent connections between social media and e-commerce, powered by the web 2.0 and the concept of user-generated content. However, because individual motivations can vary significantly, consumers may decide to create user-generated content for different reasons (Daugherty et al., 2008). Previous research has also explored topics associated with user-generated content such as customer engagement, electronic word-of-mouth, online brand reputation management, customer relationship management, and social network analysis (Hazari, Bergiel, & Sethna, 2016). Of these, we find electronic word of mouth of particular relevance for this study, due to its connection to "sharing" activities. Therefore, it is important to explore the field of online user behaviors, with both the concept of user-generated content and the topic of electronic word-of-mouth.

Online User Behaviors

The popularity and importance of online communication generated by users (UGC) and e-Wom has become relevant in the context of e-commerce in the sense that both generate information for potential customers in an unprecedented scale and with a great diffusion speed, that can lead to a sense of trust (Chang & Wu, 2014). Many e-commerce websites actively encourage their customers to produce e-WOMactually based on this increased sense of trust in potential customers, turning e-WOMinto a viable marketing strategy for attracting new customers and retaining existing ones (Yoo, Sanders, & Moon, 2013). In this perspective it should also be noted that the type of WOM, whether positive or negative, also has a very powerful effect on behavior (Alexandrov, Lilly, & Babakus, 2013). Individuals have a tendency to seek information before making some decisions. Positive information can lead to more positive attitudes and increase purchase intention, for instance, whereas negative information can have the opposite effect, generating a negativity-oriented attitude which impacts purchase intention reversely (Chang & Wu, 2014). In particular, negative WOM communication can have an adverse effect in attitudes and purchasing intentions of customers and a firm's brand image, which can lead to undesirable long-term outcomes, such as brand dilution, volatility in stock returns and the overall erosion of firm value (Balaji, Khong, & Chong, 2016). Nevertheless, if consumers are not willing to accept these negative messages nothing will change despite their exposure to a negative e-Wom message (Chang & Wu, 2014).

Customers experiencing very high levels of both satisfaction or dissatisfaction are also more likely to share experiences than customers with more neutral opinions (Alexandrov et al., 2013). Human beings have a natural tendency to share emotional experiences with others and the social environment in which they live, motivates the expression of emotions with other people around them, in order to obtain help and support, vent, bond or achieve some sort of validation (Kim, Wang, Maslowska, & Malthouse, 2016).

By this stage it is clear that the concepts of user-generated content and e-WOM are inextricably connected and, as seen above, e-WOMis particularly interesting for us because of the link it appears to have to "sharing" in the sense that, as Cheong and Morrison (2008) put it, is defined by the conveying of content rather than its creation. It is this conveying of content which interests us and, in particular, the motivations which may precede this behavior. In this sense, it becomes essential to explore precisely the field of motivation and behavior, to unravel possible avenues of enquiry in this study.

Theories of Human Behavior and Motivation

Viewing e-WOM, for instance, as a conversation between two sources, implies a need to understand the process involved in the transmission of information from person to person (Ho & Dempsey, 2010). In previous studies on areas related to the forwarding of information online, in which websites and blogs were the main focus, the forwarding of messages has mainly been influenced by motivation to share, without which information flow is hindered, and also by individual cognitive and social influences (Chih-Yu, Hsi-Peng, & Chao-Ming, 2015).

There have also been a significant number of theories and models applied in the field of social media research to study the socio-psychological behavior of social media users and other stakeholders, such as marketing professionals and customers. For the purpose of the current review, we will refer to the work of Ngai, Tao and Moon (2015) and their review of the main theories used on social media research from 2002 to 2011. The authors have identified three main groups of theories (summarized in Table 1) used in the field of social media Research: (i) *Personal Behavior Theories*, aimed at explaining the behavior of human beings at a personal/individual level; (ii) *Social Behavior Theories*, attempting to explain individuals' behavior toward social media in a social context and; (iii*) Mass Communication Theories*, whose purpose lies in understanding the influence of Mass communication on people's behavior.

Table 1. Theories and models used in social media research

Personal Behavior Theories	Social Behavior Theories	Mass Communication Theories
Attribution theory	Cognitive map	Media richness theory
Elaboration likelihood model	Effectuation process	Para-social interaction
Existence, relatedness, growth theory	Involvement theory	Uses and gratifications theory
Expectation and disconfirmation paradigm	Justice theory	
Goal-directed behavior model	Social capital theory	
Hofstede's theory of cultural difference	Social Exchange theory	
Personality traits	Social identity theory	
Psychological choice model	Social influence theory	
Risk perception theory	Social interaction theory	
Social cognitive theory	Social loafing	
Switching behavior	Social network analysis	
Task-technology fit model	Social power	
Technology acceptance model (TAM)	Social ties	
Theory of planned behavior (TPB)		
Theory of reasoned action (TRA)		

Source: Adapted from Ngai et al. (2015)

RESEARCH QUESTIONS

For the purpose of the current study, we will follow a combination of theoretical models. Although the main focus is on motivations behind the intentions to share content from e-commerce websites into social media, we believe that motivation theory should be complemented with behavior theories, which should aid in giving a more robust theoretical background for the formulation of research questions as well as to the analysis of the data generated in the Focus group interviews. Therefore, the adopted approach will be based on concepts extracted from the Social Cognitive Theory, Social Exchange Theory and Uses and Gratifications Theory which, combined, should provide a solid background for the understanding of behavior on a Personal and Social levels (Social Cognitive and Social Exchange Theories), as well as providing a view of how individuals act in the context of the potential for Mass communication offered by the internet (Uses and Gratifications Theory). These approaches, as mentioned above, will be combined with concepts from Motivation theory. According to Oh and Syn (2015), an analysis on the study of motivations reveals that there are three fundamental theories/models that have been widely adopted in research on the topic: i) Maslow's hierarchy of needs ii) the Intrinsic and Extrinsic motivation model and iii) Herzberg's two factor theory. In the present study, we will apply the Intrinsic and Extrinsic motivations approach to help us understand what can lead individuals to share content from e-commerce websites on social media.

Table 2 below summarizes the aforementioned research questions and respective theoretical approaches which will frame this study and Table 3 provides an overview of how the main research questions are linked to the support questions.

Table 2. Main research questions and theoretical foundations

	Research Question	TheoryGroup	Theoretical Domain	Literature
RQ1	What types of internal and external rewards motivate individuals to share content from e-commerce websites into social Media platforms?	Motivation Theories	Intrinsic and Extrinsic Motivation	Deci, 1971; Ryan & Deci, 2000a;Ryan & Deci, 2000b;Oh & Syn, 2015
RQ2	When sharing content from e-commerce websites with one or many individuals, do people act based on self-interest, reciprocating a similar behavior towards them or, do they act based on the concept of generalized reciprocity?	Social Behavior Theories	Social Exchange Theory	Blau, 1964; Constant, Kiesler, &Sproull, 1994; Lambe, Wittmann, & Spekman, 2001; Hall, 2003 Molm, Collet & Schaefer, 2007; Oh & Syn, 2015
RQ3	How are the content sharing intentions and behaviors of individuals affected by e-commerce website characteristics such as website design and product/service typologies?	PersonalBehavior Theories	Social CognitiveTheory	Bandura, 1989; Wood & Bandura, 1989; Compeau & Higgins, 1995; Lin, Hung, & Chen, 2009
RQ4	Which channels individuals commonly prefer to share content from e-commerce websites and how purposive is the selection of these channels?	Mass-communication Theories	Uses and Gratifications Theory	Flanagin & Metzger, 2001; Dholakia, Bagozzi, & Pearo, 2004; Rubin, 2009; Chen, 2011 Sundar & Limperos, 2013

Source: Authors

Table 3. Main research questions and related support questions

	Research Question		Support Question	Literature
RQ1	What types of internal and external rewards motivate individuals to share content from e-commerce websites into Social Media platforms?	SQ A	Would the existence of monetary rewards such as discounts, vouchers, free gifts, etc encourage you to share content from e-commerce websites into any social media platform you use?	Yoo, Sanders & Moon, 2013 Liu, Cheung & Lee, 2016 Oh &Syn, 2015
		SQ B	Would you consider any level of personal satisfaction could arise from sharing content from e-commerce websites into social media platforms? Examples may include recognition by peers, help a friend, establish a personal position or opinion.	
RQ2	When sharing content from e-commerce websites with one or many individuals, do people act based on self-interest or reciprocating a similar behavior towards them?	SQ C	When sharing content from E-commerce websites are individuals more prone to engage in more direct (one-to-one) or indirect (one-to-many) exchanges and why?	Molm, Collet & Schaefer, 2007
		SQ D	Which examples of self-interested motives, from material rewards, to hedonic pursuits, to direct impact on their lives do people consider would make them more prone to share content from e-commerce websites into social media?	Pelaprat & Brown, 2012 Kim, 2014
RQ3	How are the content sharing intentions and behaviors of individuals affected by e-commerce website characteristics such as website design and product/service typologies?	SQ E	What sort of products make or would make you more prone to share their information through a social media platform. For instance, would there be a difference between fashion items or consumer electronics?	Tsao&Hsieh, 2015 Chen&Berger, 2016
		SQ F	What sort of website characteristics make or would make it easier - or harder - for you to consider sharing their contents into social media networks? Examples may include website design, website fame, number of clicks or actions required to share, etc.	Green &Pearson, 2011 Ling&Salvendy, 2013
RQ4	Which channels individuals commonly prefer to share content from e-commerce websites and how purposive is the selection of these channels?	SQ G	When or if you would share content from e-commerce websites which channels would you select preferentially? (This may be specific social media platforms or communication tools like, for instance, e-mail or Whatsapp).	Chen, 2011 Berger & Iyengar,2013 Dolan, Conduit, Fahy, & Goodman, 2016

Source: Authors

METHODOLOGY

The main objective underlying this study is to enrich the field of social media and e-commerce research, uncovering some factors which may explain the motivations of the users of e-commerce to share the content on social media networks. Due to the exploratory nature of the study, it is assumed that a qualitative approach will be, in general, more appropriate in this specific scenario and, specifically, the organization of a focus group. Participants were provided a brief questionnaire with the purpose of profiling them as e-commerce and social media users. The following framework of reference was used to classify their self-assessed usage levels:

The Focus Group session took place in 2017 and was comprised of 7 participants. The group possessed a certain degree of heterogeneity in terms of gender, age, background and professional occupation, as shown in Table 5.

The focus group interview was tape-recorded and transcribed. The discussion took place in the main language of the participants which is Portuguese. A great effort has

Table 4. Participants self-assessed usage levels of E-commerce and social media

# of purchases done on e-commerce annually	UsageLevel	Time spent on social media daily	UsageLevel
1 to 5	Low	1 minute to 1 hour	Low
6 to 10	Moderate	1 hour to 2 hours	Moderate
11 andhigher	High	2 hoursor more	High

Source: Author

Table 5. Participants list and demographic information

Subject Identifier	Gender	Age	Occupation	E-commerce Usage	Social Media Usage	# of Active Social Media Accounts
A	Female	33	Medical Doctor	High	Low	4
B	Male	30	Audiovisual Agent	High	Moderate	9
C	Male	32	Sales Representative	High	Moderate	7
D	Female	26	ChemicalLabAssistant	Moderate	Moderate	4
E	Female	27	Professional Makeupartist	High	High	8
F	Male	29	AirforceSargeant	High	Moderate	7
G	Male	56	PublicAgent	High	High	4

Source: Authors

been done to ensure an accurate translation in terms of the words and expressions used, as well as the meaning that the participants wanted to give to their comments.

A preliminary stage of analysis consisted in reading the transcript of the session in order to gather a general sense of the data, prior to the coding of main themes. Data analysis used computer software Nvivo 11. We had 4 main nodes labeled Question 1, Question 2, Question 3 and Question 4.

For each of these questions, an analysis of the main themes reflecting ideas and thoughts of the participants was conducted. These were aggregated into child-nodes, pertaining to each of the specific Questions mentioned above. Some interesting themes, indirectly connected to the main points also emerged, mainly connected to Location-Tagging, Service Levels of e-commerce websites and sharing as Spam and the potential it has to bother others.

RESULTS

Table 6 below shows the node classification and the number of references under each specific node:

Internal vs External Rewards

In terms of external rewards, connected to extrinsic motivation, several themes arose mainly connected to references to discount or vouchers, professional motives, which include the possibility of being paid to share and the possibility of receiving free products as a reward for sharing. In terms of internal rewards, connected to intrinsic motivation, some generic comments on personal satisfaction arose, accompanied by the manifest will to protect others from negative experiences.

The results of the analysis seem to only partially confirm similar research found in the literature. Liu, Cheung and Lee (2016), in their study on information sharing behavior on social commerce sites, noted that individuals who feel good about helping others can be more disposed to share information online without expecting direct rewards in return. This appears to be true to some extent as the following comments indicate:

My opinion can be important for someone.

My benefit is always aligned with what good I'm able to give to the community who follows me.

Table 6. Focus group main themes and number of references

Name	# References
Research Question 1	
ExternalRewards	12
Discount - Voucher - Free Products	6
Emerging Theme – Spam vs. Monetary incentives	8
Professional Reasons - Being paid to share	4
InternalRewards	14
PersonalSatisfaction	5
Protect other from negative experiences	7
Research Question 2	
One-to-One	9
Motivations	5
Self-interest	3
Motivations	8
Research Question 3	
Product-ServiceTypology	8
Experiences	6
EmergingTheme- Location-tagging	2
PhysicalProducts	6
Website Design	11
Ease-of-use	6
EmergingTheme- ServiceLevels	2
Simple Design	3
Research Question 4	
E-mail	4
Purposiveness	3
Instagram	6
Purposiveness	3
Whatsapp – Messenger	9
Purposiveness	6

Source: Output Nvivo 11

There are people who follow my work and who are looking for opinions specifically and, as such, I do it in that sense: of being able to bring some good and a positive influence.

These expressions revealed a certain degree of personal satisfaction in sharing, with concepts of being able to help and inform the community and be able to have pleasant feelings which is aligned with the realization that Intrinsic motives do appear to lead to e-Wom participation, in the form of sharing, through association with positive sensations of enjoyment, friendship, and pleasantness as apparent in the literature (Yoo et al., 2013).

A second topic connected to Intrinsic motivation was the realization that the individuals in the study were more inclined to share if they felt some degree of dissatisfaction and felt like they were somehow protecting others from feeling the same dissatisfaction they felt with a product or service. This seems to be consistent with our findings in the literature, especially in what concerns negative e-WOM, in the sense that high levels of satisfaction or, in this case, dissatisfaction make customers more prone to share experiences than customers with more neutral opinions (Alexandrov et al., 2013). Interestingly, although the literature seems to suggest that high levels of satisfaction also make customers more prone to share these experiences, the focus group responses were almost exclusively biased towards dissatisfaction and negative e-WOM, with seven references to this topic and with clear statements such as:

(…) I would only share in the event that I was very dissatisfied with the product, in the sense of trying to protect others from this product.

I shared products which I didn't like, also in the sense of alert and so that people know what's good and what's not.

If I did (share it) it would be to alert towards a negative aspect of the product.

As for external rewards which can be promoted by offering monetary benefits, such as gift certificates or other prizes (Yoo et al., 2013) the comments of the participants reported a considerable negatively-charged sentiment towards how these would affect their motivation to share. This is remarkable as it seems to contradict to some extent findings mentioned in the literature such as the results of Liu, Cheung and Lee (2016) which appear to indicate that extrinsic rewards maybe more important than intrinsic returns to motivate information sharing, and is particularly in line with specific findings in terms of monetary-rewards in the sense that they may have potential negative consequences even when they appear to be good marketing tools (Reimer & Benkenstein, 2016). Mentions in the discussion to discounts and vouchers, particularly, revealed the most negative sentiments towards these incentives to sharing:

I'm not a fan. I don't do it with supermarket vouchers and I would not do it also in this situation only because I would benefit from a discount, a promotion or some sort of benefit.

I'm very suspicious of these promotions or bonuses they offer because I think it's a gift in disguise so they can benefit from it. So, I completely refuse to do it.

I do not share with other people with the purpose of obtaining monetary rewards or vouchers.

Under the context of external rewards, the analysis revealed that professional reasons were also mentioned as a potential motivation for sharing. One of the participants, *Subject E*, described herself as a digital influencer and assumed that there was a clear relationship in some cases between the external rewards received and her sharing activities:

In my case it is almost a professional matter. I work in partnership with several brands, several e-commerce websites so it's normal that I have some interest there as there is something to be gained (…) and being paid to share.

Although all the comments under this particular node revealed very little extensiveness as they all pertained to *Subject E*, it was relevant to mention this as, although no other participants made comments in this sense, their body language revealed that they understood and approved the coherence of these comments, which seemed to suggest that for them it was obvious why *Subject E* was making them and that it appeared logical to them that in that situation, external rewards obviously had a role to play in terms of motivating individuals to share content from e-commerce websites into social media.

An interesting theme arose in the context of the discussion connected to monetary rewards. We categorized it as an Emerging theme related to spam vs. monetary incentives. These were references made to the fact that sharing had the possibility of being abusive and could have a negative impact on the recipients of the shared content. Some of the expressions and comments made to the theme were:

(…) I don't feel good as being another one adding 'spam' on the social network. And I don't feel good by spamming and for that I don't share.

I share the opinion of some people here in the sense that it is a type of sharing which can be abusive.

(…) and by doing that I would be bothering others. And I'm careful with that.

This was not a theme included in the literature review but, consistently following Krueger and Casey's (2014) approach, this theme was noteworthy, not only due the frequency of the comments made, but also because the comments showed a notable level of specificity, emotion and extensiveness in the group.

Also of interest, and likely one of the key-findings of the focus group analysis, was the fact that, although the abovementioned concern about the potential impact that sharing content from e-commerce websites on social media could have on the recipients and its equation to the normally negatively-charged concept of 'spam', some participants brought forth the idea that there could be a "threshold" for these discounts which could counteract this feeling and that it could potentially ease the unpleasantness of "bothering" others and eventually make it worthwhile. This was patent in comments such as:

It would have to do with the balance between my compensation and "bothering" others. If I thought that it would be worth it to "bother" others to obtain a discount...i don't know, I'm guessing…15 or 20% of a product with a high price, that's fine. (…) For a product costing 2 Euros and a discount of 20 cents I would never "bother" anyone.

Now how much is the "feel-bad" factor actually worth? Because that really exists. Because I would be bothering my list of friends. The social networks are weird and you don't know if you are sharing something for a 30-cent discount and it's not worth it because you also don't want to bother other people.

I don't need to share or spam on social networks for a 10% discount.

(…) the fact that I would feel bad for bothering others would have to be compensated by the factor that, monetarily, I would not spend as much.

This appears to be in line with the literature reviewed in the sense that the amount of compensation obtained from these monetary rewards can directly impact the level of effort and that the introduction of "money" in the equation seems to have a negative effect on cooperative, communal, and altruistic behaviors (Jin & Huang, 2014). In the literature review we did not find any references to the particular subject of how people's behaviors could be influenced by the breaking of the "thresholds" mentioned above nor on the effect this could have on peoples' motivations to share online. However, the fact that it emerged on the focus group discussion, with undeniable weight, is intriguing and can perhaps present a fertile ground for future investigation and broadening of knowledge in this field. For instance, questions such as how much discount would be necessary to start overcoming the feel-bad factor associated with bothering others or if there is an upper-limit after which this stops making a difference come to mind.

Reciprocity, Self Interest and Sharing Orientation

For RQ2 we looked into the concept of reciprocity as an important determinant of human behavior (Surma, 2016) and it's dyadic or collective orientation (Molm et al., 2007) *versus* the role of self-interest as also a primary driver of that behavior (Kim, 2014). Specifically, we wanted to understand how both concepts fared against one another and whether the participants could provide clues as to what motivations would be behind the particular inclination towards one or the other.

Although the literature reviewed does mention the importance of the concept of reciprocity in people's behavior (Surma, 2016) and even of generalized reciprocity as an important factor in motivating individuals to participate in knowledge sharing in virtual communities (Oh & Syn, 2015), in the context of the focus group, these concepts did not arisein the particular context of sharing content from e-commerce websites into social media.

The concept of self-interest, on the other hand, appeared to be more clearly recognized by the participants in the sense that there were comments directed towards the role that it may play in motivating them to share. One of the participants, *Subject C,* although not directly referring to e-commerce, did mention, due to his involvement in event organization that:

We organize events to earn Money. And the social media platforms are very important for us to attract peoples' attention.

Other comments, categorized under the same node, which also appeared to reveal a clear self-interested posture were, for example:

With the general public, the only thing I recall sharing was a car which I was trying to sell and I shared it due to self-interest.

Personally, I've also done it (sharing) for my sister's shoe brand...

(Talking about wife's business) I did it for her when she started her business, to help her out.

We end up having to share due to personal and professional interest for our company.

Common measures of self-interest include, among other things, the motivation to maximize material resources, hedonistic motives to pursue feeling good, and psychological impacts of being involved in a particular outcome (Kim, 2014). Although the broad scope of these concepts may leave to the feeling that everything that one does is rooted in self-interest (Pelaprat & Brown, 2012), it is nevertheless necessary to note that self-interest does seem to play a pivotal role on the motivations for sharing content from e-commerce websites into social media, confirming previous views brought forth by other authors.

One of the supporting questions in our study was connected to the directness or indirectness of reciprocity and two related structural differences: whether exchange is dyadic or collective (Molm et al., 2007). We tried to explore whether participants would be more prone to engage in one-to-one or one-to-many exchanges. Although initially connected to the base concept of reciprocity in the literature, in the context of the group conversation appeared in a looser manner, not necessarily connected to the concept of reciprocity. The view of several participants of the focus group revealed that their inclination tended more towards a more direct exchange, and that the concept of one-to-one sharing emerged as predominant. It could be understood that participants felt more at ease with more directed, private and personal sharing. This was corroborated by several comments from different participants such as:

It would probably be easier for me to share with one person in particular.

I'm not saying that I do it exclusively one-to-one but, like I said, I normally do it in a private manner, through direct messages.

I do it but in a more personal manner (…) Customized. Not generalized.

This tendency to prefer one-to-one exchanges appeared to reveal some connection with some of the reasons or motives which could be uncovered in the analysis of the comments. Participants appeared to link this directness in the exchanges with their connection to a closer circle of relationships and the nurturing or these relationships or to the need to help a member of this narrower circle. This was, to some extent, patent in comments such as:

One-to-one sharing happens several times. When (we are talking about) friends, clients too, close people which I happen to know need something…

(if) I'm pleasing a friend, of course I'll share one-to-one.

I have shared things which I think people can take advantage of (...) I do that when I believe it's interesting. That kind of sharing is one-to-one.

(one-to-one or one-to-few) I do several times because I know it pleases that group of friends.

Interestingly, one can be inclined to deduce a level of self-interest in these reasons, recognizing possible social rewards like emotional satisfaction (Lambe et al., 2001) and hedonistic drives to pursue feel-good sensations (Kim, 2014). This provide consistency to the participants view, by linking the concept of self-interest to a more direct and personal level in their exchanges, with one-to-one interactions (or, at most, one-to-few) being the preferred way of interaction for the participants when sharing content from e-commerce websites via social media.

Website Design and Product/Service Typologies

Under RQ3 we tried to uncover how the external environment, in this case, in the form of e-commerce websites' design and usability characteristics, could impact the motivations for the participants in the study to share content from these platforms into social media as well as the potential impact different products and/or services could also have in these motivations.

The literature established that aesthetics in website interface design can serve as an important predictor of customer's emotions, perception, and action toward the website (Deng & Poole, 2012). Findings from the analysis of the focus group discussion appear to confirm this in the sense that the design of websites can have, to some extent, a direct impact on the actions and willingness of the participants to share content from them into or through social media. Also, in line with previous research (Molinillo et al., 2018), concepts such as cleanness and clarity in the design were directly associated by several participants to their intent to share their content. This is definitely visible in comments such as:

I would only share if the website 'deserved' it. If it was a clear website, evident, without subterfuges...there are complicated websites in which you get lost (...) only if it was a good website...

(...) having a clean and direct image of course it influences (sharing).

Regarding the aspect of the websites, of course a clean design makes it easier.

Another point raised during the discussion pertained to the ease-of-use of e-commerce websites. Participants associated positively websites which are easy to use with the possibility of sharing content from those websites:

(…) I think I would share more easily all websites which are easy to use.

I would easily share if it's easy to buy in that website.

Regarding websites, they need to be easy in terms of access…if I have to make a lot of clicks… no.

This seems to be in direct alignment with the notions advanced in the literature that the success of B2C websites is directly affected by their usability (Ling & Salvendy, 2013) and that specific usability-related design attributes such as design credibility, content, interactivity, navigability and responsiveness play an important role in the online shopping experience (Green & Pearson, 2011).

In terms of ease-of-use and design, participants made a link between the websites and the sharing widgets present in them and remarked at how impractical these seemed to be when the intent is making a more targeted share and even how that could serve as a detractor for sharing:

Although those buttons seem very practical, I find it very hard to make a more targeted sharing. (…) If you want to share to a few people only, when possible, it's not practical. If you want to share with three different people you have to send an individual message to each. It's not practical.

I think social networks facilitate more generalized sharing. Everything else starts becoming more complex. For starters, you waste more time sharing individually, it's not as intuitive. What's intuitive and easier to access is what suits them the most which is sharing with everyone

(…) only they then lose the greater number of people who don't want to share at a more generalized level.

A particular comment spiked our interest in the analysis, in the sense that it expanded on the concept of design and usability to include the concept of service as a whole in which became an interesting emerging theme.Both references made to this theme are shown below, in an interaction with the moderator of the focus group:

Subject A – Now, if everything's very simple, you buy, you pay and the next day you're getting a message saying that they will deliver in 48 hours you think: 'this is really effective, it's worth buying here (…) I would easily share if the website is easy to buy in and also if the service is really effective, if it is delivered quickly….

Although not part of the original scope of the question and not discussed in our literature review, this mention to service as a part of the considerations for sharing content from an e-commerce website, bundled with concepts of design and usability seemed, nevertheless, worthy of being mentioned as a potential topic to be further explored in other studies. As seen previously, empirical evidence suggests that most of the products discussed on the internet are mostly search goods, like consumer electronics, house appliances, and vehicles, and experience goods such as hotels and restaurants (Tsao & Hsieh, 2015). The findings of the focus group discussion appeared to confirm this evidence, as the references revolved around physical products and experiences. However, the references to the sharing of products had more negatively-charged comments, whereas the references to experiences evoked more positive comments.

Eventually a product of my interest but with a one-to-one objective to share it with that particular person.

(…) I would very hardly share something which was a real product…like a shirt or something. I don't recall sharing something like that...only if it was a personal request because, due to my job, a lot of people come to me for an opinion but this sharing is more because others ask me than by my own initiative.

I find it less likely when it comes to products.

This seems to show that participants, although not excluding the possibility of sharing products, revealed in their speech expressions of resistance like "eventually", "hardly" and "less likely" when it came to discussing if or why they would share actual physical products. When it came to experiences, however, the participants showed more openness and willingness to share in general. References to experiences were linked to terms such as "satisfaction", "liking", or "emotion" for instance:

(…) I think that experiences as a products don't stop being something more personal and the satisfaction you had (…) everyone will like and I think you're not 'pushing' but rather informing.

I would more easily share experiences, which transmit emotion and liking and are moments of peoples' lives.

This finding also seems to be consistent with the literature, as was noted previously by Chen and Berger (2016), for instance, that products and information which stir up more interest, arouse more emotion and arousal or contain more useful information get shared more. Participants appeared to be more "at-ease" with experience-sharing online than with products and one comment from *Subject C* revealed consistency with the previously discussed emerging theme of 'Spam-Bothering others' in the sense that this subject equated the sharing of an experience to guiding or informing someone through his experience rather than just bothering others through the intrusive sharing of products:

(An) experience leaves me on a different level...because sharing an experience like a restaurant or a hotel I would be more 'at-ease' to do. Because I would be (sharing) in the sense of guidance and not spamming (...) with a product I feel like I'm 'pushing' something. With an experience I feel more like I'm 'informing' than anything else.

During the discussion of RQ3 an interesting topic was raised by two participants. This concept was Location-tagging or Geo-Tagging.

The two comments related to this theme, coming from two different subjects, are shown below:

(...) generally I would not go to a restaurant's page and share it but if I have a good experience I might share and recommend...for instance through the location. The GPS will give you the location and by sharing that location, you are already advertising it (the restaurant).

(For) experiences mainly Instagram where I can take picture and add the location.

This concept arose particularly connected to the discussion of Experiences and it was interestingly linked by one of the participants, as seen in the comments above, as a tool to advertise an experience by linking it to its location. Time on the focus group session proved insufficient to explore this new theme but we feel this has potential to broaden the areas of research on motivations to share into social media.

Main Channels and Purpose in Selection

The analysis of the focus group discussion revealed that E-mail, Instagram and Whatsapp/Messenger messaging services were preferentially used by the participants in this particular group.

With an average of six active social media accounts, it was interesting to note the emergence of these three communication media as preferential, especially considering that three of them are more directed to personal rather than collective sharing. Taking the U&G theory as the background for this question, we tried to understand if individuals are purposive and active and select media based on their needs (Flanagin & Metzger, 2001) and if they would be goal-oriented and consistent they would be with their choices of medium to share the message (Rubin, 2009). The findings seem to agree with the literature, in the sense that there appears to exist some coherence in the views of the participants, especially when linking these to the findings of RQ2, in which one-to-one sharing took prominence over one-to-many sharing scenarios. For E-mail for instance, participants made reference to the "personal", "direct" and "formal" characteristics of the mean:

I would say E-mail. Precisely because it's more formal. If you get an e-mail from me you will be more interested in checking in out.

I share by e-mail because it's more personal and directed. I share with whom I want, direct the content...

It's more direct and guided, because I will not send an e-mail (about a watch) to someone who is not interested.

These references to e-mail were made specifically by *Subjects* A and *G,* who were the two oldest of the group, and consistently revealed throughout the study some resistance to the concept of sharing directly from e-commerce into social media, with some of the most negatively-charged comments, and this may raise an interesting case towards the usage of e-mail rather than another particular medium.

This can be corroborated by the views of some of the other participants who mainly mentioned Whatsapp and Messenger as preferred methods as opposed to the "formality" of E-mail. *Subject C* made a specific remark concerning this specific point which can serve as a link between both topics: *I do not share 'formally' because I'm going to recommend products to strangers...it's always more personal so it will be through Whatsapp or Messenger.*

Other participants' comments, similar to *Subject C's* view, show a more favorable view towards using Whatsapp and Messenger as their preferential means of sharing, while also using terms such as "directed" and "private", apparently linking these notions to the purpose of keeping these interactions on a more one-to-one or one-to-few basis:

If it's a product, from an e-commerce page, it will always be by Messenger or Whatsapp

Basically, the sharing I make it's always directed and always via Messenger or Whatsapp…never a general share if it's a product.

Messenger and Whatsapp are the social media that I use more often to share with my closest circle of friends.

(…) Messenger and Whatsapp in a more private manner.

As for the references made to Instagram, it was interesting to note that most participants held this social network in highest regard when compared to other available networks such as Facebook, even when it came to generalized sharing. This appeared to be due to its more visual nature and simplicity, as some comments seem to reveal:

In what concerns public sharing I normally use Instagram. That' because normally that sharing is more visual, through images, and images transmit more than words when it comes to experiences and sensations in a more direct manner.

Facebook has become very textual, with a lot of confusion and Instagram is more visual.

This appears to reveal some measure of consistency in the participants, as they also mentioned that cleaner designs are favored in terms of e-commerce websites and this notion can spill into the design of social media platforms. Although this remains unproven, as it was not discussed at length and it was not included in the original scope of this study, this notion can be worth exploring. However, despite references to Instagram as a potential preferential platform for more generalized sharing, no real indication in the discussion appeared to reveal its use for sharing content from e-commerce websites into social media, with the main references to this, as seen above, always being connected to more direct and private means such as E-mail, Whatsapp and Messenger. Consistency in the opinions of the participants also appears to exist on this point in connection to the findings of the previous section, when participants also noted some dissatisfaction towards the fact that the sharing interfaces on websites appear to facilitate generalized sharing as opposed to more targeted, direct sharing, which may serve as a detractor to the activity due to their more one-to-one sharing preferences.

CONCLUSION

The present study was aimed at uncovering motivations for sharing content from e-commerce websites into social media through a series of research questions founded in theories of motivation and human behavior. Through the use of a focus group, the main conclusions appear to be that intrinsic motivation, with sensations of personal satisfaction, appears to take on a more relevant role than extrinsic motivation prompted by external rewards. Although results in other studies such as those of Liu, Cheung and Lee (2016), suggest extrinsic rewards appear to have a prevalence over intrinsic ones, this study revealed otherwise and found that people can, actually, have a more negative perception of these rewards, in line with what was previously suggested by Jin and Huang (2014) and Reimer and Benkenstein (2016), which may lead to distrust and even serve as a detractor for sharing content from e-commerce websites into social media. Dissatisfaction proved to be a powerful motivator to share content from e-commerce websites into social media, confirming similar views brought forth in the literature (Alexandrov et al., 2013) as powerful sensations, of dissatisfaction in this particular case, appear to be prime motivators for the generation of negative e-Wom. Findings also appear to indicate that people show some aversion to abusive sharing and to spamming and that they believe that sharing can have the potential to bother other people and that their sharing activities are moderated by the acknowledgement of that reality although, interestingly, it also appears that external rewards such as vouchers or discounts obtained through sharing activities can eventually motivate them to share, if the discount or benefit overshadows their negative feelings associated to bothering others and the benefit is appealing enough.

Reciprocity phenomena (Oh & Syn, 2015; Surma, 2016) failed to obtain any real prominence in the participants minds and self-interest appeared to play a more relevant role in peoples' motivations to share content from e-commerce websites into social media. This does not mean that reciprocity is not an important factor to consider, but participants revealed to be less prone to sharing because someone shared something with them, but rather would do it out of self-interested motives, like the personal satisfaction and social rewards obtained for helping others or pleasing a friend. This was consistent with the direction of the reported sharing activities, as one-to-one sharing was mentioned and noted as the most common direction of these activities, suggesting that people may actively engage in more direct and personal exchanges, rather than more generalized ones, when talking about sharing content from e-commerce websites, especially when it comes to physical products.

The research revealed that website characteristics have an important impact on peoples' intentions to share, confirming similar views in the literature (Molinillo et al., 2018), that aesthetics in website interface design can serve as an important predictor of customer's emotions, perception, and action toward the website (Deng & Poole, 2012). People appear to be more inclined to share from a given e-commerce website if they find that the website is easy to use, with a clean and unobtrusive design. They also appear to bundle the website characteristics to the overall service provided when making a judgment on the websites worthiness of being shared and that one-to-one sharing is made unnecessarily more difficult than generalized sharing. Although people can and do share products from e-commerce websites into social media, they appear to prefer to share experiences which may, or may not be entirely connected to a traditional e-commerce website, but may include services such as restaurants and hotels. When it came to experiences, however, due to their more emotional nature, participants felt more likely to share these in a generalized manner but with a focus on guidance and information and not with the specific purpose of "pushing" the experience, like they would do with actual physical products. Under this thematic, the topic of Location-tagging or Geo-tagging was connected to the sharing of experiences and the promotion of businesses, in the participants' opinion.

Participants showed a more favorable inclination towards the use of more one-to-one exchange methods, like e-mail and social messaging applications such as Whatsapp and Messenger, purposively selecting them for their more directed and personal characteristics, especially when considering sharing information of physical products from e-commerce websites. This is in line with the Uses and Gratifications literature explored previously, for instance Rubin (2009), in the sense that individuals do appear to be goal-oriented and consistent with their choices of the medium in which the message is shared, going for more direct means rather than generalized ones. Experiences were again mentioned and associated to more open platforms such as Instagram, because they were not related to product-pushing and because of the appeal of a simple design, which was also proven to exist when discussing e-commerce websites characteristics.

REFERENCES

Alexandrov, A., Lilly, B., & Babakus, E. (2013). The effects of social- and self-motives on the intentions to share positive and negative word of mouth. *Journal of the Academy of Marketing Science*, *41*(5), 531–546. doi:10.100711747-012-0323-4

Aluri, A., Slevitch, L., & Larzelere, R. (2015). The effectiveness of embedded social media on hotel websites and the importance of social interactions and return on engagement. *International Journal of Contemporary Hospitality Management*, *27*(4), 670–689. doi:10.1108/IJCHM-09-2013-0415

Balaji, M. S., Khong, K. W., & Chong, A. Y. L. (2016). Determinants of negative word-of-mouth communication using social networking sites, Information & Management, 53(4), 528.

Bandura, A. (1989). Human agency in social cognitive theory. *The American Psychologist, 44*(9), 1175–1184. doi:10.1037/0003-066X.44.9.1175 PMID:2782727

Berger, J., & Iyengar, R. (2013). Communication channels and word of mouth: how the medium shapes the message. *The Journal of Consumer Research, 40*(3), 567–579. doi:10.1086/671345

Blau, P. M. (1964). *Exchange and power in social life*. Transaction Publishers.

Cappel, J. J., & Zhenyu, H. (2017). An analysis of social media presentation at company websites. *Journal of International Business Disciplines, 12*(1), 1–17.

Chang, H. H., & Wu, L. H. (2014). An examination of negative e-Wom adoption: Brand commitment as a moderator. *Decision Support Systems, 59*, 206–218. doi:10.1016/j.dss.2013.11.008

Chen, G. M. (2011). Tweet this: A uses and gratifications perspective on how active Twitter use gratifies a need to connect with others. *Computers in Human Behavior, 27*(2), 755–762. doi:10.1016/j.chb.2010.10.023

Chen, Z., & Berger, J. (2016). How content acquisition method affects word of mouth. *The Journal of Consumer Research, 43*(1), 86–102. doi:10.1093/jcr/ucw001

Cheong, H. J., & Morrison, M. A. (2008). Consumers' reliance on product information and recommendations found in UGC. *Journal of Interactive Advertising, 8*(2), 38–49. doi:10.1080/15252019.2008.10722141

Chih-Yu, C., Hsi-Peng, L. U., & Chao-Ming, W. U. (2015). Facebook users' motivation for clicking the "Like" button. *Social Behavior and Personality, 43*(4), 579–592. doi:10.2224bp.2015.43.4.579

Compeau, D. R., & Higgins, C. A. (1995). Computer self-efficacy: development of a measure and initial test. *Management Information Systems Quarterly, 19*(2), 189–211. doi:10.2307/249688

Constant, D., Kiesler, S., & Sproull, L. (1994). What's mine is ours, or is it? A study of attitudes about information sharing. *Information Systems Research, 5*(4), 400–421. doi:10.1287/isre.5.4.400

Daugherty, T., Eastin, M. S., & Bright, L. (2008). Exploring consumer motivations for creating user-generated content. *Journal of Interactive Advertising, 8*(2), 16–25. doi:10.1080/15252019.2008.10722139

Deci, E. L. (1971). Effects of externally mediated rewards on intrinsic motivation. *Journal of Personality and Social Psychology, 18*(1), 105–115. doi:10.1037/h0030644

Deng, L., & Poole, M. S. (2012). Aesthetic design of e-commerce web pages – Webpage Complexity, Order and preference. *Electronic Commerce Research and Applications*, *11*(4), 420–440. doi:10.1016/j.elerap.2012.06.004

Dholakia, U. M., Bagozzi, R. P., & Pearo, L. K. (2004). A social influence model of consumer participation in network- and small-group-based virtual communities. *International Journal of Research in Marketing*, *21*(3), 241–263. doi:10.1016/j.ijresmar.2003.12.004

Dolan, R., Conduit, J., Fahy, J., & Goodman, S. (2016). Social media engagement behaviour: A uses and gratifications perspective. *Journal of Strategic Marketing*, *24*(3-4), 261–277. doi:10.1080/0965254X.2015.1095222

Flanagin, A. J., & Metzger, M. J. (2001). Internet use in the contemporary media environment. *Human Communication Research*, *27*(1), 153–181. doi:10.1093/hcr/27.1.153

Green, D. T., & Pearson, J. M. (2011). Integrating website usability with the electronic commerce acceptance model. *Behaviour & Information Technology*, *30*(2), 181–199. doi:10.1080/01449291003793785

Hall, H. (2003). Borrowed theory: Applying exchange theories in information science research. *Library & Information Science Research*, *25*(3), 287–306. doi:10.1016/S0740-8188(03)00031-8

Hazari, S., Bergiel, B. J., & Sethna, B. N. (2016). Hedonic and utilitarian use of user-generated content on online shopping websites. *Journal of Marketing Communications*, 1–20.

Hess, T., Lang, K. R., & Xu, S. X. (2011). Social embeddedness and online consumer behavior. *Electronic Markets*, *21*(3), 157–159. doi:10.100712525-011-0071-1

Ho, J. Y. C., & Dempsey, M. (2010). Viral marketing: Motivations to forward online content. *Journal of Business Research*, *63*(9–10), 1000–1006. doi:10.1016/j.jbusres.2008.08.010

Huang, Z., & Benyoucef, M. (2013). From e-commerce to social commerce: A close look at design features. *Electronic Commerce Research and Applications*, *12*(4), 246–259. doi:10.1016/j.elerap.2012.12.003

Jin, L., & Huang, Y. (2014). When giving money does not work: The differential effects of monetary versus in-kind rewards in referral reward programs. *International Journal of Research in Marketing*, *31*(1), 107–116. doi:10.1016/j.ijresmar.2013.08.005

Kietzmann, J. H., Hermkens, K., McCarthy, I. P., & Silvestre, B. S. (2011). Social media? Get serious! Understanding the functional building blocks of social media. *Business Horizons*, *54*(3), 241–251. doi:10.1016/j.bushor.2011.01.005

Kim, A. (2014). The curious case of self-interest: inconsistent effects and ambivalence toward a widely accepted construct. *Journal for the Theory of Social Behaviour*, *44*(1), 99–122. doi:10.1111/jtsb.12032

Kim, S. J., Wang, R. J.-H., Maslowska, E., & Malthouse, E. C. (2016). "Understanding a fury in your words": The effects of posting and viewing electronic negative word-of-mouth on purchase behaviors. *Computers in Human Behavior*, *54*, 511–521. doi:10.1016/j.chb.2015.08.015

Lambe, C. J., Wittmann, C. M., & Spekman, R. E. (2001). Social exchange theory and research on business-to-business relational exchange. *Journal of Business-To-Business Marketing*, *8*(3), 1–36. doi:10.1300/J033v08n03_01

Lin, M.-J. J., Hung, S.-W., & Chen, C.-J. (2009). Fostering the determinants of knowledge sharing in professional virtual communities. *Computers in Human Behavior*, *25*(4), 929–939. doi:10.1016/j.chb.2009.03.008

Ling, C., & Salvendy, G. (2013). Prioritising usability considerations on B2C websites. *Theoretical Issues in Ergonomics Science*, *14*(1), 69–98. doi:10.1080/1464536X.2011.573012

Liu, L., Cheung, C. M. K., & Lee, M. K. O. (2016). An empirical investigation of information sharing behavior on social commerce sites. *International Journal of Information Management*, *36*(5), 686–669. doi:10.1016/j.ijinfomgt.2016.03.013

Molinillo, S., Liébana-Cabanillas, F., & Anaya-Sánchez, R. (2018). A social commerce intention model for traditional e-commerce sites. *Journal of Theoretical and Applied Electronic Commerce Research*, *13*(2), 80–93. doi:10.4067/S0718-18762018000200107

Molm, L. D., Collett, J. L., & Schaefer, D. R. (2007). Building solidarity through generalized exchange: A theory of reciprocity. *American Journal of Sociology*, *113*(1), 205–242.

Murugesan, S. (2007). Understanding Web 2.0. *IT Professional*, *9*(4), 34–41.

Ngai, E. W. T., Tao, S. S. C., & Moon, K. K. L. (2015). Social media research: Theories, constructs, and conceptual frameworks. *International Journal of Information Management*, *35*(1), 33–44. doi:10.1016/j.ijinfomgt.2014.09.004

Oh, S., & Syn, S. Y. (2015). Motivations for sharing information and social support in social media: A comparative analysis of Facebook, Twitter, Delicious, You Tube, and Flickr. *Journal of the Association for Information Science and Technology*, *66*(10), 2045–2060. doi:10.1002/asi.23320

Pelaprat, E., & Brown, B. (2012). Reciprocity: Understanding online social relations. *First Monday*, *17*(10). doi:10.5210/fm.v17i10.3324

Qu, Z., Wang, Y., Wang, S., & Zhang, Y. (2013). Implications of online social activities for e-tailers' business performance. *European Journal of Marketing*, *47*(8), 1190–1212. doi:10.1108/03090561311324282

Reimer, T., & Benkenstein, M. (2016). Altruistic eWOM marketing: More than an alternative to monetary incentives. *Journal of Retailing and Consumer Services*, *31*, 323–333. doi:10.1016/j.jretconser.2016.04.003

Rubin, A. M. (2009). Uses-and-gratifications perspective on media effects. In J. Bryant & M. B. Oliver (Eds.), *Media effects: Advances in theory and research*. Routledge.

Ryan, R. M., & Deci, E. L. (2000a). Intrinsic and extrinsic motivations: classic definitions and new directions. *Contemporary Educational Psychology*, *25*(1), 54–67. doi:10.1006/ceps.1999.1020 PMID:10620381

Ryan, R. M., & Deci, E. L. (2000b). Self-determination theory and the facilitation of intrinsic motivation, social development, and well-being. *The American Psychologist*, *55*(1), 68–78. doi:10.1037/0003-066X.55.1.68 PMID:11392867

Song, S., & Yoo, M. (2016). The role of social media during the pre-purchasing stage. *Journal of Hospitality and Tourism Technology*, *7*(1), 84–99. doi:10.1108/JHTT-11-2014-0067

Sundar, S. S., & Limperos, A. M. (2013). Uses and Grats 2.0: New gratifications for new media. *Journal of Broadcasting & Electronic Media*, *57*(4), 504–525. doi:10.1080/08838151.2013.845827

Surma, J. (2016). Social exchange in online social networks. The reciprocity phenomenon on Facebook. *Computer Communications*, *73*, 342–346. doi:10.1016/j.comcom.2015.06.017

Tsao, W.-C., & Hsieh, M.-T. (2015). eWOM persuasiveness: do eWOM platforms and product type matter?, *Electronic Commerce Research, 15*(4), 509-541.

Wood, R., & Bandura, A. (1989). Social cognitive theory of organizational management. *Academy of Management Review*, *14*(3), 361–384. doi:10.5465/amr.1989.4279067

Yoo, C. W., Sanders, G. L., & Moon, J. (2013). Exploring the effect of e-Wom participation on e-Loyalty in e-commerce. *Decision Support Systems*, *55*(3), 669–678. doi:10.1016/j.dss.2013.02.001

Zhao, J. J., Truell, A. D., Alexander, M. W., Sharma, S., & Smith, S. M. (2013). Strategic use of social media on companies'e-commerce sites. *The Journal of Research in Business Education*, *55*(2), 50–68.

KEY TERMS AND DEFINITIONS

Electronic Word of Mouth (e-Wom): Positive ornegative statement made by potential, actual, orformer customers about a product or company, whichis made available to a multitude of people and institutionsvia the Internet.e-WOMcan be articulated in many different forms such as opinions, online ratings, feedback, reviews, comments and experience sharing on the internet and through many different channels which range from blogs to discussion forums as well as online retailers and social networking sites.

User Generated Content (UGC): Content coming from regular people who, voluntarily, contribute data, information, or media that then appears before other people in a useful or entertaining way, usually on the web.

Chapter 7
Empowering the Economic Impact of Virtual Communities:
Managing Trust in the Sharing Economy

Tuğçe Aslan
https://orcid.org/0000-0002-5556-225X
Duzce University, Turkey

Adem Akbıyık
https://orcid.org/0000-0001-7634-4545
Sakarya University, Turkey

ABSTRACT

Developments in information and communication technologies have led to changes in the consumption patterns of individuals and the distancing of businesses from traditional business models. Globally, the digital transformation process has led businesses to more innovative and flexible business models. Sharing economy is a type of digital economy in which goods or services are shared through digital networks, is an innovative and flexible business model. One of the key factors in sharing economic business models is the perception of trust. The term trust has been called the currency of the sharing economy. This chapter examines trust issues in sharing economy to empower the economic impact of virtual communities because trust is a key element in strengthening participation or knowledge sharing in virtual communities. In this respect, the concept of virtual communities and trust is explained. Moreover, the concept of trust in virtual communities and the effects of virtual communities on the economy are evaluated within the framework of sharing economy.

DOI: 10.4018/978-1-7998-2185-4.ch007

INTRODUCTION

The emergence of information communication technologies and especially the internet has enabled the communities formed in physical environments to move to the digital world. The Internet connects people from all over the world to create virtual communities by eliminating time limits (Ridings, 2000). Understanding virtual communities can provide valuable information about the digital economy. In the digital economy, the purchase and sale of goods and services among peers are done through technological processes (Hojeghan & Esfangareh, 2011). The rapid development of technological developments and the intense information of individuals affect trust in digital environments.

As trust represents the primary building block of society, it plays a vital role in the formation and development of interactions and relations while sharing commercial services. (Mazzella, Sundararajan, Butt d'Espous, & Möhlmann, 2016; Westrøm et al., 2015). Trust in collaborative consumption is among peers, and therefore, different from online stores, systems, or trust in shopping (Lu, Zhao, & Wang, 2010). Vendor identification on the web is generally unknown, and buyers do not have direct contact with the offered products and have uncertainties about product quality (Bauerly, 2009). It is imperative to build trust within the sharing economy to reduce the uncertainties felt (Botsman & Rogers, 2010, p. 15). In a virtual environment, participants are usually anonymous and cannot perform direct face-to-face communication. In this context, the social network helps to increase the degree of trust that allows a stranger to use his vehicle, house, or other personal belongings. Buyers and sellers who connect through social networks can view their online profiles. The social profiles of the participants reduce the risk of a transaction in an online environment. In order to create a reliable online reputation, both sellers and buyers must take full advantage of social networks (Nadler, 2014).

This chapter aims to examine trust issues in sharing economy in order to empower the economic impact of virtual communities. In this respect, firstly, the concept of trust has been discussed in general terms, and the concept of trust in online communities has been put forward with differences. Then, the economic effects of trust in online communities were evaluated within the framework of the sharing economy by giving examples from the literature. Moreover, the relationship between culture and trust was examined. Also, the concept of risk and reliability associated with trust is tried to be explained. Finally, general evaluations were made in the light of the suggestions and future topics.

Virtual Communities

The emergence of information and communication technologies, especially the internet, has brought face-to-face and physically formed communities into a virtual environment. This community is a virtual community when interpersonal interaction occurs with electronic means, and communication is enabled by technology. Virtual communities do not have an agreed and defined partner definition (Ma, 2005). In general, virtual communities are defined as groups of people who share common interests, ideas, and feelings that communicate regularly and over a while over the internet (Ridings, 2000). Preece (2003) proposed that a virtual community has four main components: human, common goal, policies, and computer systems. The interaction environment and social norms supported by information technologies determine how social information is presented and communicated while affecting interpersonal relationships. In summary, both social and technical factors will affect the development of a virtual community (Ma, 2005).

Hagel and Armstrong (1997) propose four main types of virtual communities based on people's desire to meet basic human needs: imagination, interest, relationship, and operation. Jones and Rafaeli (2000), on the other hand, differentiate virtual communities based on social structure and technology base. Finally, Macchiette and Roy (1992) proposed a typology that can be used to classify virtual communities. They suggested that communities can be classified as professional individuals, people with common goals, and people with the same demographic characteristics. In another study, virtual communities are classified into four main groups as formal, informal, commercial, and non-commercial communities (Roy, 2015).

The need to exchange or change goods, services, or information has started the era of the digital economy. The new digital economy leads to many virtual communities. Understanding virtual communities can provide valuable information about the digital economy. Virtual communities are places where people with common interests share information. For this reason, businesses care about building a community to develop relationships with their customers. As a result, virtual communities can be much more important to both the community's knowledge base and businesses (Ridings, Gefen, & Arinze, 2002).

Trust has been identified as a critical element in strengthening participation or knowledge sharing in virtual communities (Andrews & Preece, 2001; Chiu, Hsu, & Wang, 2006). For this reason, this paper is handled mainly in trust.

The Term Trust

Trust from past to present has always been an essential factor since it reduces the uncertainty and risk of both social and business life. Although many kinds of research have been done in the past on the concept of trust, which has become increasingly important with developing technology, there is no standard definition of this concept. This uncertainty arises from the fact that trust is an abstract concept.

Due to the multidimensional nature of the concept, it has been tried to be explained with different perspectives under multiple disciplines.

Initial research on trust began in military organizations under the influence of the cold war period after World War II (Deutsch, 1958). Then, trust studies were continued in psychology (Rotter, 1967). By the 1980s, researches began to shift to sociology (Rempel, Holmes, & Zanna, 1985) and in the 1990s, the concept of trust with developing technology became the subject of economics (Coleman, 1990). Today, studies on the concept of trust in various sciences and disciplines are continuing.

Trust, which is a very complex and multidimensional concept, has been studied in different disciplines in sociology, psychology, and economics (Conte, 2016; Gambetta, 1988; Kim & Benbasat, 2009). Every science has taken the concept of trust within its framework, and the concept is defined in many different ways. Everyone generally understands trust, but it is a concept that is difficult to explain and define (Demircan & Ceylan, 2003, p. 141). This situation made it difficult to make a standard definition of trust and explain it. When the studies are examined, the definitions about the concept of trust are as follows;

In general, trust can be defined as a mobilization mechanism that allows individuals to navigate the environmental complexity of modern society and to respond to expectations despite the existing risks (Finley, 2012). Trust reduces uncertainty about what will happen, and people make willing to take risks for productive social changes (Tyler, 2001). The sense of trust also makes life more comfortable in the social sphere, in different societies and humans. Trust is a phenomenon affected by individual differences and situational factors (Lewis & Weigert, 1985). Gefen (2000) ties this situation to its complex and multidimensional nature by its nature. Rempel et al. (1985) stated that the trust of an individual has improved with the experiences and past interactions. Therefore, since each person's personality and experiences are different, their trust levels will be different.

Finally, the meaning of the concept of the dictionary, trust in the Oxford dictionary is defined as a strong belief in the reliability, accuracy, or ability of someone or something (Oxford Dictionary, 2018). With all these definitions, a brief summary of the concept of trust is needed; it is a multi-faceted concept of trust, goodwill, and risk.

When the definitions made about the concept of trust are examined, it is necessary to summarize the characteristics of the concept of trust based on common points in the definitions and will be necessary for a better understanding of the concept (Bhattacharya, Devinney, & Pillutla, 1998; Çabuk et al., 2000; Divsalar & Azgomi, 2010; Subaşı, 2012).

- Trust occurs in the environment of uncertainty and risk.
- Trust reflects expectations.
- The degree of trust is directly and statistically related to the size of the expectation.

- Mutual parties are required to establish trust.
- Trust deals with positive results.
- Trust has a dynamic structure. Experience and recommendations increase or decrease the trust level.
- Trust is sensitive. There may not be any wrong or immediate error.
- Trust is subjective. Individuals may have different perceptions of the reliability of the same tool.

Trust is based on past experiences. As everyone's experience and experience will be different, trust levels will be different. In the light of these explanations and definitions regarding the concept of trust, trust can be defined as the positive belief of one party to the other in uncertain and risky situations. Another issue in the literature about the concept of trust is trust types. Many researchers have examined the concept of trust in different dimensions. In general, Trust is divided into three dimensions as individual trust, interpersonal trust and organizational trust (Lai, 2003; Tan & Sutherland, 2004; Yang, 2017; Yıldırım, 2017).

- **Individual Trust:** This type of trust, also called trendy trust, is treated from a psychological point of view. Expresses the tendency of people to trust others and focus on the personality traits of the individual(Yang, 2017; Yıldırım, 2017). Past experiences affect the tendency to socialize and trust culture. Thus, trust is a prerequisite for another trust dimension so that it can be seen as a necessary foundation for trust (Tan & Sutherland, 2004).
- **Interpersonal Trust:** A social trust level that focuses on the factors create or destroy trust relationships between individuals (Lai, 2003). It expresses the desire of one side to trust and believe in the other side (Yang, 2017). Generally, it is considered as the expectations of a person in another person.
- **Organizational Trust:** This type of trust dealt with by sociologists is the level of trust that focuses on the development of trust in other groups of people. In itself are divided into two groups as institutional trust and system trust. Institutional trust is a level of social trust that focuses on the development of trust between individuals and institutions. System trust is placed on the perceived characteristics of the system in which a trusted person works, not the trust of a person, not another person or an institution (Lai, 2003).

Trust in Virtual Communities and Its Economic Impact

Trust is recognized as an important pioneer of information systems group performance, online transactions, corporate value creation, and information sharing in virtual communities (Chiu et al., 2006). The sense of trust required for the continuity of a community is essential in virtual communities (Lee, Ahn, Kim, & Lee, 2014) People in communities work better with people they trust and avoid contact with people they do not interact with (Lee et al., 2014). Therefore, the sense of trust in virtual communities has been identified as a key element in strengthening participation level or knowledge sharing (Andrews & Preece, 2001; Chiu et al., 2006).

The feeling of trust among peers makes the parties more willing to cooperate (Nahapiet & Ghoshal, 1998). Therefore, interpersonal trust is argued to be an essential factor in sharing information in communities and organizations (Nonaka, 1994). However, increasing the social connection between buyers and sellers is ensured by a sense of trust (Ma, 2005).

Most economical, social, and political environments involve people whose behavior is not always predictable (Knack & Keefer, 1997). At this point, trust is a crucial factor in consumer decision making by reducing risk and uncertainty. Online trust differs from general trust because it covers the trust between the customer and the Internet (Bart, Shankar, Sultan, & Urban, 2005).

Trust in technology and trust in people are different. Social trust is often based on face-to-face interactions and relationships where trust is more comfortable to establish. Online trust, on the other hand, is a complex issue because it is based on a virtual environment. When consumers feel comfortable interacting with a website, they can develop trust in the website and trust is becoming the primary strategy for dealing with uncertainty and fear (Jarvenpaa, Tractinsky, & Saarinen, 2000). Trust on the platform has proven to have a positive impact on the trust in the Internet environment (Wei, Zha, & Sun, 2014). Unlike traditional face-to-face interaction, the primary interface between consumers and firms are online environments. Therefore, in order for consumers to develop positive relationships with online firms, trust must be established in the online environment or internet technologies (Ye, 2013). Trust in the online environment plays an essential role in the satisfaction of online transactions and the expected results. The development of trust in the online environment is also crucial for the success of sharing economy services. Because the consumer's trust in the online environment will affect their trust in sharing services (Finley, 2012).

The emergence of Internet technologies affects the nature of trade and peer relationships, thus providing a unique environment for trust research (Freedman & Zhe Jin, 2008). In a study, consumer trust has been shown to have a direct positive impact on the intention to trade online (Kim, Ferrin, & Rao, 2009).

With the unknown, the online environment can be seen as a high-risk environment where traditional rules and daily experience knowledge are not applied (Rutter, 2001). At this point, trust in the online environment has become an area of interest for studies. The exciting feature of this area is reflected in the studies. Researchers have addressed online trust in several ways. For example, Shankar, Urban, & Sultan (2002) found that features such as consumer online shopping experiences and technology propensity affect online trust. Other studies in the literature have confirmed this effect (Walczuch & Lundgren, 2004;Yoon, 2002). Also, it is argued that individual trust is decisive in the formation of online trust (Brown, Poole, & Rodgers, 2004) and personality traits affect online trust (Tan & Sutherland, 2004). In a study, it was found that online trust that affects purchase intention has a more significant impact than perceived risk (Wu, 2010). In their study, Chung & Shin (2010) stated that perspectives on the characteristics of the website, such as website design, may affect the intention to use the platform. In other words, the ease of use of the online platform and perceived security control have a significant impact on trust formation (Koufaris & Hampton-Sosa, 2004).

Each individual's tendency to trust is different. Some individuals are more likely to trust the other side (Gefen, 2000). This is because the experience and experience of online shopping vary from person to person. Experiences from the shopping affect the tendency to trust positively or negatively. An understanding customer who is familiar with online shopping will be more likely to trust online sellers (Weisberg, Te'eni, & Arman, 2011). Besides, the higher the level of consumer trust, the higher the intention to purchase, and the lower level of consumer trust is the main reason why people avoid online shopping (Gefen & Straub, 2004).

While offline trust covers only an individual or a company, an online trust includes an online information system in addition to an individual or a company (Yang, 2017). However, among these factors, the online information system is the first factor that affects the trust of consumers. Because, this information system is the interface that consumers first encounter when shopping online. Consumers find websites (interfaces) that have poor design and complex layout look unreliable (McCloskey, 2006), whereas websites (interfaces) that offer high-quality information and original content are more reliable (Weisberg et al., 2011).

Consumers who shop online are mostly concerned with the risk of payment or personal risk, which is dependent on security. Liao & Cheung (2002) investigated the attitudes towards internet-based e-banking and found that system security is an essential determinant of customer attitudes towards system use. In another study, the perceived quality of the website was found to have a positive effect on trust (Jones & Leonard, 2008; Yoon & Occeña, 2015). According to another study, it was found that the quality of website design is more critical than store reputation (Liang & Lai, 2002). From this point of view, it can be interpreted that the trust of a company's website affects customers' attitudes towards the company and their desire to purchase.

Ensuring customer trust can significantly contribute to the growth of sales through customer acquisition and the acquisition of customer loyalty. For re-purchases, customer trust in a company is the crucial instrument between product or service characteristics and customer retention (Garbarino & Johnson, 1999).

Sharing economy is a kind of digital economy. In the sharing economy, the trade of physical assets and services is carried out through technological systems. People who buy and rent from these markets are identified as consumers, and the people who sell or provide these services are called micro-entrepreneurs (Sundararajan, 2014). In this model, consumers and micro-entrepreneurs are defined as peers. Peers are often connected through social networks, and the pitfall of these relationships are cooperation and trust to achieve successful shopping (Conte, 2016). With the trust of peers, the system begins to operate and is willing to cooperate with peers who trust each other.

It is trust that makes the sharing economy move forward rapidly. A sense of trust allows a person to get into someone's car or rent a room from someone he has never met (Ufford, 2015). According to a study conducted in 2012, 67% of the respondents stated that the main obstacle to participating in the collaborative consumption service was the problem of trust. Besides, the study revealed that participants were concerned that the items would be broken or stolen and that there were trust issues against foreigners (Davis, 2012; Olson, 2012). According to the PwC report, trust is the cornerstone of sharing platforms (PwC, 2015). So if there is no trust, a sharing platform will not work (Tosuner, 2012, p. 9). Möhlmann (2015) found that trust affects both the willingness to use the service and a significant impact on the satisfaction of consumption and that it affects the likelihood of the consumer selecting a service again.

The role of trust in economic changes has been investigated by some researchers, and this effect has been confirmed (Fukuyama, 1995; Inglehart, 1999). It is claimed that trust is an indicator of economic growth. Because trust in the economy facilitates economic transactions, reduces costs between the parties, opens new ways of cooperation, and encourages business activities (Morgan & Hunt, 1994). In a study, a higher level of social security was positively correlated with economic development (Zak & Knack, 2001). From this point of view, it can be concluded that the level of trust in society is one of the precursors of economic and social development.

In the Traditional World, trust was easy to create and grasp. In this world, people did not have access to technology and were mostly communicating with the family, not with other individuals (Durkheim, 1964; Samadi, 2015). However, trust in today's World is more complicated. With the emergence of information communication technologies and spreading rapidly all over the world, interpersonal communication has become a significant value. It starts with the trust of the parties in a healthy and fruitful communication between individuals. As a result, trust is an essential factor inherent in all trade sector activities and affects society in various ways.

The concept of online trust has attracted much attention in several disciplines, such as marketing, management, information systems, organizational behavior, psychology, and social psychology (Ye, 2013). Among the predecessors of trust, the relationships between offline trust and online trust are examined from the perspective of company/organization design of web sites, individual customers' characteristics and culture (Yang, 2017).

Other Concepts Related to Trust

This section will provide detailed explanations of risk and reliability concepts that are strictly related to trust.

Risk

When the studies on trust in the literature are examined, it is observed that the researchers frequently touch on the concept of risk as well as the concept of trust. Some have agreed that there is no need for trust in the absence of risk (Mayer et al., 1995; Morgan & Hunt, 1994). At this point, a risk emerges as a factor that constitutes trust (Gambarov, 2014).

It is claimed that the trust function reduces environmental complexity. Reducing complexity also allows individuals to adapt to the uncertain and complex situations in contemporary societies that they are increasingly challenged to do and to do their jobs easily (Finley, 2012; Welch et al., 2005). The current structure of social uncertainty throughout all social changes emphasizes the inevitable relationship between trust and risk (Coleman, 1990).

The level of participation in the sharing economy is also linked to the degree of risk. According to the results of the survey conducted in 2014, it was revealed that the participants stated the risk factor as the first obstacle to participate in the sharing economy (Burnett, 2014). Individuals with lower risk aversion levels are more likely to use websites that provide sharing services. It means that those who participate more often in the sharing economy avoid less risk than those who participate less often. This reluctance to take risks can be defined as a dynamic characteristic of the participants in the sharing economy because the participants' positive or negative experiences about the sharing economy can change (Cialdini, 2009; Conte, 2016). In this context, the dynamic aspect of the risk aversion attitude depends not on how often a party is involved in the sharing economy, but on the quality of the participation experience. This supports the idea that risk attitudes may change as a result of an experience in the sharing economy (Conte, 2016; Santana & Parigi, 2015).

The degree of risk aversion differs from culture to culture, just like trust. In other words, cultural aspects also affect risk perception. Some cultures have a high level of risk, while others have a low level of risk perception (Koç, 2015; Yamagishi & Yamagishi, 1994). As a result, the risk is the essence of trust, and essentially means trust, willingness to take risks and to be vulnerable to the actions of others (Das & Teng, 1998). So trust is not willing to take risks, but a willingness to take risks (Mayer et al., 1995).

Looking at risk-related studies, Santana and Parigi (2015) investigated whether participation in the sharing economy is related to the risk attitude and found that consumers participating in the sharing economy have an equally high-risk level. He also argued that consumers with low-risk aversion levels are more likely to use sharing economy websites. In another study, it was found that risk-sensitive individuals were less likely to present their products to others (Gupta, Esmaeilzadeh, Uz, & Tennant, 2019).

Reliability

Reliability is the possibility that a product, a part or a system, can perform the expected function in a predetermined time and under certain conditions without any problems. The concept of reliability, in this case, can cover every area such as a computer, website, private companies, e-commerce companies (Bakkurt, 2004). In this case, reliability is one of the most critical criteria for product or service quality.

Trust is the property of the trusting party, while reliability is the property exhibited by the trusted party (Mayer et al., 1995; Subaşı, 2012). In other words, reliability is two different phenomena that belong to the trusted side and trust to the trusted side. However, it was found that trust was associated with reliability and the reliability level of the individuals with high tendency to trust increased (Tschannen-Moran & Hoy, 2000).

Given the importance of trust in P2P markets, the perceived credibility of vendors has a central role. After consumers rely on the online environment, they begin to look for other reasons to make the final decision. The first is the reliability of the other party. As a result of the studies on reliability, it has found that perceived reliability has a positive effect on consumer decisions (Duarte, Siegel, & Young, 2012; Ert, Fleischer, & Magen, 2016).

In addition to reliability, fame, and perceived fame are also essential factors in the literature. Although the concepts of reputation and trust are interrelated, they are different. Reputation can be defined as a general view that expresses a general assessment of an individual's characteristics. Some studies have found a relationship between perceived reputation and online trust, and perceived reputation has a significant impact on online trust (Jarvenpaa et al., 2000). In another study, a study was conducted to examine the premise of consumer confidence. According to the results of this study, perceived reputation, system security, and trust tendency are the determinants of consumer confidence (Teo & Liu, 2007).

BlaBlaCar, Airbnb and Uber

For thousands of years, trust has been limited to close family and friends. But by the end of the 20th century, trust expanded globally through institutions and brands around the world. Businesses have evolved from small-scale shops with a well-known customer base to larger-scale organizations that meet the needs of a wider audience in a competitive marketplace. Regulations and contracts supported by legal and financial institutions have enabled people to trade directly beyond their trusted environment (Möhlmann, 2016).

Online platforms, databases, search engines and connectivity are creating new systems for ensuring and nurturing interpersonal digital trust. With these developing technologies, individuals become a part of the digital trust wave by establishing reliable connections not only with their friends and families but also worldwide. With the development of information technologies, economic growth is accelerating in the same direction.

The survey, conducted in 2015 with more than 18,000 BlaBlaCar members from 11 countries, has been one of the largest studies on online trust to date. And as a result, 88% of people showed that the profile of BlaBlaCar members trusted the full ones. This level of trust is as high as the level of trust we have in someone we know (Möhlmann, 2016).

BlaBlaCar has developed a set of trust tools that allow its members to trust each other, choose who to travel with and share a journey with confidence. These are listed in the following five items (Möhlmann, 2016).

1. **Declarative Information:** The information declared in the system is required for a reliable online profile. This information is considered the first step in ensuring online trust. Users can share their names, photos, preferences and make their own definitions. Thus, the confidence of the other side develops. It was observed that the members needed information such as the name of the person they would travel to and the photograph. A stranger with a name and face was found to be more reliable and the system was designed accordingly.
2. **Verification:** It was understood that the phone numbers needed to be verified. And the verification system was improved.
3. **Ratings:** Ratings allow collection of incoming feedback. Ratings enable individuals to build dignity and build interpersonal trust. A rating system has been developed so that drivers do not have to prove their reliability from scratch when they re-enter the system later.
4. **Booking System:** With this system, drivers can view the passenger profile before accepting a request to share a ride.
5. **Two-way Ratings:** When a member receives a rating, it's undisclosed until they leave one in return. This process allows members to leave a completely honest rating, because they know the other member can't leave a negative rating as revenge, in response.

Airbnb has developed trust tools in three important ways for trust (Maier, 2016). Airbnb has discovered that creating a profile with photos of hosts and guests reinforces mutual trust. The second instrument of trust is comments. According to Airbnb, a host with no comment is four times less likely to book with at least one person. A landlord with 10 comments is 10 times more likely to book a house. Reviews are therefore one of the most successful ways Airbnb creates trust between users. Another way Airbnb promotes trust is to enable people to make more meaningful interactions with each other. In addition, Airbnb also has a risk scoring system. Accordingly, each Airbnb booking is scored for risk before being approved. This system ensures that suspicious activities occur in advance (Airbnb, 2019).

Uber has developed trust vehicles in several ways to improve trust between passengers and drivers (Uber, 2019). These:

- Anyone involved in Uber undergoes multi-stage safety checks, including driving violations, violent offenses and other checks. In addition, Uber investigates drivers and their problems every year.
- In case of an emergency, you can view your live location and travel information in Uber app and forward it to the authorities. This information is automatically provided to the authorities by the uber when deemed necessary. Your friends and family can also follow your route on request.
- Uber has developed a warning system called RideCheck. RideCheck using sensors and GPS data, it helps to determine if a trip is off course in an unusual way. If anything out of the ordinary is noticed, the tools for assistance are provided.
- Uber support is available 24 hours a day, 7 days a week and is provided by trained security guards.
- When communicating through the Uber app, neither drivers nor passengers can see each other's phone numbers.
- Uber uses a system to determine whether there is a new offense involving an active driver and to detect offenses that prevent the driver from driving.

CONCLUSION

The emergence of information and communication technologies, especially the internet, has brought face-to-face and physically formed communities into a virtual environment. People participate in virtual communities because they join a physical community. The need to share experiences, emotions, and interests with others leads people to come together. The need to exchange or change goods, services, or information has started the era of the digital economy.

It combines demand and supply at an unprecedented speed and scale through networks and platforms generated by technology. Sharing economy is a type of digital economy where goods or services are shared through digital networks. In sharing economy business models, goods, or services are usually shared among individuals connected via virtual networks. Thanks to advancing technology, individuals can share goods or services faster and less costly with their peers on a global scale.

One of the critical factors in sharing economy business models is the perception of trust provided by the platform in the role of buyers, sellers, and intermediaries. As it can be seen in the relationship between trust between countries, trust is one of the essential indicators of economic growth. Because it makes economic transactions run faster, reduces transaction costs, and thus supports commercial activities. This also applies to the sharing economy. A sense of trust allows individuals to share or aspire to share what they have.

One of the determinants of participation in the sharing economy is related to the degree of risk. Depending on the level of risk aversion, people have an attitude towards the sharing economy. It is seen that consumers are taking high-level risk-benefit more from the sharing economy. Again, it was found that individuals who are anxious about taking risks prefer to be on the consumer side in the sharing economy, but are reluctant to share their products or services.

Another factor affecting the sharing economy is reliability. There is a close relationship between trust and reliability. Because, the reliability level of individuals with high tendency to trust is high. The economic impact of these two concepts, which are critical for the sharing economy, is quite high. Like the sharing economy, the rapidly growing peer-to-peer trade demonstrates the benefits of collaborative consumption and raises questions. Therefore, the social and economic structures created in the digital environment; new assessments regarding the sense of trust, risk perception, and reliability.

The companies we have cited above have developed various trust tools to improve trust among peers. This increased the trust of the users in the system and their peers. For example, uber uses technology that keeps phone numbers private. Airbnb also has a risk scoring system. Accordingly, each Airbnb booking is scored for risk before being approved. This system ensures that suspicious activities occur in advance. Such measures enable individuals to trust each other in virtual communities.

Increasing trust and risk aversion level of individuals, Initiatives or measures that can keep the credibility of the sharing economy parties at the highest level will pave the way for economic activities to be carried out in the digital environment.

FUTURE RESEARCH DIRECTIONS

Developments in information and communication technologies have changed the life and consumption habits of societies by eliminating physical boundaries and regional time differences. Technological innovations that have entered our lives very quickly have facilitated the sharing of products and services through virtual environments and a more innovative and flexible consumption model has emerged under the name of sharing economy. The sharing economy is a type of digital economy in which goods or services are shared through digital networks. Individuals connected with virtual networks make sharing goods or services faster and less costly with other users globally. Also, studies on the sharing economy gain importance when increasing over consumption, global warming, and depletion of natural resources are taken into consideration.

The role of trust in sharing services offered via online or mobile platforms for consumers and service providers is recommended for future studies. Also, intercultural comparisons, including various cultures, are recommended for future studies.

REFERENCES

Andrews, D., & Preece, J. (2001). A conceptual framework for demographic groups resistant to online community interaction. *Proceedings of the 34th Annual Hawaii International Conference on System Sciences (HICSS-34)*-Vol. 7, *00*(c), 7013. 10.1109/HICSS.2001.927044

Andrews, D., & Preece, J. (2001). A conceptual framework for demographic groups resistant to online community interaction. *Proceedings of the 34th Annual Hawaii International Conference on System Sciences (HICSS-34)*-Vol. 7, *00*(c), 7013. 10.1109/HICSS.2001.927044

Armstrong, A., & Hagel, J. (1997). Net gain: expanding markets through virtual communities. Retrieved from http://www.techsoc.com/netgain.htm

Bakkurt, A. T. (2004). *Hizmet İşletmelerinde Güvenilirlik Güvencesi Programları ve Bir HTEA Uygulaması.*

Bart, Y., Shankar, V., Sultan, F., & Urban, G. L. (2005). Are the drivers and role of online trust the same for all web sites and consumers?: a large-scale exploratory empirical study. *Journal of Marketing*, *69*(4), 133–152. doi:10.1509/jmkg.2005.69.4.133

Bauerly, R. J. (2009). Online auction fraud and eBay. *Marketing Management Journal, 19*(1), 133–143. Retrieved from http://www.mmaglobal.org/publications/MMJ/MMJ-Issues/2009-Spring/MMJ-2009-Spring-Vol19-Issue1-Bauerly-pp133-143.pdf

Bhattacharya, R., Devinney, T. M., & Pillutla, M. M. (1998). A formal model of trust based on outcomes. *Academy of Management Review, 23*(3), 459–472. doi:10.5465/amr.1998.926621

Botsman, R., & Rogers, R. (2010). *What's mine is yours: the rise of collaborative consumption*. Harper Business.

Brown, H. G., Poole, M. S., & Rodgers, T. L. (2004). Interpersonal traits, complementarity, and trust in virtual collaboration. *Journal of Management Information Systems, 20*(4), 115–138. doi:10.1080/07421222.2004.11045785

Burnett, L. (2014). *The sharing economy - where we go from here*. Leo Burnett Inc.

Çabuk, S. DOĞAN SÜDAġ, H., Zeren, D., Kelimeler, A., ĠletiÇimi, P., KarÇıtlığı, T., & PaylaÇımı, O. (2000). Sahip Olmak Yerine Paylaşmak: Tüketicilerin Paylaşma Davranışlarının Unsurlarını Belirlemeye Yönelik Bir Çalışma Sharing versus having: a study of determining the factors of consumer sharing behaviour. *Çankırı Karatekin Üniversitesi Sosyal Bilimler Enstitüsü Dergisi Cankiri Karatekin University Journal of Institute of Social Sciences, 6*(61), 151–168. Retrieved from https://pdfs.semanticscholar.org/6f12/7e35044fcef9d04d628a15a614d74d74cda3.pdf

Chiu, C. M., Hsu, M. H., & Wang, E. T. G. (2006). Understanding knowledge sharing in virtual communities: An integration of social capital and social cognitive theories. *Decision Support Systems, 42*(3), 1872–1888. doi:10.1016/j.dss.2006.04.001

Chiu, C. M., Hsu, M. H., & Wang, E. T. G. (2006). Understanding knowledge sharing in virtual communities: An integration of social capital and social cognitive theories. *Decision Support Systems, 42*(3), 1872–1888. doi:10.1016/j.dss.2006.04.001

Chung, K., & Shin, J. (2010). The antecedents and consequents of relationship quality in internet shopping. *Asia Pacific Journal of Marketing and Logistics, 22*(4), 473–491. doi:10.1108/13555851011090510

Cialdini, R. B. (2009). *The psychology of persuasion*. Retrieved from http://elibrary.bsu.az/books_400/N_232.pdf

Coleman, J. (1990). *Foundations of social theory*. Cambridge, MA: Harvard University Press.

Conte, C. (2016). *The triangular trust in the sharing economy*. (Bachelor's thesis, Università Ca'Foscari Venezia).

Das, T. K., & Teng, B.-S. (1998). Between trust and control: developing confidence in partner cooperation in alliances. *Academy of Management Review*, *23*(3), 491–512. doi:10.5465/amr.1998.926623

Davis, P. (2012). Trust is #1 barrier to sharing | Deskmag | Coworking. Retrieved from http://www.deskmag.com/en/trust-is-1-barrier-to-sharing-coworking-shareable-491

Demircan, N., & Ceylan, A. (2003). Örgütsel Güven Kavram : Nedenleri ve Sonuçlar. *Yönetim ve Ekonomi, 10*(2). Retrieved from http://webcache.googleusercontent.com/search?q=cache:http://www2.bayar.edu.tr/yonetimekonomi/dergi/pdf/C10S22003/ndac.pdf

Deutsch, M. (1958). Trust and suspicion. *The Journal of Conflict Resolution*, *2*(4), 265–279. doi:10.1177/002200275800200401

Dictionary, O. (2018). Trust | Definition of trust in English by Oxford Dictionaries. Retrieved from https://en.oxforddictionaries.com/definition/trust

Divsalar, M., & Azgomi, M. A. (2010). A computational trust model for e-commerce systems. *Lecture Notes of the Institute for Computer Sciences, Social-Informatics and Telecommunications Engineering, 21 LNICST*, 9–18. doi:10.1007/978-3-642-11532-5_2

Duarte, J., Siegel, S., & Young, L. (2012). Trust and credit: the role of appearance in peer-to-peer lending. *Review of Financial Studies*, *25*(8), 2455–2484. doi:10.1093/rfs/hhs071

Durkheim, E. (1964). *The rules of sociological method*. Retrieved from http://www.worldcat.org/title/rules-of-sociological-method/oclc/220073686

Ert, E., Fleischer, A., & Magen, N. (2016). *Trust and reputation in the sharing economy: The role of personal photos in Airbnb*. doi:10.1016/j.tourman.2016.01.013

Finley, K. (2012). *Trust in the sharing economy: an exploratory study.*

Freedman, S., & Jin, Z. G. (2008). *Do social networks solve information problems for peer-to-peer lending? Evidence from Prosper.com**. Retrieved from www.netinst.org

Fukuyama, F. (1995). *Trust: the social virtues and the creation of prosperity.* Retrieved from https://www.worldcat.org/title/trust-the-social-virtues-and-the-creation-of-prosperity/oclc/32547174

Gambarov, V. (2014). *Elektronik Ticarette Güven Oluşturan Faktörler Ve Satınalma Niyetine Etkileri Üzerine Bir Araştırma*. doi:10.1192/bjp.205.1.76a

Gambetta, D. (1988). *Can we trust trust?* Retrieved from https://philpapers.org/rec/GAMCWT

Garbarino, E., & Johnson, M. S. (1999). The different roles of satisfaction, trust, and commitment in customer relationships. *Journal of Marketing, 63*(2), 70–87. doi:10.1177/002224299906300205

Gefen, D. (2000). *E-commerce : the role of familiarity and trust. 28*, 725–737. doi:10.1016/S0305-0483(00)00021-9

Gefen, D., & Straub, D. W. (2004). Consumer trust in B2C e-Commerce and the importance of social presence: Experiments in e-Products and e-Services. *Omega, 32*(6), 407–424. doi:10.1016/j.omega.2004.01.006

Gupta, M., Esmaeilzadeh, P., Uz, I., & Tennant, V. M. (2019). The effects of national cultural values on individuals' intention to participate in peer-to-peer sharing economy. *Journal of Business Research, 97*(September 2017), 20–29. doi:10.1016/j.jbusres.2018.12.018

Hojeghan, S. B., & Esfangareh, A. N. (2011). Digital economy and tourism impacts, influences and challenges. *Procedia: Social and Behavioral Sciences, 19*, 308–316. doi:10.1016/j.sbspro.2011.05.136

Inglehart, R. (1999). Trust, well-being, and democracy. In M. E. Warren (Ed.), *Democracy and trust* (pp. 88–120). doi:10.1017/CBO9780511659959.004

Jarvenpaa, S. L., Tractinsky, N., & Saarinen, L. (2000). Consumer trust in an internet store: a cross-cultural validation. *Journal of Computer-Mediated Communication, 5*(2), 0–0. doi:10.1111/j.1083-6101.1999.tb00337.x

Jones, K., & Leonard, L. N. K. (2008). *Trust in consumer-to-consumer electronic commerce*. doi:10.1016/j.im.2007.12.002

Jones, Q., & Rafaeli, S. (2000). Time to split, virtually: 'discourse architecture' and 'community building' create vibrant virtual publics. *Electronic Markets, 10*. doi:10.1080/101967800750050326

Kim, D., & Benbasat, I. (2009). Trust-assuring arguments in B2C e-commerce: impact of content, source, and price on trust. *Journal of Management Information Systems, 26*(3), 175–206. doi:10.2753/MIS0742-1222260306

Kim, D. J., Ferrin, D. L., & Rao, H. R. (2009). Trust and satisfaction, two stepping stones for successful e-commerce relationships: a longitudinal exploration. *Information Systems Research, 20*(2), 237–257. doi:10.1287/isre.1080.0188

Knack, S., & Keefer, P. (1997). Does social capital have an economic payoff? A cross-country investigation. *Quarterly Journal of Economics 112*(4), 1251-1288 | socialcapitalgateway.org. Retrieved from http://www.socialcapitalgateway.org/content/paper/knack-s-keefer-p-1997-does-social-capital-have-economic-payoff-cross-country-investiga

Koç, E. (2015). *Tüketici Davranışı ve Pazarlama Stratejileri: Global ve Yerel Yaklaşım.*

Koçgar, M. E. (2013). *Tüketici Davranışlarını Etkileyen Faktörler Ve Kültür: Eskişehir'de Kültürün Tüketim Tercihleri Üzerine Etkisi.*

Koufaris, M., & Hampton-Sosa, W. (2004). The development of initial trust in an online company by new customers. *Information & Management, 41*(3), 377–397. doi:10.1016/j.im.2003.08.004

Lai, B. S. T. (2003). *Trust in online trading systems.* (Doctoral dissertation, University of Auckland).

Lee, H.-Y., Ahn, H., Kim, H. K., & Lee, J. (2014). Comparative analysis of trust in online communities. *Procedia Computer Science, 31*, 1140–1149. doi:10.1016/j.procs.2014.05.370

Lee, H.-Y., Ahn, H., Kim, H. K., & Lee, J. (2014). Comparative analysis of trust in online communities. *Procedia Computer Science, 31*, 1140–1149. doi:10.1016/j.procs.2014.05.370

Lewis, J. D., & Weigert, A. (1985). Trust as a social reality. *Social Forces, 63*(4), 967–985. doi:10.2307/2578601

Liang, T. P., & Lai, H. J. (2002). Effect of store design on consumer purchases: An empirical study of on-line bookstores. *Information & Management, 39*(6), 431–444. doi:10.1016/S0378-7206(01)00129-X

Liao, Z., & Cheung, M. T. (2002). Internet-based e-banking and consumer attitudes: An empirical study. *Information & Management, 39*(4), 283–295. doi:10.1016/S0378-7206(01)00097-0

Lu, Y., Zhao, L., & Wang, B. (2010). From virtual community members to C2C e-commerce buyers: Trust in virtual communities and its effect on consumers' purchase intention. *Electronic Commerce Research and Applications, 9*(4), 346–360. doi:10.1016/j.elerap.2009.07.003

Ma, M. (2005). *It design for sustaining virtual communities: an identity-based approach.* (Doctoral dissertation).

Maier, S. (2016). Learn from these 3 ways AirBNB won the trust it needed to succeed. Retrieved from https://www.entrepreneur.com/article/280224

Mayer, R. C., Davis, J. H., & Schoorman, D. F. (1995). An integrative model of organizational trust. *Academy of Management Review*, *20*(3), 709–734. doi:10.5465/amr.1995.9508080335

Mazzella, F., Sundararajan, A., Butt d'Espous, V., & Möhlmann, M. (2016). How digital trust powers the sharing economy: the digitization of trust. *IESE Insight*, (30), 24–31. doi:10.15581/002.ART-2887

McCloskey, D. (2006). *The bourgeois virtues: ethics for an age of commerce*. Retrieved from http://www.deirdremccloskey.com/docs/bv_selection.pdf

Möhlmann, M. (2015). Collaborative consumption: Determinants of satisfaction and the likelihood of using a sharing economy option again. *Journal of Consumer Behaviour*, *14*(3), 193–207. doi:10.1002/cb.1512

MöhlmannM. (2016). *Trust age*.

Morgan, R. M., & Hunt, S. D. (1994). The commitment-trust theory of relationship marketing. *Journal of Marketing*, *58*(3), 20–38. doi:10.1177/002224299405800302

Nadler, S. (2014). *The sharing economy: What is it and where is it going?* (Doctoral dissertation, Massachusetts Institute of Technology).

Nahapiet, J., & Ghoshal, S. (1998). Social capital, intellectual capital, and the organizational advantage. *Academy of Management Review*, *23*(2), 242. doi:10.2307/259373

Nahapiet, J., & Ghoshal, S. (1998). Social capital, intellectual capital, and the organizational advantage. *Academy of Management Review*, *23*(2), 242–266. doi:10.5465/amr.1998.533225

Nonaka, I. (1994). A dynamic theory of organizational knowledge creation. *Organization Science*, *5*(1), 14–37. doi:10.1287/orsc.5.1.14

Olson, K. (2012). National study quantifies the "sharing economy" movement. Retrieved from https://www.prnewswire.com/news-releases/national-study-quantifies-the-sharing-economy-movement-138949069.html

PwC. (2015). The sharing economy: how is it affecting you and your business? *PwC*, (January), 1–10. Retrieved from http://pwc.blogs.com/files/sharing-economy-final_0814.pdf

Rempel, J. K., Holmes, J. G., & Zanna, M. P. (1985). *Trust in close relationships, 49*(1), 95–112. Airbnb. (2019). Airbnb Güven ve Güvenlik - Güvenliğiniz bizim önceliğimiz. Retrieved from https://www.airbnb.com.tr/trust

Ridings, C. M. (2000). *Determinants of trust and use in virtual communities*. Drexel University.

Ridings, C. M., Gefen, D., & Arinze, B. (2002). Some antecedents and effects of trust in virtual communities. *The Journal of Strategic Information Systems, 11*(3-4), 271–295. doi:10.1016/S0963-8687(02)00021-5

Rotter, J. B. (1967). A new scale for the measurement of interpersonal trust1. *Journal of Personality, 35*(4), 651–665. doi:10.1111/j.1467-6494.1967.tb01454.x PMID:4865583

Roy, A. (2015). *A typology of virtual communities on the internet: contingency marketing approaches*. 22–24.

Rutter, J. (2001). From the sociology of trust towards a sociology of "e-trust." *International Journal of New Product Development & Innovation Management, 2*(4), 371–385. Retrieved from http://www.ncsa.uiuc.edu/SDG/Software/XMosaic/

Samadi, B. (2015). Factors influencing organisational trust and knowledge sharing behaviour in MSC status companies (Doctoral dissertation, Multimedia University, Malaysia).

Santana, J., & Parigi, P. (2015). Risk aversion and engagement in the sharing economy. *Games, 6*(4), 560–573. doi:10.3390/g6040560

Shankar, V., Urban, G. L., & Sultan, F. (2002). Online trust: a stakeholder perspective, concepts, implications, and future directions. *Journal of Strategic Information Systems, 11*, 325–344. Retrieved from www.elsevier.com/locate/jsis

Subaşı, H. H. (2012). *Elektronik Ticaret ve Güven: Bir Araştırma*.

Sundararajan, A. (2014). *Peer-to-peer businesses and the sharing (collaborative) economy: overview, economic effects and regulatory issues*. Retrieved from http://www.collaborativeconsumption.com/directory/

Tan, F. B., & Sutherland, P. (2004). Online consumer trust : A multi-dimensional model. *Journal of Electronic Commerce in Organizations, 2*(3), 40–58. doi:10.4018/jeco.2004070103

Teo, T. S. H., & Liu, J. (2007). Consumer trust in e-commerce in the United States, Singapore, and China. *Omega, 35*(1), 22–38. doi:10.1016/j.omega.2005.02.001

Tosuner, A. (2012). *Tüketim Davranışının Azaltılması için İnternetin Kullanılması: Ortak Kullanım Ağları. XVII.* Türkiye'de İnternet Konferansı.

Tschannen-Moran, M., & Hoy, W. K. (2000). A multidisciplinary analysis of the nature, meaning, and measurement of trust. *Review of Educational Research*, *70*(4), 547–593. doi:10.3102/00346543070004547

Tyler, T. (2001). Trust in society. In *The Russell Sage Foundation Series on Trust, Vol. 2*. Retrieved from https://ostromworkshop.indiana.edu/library/node/67979

Uber. (2019). *Our approach to safety.* Retrieved from https://www.uber.com/us/en/safety/

Ufford, S. (2015). *The future of the sharing economy depends on trust.* Retrieved from https://www.forbes.com/sites/theyec/2015/02/10/the-future-of-the-sharing-economy-depends-on-trust/#2648cbcf4717

Walczuch, R., & Lundgren, H. (2004). *Psychological antecedents of institution-based consumer trust in e-retailing.* doi:10.1016/j.im.2003.12.009

Wei, K., Zha, Y., & Sun, H. (2014). *A comparative study of buyers' and sellers' transaction intentions in consumer-to-consumer emarketplaces.* Retrieved from http://aisel.aisnet.org/pacis2014/103

Weisberg, J., Te'eni, D., & Arman, L. (2011). *Past purchase and intention to purchase in e-commerce: The mediation of social presence and trust Article information, 21*(1), 82–96. doi:10.1108/10662241111104893

Welch, M. R., Rivera, R. E. N., Conway, B. P., Yonkoski, J., Lupton, P. M., & Giancola, R. (2005). Determinants and consequences of social trust. *Sociological Inquiry*, *75*(4), 453–473. doi:10.1111/j.1475-682X.2005.00132.x

Westrøm, H., Kristjansson, S., Investigation, A., Behaviour, C., Westrøm, H., & Kristjansson, S. (2015). Sharing economy in Denmark. An investigation of consumer behaviour.

Wu, D. M. (2010). *Culture, trust, and security – an empirical study of consumer attitudes towards B2C e-commerce in Chinese societies.* (Doctoral dissertation, Edinburgh Napier University).

Yamagishi, T., & Yamagishi, M. (1994). Trust and commitment in the United States and Japan. *Motivation and Emotion*, *18*(2), 129–166. doi:10.1007/BF02249397

Yang, L. (2017). *Effect of product review, interactivity, social inequality, and culture on trust in online retailers: a comparison between China and the U.S.* (Doctoral dissertation, Bowling Green State University). doi:10.2202/1935-6226.1069

Ye, C. (2013). *Toward an integrated understanding of online trust.* Retrieved from https://vpn.utm.my/docview/1448297657?accountid=41678

Yıldırım, L. (2017). *Online Alışveriş Sitelerinde Uygulanan Canlı Destek Sistemlerinin Tüketicilerde Oluşturduğu Güvene Etkisi: Bir Araştırma.*

Yoon, H. S., & Occeña, L. G. (2015). Influencing factors of trust in consumer-to-consumer electronic commerce with gender and age. *International Journal of Information Management, 35*(3), 352–363. doi:10.1016/j.ijinfomgt.2015.02.003

Yoon, S. J. (2002). The antecedents and consequences of trust in online-purchase decisions. *Journal of Interactive Marketing, 16*(2), 47–63. doi:10.1002/dir.10008

Zak, P. J., & Knack, S. (2001). Trust and growth. *Economic Journal (London), 111*(470), 295–321. doi:10.1111/1468-0297.00609

KEY TERMS AND DEFINITIONS

The Term Trust: Trust from past to present has always been an essential factor since it reduces the uncertainty and risk of both social and business life. Although many kinds of research have been done in the past on the concept of trust, which has become increasingly important with developing technology, there is no standard definition of this concept. This uncertainty arises from the fact that trust is an abstract concept. Due to the multidimensional nature of the concept, it has been tried to be explained with different perspectives under multiple disciplines.

Virtual Communities: The emergence of information and communication technologies, especially the internet, has brought face-to-face and physically formed communities into a virtual environment. This community is a virtual community when interpersonal interaction occurs with electronic means, and communication is enabled by technology.

Chapter 8
Social Media:
Concept, Role, Categories, Trends, Social Media and AI, Impact on Youth, Careers, Recommendations

Priyanka Garg
Jamia Milia Islamia University, India

Saloni Pahuja
https://orcid.org/0000-0002-0500-0777
Amity University, Noida, India

ABSTRACT

In this age of digitisation social media has become an integral part of our lives. It is an important tool for business decision makers as it enables them to stay connected with their consumers. The firms intend to make profitable use of social media applications such as YouTube, Facebook, Twitter, Pinterest and Mobile Apps. This chapter details out the concept of social media, how it differs from traditional media, the specific categories such as content communities, micro blogging, collaborative websites, social networking sites, live casting, virtual game and social worlds, etc. Further the impact of social media on youth is highlighted. This chapter presents guidelines regarding optimum utilization of social media. Also the strategies to handle different social media activities are discussed

DOI: 10.4018/978-1-7998-2185-4.ch008

INTRODUCTION

When term Social comes we all have a need to be around with like- minded people where we feel comfortable and we can express our ideas, thoughts and expressions. And Media is a medium through which we can connect with others like television, radio, mobile phones, text messages, e-mail, websites, audio, video. Social Media is the way how we use technologies to connect with others and create relationships and build trust. By social networking you are developing and opportunity to create trust which may further lead to more sales. Like if you have any good and bad experience and you want others should know about your experiences then the list is very limited if you share it personally but if you take help of social media it can increase to millions or billions which can influence the reputation of the firm.

"Social media employ mobile and web-based technologies to create highly interactive platforms via which individuals and communities share, co-create, discuss, and modify user-generated content. Given the tremendous exposure of social media in the popular press today, it would seem that we are in the midst of an altogether new communication landscape" (Kietzmann, Hermkens, McCarthy, & Silvestre, 2011).

BACKGROUND

Traditional Media (Radio, Newspaper, Television, Film etc.) was a form where media connects with the people. These act as interface between media and people but it was more of one way communication as we can only know about what media wants to convey but we cannot convey our ideas and views. It started as communication tool when computers were designed and people used websites as medium to share information. It was used by consumers as a platform where they can read, write and can use this media to buy products and services. There was time when we just recognize this media as Facebook and Twitter. The technology has changed exponentially and so are the social media trends. Now the media act as omnipresent as anyone can scroll down the information.

Currently we refer the media which helps us to share the information fast in real time is social media. It is fast and emerging Information exchange. It has actually transformed our life from websites in computer to applications in our smartphone. It transformed the whole interaction. Markets revive and Business has changed the way it does its transactions when attention towards this media has increased. New Virtual market evolved both customers and marketers now treat each other with more respect and pay attention to other needs. The whole way of dealings in the business transformed. It has been started as measuring tool for marketers to measure their results. Lot of marketing efforts is required to make it more successful. This virtual market has shaken the entire business and they have to revive their strategies to survive in this competitive and challenging era where anyone can write anything on social media and has got so much power that it can help in getting fame and can also defame in just one single night. Consumers started utilizing this platform for sharing their views, their contents, their knowledge, their skills, their blogs and the like. It is influencing the whole Market and even the survival of the business. This Media has so much power that it can influence the firm's reputation and even its survival. One has to be updated to survive in this technology driven era. Whether you prefer or not the youth of today is highly influenced by this Media and to meet their demands one must learn this new technique of interacting and engaging.

The current social media has become more user friendly and interactive as communication is two way and it is easier for marketer and customer to spread the news. In early days of this marketing it was difficult to get attention in short time span but now it is very easy to catch the attention of entire word in just one night. From Advertisements to headlines to Facebook to Instagram to twitter to other application based media so many transitions. Social Media is used for sharing, interactions, to mark presence, to build relationships and networking, to influence the consumers, to create image and for some specific purpose as groups. Different social media are defined for each purpose. And thus, each has its own implications and firm should be aware of its purpose and the thus focus on its way of engaging in the social media as per its purpose.

ROLE OF SOCIAL MEDIA IN COMMERCE

Social media, is not just a virtual hangout these days. It is much beyond that, social media is an ecosystem in itself which is affecting individual's life and society at large. Besides having a huge commercial importance, it is also playing a transformational role in affecting the way information being consumed by individuals (Drahošová, Martina, Balco & Peter, 2017).

ROLE IN BRAND MANAGEMENT

When social media site was started, it has an aim to connect people at virtual platform to socialize virtually. But, how would have revenue been generated? If social media would have started its membership fees, then usage would have been much lower. So, the way of generating revenue was providing marketing solutions to advertisers, who pay for the advertisements. Slowly, this media has become the most lucrative way of advertising because of the following reasons:

- **Reaching Target Audience**: These platforms, give choice of targeting audience which seems to be potential customer. An advertiser can choose location based, demographics based or interest based potential customers for targeting instead of targeting the whole mass.
- **Value for Money**: Advertisements here starts at very low rate, and supported with other factors make it value for money as compare to other media.
- **Interactive:** That is the most important part of social media marketing, that it is two-way communication. Marketer can interact with consumers and vice versa. It helps them in market research, taking insights and be more consumer centric.
- **Measurable:** In social media marketing, the budget spent on advertising and ROI achieved can be easily measured. It also gives exact number of the leads generated, audience engaged etc.
- **Responsive to Consumer Complaints**: Earlier, many complaints were never reached to the senior management of the company and were not solved by lower management, which could lead to frustration in consumer, loss of customer and even bad Word of Mouth. Now, many companies have made special pages for resolving consumer complaints immediately.

Social media marketing in itself a domain which has now come up with very innovative way of marketing and influencing customers. No business, whether small or big can afford to have social media absence (Jayasuria et al., 2018).

News Delivery

It is the most used media of reading news. There has been a great drop in the number of newspapers and magazines sold. It has been reported in research studies, that people rely on news which come on social media more compared to traditional source. Moreover, it is convenient and responsive platform for news followers.

Many news channels have started live streaming's on Facebook, a page that is regularly updated. It is advantageous for news company also, as it saves cost and gives measurable audience (Bergström, Annika, & Wadbring, 2010.)

Best part of news at social media is, that it can be reported and delivered by any person (not even journalist). Some of the local news, which is not covered by any newspaper or news channel have become viral on social media and gained attention of public at large.

It also helps in massive social protest against any ongoing or new emerging issue in any area. It calls for an immediate action by the accountable authorities.

For e.g., People tweet if police are not taking action against the complaint, then it calls for immediate action as it reaches to superior authority and general public.

ROLE OF SOCIAL MEDIA IN SOCIETY

Once upon a time social media was not even a known term, but in the past decade, it has led to user addiction owing to greater usage of smartphones, faster internet speeds and increased internet bandwidth. Information is available to users in seconds.

Following ways, it plays a critical role in our life and society in the following ways-

Knowledge Sharing and Skill Building

Social media allows people to share their knowledge and build online community without borders. There are so many pages, social groups, YouTube channel where experts come up with their knowledge and share with public. It is very transformational, as it reaches to even remote areas where they don't get experts in the particular domain.

Not only experts, but novice also gets the opportunity to showcase their talent in the field and gain experience. People can also collaborate with each other, share their skills in particular projects (Ghazali et al., 2016).

Virtual Networking

Social media platforms give everyone an opportunity to be part of virtual network and improve their networking at very little or no cost. People make new alliances, new community and even collaborate to make companies together.

Platform like LinkedIn, which gives professional networking, opens the ocean of opportunity for professionals and job seekers (Mago, Zdenko, 2015).

Virtual Simulating Games

Social media sites like Facebook, have a very good strategy to keep consumers engaged and addicted to the site. That is through virtual games, it requires person to come again and again on site to play next level. People find it very entertaining and simulating to engage in new virtual games. Different kinds of games are there, according to different people's interests (Mago, Zdenko, 2015).

In research, people have said that it helps them releasing their stress too.

Leisure Time/ Social Time

Most of the time, people keep scrolling their social media news' feed just to pass their time. There are some entertaining posts, live video streaming, entertaining videos etc. That keep them busy and enjoying. Tiktok is the good example of using social media apps for time pass, it engages people in making videos and sharing to showcase their talent.

Help in Social Causes

Apart from fun activities, social media has played a significant role in collecting relief funds for social causes. Many crowdfunding organizations, charity organization, disaster relief funds and NGOs have directly collected funds from public at large through social campaigns. Despite of their origin, country base or origin, people come forward in large numbers and have contributed to social causes in best possible way (Akram & Waseem, 2018).

Celebrities' Fan Following

Almost all the celebrities around the world have their social media presence in form of Facebook page, Instagram handle, twitter handle, YouTube channel etc. The celebrities cannot afford to lose their fan following because of social media absence. Every celebrity keeps posting about their updates, regular live streams, new upcoming events and all. These help celebrities in managing and expanding their fan base through interactive media.

In social media, there are new apps and websites coming with added new features to attract more consumers. But still, Facebook and YouTube are the most used platforms.

Categories of Social Media

Social Media is a form of forums which includes different form of medium of spreading the word of mouth including blogs, e-mail, various websites related to product and service ratings and company sponsored discussion boards, Internet discussion forums and chat rooms, microblogs (sites containing digital audio, images, movies, or photographs), and social networking websites, to name a few (Bicen, Huseyin, Cavus & Nadire, 2010).

In some previous studies on social media the categorization of social media has been done on the basis of two characteristics of social media (Zhu & Chen, 2015) that are nature of connection and the level of customizing the messages according to individual particular preferences

Together these two defining characteristics lead to four categories of social media:

1. **Relationship** it represents those platforms which help people in building a relationship with individuals and society at large and personally also. This category is well exemplified by the platforms such as Facebook and LinkedIn.
2. **Self-media** are also profile based platforms with the service of managing their own social media communication channel. The best example is Twitter.

3. **Creative Outlet** are those platforms which are content based and allow users to show their own personal interests and talent. Example of these platforms are Tiktok, YouTube and Instagram.
4. **Collaboration** platforms are content based which help in building a community of likeminded people coming together and sharing questions, advice, news and content of the day example of this are Pinterest, whatsapp group, Facebook groups.

It has various forms of social media application widely used some of them are mentioned in the below:

Audio

It is also a very powerful medium where one can retrieve the information by listening the content, tone, dramatic pauses and all. You have to sit down, relax and hear the sound. It is more interesting way than reading text as it will help you to move to imaginary world and you start thinking creatively and can relate the content you are listening with associated images.

Video

One picture is worth thousand words that is why everyone loves to watch videos and people can retain and connect more through this medium. People trust more on this form of media. They can hear the words, can imagine and connect with what other person is saying, observe the body language and expressions of the person conveying message and thus feel more connected and involved emotionally and mentally. It is said that maximum communication is through body language then through voice and very less through words. So person can have all through this medium. That is why people prefer this form of media.

Microblogging

It is the online medium or form of blogging where the content is short and it is immediately available to the subscribers of the group. It is a mix of blogging and instant messaging and convenient form of messaging like twitter. One can have quick interactions with the subscribers and can share the information with audience instantly. Posts are brief typically 140-200 words and one can read and update it anytime anywhere through any device. It allows text, images, hyperlinks, audio and videos messages. It evolved at the end of WEB 2.0 era. It is easier, more direct way to communicate, time sensitive, convenient and faster mode of communication. Subscribers are also given details about what is relevant for them. Examples of this form of Media are twitter, Instagram and Tumblr. You spent less time in writing and as the content is short you can read more posts and more information in limited time.

Social Networks

It is referred to the virtual community set on common platform, where people make their profile and bring together with other people to interact and share common interests. It has benefit over traditional media, as one can come across of millions of people together for networking.

Examples of social networking are like Facebook, Instagram, pinterest, Linkedin, classmates, twitter, tumblr etc.

Publish

Publish allows to create and publish your content. It can be in the form of blog, picture, graphic or videos. One can publish content on their own account or page which reaches to all the followers at the same time. Publishing can be future scheduled also.

Livecasting

This is widely used application across social media, where you can live cast your events, movies, wedding to those who are unable to attend it physically. Live casting helps in real time interaction of celebrities with fans.

Virtual World

People make social media groups, and find comfort in virtual world. In these virtual community, they share good interpersonal relationship and have quality communication.

Gaming

There are many virtual gaming sites and app, where user can download and play those games with other members virtually, they can collaborate and form teams, without actual presence.

RSS

RSS means Really simple syndication, in this files are read by computer called XML files, that help in automatically updating of information. The information is fetched by user's RSS feed reader, which converts the files into updates (latest) from websites in easy interface. It helps in feed of headlines, notices etc. All content is distributed in real time.

Search

Search options helps in searching anything on the network which is related to the keywords. It goes through the algorithm and bring out close results of desired search. Search Engine Optimization, if you want your customers will be able to find you then you have to make things simple for them (Gironda et al., 2014).

TRENDS IN SOCIAL MEDIA

Popularity of Influencers: Micro celebrities, who have gained huge number of followers on social media through their popular content are called as influencers. Influencers are becoming popular among marketers also, for endorsement of their products.

Realities are Changing with Technology: Realities of life is also highly affected by the technology; it is changing the way we used to live life in traditional times.

Dating is Merging

Online dating is not a new concept, now it is merging with social media as well. Many dating apps link your social media account to dating app which help them finding suitable matches by using machine learning logics.

Serious News Replaced with Trending

People take interest in those news which are trending on social media, they like to comment on that, share that and talk about such news only. On social media, the news which could not become viral is not important at all.

Conversation Through MEMES

People love using memes, stickers and emoji to express their words instead of using actual words.

Social Media and AI (Artificial Intelligence)

As social media is very popular and has the potential to grow in coming times. The use of Artificial Intelligence in social media is imperative to the filter the required information from the ocean of information available. Artificial intelligence through its algorithms has the capacity to filter out the information, it connected with neural networks which helps in location recognition, tagging, image recognition. It gives the closest search result as desired by the person even with common keywords. AI is making its way by giving best user experience on social platforms.

Artificial can read all the digital footprints of the consumer and help in predicting its behaviour by using propensity modelling for predictive analysis. So artificial intelligence is widely used by marketers to reach the targeted audience in minimum cost. It also helps companies in analyzing the consumer insights through the comments or hate speech (Thiraviyam, 2018).

Twitter is using advance AI apps to even crop the photographs for maximizing their aesthetic output. In this machine learning reads eye track, it records where the person look at first and the most, and this way AI helps making photograph more appealing. It helps marketers in continuous and personalised marketing to the consumers (Zeng et al., 2010).

Impact of Social Media on Indian Youth

Youth now a day is all time busy and engaged in various forms of Social Media. This is the most common routine activity of them. Websites that allow any form of social interaction is social media website like Facebook, twitter, Instagram, snapchat, Face-App, Gaming sites, Virtual worlds, video streaming such as you tube, blogs writing and many more. Now interaction is not just limited to one room or building but you can connect to all the persons having same interests around the world. The usage of social media sites has exponentially increased in recent time. Youth enjoys the content and have more options to share their ideas, experiences, thoughts and building relationships. It has both positive and negative impact on the Youth. On one side they will be able to have more information, knowledge sharing, new ways of learning and awareness about everything around them, build connections, enhance their technical skills on other side if not used in a proper and healthy way it can result into various problems related to emotional, physical and mental health such as cyberbullying, depression, frauds, sexting, exposure to inappropriate content and many more. As the deviations are increasing so parents have to me more aware and thus restrict their usage to only those sites which are relevant for them and make sure they track their activities so that they can help, safeguard and guide them properly when required.

Social media give more learning opportunities to the Youth, they can explore new angles, socialize, communicate, enhance their creativity, generate new ideas, get information related to health so many endless benefits if used in proper way. Effects of SNS on Social and emotional development of child are many (Christofferson, 2016). But as we all know excess of everything is bad and youth is giving much more time and energy to this media leading to addiction. More usage can lead to addiction and sleep related issues also.

On the other hand, it is very difficult for parents to track every activity of their child on this platform. Not every parent is aware of the usage and technicalities of this media. There is a gap between the knowledge and skills of child and parent. They cannot relate to all their activities as they are not tech savvy. Parents having digital awareness can guide more but still deviations are many.

There is numerous education related sites where students can collaborate and exchange information. They help them in learning new skills, enhancing their creative side, increasing knowledge and also give chances to explore and showcase their creative side by content creation activities. There are dating sites which can distract the youth if used before the required age. Adolescent age is the most challenging age for parent to handle. During last few years' usage of this media has increased by teenagers. They visit sites more than 10 times a day. Almost 75% of teenagers are on social media despite of having knowledge about what they should post and what not. They just enjoy the entertainment, likes and comments.

This Generation social, mental and emotional development is majorly dependent on the social media. As they experiment more, less self-regulated and are more susceptible to peer pressure so the risk associated are more such as Cyber bullying, privacy issues, Facebook depression, sexual experimentation, peer-to-peer pressure, inappropriate content; third-party influences (O'Keeffe & Clarke, 2011).

So this social media is impacting the youth and their value system also. Young adults likely to own their mobile phones and from watching current news to posting personal information to listening music, video streaming, Online Shopping, gaming, getting fitness and health related information and the like they are depend on Social media. They know the power of this form of media thus always prefer to be updated and visit regularly on this platform. They love to spend much time on Social networking sites. Teens also started demanding laptops and mobile phone as they want to be updated and to have more technical skills required for keeping pace with current advance scenario and peer pressure. With less awareness about the technicalities and terms and conditions they are more prone to negative effects of this media. (Lenhart et al., 2010) Teens spend their time watching videos, handling various apps which can leak their personal information, on gaming sites and all. It is affecting their concentration, learning abilities, mental development making them addictive and facing much big problems related to health and emotional well-being.

With more advancement and more distractions there come more responsibility of parents and other government authorities. Many researches have proved that this media is impacting the overall life of adults, teens, adolescents and their families. It has both positive and negative impact. The effects are accordingly how we are using this platform. Uses are endless if used in proper way with proper awareness and care.

CAREERS IN SOCIAL MEDIA

Since past decade, Social Media has become a big domain of career choice and has good demand in industry. Social media is being taught has separate course in many education institutes, which helps people in gaining the skills required for the job. Social media career is growing at faster pace than traditional marketing jobs. One can find lucrative career in social media with growing demand and salary.

Following are few career options which are currently in demand:

Director of Social Media

With a degree in marketing or management, one can learn social media marketing tools. Director of Social media marketing is role where complete planning, developing and implementation of social media for company is required to be done. This role is overseeing role and expect director of social media to be responsible and work with multiple social media platforms at the same time.

Brand Manager

Brand manager requires strong marketing communication and analytical skills. Brand Manager will be responsible in promoting the brand's identity across all social media platforms and networking sites. Brand manager can work as in-house for single brand management or can work with agency handling multiple brands' social media profile to create strong brand value.

Digital Content Manager

Digital content manager will be responsible for streamlining digital identity of an organization across social media platforms. Job responsibilities will be content development, creating schedule to post social media content and also optimizing webs content for organic search. Digital content manager needs to have strong communication skills with degree in Mass media, advertising, or content writing (Anonymous, 2016).

Business on Social Media

Social media sites like Facebook, Instagram have created many small businessman and trader, who can do reselling of the product through their social network. Many people are selling their self- manufactured through social media sites only. Service providers like accountants, lawyers, photographers, wedding planners have also built their business through social media. It gives wide reach across the globe, even without having physical workplace.

Youtuber/ Video Blogger

YouTube has given birth to altogether a new lucrative career stream, which is named as "You Tuber"; this career is very famous not only amongst youngsters but housewives, kids and oldage people also. For this career, person doesn't need any degree, it requires only showcasing of talent. Successful youtubers are earning in millions which one can never earn in conventional jobs. In this person can upload its informative or entertaining video, according to number of views and ads clicked on that video, YouTube will pay the uploader. Moreover, if someone has built good subscribers' list on YouTube one can earn by becoming influencer of brand through his videos.

RECOMMENDATIONS TO HANDLE SOCIAL MEDIA

Be Active: You must be active on Social Media if you want to have its benefits otherwise it can create a bad image of your business i.e. Create accounts on relevant platforms where you can regularly visit and engage actively. Just for the sale of marketing do not open so many accounts and end up as pretender having list of inactive accounts with no activity. Users do not like such retailers who do not engage actively and do respond to their queries timely. It is better to not enter into this pool if you cannot actively engage on daily basis.

Focus on What is Relevant for Customer Not Just About You: Retailers generally make this mistake by just talking about what is important for them rather than customer. You must provide the details which are relevant for your customers and engage them so well that they share your information with others. Ask for their opinions, their preferences, expectations, create a dialogue so that they feel concerned and connected leading to engaged followers.

Make it Impressive by Including Images

Whenever you share content and want your post to go viral try to make it more interactive and impressive by including images in your posts. Your aim is to increase your followers which will be possible when the content posted by you will be shared largely. The chances of getting sharing post over any network increases when it has images with clear content. Thus one can build large networks.

Do Not Exaggerate and Modify the Facts

Public is very smart now a day. They have so many channels of communication and information sharing. Share what is relevant and true. Do not include doubtful information as it can be problematic for you and can result in defame and bad reputation in the market.

Research and Then Post

Social Media is very quick but again it demands time and your intellect if you are spreading information related to your business. Do your homework prior to posting anything such as what will be the target audience which should be targeted for spreading of information, who should see and how to post the content to have maximum chances of sharing of that information among your target audience and the like. Right time and right way of posting the details about your product and services is very important. You can take help of experts if you are not having knowledge in this area.

DISADVANTAGES OF SOCIAL MEDIA

Exposure to too Much of Information

As social media is flooded with news feed, some of them are not even relevant to us and at times misleading. Also, marketers in order to promote their product send updates daily, which creates lot of white noise. When a person scrolls through such information, subconsciously he is consuming bit of every information which may affect him adversely. For example, political arguments in which lot of people impose their opinions on every other person reading it, it is very disturbing to be part of such virtual arguments.

At times, people keep sharing any news without even checking its credibility, and later it is discovered that it was fake or distorted. In fact, fake news gets more attention and get viral as compare to original important news (Browning, Gerlich, &Westermann, 2011).

Privacy Issues on Social Sites

This is much considered issue by consumers and service providers also. Since beginning, people are very much concerned about their privacy. As when you share your data through social media, its copy is created and kept in cloud storage by service provider, if it is hacked your personal data will be stolen easily.

Service providers have provided lots of privacy settings, which enables users to provide access of your data to the people you want. Still, when you are doing social networking, trust issues are there. Many people make fake account and socialize for malice intention behind.

The user agreements by service providers of social media apps makes you agreed while signing up that they can keep your content and can even use it without attribution, including all your information (K. Wong, A. Wong, Yeung et al., 2014).

It is even more dangerous to share your current location, through which hacker can trace your address and can be used in crimes (W. Luo, Y. Lu, Zhao et al., 2017).

You might become a target if you share your current location over social media. Your employer can choose to fire you if they disagree with something that you shared over your network. If you share too much with the public, there could be problems that develop which will never resolve as the information releases.

There is concern of nudity over social media, people misusing personal photographs (Kim & Kim, 2017).

Stress of Peer Pressure

As lot many people share their about life's happening on social media, it creates lot of peer pressure on other people to do that much in their lives to show off.

"If you are not sharing your hotel check ins, airport check ins, foreign travel stories, then people start taking you for granted on social media as you if you are a looser", this is the opinion shared by most of the Facebook users.

Lot of many people get complexed by seeing other people's achievements, travelling to exquisite places, showing off new car etc. It makes people feel lot of stress, when they can't do more such things which they can show off. They feel struggle to fit in the groups of peers online.

Cyber Stalking

Social media made easier for stalkers to get the information which was not otherwise available. When people share about their life's daily events, sharing locations with check ins, stalkers easily get all the where about even without visiting the place. This can lead to planning of serious crimes also.

Cyber Bullying

This impacts teens and young adults the most. When some of the classmate starts negative comments online, it spread even at faster rate which leads to joining more other people in bullying. Such bullying comments lead to anxiety, loss of control, depression and high level of stress. At times, people use fake accounts to bully other, so it becomes even more difficult to control such acts. It has been reported that people who are bullied online are more likely to attempt suicide or harm themselves in other ways (Kiriakidis & Kavoura,2010)

There must be awareness campaigns regarding such activities, which must involve parents for counselling and training (Mesch, 2009).

Substituting Online Interactions for their Offline Relationships.

As we can connect to any number of people online, we can interact with them without even taking physical efforts to meet. It saves time, but it has been seen that people who are very active on social media are not as confident in meeting people in real. When we meet people in person, it strengthens our relationships and interpersonal skills. Moreover, people behave differently online as they are not actually, which may lead to different personality disorder. (Mesch, Gustavo, & Ilan, 2006)

No Outdoor Activities

Social media is so engaging and addictive that people prefer not to go out and do some physical activities. This is causing serious health problem, as exposure to screen time is increasing, body is becoming lethargic. When a person doesn't do physical exercise, it makes him weak and more prone to diseases.

Severe Addiction and Distraction for Some People

Some people specially youngsters spend too much time on social media, that can lead to behavioural addiction, according to psychology this can lead to problematic behaviour in other areas of life. (Kandell, 1998; Griffiths, 2000).

Social media apps cause severe distractions, as it never sleeps. Every minute you keep getting some or other notifications to distract. People have cultivated an addiction to check their phones again and again even if there is no notification. Normally a person has average screen time of 4-5 hours per day, which costs you lot of important things which could have been done (Charlton, 2002).

This can be minimized, by fixing the time per day to check your social media profile instead of going through it multiple times per day.

Disrupting Sleep Cycle

When you are exposed to screens of Smartphones, TV or laptop, the radiations affect your brain, it can change your sleeping pattern. It can even lead to insomnia or difficulty in falling asleep. The blue light radiations that come from electronic devices is simulating as well, but most important cause of sleeplessness is your brain start thinking about other people's profile and comparing their life.

CONCLUSIONS

Social media and networking is revolutionary advancement in the way people interact with each other and the world at large. Its customization and yet wide reach gives an edge over other medias. It helps us to stay connected with our family and friends even if there is physical distance. It has given contribution in helping people learn new skills, participate in debates, attending current events through live cast and networking by building a borderless community. Social Media has given a virtual platform and has changed the way business used to perform, it has changed the way consumers used to consume information. Yet there is a dark side of social media which has not only affected privacy of people by having access to their data, but has also given rise to cybercrimes through it. Companies are using data unethically to manipulate people about their products. There must be strict rules and laws pertaining to data usage by the corporates.

Though there are Pros and Cons of Social Media, but it cannot be avoided by anyone. One must take care of the disadvantages of social media, use it optimally and carefully in order to avoid any problems to ourselves or any other person.

REFERENCES

Agarwal, N., Liu, H., Tang, L., & Yu, P. S. (2008). *Identifying the influential bloggers in a community*. WSDM. doi:10.1145/1341531.1341559

Akram, W. (2018). A study on positive and negative effects of social media on society. *International Journal on Computer Science and Engineering*, *5*. doi:10.26438/ijcse/v5i10.351354

Anonymous. (2016, Nov. 24). *Careers in communication*. Retrieved from https://study.com/articles/careers_in_social_networking.html

Bergström, A., & Wadbring, I. (2010). The contribution of free dailies and news on the web: implications of media structural changes for the Swedish newspaper readership market. *Northern Lights*, *8*(1), 139–155. doi:10.1386/nl.8.139_1

Bicen, H., & Cavus, N. (2010). The most preferred social network sites by students. *Procedia: Social and Behavioral Sciences*, *2*(2), 5864–5869. doi:10.1016/j.sbspro.2010.03.958

Brin, S., & Page, L. (1998). The anatomy of a large-scale hypertextual Web search engine. *Computer Networks and ISDN Systems*, *30*(1-7), 1–7. doi:10.1016/S0169-7552(98)00110-X

Browning, L., Gerlich, R., & Westermann, L. (2011). The new HD classroom: A “Hyper Diverse” approach to engaging with students. *Journal Of Instructional Pedagogies,* 1-10. Retrieved from http://www.aabri.com/manuscripts/10701.pdf

Cha, M., Haddadi, H., Benevenuto, F., & Gummadi, K. P. (2010): Measuring user influence in Twitter: the million follower fallacy. In 4th International AAAI Conference on Weblogs and Social Media, ICWSM (2010).

Charlton, J. (2002). A factor-analytic investigation of computer ‘addiction’ and engagement. *British Journal of Psychology*, *93*(3), 329–344. doi:10.1348/000712602760146242 PMID:12230834

Drahošová, M., & Balco, P. (2017). The analysis of advantages and disadvantages of use of social media in European Union. *Procedia Computer Science*, *109*, 1005–1009. doi:10.1016/j.procs.2017.05.446

Galuba, W., Aberer, K., Chakraborty, D., Despotovic, Z., & Kellerer, W. (2010): Outtweeting the Twitterers - predicting information cascades. In Microblogs 3rd Workshop on Online Social Networks, WOSN (2010).

Ghazali, Saadiah&Sulaiman, Nor Intan, & Zaibidi, Nerda, & Omar, MohdFaizal, & Alias, Rose. (2016). The impact of knowledge sharing through social media among academia. doi:. doi:10.1063/1.4966060

Gironda, J. T., & Korgaonkar, P. K. (2014). Understanding consumers’ social networking site usage. *Journal of Marketing Management*, *30*(5–6), 571–605. doi:10.1080/0267257X.2013.851106

Grifiths, M. (2010). Internet abuse and internet addiction in the workplace. *Journal of Workplace Learning*, *22*(7), 463–472. doi:10.1108/13665621011071127

Jansen, B., Zhang, M., Sobel, K., & Chowdury, A. (2009). Twitter power: Tweets as electronic word of mouth. *Journal of the American Society for Information Science and Technology*, *60*(11), 2169–2188. doi:10.1002/asi.21149

Jayasuriya, N., Azam, S. M., Khatibi, A., & Dharmaratne, I. (2018). The role of social media marketing on brand equity-a literature review. *Global Journal of Management and Business Research*, XVIII.

Kandell, J. (1998). Internet addiction on campus: The vulnerability of college students. *Cyberpsychology & Behavior*, *1*(1), 11–17. doi:10.1089/cpb.1998.1.11

Kietzmann, J. H., Hermkens, K., McCarthy, I. P., & Silvestre, B. S. (2011). Social media? Get serious! Understanding the functional building blocks of social media. *Business Horizons*, *54*(3), 241–251. doi:10.1016/j.bushor.2011.01.005

Kim, B., & Kim, Y. (2017). College students' social media use and communication network heterogeneity: Implications for social capital and subjective well-being. *Computers in Human Behavior*, *73*, 620–628. doi:10.1016/j.chb.2017.03.033

Kiriakidis, S. P., & Kavoura, A. (2010). A review of the literature on harassment through the internet and other electronic means. *Family & Community Health*, *11*(2), 82–93. doi:10.1097/FCH.0b013e3181d593e4 PMID:20216351

Leskovec, J., Adamic, L. A., & Huberman, B. A. (2006). The dynamics of viral marketing. In *Proceedings of the 7th ACM Conference on Electronic Commerce (pp. 228-237).*

Luo, W., Lu, Y., Zhao, D., & Jiang, H. (2017). On location and trace privacy of the moving object using the negative survey. IEEE Transactions on Emerging Topics in Computational Intelligence, 1(2), 125-134.

Mago, Z. (2015). Games on social networks and the promotion within. Studia Ekonomiczne: Marketing communication – selected issues, 14. 49-58.

Mangold, W. G., & Faulds, D. J. (2009). Social media: The new hybrid element of the promotion mix. *Business Horizons*, *52*(4), 357–365. doi:10.1016/j.bushor.2009.03.002

Mesch, G., & Talmud, I. (2006). The quality of online and offline relationships: the role of multiplexity and duration of social relationships. *The Information Society*, *22*(3), 137–148. doi:10.1080/01972240600677805

Mesch, G. S. (2009). Parental mediation, online activities, and cyberbullying. *Cyberpsychology & Behavior*, *12*(4), 387–393. doi:10.1089/cpb.2009.0068 PMID:19630583

Mesch, G. S. (2009). Parental mediation, online activities, and cyberbullying. *Cyber Psychology & Behavior, 12*(4), 387-393. doi:10.1089/cpb.2009.0068

Weng, J., Lim, E.-P., Jiang, J., & He, Q. (2010, February). Twitterrank: finding topic-sensitive influential twitterers. In Proceedings of the third ACM international conference on Web Search and Data Mining (pp. 261-270). ACM.

Wong, K., Wong, A., Yeung, A., Fan, W., & Tang, S.-K. (2014). Trust and privacy exploitation in online social networks. *IT Professional, 16*(5), 28–33. doi:10.1109/MITP.2014.79

Zeng, D., Chen, H., Lusch, R., & Li, S. (2010). Social media analytics and intelligence. *IEEE Intelligent Systems, 25*(6), 13–16. doi:10.1109/MIS.2010.151

Zhu, Y.-Q., & Chen, H.-G. (2015). Social media and human need satisfaction: implications for social media marketing. *Business Horizons, 58*(3), 335–345. doi:10.1016/j.bushor.2015.01.006

KEY TERMS AND DEFINITIONS:

Artificial Intelligence: The ability of a digital computer or computer-controlled robot to perform tasks commonly associated with intelligent beings. It refers to the simulation of human intelligence in machines that are programmed to think like humans and mimic their actions. The term may also be applied to any machine that exhibits traits associated with a human mind such as learning and problem-solving.

Blogs: A website or web page which is updated regularly and typically run by an individual or small group on which contents or text is written in an informal or conversational style.

Competitive Advantage: A competitive advantage is the unique ability of a firm to utilize its resources effectively, managing to improve customer value and position itself ahead of the competition. In other words, it's something that a company does better than its competitors because of some proprietary process, service, or brand.

Content Communities: Content communities allow users to share online multimedia materials. Popular content communities include YouTube, Flickr, and SlideShare. After registering for an account, individuals upload their materials, describe them, and make them publicly available.

Live Casting: A webcast that is streamed live, often combined with an integrated chat forum for those watching.

Media Trends: Anything which is trending can be any topic, event or individual which a lot of people are discussing or mentioning on social media.

Microblogging: Microblogging is a web service that allows the subscriber to broadcast short messages to other subscribers of the service. Micro-posts can be made public on a Web site and/or distributed to a private group of subscribers. Subscribers can read microblog posts online or request that updates be delivered in real time to their desktop as an instant message or sent to a mobile device as an SMS text message.

Social Media: Websites and applications that enable users to create and share content or any medium that helps the users to participate in social networking.

Social Networking Sites: A social networking site is an online platform that allows users to create a public profile and interact with other users on the website. Social networking sites usually have a new user input a list of people with whom they share a connection and then allow the people on the list to confirm or deny the connection.

Virtual Market: A simulation of the real marketplace where buyers and sellers meet to negotiate transactions.

Chapter 9
Social Media Usage in Online Consumer Decision Process and Buying Behaviour

Lydia Andoh-Quainoo
Pentecost University College, Ghana

ABSTRACT

This chapter examines the usage of social media in predicting consumer buying process. A mixed method approach has been applied, a cross sectional survey and in-depth interviews were conducted in three universities in Ghana. The responses were collected from individuals in the age group of 18 -30. Data was analysed using Logistics Regression and Thematic analyses. The findings revealed that the social media behaviour of young consumers could significantly influence their behaviour at the pre-purchase information search and evaluation levels. The findings suggest young consumers are more likely to use social media for marketing activities such as purchasing, hence industries should redirect more activities towards this digital channel. This implies that social media is driving young consumers into e-commerce and that presents a huge opportunity for business and marketers.

INTRODUCTION

Social media has emerged as technology beyond cell phone and one of the most dynamic, interdisciplinary socially facilitated media of contemporary society (Kaplan & Haenlein, 2010; Hjorth & Hendry, 2015). Social media combines wed 2.0 and social networking technological applications to connect users to a wide range of sites such Facebook, Wechat, Instagram etc. (Wei, Huang & Zheng, 2018). Social media

DOI: 10.4018/978-1-7998-2185-4.ch009

comprises of different digital network platforms including Social Networking Sites (SNS). SNS's are platforms where individuals are able to connect with others on sites such as Facebook, Myspace, Whatapp, Instagram, Twitter, Wechat, Snapchat, etc to share information, personal images, blogs and others (Khan, 2017; Pookulangara & Koesler, 2011). Social networking sites have become the most popular aspect of social media and it is used for social connection, for sharing of media content, for academic work and searching for and buying of goods and services generated by these contents (Watulak & Whitefield, 2016). This is followed by social news sites, internet sites that feature users-posted stories. Such stories are graded based on popularity, as voted on by other users of the site or by site administrators. It's also known as Social Bookmarking sites and they include Digg, Reddit, and Scoop. Another aspect of social media is the media sharing sites which permits users to upload your photos, videos and audio to or from other sites anywhere in the world. One predominant example of social media sharing site is YouTube.com where most people share videos with others and tag them. There is also yet another form of social media referred to as blogging which is publication on the World Wide Web consisting of discrete, diary-style entries referred to as post.

Emergent usage behaviour on social media and social networking sites is growing higher among young consumers especially college students. Carter & Yeo (2016) reported that young university students both undergraduates and postgraduates on daily basis averagely use chat about 20 times especially familiar social networking sites such as Wechat, Twitter, Facebook, Whatsapp and Instagram (Khan, 2017; Whiting & Williams, 2013). Due to the prolific usage of social media, its usage in businesses is becoming growing significantly (Ioanas & Stoica, 2014). Although, Social media presents a digital media challenge to businesses and marketers in view of the fact that it is totally different from traditional media and other digital media. It portrays a dual communication channel which demonstrate superior business interaction and effective tool which offers more power to customers (Keegan & Rowley, 2017). Yet there is an increasing usage for this digital media at different levels of business processes

The important role of social media in emergent business and marketing practices cannot be over emphasized as it serves different functions in e-commerce processes including communication, brand building, market space, customer engagements, customer relationship management and market research and intelligence (Ioanas & Stoica, 2014; Song &Yoo, 2016; Zhang, 2017). Social media in recent times has taken dominance in communicating the value of products and services and creating a superior customer experiences in digital marketplace. Businesses and marketers are engaging in social media strategies to reach and engage customers in various ways such as advertising, promotion, branding, data and viral marketing, other commercial activities on social media. Social networks have become a platform for enhancing the overall marketing strategy Social Media content are used to access and generate product and services and build product referrals and responses (Dolan et al., 2015).

Customers are be able to monitor their favorite brands, post questions and make comments related to services or products on social media platforms like Facebook, Twitter, Youtube and Instagram. Businesses on the other hand have developed digital competences to connect directly with consumers, engage in business interactions and ascertain discussions about their brands through these social media platforms. Due to the usage of social media in the shopping experiences of consumers there is growing interest in social media consumer decision and buying behaviour (Ioanas & Stoica, 2014; Pookulangara & Koesler, 2011; Zhang et al., 2017)

However, there has been limited research focus on online social media and consumer decision making. Few studies have been directed at the social media decision making at managerial level. For instance, Keegan and Rowley (2017) posit that social media should be planned, implemented and evaluated at the managerial levels to ascertain the achievement of marketing objectives based on key performance indicators. Some have researches have also focused on smart phone usage online purchasing behaviour (Arif, Aslam & Ali, 2016; Byrne & Rowley, 2013). While a few have concentrated on the use of social media in the various stages of the consumer decision process (Song & Yoo, 2016). However the extent to which social media is used in daily information searching, selection and choosing products and services online is low and that provides more room for research in this aspect of social media.

This chapter therefore seeks to explore the extent to which Social media is used in consumer decision process or how it can be applied in social media purchasing behaviour by young consumers. The core contribution of this chapter is to contribute to knowledge on social media facilitated daily consumer decision and buying activities and the integration into online consumer decision process and buying behaviour.

THEORETICAL BACKGROUND

Consumer Buying Behaviour

Consumer behavior is the study of individuals, groups or organizations and the behaviour they exhibit during the selecting, securing, using of product and services to satisfy their needs . Consumer behavior can be defined as the behavior consumer's display in searching for, purchasing, using, evaluating, and disposing of products and services that they expect will satisfy their need. (Schiffman & Kanuk, 2010). It focuses on what people spend valuable resources such as money, time and energy in consumables. Consumer behaviour involves studying how people buy, what they buy, when they buy and why they buy when consumers are making purchasing decisions, the pass through the processes of recognition, (Blackwell, Miniard, & Engel, 2006). Consumer buying behaviour is influenced by two major factors. These factors are individual and environmental. The major categories of individual psychological factors affecting consumer behaviour are, consumer Knowledge, perception, learning, motivation, personality, beliefs, attitudes and life styles. The second category of factors is environmental factors. Environmental factors represent those items outside of the individual that affect individual consumer's buying behaviour process. These factors include culture, social class, reference group, family and household. The above mentioned factors are the major determinants behind the firmness of consumers to opt for a given good or service (Blackwell, Miniard, & Engel, 2006). Consumers' physical and social environment has huge influences on consumers' buying behaviour and can make a big difference in their desire and motives for product purchase.

In recent times the emergence digital media has transformed consumer buying behaviour due to the shift in retail platforms to the digital market space. Digital media consumer behaviour such as smart phone and social media behaviour has become distinct from offline buying behaviour and has emerged as online buying, significant to consumer buying and consumption behaviours. Through social media consumers have access to a global retail market both locally and far from their domestic market. This offers them a numerous opportunity to have more product information such as product offering, prices and demand for customized services (Holmes, Byrne & Rowley, 2013; Sunil, 2015). This has offered more opportunities for consumers to have access to a huge amount of information and social media has become a major channel for the supply of such information. Customers disseminate voluntarily information to one another through social media (Ioanas & Stoica, 2014; Pookulangara & Koesler, 2011). Consumers also search for a lot of information about products and services which they expect will satisfy their needs better. They also receive ratings and feedback from rated consumer experiences (Sunil, 2015) through the use of social media. Social media therefore plays a key role in the whole decision process. Consumers have a higher need for information particularly, product information. Social media has improved significantly the manner in which consumers receive information from different industries on many products and services. It has also influences the information needs; information obtained and has transformed the way consumers integrate information searching at during the various stages in the Consumer Decision Process (CDP) (Zha, 2019; Zhang, 2017).

The Consumer Decision Model

Consumer decision-making models have been widely used in consumer behavior studies especially for offline consumer behaviour. Consumer decision-making

Figure 1. Consumer decision model

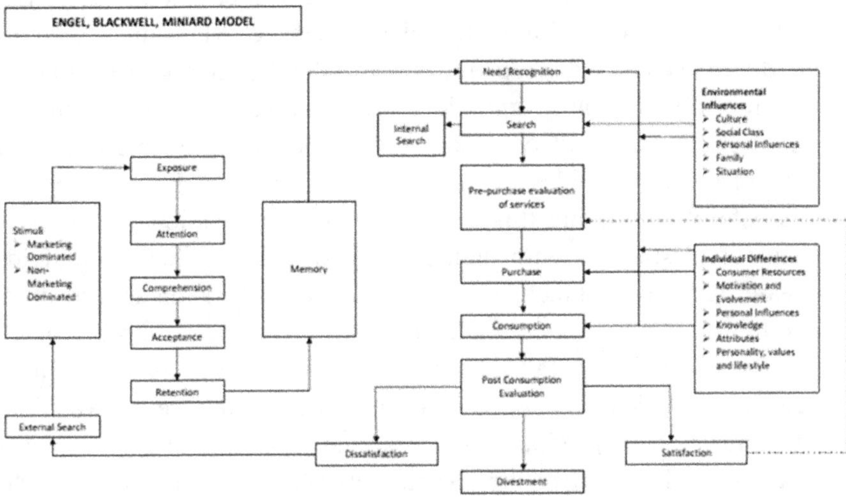

Source: Blackwell, Miniard and Engel, 2001: Rau and Samiee, 1981; Foxall, 1980.

has long been of interest to researchers leading to a number of models that try to explain the stages that a consumer goes through when making a buying behavior. However, one of the most popular contemporary consumer behavior model is the Engel-Blackwell-Miniard Model which has receive constant advancement for the last four decades, improving understanding of consumer behavior theory and knowledge by (Blackwell et al., 2001)

There are three major stages involved as consumers attempt to buy before the final action of buying. These include; pre-purchase, purchase and post purchase. The cognitive decision sequence are further broken down into core seven -point model based on; problem identification, search for information search (internal and external), evaluation of alternatives, purchasing and post purchasing decision. The seven point decision process can be categorized broadly into pre-purchase, purchase and post purchase and are discussed below:

Pre-Purchase Stage

The pre-purchase stage is considered to be a preliminary stage whereby the consumer can get know needs and make the necessary steps towards fulfillment of the need. The pre-purchase stage is where consumers recognize a need, search for information and conduct pre-purchase evaluations to decide ad select the best option of the product or service they intend to buy.

Problem recognition is the first step of consumers' buying behaviour process that may occur because consumer has an expected state desired to be attained than the current state. Problem recognition takes place whenever a consumer recognizes a significant difference and a discrepancy between the desired and the actual state of affairs, which is in sufficient magnitude to arouse and activate the buying process (Schiffman & Kanuk, 2010). Consumers' buying behaviour begins with the result of problems or a single problem. Consumers at different stages portray different behaviours before buying and this stage give them motivation to continue with other behaviours associated with their need recognition. When an individual is triggered externally, for instance, a person may see a television advertisement for a vacation, the stimuli triggers thoughts or ideas about the possibility of making a buying (Kotler and Keller 2009). Digital technologies such as Smart phone and social media has drastically changed consumer needs and have allowed for much greater customization of products, services, and promotional messages than do older marketing tools (Schiffman & Kanuk, 2010). These technological changes have been designated as one of the major factors causing changes in the market and customers behaviour.

Once a problem is recognized, consumers begin to seek pertinent information from internal and external sources about the product and services they desire. Internal search involves the consumers' memory on what is known about the product, while external search includes word of mouth, stores visit, trial and online, information, advertisements and social media. The social media environment effectively allows consumers to use such tools in buying behaviour and the Internet has become an important tool for information search.

Information search is very critical in consumer buying decision and behaviour and social media has become an important source of information in online consumer behaviour. For instance, in the Hotel Industry, it has been found that social media plays a critical role at the pre-travel stage in searching for and obtaining the relevant information. That is, social media becomes the main tool used in travel arrangement by customers before moving (Varkaris & Nuehofer, 2017).

The next step to evaluate available options from the total consideration set to the choice set of two or three products. Alternative evaluation process sets in and depending on their motives or goals of purchase; consumers establish criteria for evaluating weighing options. Based on set criteria consumers start to compare and evaluate several alternatives in terms of products features and their desires. Sometimes consumers' choices may be complex and may the consideration of alternatives best to fulfill their needs (Blythe, 2008; Schiffman & Kanuk; 2010).

Purchase Decision and Consumption

When consumers find alternatives and evaluate them based on their selection criteria, they make their choice among the alternatives by purchasing them. The choice can be influenced by the gathered information from different including mobile phone and social media (Hawkins & Mothers Baugh, 2010; Song & Yoo 2015). Purchase behaviour also include the consumption of goods and services.at the consumption stage consumers seek information on how the product or service is used.

Post Purchase Evaluation Behaviour

After the consumption, the consumer then experiences certain levels of satisfaction or dissatisfaction, and evaluates the wisdom of the choice made in selecting the alternative. Two potential outcomes are derived from this phase – satisfaction or dissonance. When consumer experiences dissonance towards the buying, the choice is 'devaluated' and the consumer begins the process of searching, obtaining information and evaluating other options for future buying decision, in which triggers new behaviour. It is a phase when the consumer decides whether or not to move from merely implementing the product to a full adaption; that is, whether to use the product repeatedly or repurchase or not. The quality of their conclusion becomes important in this stage of steps and how well the choice worked out. Consumers compare their perceptions and experiences of the product with their expectations.

With the advent of digital media such as computer, smart phone and social media, consumers are constantly online creating and sharing content with others. Such technological behaviour has also influenced the behaviour of consumers in online purchasing decisions and behaviour in this new digital market. At the post purchase stage evidence suggest that consumer experiences and satisfaction influence the word of mouth and repeat purchase in mobile and social media commerce (San-Martin et al., 2016). Once more, the process of shopping has also evolved and revolutionized since the emergence of digital media technology. Consumers search for products and services and others needs through digital means such as smartphone and social media (Sunil, 2015). It is therefore important to explore the use of social media in online consumer decision and behaviour.

The Influence of Social Media in the Online Consumer Decision Process

Consumer decision process has been migrated unto the digital media platform where there is pre-purchase, purchase and post purchase activities are displayed. In applying the consumer decision model to the digital media online buying behaviour researchers have considered the use of smart phone and social media in the different stages of the model that can be well applicable and better utilized by online consumers in order to facilitate effective online customer strategy. Others have also focused on industries and online products which yield themselves better for the application of the consumer decision model (Song &Yoo, 2015; Varkaris & Neuhofer, 2017). Findings suggest that using smart phone and social media remains relevant and significantin the online consumer decision process and buying behaviour (Holmes et al., 2013; Song &Yoo, 2015; Sunil, 2015; Varkaris & Neuhofer, 2017). Holmes et al., 2013 reported that in the UK smart phone usage remains highest with products which have higher emotional involvement. Also, there is high usage of smart phone at the pre-purchase stage where needs are recognized, information is searched and alternatives are evaluated than during actual purchase.

According to Varkaris and Neuhofer, (2017) consumer decision making using social media has not changed but it rather been adapted in the new digital system where brands on social media are observed and selected based online reviews help consumers to come up with consideration set and pre purchase evaluation. Although not much has been done on social media, evidence from some studies suggest a remarkable usage of social media in searching for and evaluating particularly at the pre purchase stages in e-commerce. In online buying process consumers use social media to identify needs, search for products and services and select product and service brands (Varkaris & Neuhofer, 2017). Other findings also suggest that using social media can be critical in pre-purchase stage when using a service and support customers in making decision for engaging in the service process (Song & Yoo, 2015; Sunil, 2013). Other reports also shows that social media benefits such as functional and monetary including convenience, and coupon all facilitate the pre purchase stage of buying particularly the pre-purchase evaluation and information search (Song & Yoo, 2015).

The Influence of Social Media in Information Search and Evaluation

Social media usage in consumer decision process remains higher at the information search level and consideration n of alternatives where they are more likely to compare brands and prices for pre-purchase evaluation, particularly, where the emotional involvement is high on the product or service in question (Byrne & Rowley, 2013; Varkaris & Neuhofer, 2017). Social media exposes consumers to new shopping related information. Zhang et al. (2017) reported that the cumulative usage of social networking sites could be positively associated with online shopping activities. This has made information generation and sharing critical at the pre-purchase information stage of consumer buying behaviour. According to Jha, (2019) social media influences information at different stages of customer's decision making particularly at the searching stage. Social media user generated information such as customer reviews creates positive perception towards online purchasing which fosters intention to buy and actual online buying. This implies that social media usage does not only foster information search but also in evaluation and actual selection.

The use of social media in service information, pre-purchase evaluation and actual buying has been high in service industries. Song and Yoo (2016) focused on the role of social media during the pre-purchase stage in hotel and restaurants and found that social media support consumer decision significantly in their selection of these services. It was reported that there is a positive relationship between function and monetary benefits obtained from social media during the pre-purchase stage. The functional benefits are mainly information search, exchange of information, past experiences from other users which monetary benefits included coupons, price rebates and special offers. This has been supported by Varkaris & Neuhofer, (2017) who also reported that in the Hospitality industry, specifically hotel search, evaluation and selection, social media plays a major role. Consumer use social media channels for comprehensive search using trip Advisor predominantly. This was followed by Facebook, Instagram, Youtube and Twitter. They use such channels to search, compare and evaluate the hotels which they have a need to use.

To this end it was necessary to examine social media use in consumer decision and buying behaviour especially at the pre-purchase stage in young consumers (Arif et al., 2016; Song & Yoo, 2015; Varkaris & Neuhofer, 2017).

Social Media Use and Information Search by Youth in Ghana

Social media usage in young people includes information gathering and sharing of content as well as interactions with friends and relatives. Social networking sites have become the most popular aspect of social media and it is used for social connection, for sharing of media content, for academic work and searching for and buying of goods and services generated by these contents (Watulak & Whitefield, 2016). In social media usage is on the ascendency in young people (Owusu-Acheaw & Larson, 2015; Yeboah & Dominic, 2014). There are only a few studies which have reported on social media behaviour of young people in Ghana. Most studies have connected the academic performances of students and social media usage behaviour. For instance, Yeboah & Dominic, (2014) reported that tertiary students spend too much time on social media which affects their concentration, and result to poor performance. This has been supported by Owusu-Acheaw and Larson, (2015) reported that social media is quiet high in some tertiary institutions where students spend between 30 minutes to three hours on social media. It was also found that there is a direct relationship between students' academic performance and the extent of social media usage. This if not controlled students' academic performance will be influenced negatively by their social media behaviour.

Other studies have also explored the social antecedents driving social media usage behaviour. Karikari et al. (2017) reported that social media support the generation social capital and user well-being but it usage can be influenced by external social pressure. Thus young people have social pressure to connect with friends through social networking sites hence the high usage behaviour. Hence, the main social factor motivating usage behaviour in social media is the need to connect with others. This is one of the few studies from an emerging economy on social media. Still most of the studies are from developed countries and this calls for more studies in the developing world to bridge the gap. Again, with the high usage rate knowledge about its usage in social commerce is still lacking hence this study explores how psychosocial drivers for engage predict social commerce in young people.

METHODOLOGY

The study adopted a mixed method approach where both qualitative and quantitative methods were employed due the research objectives. The survey method which is a widely used data collection in measuring multiple variables and hypotheses testing was used to collect quantitative data while in-depth interviews were used for the qualitative data. The Survey method allowed for a deductive approach based on theoretical framework with empirical measurement through data analysis and interview complemented the survey data. Using both qualitative and quantitative methods added richness and details to research results which might be lacking when using just one method.

Sampling and Data Collection

The target population was young consumers from age 18-35 currently pursuing tertiary education at the various universities. They being in their prime ages from 18-35 years gave them more time to use social media and to explore its functions more because majority of them are not in employment. They are the most active users of digital media because they are the generation who has been exposed widely to mobile phone since they were born (Karikari et al., 2017). The Universities were considered to be concentrated convergence point for most young people at the prime age in the country. To ensure sample representativeness, a probability sampling specifically a two stage cluster sampling where clusters were selected purposively and respondents were also selected at random from this cluster. Three faculties were selected at random from each university and students were randomly selected for the

Table 1. Characteristics of respondents

Variables	Frequency	Percent
Institution: U.G	201	33.3
U.C.C	222	36.8
KNUST	182	30.0
Age: 20 years & below 21-25 years 26-30 years 31-35years 36 years and above	210 252 115 25	34.8 41.7 19.0 4.2 0.3
Sex: male	292	48.3
Female	312	51.7
Frequently used S. media		
Facebook	211	34.9
Whatsapp Twitter Instagram	158 116 72	26.2 19.2 11.9

survey. Each member of the population had an equal chance of being selected for survey. Each member of the population had an equal chance of being selected for survey. A total population of 605 was selected randomly for the study. Out of these 30 students who were considered to be active users were selected as key informants for in-depth interview as well.

Instrument and Measures

The survey questionnaire was made of questions assessing the social demographic data such as age, gender and which type of social media they frequently used. The questionnaire also captured the use of social media in searching for products and buying . All variables were measured using a five-point Likert scale anchored from 1 to 5 and categorized into various responses ranging from (5) strongly agree to strongly disagree (0)All variables were measured using a five-point Likert scale anchored from 1 to 5 and categorized into various responses ranging from (1)strongly factors. All variables were with the acceptable range for Cronbach's Alpha .75 -.899 which suggests robust reliability levels. The qualitative data was collected with an interview guide and solicited for information on social media daily usage practices and usage in the consumer decision process. Both questionnaire and interview guide were adapted from Consumer Decision Model from (Blackwell et al., 2001 Song & Yoo, 2015; Varkaris & Neuhofer, 2017).

Data Collection and Analysis

Prior to data collection, there were preliminary visits to the selected public universities for permission from appropriate authorities through a letters. Students were contacted and invited for participation at the lecture halls. After seeking consent of students, initial briefing was also give before participation, participation was purely optional. Students were randomly selected, to respond to questions by completing the questionnaire while those selected for qualitative data were interviewed and recorded with their consent. In all 604 questionnaires were fully completed and were subjected to analysis using descriptive analyses and Logistic Regression. Data from interviews were transcribed and subjected to thematic analysis. The results are presented and discussed below;

Generally, Social media usage showed alikelihood **of (OR 2.422)** significant at **P<0.000** displaying a strong significance. This means consumers who use social media are twice likely to search for products and buy products online through their social media platform. This also further tested on specific social media platforms and it was observed that specific social media platforms differ in the extent to which they could be used in business and the buying behaviour.

This table compares the purposes for which people use mobile and their respective connections to using social media in buying or shopping behaviour. The table shows that there is a significant positive relationship between high users of Facebook, Instagram, Whatsapp, and Youtube in the use of social media in buying processes and

Table 2. Integration of social media in buying decision and behavior

Buying Beh	Odds Ratio	Std. Err.	Z	P<z	[95%Conf. Interval]
S. MEDIA	2.422	.47835	4.48	0.000	1.645211 3.567495

Table 3. Specific social media platforms and usage in online buying process and behavior

S. Media usage &consumer decision	Odds Ratio	Std. Err	Z	P>z	95% Conf. Interval
Facebook	5.5225	1.9085	4.94	0.000	2.805277 10.8718
Youtube	4.5876	.96988	7.21	0.000	3.031344 6.942967
Instagram	2.0292	.35928	4.00	0.000	1.434301 2.87109
Twitter	.37298	.07413	-4.96	0.000	.2526371 .5506562
Whatsapp	3.6015	1.2821	3.60	0.000	1.792469 7.236347

behaviour as shown in the Table 2 above demonstrated by the odds ratios as follows Facebook **(OR=5.5225),** Youtube **(OR=4.5768), WhatSapp (OR=3.6015),** and Instagram **(OR=2.0292),** all significant at **(P<0.000)** with the exception of Twitter which did not show significant relationship. This means that users of Facebook use the media for buying process and decisions than the other social media platforms. This could probably be due to the time of its emergence as Facebook appears to be older than the other platform.

Daily Social Media Usage Practices of Social Media in Online Buying Behavior

Concerning daily usage lifestyle and practices, it was found that users have well integrated the mobile phone and social media into every fiber of their day's activities to the extent that the mobile phone and social is the first thing consumers wake to and say good morning to and the last activity for the day as shown in their responses;

Right from bed, I go in for my phone and I browse Facebook to see what is I missed while asleep. I update my status religiously. It makes me feel happy and belonging (ST 6).

It is my phone alarm which wakes me up and I consult it almost every 10 seconds to check my messages on social media. (ST8)

This respondent admitted how strongly attached she is to her smart phone and social media as she uses it within her daily routines all the time. In fact, it is her first priority after waking up from sleep.

Aside using social media for daily routines and coordination, some respondents believed that social media can be used for searching for products and services at the pre-purchase stage but its might not be safe for purchasing

I have not made any online purchase yet but I do go for window shopping on social media. I do not special reason I just don't feel comfortable to purchase items online (ST 4).

I use my phone in searching for products on social media and other sites such as a shoe and other cloths but I do not buy from any websites such as Tonaton (24).

I only search for information about the products (ST 22)

Some of the respondents were not comfortable probably due to security risk and other fraudulent activities reported in online buying. These make online shopping such as social media particularly challenging in some parts of Africa. The reports on security issues were something running through the thoughts of respondents.

I do buy stuff on social media with my phone. I don't do that regularly because it is quite difficult closing buying deal with a mobile phone. It's comes with its own security issues. It is complicated so I prefer doing that on a computer than on my phone (ST 17).

Yes, I do buy online but I do buy from some selective sites that I am sure about (ST5)

Despite the challenges associated with the social media buying, there are some people who still take the risk to buy from social media sites. There are those who are online buyers through their phones and social media

Yes, I do I love to buy sneakers online directly from the manufactures and I do that a lot from England. (ST 15)

I have bought items online before from websites and social media, I love to browse through jewelry shops and places where they sell ladies items (ST 13).

Yes, I bought a beauty cream based on the health benefits that I read about from the social media (ST 22).

Yes I do online purchases items via the internet and social media from time to time using my mobile phone (ST 19).

Yes I do buy items online and I can recall that I last bought a make-up set from Facebook but I prefer Facebook because in most cases you pay at the point of delivery (ST 11).

Yes I do that a lot. Especially when am in Nigeria (ST 10)

However, for some respondents they neither buy nor search for products and services with their mobile phone and their main reason is the security and trust issues in social media commerce e.g Security issues and fear of losing money. These comments below also show a knowledge and perception gap which could be addressed if m-commerce and s-commerce will succeed

I have never bought any product from social media before, to me its quit complicated (ST2).

I don't really trust these online sales. So I don't buy from them (ST 18)

I have never tried buying online because I do not have a bank account (ST 19).

I don't buy items online or social media using because I do not trust these sites (ST17).

The reasons above also suggest the some consumers have already formed some wrong perceptions about buying through the internet. However, some consumers also do not buy due to other reasons either than online security issues.

The findings revealed that general social media usage behaviour is predictor of its usage in online buying behaviour. It shows that users of social media are two times likely to use social media in buying decisions and behaviour. This means that users of social media have assimilated social media into their online buying decision process and behaviour.

These findings suggest that social media has a significant relationship with consumer buying behaviour, meaning that consumers who are dependent on social media are likely to engage in buying activities including searching for products and services and buying. If so then young people's involvement with social media can be redirected into other productive activities including business and buying. Although not many works have connected social media usage and commerce, it was very important to explore social media as a platform for marketing and business as well as engaging young consumers for business growth sustainability. This seem to be confirmed Varkaris & Neuhofer, (2017) researched on how consumers use social media in UK at the pre-purchase stage for hotel selection. The study supports the findings of this study about remarkable use of social media in search for and evaluating hotel services options before selection of choices, which hitherto was not the case in the absence of social media era. For instance, some studies in confirms that sizeable number of young people prefer searching for all the options online and the daring ones who are risk takers and have the online buying requirements such as payment systems and know-how of the procedure can buy. This seem to be social exclusion where those who lack the know-how, are risk averse and lack the digital resources are not enthused about buying from online. The findings shows that truly young consumers engage social media in their daily consumption and primary at pre-purchase stage supporting finding by Song and Yoo (2016) that the use of social media in service information, pre-purchase evaluation and actual buying has been high but not consistent with service industry per se.

The findings from the qualitative data on social media consumer decision and buying behaviour of young people throws more light on the use social media in prediction social media engagement in searching for products and services, consumer decision process and online buying behaviour. The findings indicated that there are three categories of online consumers; the majority who mostly search for products and services but buy offline, those who search products and buy and those who do not search or buy due to security threats. For most people searching for information is the safest place to be hence more and younger people search for all kinds of products online through social media and mobile phone particularly fashion and electronic products. According to the Consumer decision Model by Blackwell et al. 2001 consumers recognize a need before searching for information and then proceed to make choices in offline buying behaviour, however in online buying process it appears that need recognition can be both online and offline and more information search is conducted online before deciding to buy online or offline. This means that the Consumer Decision Model can be applied depending on the market segment, the digital media used, the product or service or even industry at stake. This confirms some of the studies in social media online behaviour suggesting that integration of social media in online decision process and buying behaviour can be high at pre purchase and evaluation stage (Blackwell et al., 2001 Song & Yoo, 2015; Jha, 2019;Varkaris & Neuhofer, 2017).

IMPLICATIONS OF THE STUDY

Social media in marketing and online buying behaviour appears to be still low, therefore Businesses and Marketers should explore the full usage of social media to target young consumers for products and services by creatively and innovatively connecting marketing communication and engagement to drive social media marketing and commerce. Young people's involvement in social media could be redirected from unhealthy behaviour on social media such too much emphasis on unacceptable relationship and wrong information or entertainment "infortainment" into other productive and responsible behaviours and activities including learning, working, commerce and buying. Social media use in commercial activities including banking, ticketing, payment of bills should be encourage at national levels just like the way the social interaction side of this digital media has been popularized.

The Consumer Decision theory as it applies in offline behaviour has been applied from pre-purchase, purchase and post –purchase. However, in online buying behavior such as m-commerce and social commerce behaviour, although digital media is well integrated it appears to be highly applied at the pre-purchase level with lower integration at purchase and at post purchase. This implies that for online consumer behaviour consumer decision and buying mostly occurs at pre-purchase with selected purchases but post purchase activities are not done offline. That means consumers use digital media to search for products and services, evaluate and d It was also found that dependence on social media has a significant relationship with commerce, meaning that consumers who are dependent on social media are likely to engage in commercial activities including searching for products and services and buying. To strengthen social media use in online consumer decision process and buying behaviour, there should be some incentives for buying online such as price rebates, and free deliveries.

Government commitment to digital business in terms of adoption and infrastructure will also be a significant driver in ensuring the growth and advancement in digital marketing. The level of commitment towards infrastructure and systems such as deliveries, payments and reduction in the risk associated with mobile commerce would all drive young people to use smartphone for online buying. The use of digital money such as mobile money should be well integrated in the economy to drive e-commerce and m-commerce.

Young people's involvement behaviour in social media should be redirected from relationship and "infotainment" into other productive activities including commerce and buying. Social media use in commercial activities including banking, ticketing, payment of bills should be encouraged at national levels just like the way the social interaction side of this digital media has been popularized.

Since pre-purchase activities are high on social media, businesses should make good use of social media platform for the influencing consumer decision process to enhance pre-purchase activities. Also innovations and applications for effective m-commerce and integration of online buying behaviour should be created to increase usage of social media in buying from the digital market. Businesses who wish to thrive in online digital markets should work on innovative ways of payment such as using mobile money and other electronic or digital means of payment since young users have a stronger propensity towards mobile commerce. If businesses and marketers could get millennial to buy online they could own them for life.

However, the study is limited to only students and other researches can also focus on the young people in general. Future research can further extend to actual commerce engagement and activities on social media and processes involved in social media buying.

CONCLUSION

There has been a phenomenon growth in social media usage in young people's new digital media usage behaviour. Consequently, younger consumers have responded to seeking some business benefits from social media. However, there has been lack of literature on social media usage and how they predict business and marketing usage. The study came to a conclusion that social media behaviour is not only concerned about usage behaviour but business and consumer buying behavior as well.

REFERENCES

Arif, I., Aslam, W., & Ali, M. (2016). Students' dependence on smartphones and its effect on purchasing behavior. *South Asian Journal of Global Business Research*, *5*(2), 285–302. doi:10.1108/SAJGBR-05-2014-0031

Barger, V., Peltier, J. W., & Schultz, D. E. (2016). Social media and consumer engagement: Areview and research agenda. *Journal of Research in Interactive Marketing, 10,* 4. pp. 268-287. doi:10.1108/JRIM-06-2016-0065

Bolton, R. N., Parasuraman, A., Hoefnagels, A., Migchels, N., Kabadayi, S., Gruber, T., ... Solnet, D. (2013). Understanding Generation Y and their use of social media: A review and research agenda. *Journal of Service Management*, *24*(3), 245–267. doi:10.1108/09564231311326987 doi:10.1108/09564231311326987

Bulduklu, Y. (2017). Mobile games on the basis of uses and gratifications approach: A comparison of the mobile game habits of university and high school students. *The International Journal of Research into New Media Technologies*, 1–17. doi:. doi:10.1177/1354856517748159

Carter, S., & Yao, A. (2016). Mobile apps usage by Malaysian business undergraduates and postgraduates: Implications for consumer behaviour theory and marketing practice. *Internet Research*, *26*(3), 733–757. doi:10.1108/IntR-10-2014-0273

Ioanăs, E., & Stoica, I. (2014). Social media and its impact on consumers behavior. *International Journal of Economic Practices and Theories*, *4*(2).

Jha, B. (2019). The role of social media in communication: Empirical study of online purchasing intention of financial products. *Global Business Review*. pp. 1-17.

Kaplan, A. M., & Haenlein, M. (2010). Users of the world, unite. The challenges and lucre of social media. *Business Horizons*, *53*(1), 59–68. doi:10.1016/j.bushor.2009.09.003

Karikari, S., Osei-Frimpong, K., & Owusu-Frimpong, N. (2017). Evaluating individual level antecedents and consequences on social media use in Ghana. *Technological Forecasting and Social Change*, *123*, 68–78. doi:10.1016/j.techfore.2017.06.023

Keegan, B. J., & Rowley, J. (2017). Evaluation and decision making in social media marketing. *Management Decision*, *55*(1), 15–31. doi:10.1108/MD-10-2015-0450

Khan, M. L. (2017). Social media engagement: What motivates user participation and consumption on YouTube? *Computers in Human Behavior*, *66*, 236–247. doi:10.1016/j.chb.2016.09.024

Lim, J. (2016). Effects of social media users attitudes and perceptions of the attributes of news agency content and their intention to purchase digital subscriptions. *New Media & Society*, *18*(8), 1403–1421. doi:10.1177/1461444814558669

Owusu-Acheaw, M., & Larson, A. G. (2015). The use of social media and its impact on academic performance of tertiary students: A study of Koforidua Polytechnic, Ghana. *Journal of Education and Practice*, *6*(6).

Pookulangara, S., & Koesler, K. (2011). Cultural influence on consumer's usage of social networks and its impact on online purchase intentions. *Journal of Retailing and Consumer Services, 18*(4), 348-354.

Sahney, S. K. (2013). "Buyer's motivation" for online buying: an empirical case of railway eticketing in Indian context. *Journal of Asia Business Studies*, pp. 43-64, doi:. doi:10.1108/JABS-07-2011-0036

Sata, M. (2013). Factors affecting consumer buying behavior of mobile phone devices. *Mediterranean Journal of Social Sciences*, *4*(12). doi:10.5901/mjss.2013.v4n12p103

Schiffman, L. G., & Kanuk, L. L. (2010). *Consumer Behaviour* (10th ed.). Prentice Hall.

Sheldon, P., & Bryant, K. (2016). Instagram: Motives for its use and relationship to narcissism and contextual age. *Computers in Human Behavior*, *58*, 89–97. doi:10.1016/j.chb.2015.12.059

Song, S., & Yoo, M. (2016). The role of social media during the pre-purchasing stage. *Journal of Hospitality and Tourism Technology*, *7*(1), 84–99. doi:10.1108/JHTT-11-2014-0067

Sundar, S., & Limperos, A. (2013). Uses and Grats 2.0: New gratifications for new media. *Journal of Broadcasting & Electronic Media*, *57*(4), 504–525. doi:10.1080/08838151.2013.845827

Sunil, D. (2015). Trends and practices of consumers buying online and offline: An analysis of factors influencing consumer's buying. *International Journal of Commerce and Management*, *25*(4), 442–455. Doi.org/10.1108/IJCoMA-02-2013-0012 doi:10.1108/IJCoMA-02-2013-0012

Whiting, A., & Williams, D. (2013). Why people use social media: A uses and gratifications approach. *Qualitative Market Research, 16*(4), 362–369. doi:10.1108/QMR-06-2013-0041

Zhang, Y., Trusov, M., Stephen, A. T., & Jamal, Z. (2017). Online shopping and social media: friends or foes. *Journal of Marketing, 81*(6), 24–41. doi:10.1509/jm.14.0344

KEY TERMS AND DEFINITIONS

Consumer Buying Behavior: Consumer behavior is the study of individuals, groups or organizations and the behavior they exhibit during the selecting, securing, using of product and services to satisfy their needs.

Consumer Decision Model: Consumer decision-making models have been widely used in consumer behavior studies especially for offline consumer behavior.

Chapter 10
Methods of Published Articles on Digital Economy:
Analysis and Reflections on Databases SCOPUS and Web of Science

Luciana Aparecida Barbieri da Rosa
Universidade Federal de Santa Maria, Brazil

Maria Carolina Martins-Rodrigues
https://orcid.org/0000-0003-2575-8611
CIEO. Universidade do Algarve, Portugal

Tais Pentiado Godoy
https://orcid.org/0000-0001-5021-5315
Universidade Federal de Santa Maria, Brazil

Waleska Yone Yamakawa Zavatti Campos
IAG Business School, Pontifical Catholic University of Rio de Janeiro, Brazil

Larissa Cristina Barbieri
Faculdade de Educação São Luis, Brazil

ABSTRACT

The digital economy is changing the way business is done and is showing tremendous potential for organisational progress and global influence.As innovative products and service offerings make the world more competitive,if created properly, digital connectivity will be able to provide new business models and faster entries into global markets (Anderson, Wladawsky-Berger,2016).This gives rise to important issues pertaining to consolidation of practices, implementation of relevant issues across global companies, and many more. Appropriate answers can be searched for these questions in the international research databases on the digital economy like Scopus and Web of Science. Research contributions of authors demonstrating scientific completeness are of great important here. Also important are databases that have been adequately cited.

DOI: 10.4018/978-1-7998-2185-4.ch010

INTRODUCTION

In the increasingly demanding society, there is a need to offer innovative products and services making it competitive (Lopes et al., 2018). In this perspective, the digital economy emerges, being a new way of business today, as well as in the formulation of new possibilities for progress and global competitiveness. If properly created, digital connectivity is capable of driving innovation toward new business models, jointly providing entry into global markets (Anderson, & Wladawsky-Berger, 2016).

According to Mašić, et al. (2018) defines digital economy as:'Digital economics is a commonly accepted term, but other terms are also used informally, such as' new economy' and 'web economy', while other similar terms related to this area have been logically derived from this term subsequently, e.g. "Information economy", "virtual economy", "Industry 4.0", denoting the fourth industrial revolution, and also "electronic business" and e-commerce, etc. (economy of digitization, e-commerce, industry 4.0, information economy, information society, knowledge economy, knowledge market, virtual economy network), p.02 .

In this regard, the OECD (2013, p.5) adds that the "digital economy includes digital technology-based markets that allow trade in goods and services through e-commerce. The expansion of the digital world has been one of the main sectors of economic growth over the last few years.

From these inferences, some questions emerge: How is the world scenario in the countries? How can consolidated practices and studies on these two themes be implemented in companies worldwide? Thus, the following question was elaborated: "What are the contributions of international publications on digital economy in the multidisciplinary databases Scopus and Web of Science. The analysis sought to incorporate the research of authors with works with scientific recognition, as well as recent articles that have not had the necessary time to be cited by researchers in scientific works.

Due to the importance of deepening and analyzing what has been researched in the national and international scenario, the following study question is presented: "What is the panorama of scientific production on Digital Economy available in the Web of Science and Base Scopus databases? Thus, this study aims to analyze the characteristics of scientific production on digital economy in the Web of Science and Scopus databases from 2000 to 2018.

The present study is a bibliometrics, characterized as the approach as descriptive quantitative, aiming to investigate the main uses of the theme digital economy in the period between 2000 and 2018, in Scopus and Web of Science, in theoretical and empirical debates.

To this end and aiming to achieve the proposed objective, the study is structured as follows: Introduction, systematic literature review, providing an overview of the main concepts of Digital Economy and the state of the art of national and international studies on the theme, method of the study, where the procedures adopted in the research are described. The following are the main results, with the analysis of the theme developed in the studies and the discussion of the results found, ending with the conclusions, limitations and future lines of investigation, ending with the bibliographical references used in this study.

BACKGROUND

The Interfaces of the Digital Economy: Perspectives in the 21st Century

We live in a new paradigm for territories grounded in learning, knowledge, and new information and communication technologies. The twentieth century was marked by several changes in the social and economic structure. So, this was a century of great change, where you developed a new structure, a new way of thinking and doing economics. Today, in a world where the economy is largely driven by a digital dimension, territories acquire a new virtual element that allows them to overcome spatial barriers and partially abolish distances (Bomsel, (2007). Thus, emerges the new economy, guided by emerging digital resources (internet) and the result of the union between information and technology, which are centered on people, institutions and the transfer of learning, information and methods (Gamaet al., 1999).

In the context of new communication, information technologies and the new economy, urban space is reborn from a framework of increasing collapse of spatial boundaries. In this way, the digital economy contributes to the development of a new development paradigm related to the valorization of essential territorial factors, for the competitiveness between territories (Herscovici, & Bolano, 2005).

In this context, the economy no longer develops by the efficiency of machines, or by the workforce it has, but by the availability of knowledge, information and knowledge and the specificity, differentiation and innovative capacity of its agents, ie companies. (Lemes et al., 2012). Thus, the digital economy ends up translating its economic paradigm into the construction and emergence of different social, cultural, economic and technology consequences, all of which are reflected in the territory, that is, aspects such as the impact of information technologies on connectivity between territories, mobility, the abolition of space barriers and the informational desertification of certain places and / or regions (Ferreira, 2004).

With the emergence of the new digital economy, man has a fundamental role to play in the growth of new global competences, knowledge territories, in the control of different processes and in the regulation of the elements of the systems, with regard to the areas of innovation, technology as well as urban, regional and industrial policies (Oliveira & Pinto, 2018).

In the pursuit of smart cities and regions, technology, innovation and knowledge policies are common elements in different realities and different actors in innovation and knowledge networks and systems. They must be designed and implemented in a collaborative environment and in a close relationship. with the new technologies and instruments of the emerging digital economy (Ferreira, 2004).

The digital economy has changed the way companies work, relate to their suppliers, customers and each other. The reconfiguration of the digital economy market, was advocated by Chris Anderson, the Long Tail model, where he states that the limitations of physical space and the bottleneck of the distribution system, in this case reduce costs to produce, consume and make products available for consumption., being the digital economy founded on demand (Anderson, 2006).

According to Bomsel (2007), the digital economy is mostly driven by the bargaining power of consumers and this phenomenon arises from the fact of the rise in the media market and the power of consumer participation. Thus, the new digital economy is a basic tool for the development of cities and regions and for the construction of knowledge territories (Oliveira, & Pinto, 2018). This economy, whose evolution is exponential and rapid, can be seen as one of the elements of smart territories, along with its system of real knowledge and innovation, the institutional resources of intellectual capital.

State of the Art: Digital Economy

Recent studies on digital economics have prioritized the challenges encountered in the industry 4.0 scenario, known as the fourth industrial revolution, or the internet of things, a scenario marked by the systemic implementation of state-of-the-art computer technologies, artificial intelligence and big data, where reality suffers cyber- physical and social influences and social media play a fundamental role in mediating human interaction and communication (Andriushchenko et al., 2019; Budanov et al., 2018).

At the heart of the new industrial revolution lies, therefore, in technological advancement, which enables the exchange of information between companies, facilities and machines throughout the value chain, which creates emerging and additional challenges in capturing and creating value for consumers innovators of the digital economy (Budanov et al., 2018; Teece, 2018).Thus, innovating in highly dynamic and technological environments becomes a challenge, as distinctive dynamic capabilities can be more easily imitated, engendering the so-called spillover, which shows that the appropriateness of a resource is challenging and may not be simply by trade secrets and / or patents (Teece, 2018)

From the point of value creation, in the digital economy scenario, multinational corporations have sought to maximize tax evasion through the transfer of profits to low tax jurisdictions through predominantly artificial internal transactions that do not affect the actual location of the company, which must be tackled by rethinking the international tax system of multinational corporations (Bacache-Beauvallet & Bloch, 2018; Ting & Gray, 2019). Thus, there are difficulties in adapting current tax principles applied to traditional economic activities in the context of the digital economy.

Regarding consumption, the creation of value for the customer is also impacted by the internet of things. The digital economy, endowed with fierce online competition, engenders constant innovation that meets and fosters consumer welfare, while imposing the need for consumer attention and protection through standards and laws that are capable of to foster sustainable, conscious and committed buying decisions for responsible online consumption (Gazzola et al., 2017).With regard to sustainability in the digital economy, it is necessary that at the micro level, individuals realize that unsustainable consumption plays an active role in the creation of pollution and in various environmental changes, while the deployment of innovative technologies must be based. sustainable development, as consequences of the digital economy have direct, indirect and structural social and environmental impacts around the world (Kostakiset al., 2016; Sui & Rejeski, 2002). According to Kostakis, et al. (2016), the direct impacts of information and communication technologies involve the manufacture, use of raw materials, transportation, energy use and disposal of electronic devices; indirect impacts of ICTs are effects on contemporary consumer culture and environmental awareness; and finally, structural impacts refer to dematerialization (resource efficiency), rebound effect (greater use of resources, although their use is more efficient). The efficient use of environmental, human and technological resources addresses another fundamental and emerging issue in the digital economy scenario: smart cities. This is because digitized infrastructures enable the design of interconnected, individual-centered products and services to improve quality of life, mobility, communication, energy, health and education in cities around the world. (Bull &Azennoud, 2016; Li et al., 2016). The use of technology in the new industrial revolution is not exclusive to companies. Governments have used the benefits of TIC`s to improve access to public information and facilitate control mechanisms that foster accountability. Thus, the development of the so-called electronic government has a strong positive and reciprocal relationship with the digital economy, highlighting the occurrence of the joint evolution between technology and organizations, with special emphasis on the social, economic, political, cultural, technological and demographic aspects, which have significant effects on the growth of the digital economy and e-government.

(Ali et al., 2018; Zhao et al., 2015).Considering the differences cited between countries and regions, which notably influence the growth of the digital economy, the discussion about the accessibility of places and people to TIC`s and the Internet in the context of the digital economy is pertinent. The accessibility of people in the digital economy is affected by functional illiteracy issues added to the difficulty of adapting to new technology skills, and therefore the literacy computer and the web accessibility are crucial issues for public policies to foster new dynamics digital economy, through programs and measures that seek to overcome technological functional illiteracy, especially in risky geographical areas. (Baskakova & Soboleva, 2019).

From a spatial point of view, the geographical accessibility of ICTs and the internet is also scattered and unequal in the world, which impacts on the configuration of the digital economy, and on the spatial configuration of certain cities in Europe, for example (Tranos et al., 2013). As a result, certain countries and regions have a higher concentration of digital economy indicators than others, causing unequal access to their benefits.

The digital economy also influences the creation of startups, which find a favorable scenario in various sectors, and presented prospects for broad growth and increased value creation for customers, especially through innovative products and services traded on digital platforms. (Ruggieri et al., 2018).

Given the complexity of the dynamics established in the fourth industrial revolution, a study by Ratzinger, et al. (2018) found that startups in the digital economy are more successful in obtaining capital investments depending on their founders' educational attainment that higher education has considerable influence on the performance of digital startups.

While the benefits of the digital economy are numerous, the challenges inherent in this new model of economic management and technological innovation need to be highlighted. In this sense, there are risks posed by digital innovation to public and private spheres that need to be considered to maintain the effectiveness of contemporary democracy. (Curran, 2018). According to the author, the first risk of the digital economy involves the lonely life and the affectation of interpersonal relationships; The second relates to the impact of artificial intelligence on intensifying unemployment-related issues, and finally, the existence of a connected digital communication ecosystem at all times.

In short, to minimize these risks and preserve the most important thing in humanity, we need to recognize human beings as legitimate partners of technology, focusing organizations and relationships on the human being, not on machines, or, in other words, Human creativity must not be undermined by technology (Holford, 2019).

METHODOLOGY

Description of Research

The present article was developed from a bibliometric research, with the objective of increasing the knowledge related to the publications related to the Digital Economy theme. Bibliometrics help to know the stage in which are searching. A given area is located mentioning the authors (Macedo et al., 1999). Also, bibliometric aims to analyse scientific activity through the quantitative study of publications, to the author Silva (2004).De according with the investigators Okubo (1997), Rostaing (1997), Araújo (2006) and Garousi (2015) bibliometric is defined like a statistical or mathematical technique that allows analysing the characteristics and development of numerous scientific areas and the calculation of citation indexes. To reduce the risk of missing documents due to different coverage of publication and research were used the two databases. The study has a quantitative approach, considering that it sought to quantify some variables related to scientific production on Digital Economy. The term "Digital Economy" was searched in all areas of research without differentiation of the words searched. All publications were surveyed in the period from 2000 to 2018, once the year 2019 is underway.

Consequently, we identified the principal authors who wrote on the subject, the growth of the researches in the terms during the period in question, in order to compare the articles collected in the Web of Science and in Scopus. In Excel, comparison tables were created to analyse the data. It is noted that there is an index of citations in both data bases, where for each article, among other items, it is mentioned the title, authors, year, number of citations, type of documents as well as the year of publication (Figure 1).

Figure 1. Distribution of articles by type of publication
Source: *Authors' elaboration.*

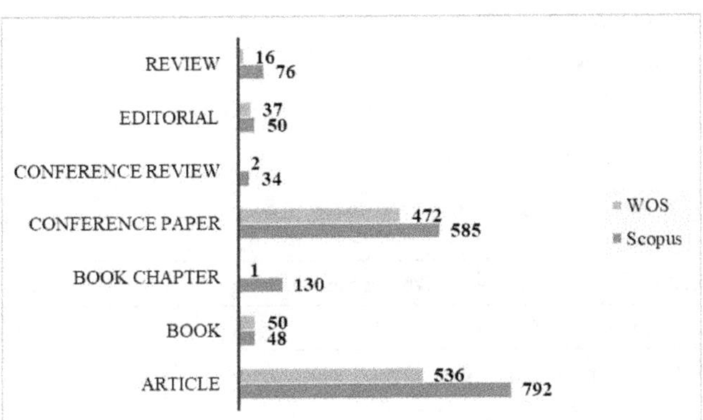

Stages of Data Collection

The development of the research occurred in two stages. The term "Digital Economy" was entered into the WOS and Scopus research field, delimiting the period between 2000 and 2018. The general characteristics of the publications were then surveyed, such as, for example, Year of publications, Authors, Title of sources, institutions, Research areas, countries and Languages, Keywords, and Financing Agencies. In the second stage, the most cited papers were compared with the authors who published the most in the same period. Figure 2 shows the steps of the research. Therefore, the bibliometric analysis of the study above was carried out, according to the steps presented in the following section.

ANALYSIS AND DISCUSSION OF RESULTS

The search results are displayed at this point. We found 2852 scientific articles distributed by Web of Science and Scopus, as indicated in Table 1.

General Characteristics of Publications

The following are the general characteristics of the publications related to the themes "Digital Economy":

1. Main authors.
2. Title of sources.
3. Main institutions.
4. Year of publications.
5. Main countries.
6. Languages.
7. Research areas.
8. Most Used Keywords.
9. Financing Agencies.

Table 1. Search terms

Terms	Web of Science	Scopus
"Digital Economy"	1098	1754

Source: Authors' elaboration.

Then, the number of publications per author and the number of citations will be displayed.

Main Authors

The Table 2 presents the 20 authors and the respective number of publications, most published on the topic "Digital Economy", in the two databases, in the analyzed period.

There was a multiplicity and diversity regarding the authorship of the works, since a small portion of these authors published a high number of articles, about the them. As for the representativeness of the articles by author, it is verified that five authors are common to both bases: Alizadeh, Boban, King, Shkarupeta, and Tolstykh. The author that leads the ranking of publications, with 12 publications in Scopus and the 5 publications in WOS was Dave King, is an Emeritus Professor in physical chemistry at the University of Cambridge, Director of the Collegio Carlo Alberto, Chancellor of the University of Liverpool and a senior scientific adviser to UBS.

Table 2. Distribution of articles by author

Author	Scopus	WOS
Alizadeh, T.	5	6
Bataev, A.V.	6	
Boban, M.	5	4
Ciocoiu, C.N.	5	
Cotet, C.E.		4
Crabtree, A.		4
Dennis, A.	12	
Dragoi, G.		5
Foster, J.		4
Geoffrion, A.M.		4
Hanson, V.L.	6	
King, D.	12	5
Ross, J.W.	6	
Shkarupeta, E.	7	5
Tolstykh, T.	7	5
Total	**71**	**46**

Source: Authors' elaboration

Main Title of the Sources

The Table 3 presents the main sources of publications related to the Digital Economy. Most of the articles have been published in proceedings which are not yet a reference as we are facing an emerging issue (Annual Hawaii International Conference on System Sciences, Lecture Notes in Computer Science, ACM International Conference Proceeding Series).Among the journals with the highest number of publications, we highlight Australian Journal of Telecommunications and the Digital Economy, Ekonomika Regiona-Economy of Region, Espacios, those that care already be a reference for issues related with the topic, which denotes therelevanceofthis theme associated with the concerns inherent in Digital Economy, which is creating a revolution in the modern economy, corroborated by unprecedented economic performance.

Table 3. Distribution of articles by title of the sources

Source Titles	Scopus	WOS
ACM International Conference Proceeding Series	22	
Advances in Intelligent Systems and Computing	17	
Australian Journal of Telecommunications and the Digital Economy	15	
Ceur Workshop Proceedings	19	
EkonomikaRegiona-Economy of Region		16
Espacios	15	
Innovation Management and Education Excellence Through Vision		11
Intertax		11
Lecture Notes in Computer Science	30	9
Modern Journal of Language Teaching Methods		7
New Challenges of Economic and Business Development - 2016		7
Proceedings 2018 Int. Conference Quality Management Transport	15	
32nd Int. Business Inf. Management Association Conference	22	
Annual Hawaii International Conference on System Sciences	39	13
Quality Access to Success	15	
Transfer-European Review of Labour And Research		6
Understanding the Digital Economy: Data, Tools, and Research		7
Total Geral	**209**	**87**

Source: Authors' elaboration.

Main Institutions

The institutions that most published works related to the theme "Digital Economy" are presented in Table 4. The institutions that published the most on scientific articles involving the subject, related to Digital Economy were: Plekhanov Russian University of Economics, Moskva, Russia, in Web of Science and University of California System, Oakland, California, in Scopus.

Articles Published per Year

According to Table 5, it is possible to follow the growth of the publications in the two databases. Both in the Web of Science and in Scopus, the ones with highest productivity were the years of 2013 - 2018.

Main Countries

The bibliometric analysis identified, at this point, the number of articles distributed by the countries of origin, the United States of America leads the ranking of

Table 4. Distribution of articles by the main institutions

Institutions	Scopus	WOS
Bucharest University of Economic Studies	17	17
Financial University under the Government Russian Federation	21	16
Indiana University	12	
Lomonosov Moscow State University	16	
Massachusetts Institute of Technology		9
Peter the Great St. Petersburg Polytechnic University	22	13
Plekhanov Russian University of Economics	30	
Queensland University of Technology QUT	14	
Russian Academy of Sciences	20	18
Russian Presidential Academy N.E. Public Administration		12
Saint Petersburg State University	13	10
The St. Petersburg State University of Economics	12	
UniversitiKebangsaan Malaysia		10
University of California System		19
University of London		15
Total	**177**	**139**

Source: Authors' elaboration.

Table 5. Total publications between 2000 and 2018 distributed per year

YEAR	SCOPUS	WOS	Total
2000	23	25	48
2001	37	24	61
2002	32	25	57
2003	41	21	62
2004	40	18	58
2005	44	17	61
2006	40	19	59
2007	38	19	57
2008	45	24	69
2009	53	34	87
2010	82	39	121
2011	78	34	112
2012	55	22	77
2013	83	32	115
2014	92	49	141
2015	86	78	164
2016	142	103	245
2017	258	198	456
2018	485	317	802
Total	1754	1098	2852

Source: Authors' elaboration.

publications, followed by Russian and England. The number of publications per country and database is illustrated in Table 6. Consequently, it can be inferred that in these countries are found most of the institutions that have research related to the theme of Digital Economy.

Main Languages

In this variable, the languages of the papers published in the study theme are presented. The preferred language is English with 2960 articles (Web of Science 1315 and 1645 Scopus), as shown in Table 7.

Table 6. Distribution of publications by country

Country	Scopus	WOS
Australia	115	58
Canada	51	32
China		50
England	202	107
France	69	31
Germany	80	33
Italy	53	
Romania	47	61
Russian	270	167
Spain	48	48
United States	310	181
Total	**1245**	**768**

Source: Authors' elaboration.

Research Areas

Regarding the main Research Areas in Digital Economy publications, there seems to be a convergence in the main research areas of most published articles as shown in Figure 2. In the next section, the keywords in the articles will be analysed.

Most Used Keywords

It was verified that in the articles of the study were found 160 key words in the text related to the theme (Figure 3). The keywords represent a source of access to scientific articles, briefly present the content used in the studies. The most used keyword was "Digital Economy", is cohesive with the purpose of the research which strengthens the selection of the Bibliographic Portfolio.

Financing Agencies

About the funding agencies of the work that includes the theme in research, we have listed those with the most significant number of publications in Table 8. These data highlight the importance of funding in the development of research worldwide.

Table 7. Distribution of articles by language

Language	Scopus	WOS
English	1645	1315
French	31	25
German	12	
Italian		4
Portuguese	7	1
Russian	41	21
Spanish	15	9
Total	**1751**	**1375**

Source: Authors' elaboration.

Figure 2. Research areas
***Source**: Authors' elaboration, using the Woldle.*

Figure 3. Keywords of the research articles
***Source**: Authors' elaboration, using the Woldle.*

Table 8. Financing agencies

Financing Agencies	Scopus	WOS
Arts and Humanities Research Council		2
Council on grants of the President of the Russian Federation	11	2
Economic and Social Research Council	6	6
Engineering and Physical Sciences Research Council	30	18
European Commission	12	2
European Research Council		2
Ministry of Education and Science of the Russian Federation	6	
National Natural Science Foundation of China		6
National Science Foundation	11	
Research Councils UK	6	
Russian Foundation for Basic Research	21	8
Russian Science Foundation	8	
Social Sciences and Humanities Research Council of Canada	5	
Strategic Research Council at The Academy of Finland		4
Total	**116**	**50**

Source: Authors' elaboration.

Relationship Among Authors with More Cited Publications and Most Cited Articles From 2000 to 2018.

Among the data from the WOS and Scopus survey on "Digital Economy", from 2000 to 2018, it is essential to highlight the main publications in several citations, shows a slight juxtaposition between the two bases. (Table 9). When comparing the Table 2 and the Table 9, it was possible to observe that only twoof the authors (Hanson, Vicki & Geoffrion, AM) who published the most in the period have their works among the 20 (twenty) most cited in the period analysed. It is important to note that among of the 20 most cited articles we have the article with the title, " Consumer surplus in the digital economy: Estimating the value of increased product variety at Online booksellers", written by Brynjolfsson, E; Hu, Y; Smith, MD, published in Management Science in 2003, with a higher number of citations (355), what is possibly a reference in the researched theme do not belong to the authors who most published on the theme "Digital Economy".

Table 9. Distribution of the most cited articles in the period from 2000 to 2018

Number of citations	Title	Author	Journal	Year
355	Consumer surplus in the digital economy: Estimating the value of increased product variety at Online booksellers	Brynjolfsson, E; Hu, Y; Smith, MD	Management Science	2003
217	Models for supply chains in e-business	Swaminathan, JM; Tayur, SR	Management Science	2003
184	Institution-based trust in interorganizational exchange relationships: the role of online B2B marketplaces on trust formation	Pavlou, PA	Journal Of Strategic Information Systems	2002
129	Research commentary: The organizing logic for an enterprise's IT activities in the digital era - A prognosis of practice and a call for research	Sambamurthy, V; Zmud, RW	Information Systems Research	2000
124	ICT and productivity: conclusions from the empirical literature	Cardona, M.; Kretschmer, T.; Strobel, T.	Information Economics And Policy	2013
113	Dynamic pricing on the Internet: Importance and implications for consumer behavior	Kannan, PK; Kopalle, PK	International Journal Of Electronic Commerce	2001
89	Price levels and price dispersion within and across multiple retailer types: Further evidence and extension	Ancarani, F; Shankar, V	Journal Of The Academy Of Marketing Science	2004
84	Measuring the digital divide: a framework for the analysis of cross-country differences	Corrocher, N; Ordanini, A	Journal Of Information Technology	2002
81	Keywords and cultural change: Frame analysis of Business model public talk, 1975-2000	Ghaziani, A; Ventresca, MJ	Sociological Forum	2005
73	Teaching for creativity: towards sustainable and replicable pedagogical practice	McWilliam, Erica; Dawson, Shane	Higher Education	2008
72	Linking innovative product development with customer knowledge: a data-mining approach	Su, Chao-Ton; Chen, Yung-Hsin; Sha, D. Y.	Technovation	2006
71	Continuous auditing: Building automated auditing capability	Rezaee, Z; Sharbatoghlie, A; Elam, R; McMickle, PL	Auditing-A Journal Of Practice & Theory	2002

continued on following page

Table 9. Continued

Number of citations	Title	Author	Journal	Year
69	An analytical framework for evaluating e-commerce business models and strategies	Lee, CS	Internet Research-Electronic Networking Applications And Policy	2001
68	Critical themes in electronic commerce research: a meta-analysis	Wareham, J; Zheng, JG; Straub, D	Journal Of Information Technology	2005
64	Knowledge management in eBusiness and customer relationship management: South African case study findings	du Plessis, M; Boon, JA	International Journal Of Information Management	2004
51	A kano-CKM model for customer knowledge discovery	Chen, Yung-Hsin; Su, Chao-Ton	Total Quality Management & Business Excellence	2006
51	Online community: enhancing the relationship marketing concept through customer bonding	Szmigin, I; Canning, L; Reppel, AE	International Journal Of Service Industry Management	2005
50	Internet of Things Applications and challenges in smart cities: a case study of IBM smart city projects	Scuotto, Veronica; Ferraris, Alberto; Bresciani, Stefano	Business Process Management Journal	2016
50	Influencing technology adoption by older adults	Hanson, Vicki L.	Interacting With Computers	2010
50	Prospects for operations research in the E-business era	Geoffrion, AM; Krishnan, R	Interfaces	2001
48	The Human Face as a Dynamic Tool for Social Communication	Jack, Rachael E.; Schyns, Philippe G.	Current Biology	2015

SOLUTIONS AND RECOMMENDATIONS

The present study aimed to verify the characteristics of the national and international scientific production that relate the theme on "Digital Economy". In order to reach the goal, a bibliometric research was carried out in the two databases, obtaining 1098 publications in the Web of Science and 1754 publications in Scopus, related to these themes, mainly in the following areas: Computer Science, Business, Management and Accounting, Social Sciences, Engineering, Economics, Econometrics and Finance, Decision Sciences, Mathematics, Arts and Humanities. It was found that the majority of publications found are articles and Proceedings, in the period between 2000 and 2018. The scientific production related to the theme gradually increased in the number of articles published per year with a "boom" in the years 2013 to 2018, in both bases. Most studies were published in the proceedings of The Annual Hawaii International Conference on System Sciences. Also, it was verified that, in both bases, USA, Russian, and England, lead the ranking of the countries that most published on the subject, and the English language is the predominant in the publications. Therefore, it can be inferred that in these countries are found most of the institutions that have research related to the theme of Digital Economy. It is worth highlighting that, Portugal and Brazil occupy the 26th and 27th position in the ranking of publications, when we consider the 30th mains countries that most published, about the them, which indicates that this theme is being worked by Portuguese researchers and Brazilians who seek originality in their work. When comparing the two tables, it was possible to observe that only twoof the authors (Hanson, Vicki L. & Geoffrion, AM) who published the most in the period have their works among the 20 (twenty) most cited in the period analyzed.

CONCLUSIONS

It can be concluded that the publications with a higher number of citations, which are possibly references in the researched theme (Brynjolfsson, E; Hu, Y; Smith, MD; Swaminathan, JM; Tayur, SR & Pavlou, PA), do not belong to the authors who most published about Digital Economy. Thus, it is observed that authors with a high number of publications may not be those who produce studies of greater impact and relevance to a given area of knowledge.

The present study found the following limitations: 1) The main limitation of this study refers to the fact that only the search term " Digital Economy " was used. 2) The results presented are limited to the articles selected only on international bases, Web of Science and Scopus.

Thus, it is suggested that for future research, 1) to select articles in others national and international bases to compare the results. 2) to seek analyse the topic in high impact journals and search with other keywords related to the theme, 3) perform the bibliometric analysis of the abstracts of the selected articles. With the development of ICT in recent decades and globalization, new trends have emerged both as behavioural and market, so it is possible to affirm that almost everything is connected, thus evidencing the concept of the digital economy. So, can perform other analyses, such for example: Which emerging themes have been worked on in Digital economy in various European countries? What is the digital economy impact on e-commerce in micro and small enterprises? What are the advantages and disadvantages of Digital Economy?

REFERENCES

Ali, M. A., Hoque, M. R., & Alam, K. (2018). An empirical investigation of the relationship between e-government development and the digital economy: The case of Asian countries. *Journal of Knowledge Management*, *22*(5), 1176–1200. doi:10.1108/JKM-10-2017-0477

Anderson, L., & Wladawsky-Berger, I. (2016). The 4 things it takes to succeed in the digital economy. Harvard Business Review. Available at https://hbr.org/2016/03/the-4things-it-takes-to-succeed-in-the-digital-economy

Andriushchenko, K., Rudyk, V., Riabchenko, O., Kachynska, M., Marynenko, N., Shergina, L., & Kuchai, O. (2019). Processes of managing information infrastructure of a digital enterprise in the framework of the «Industry 4.0» concept. *Eastern-European Journal of Enterprise Technologies*, *1*(3), 97. doi:10.15587/1729-4061.2019.157765

Araújo, C. A. (2006). Bibliometria: Evolução histórica e questões atuais. *Em Questão, Porto Alegre*, *12*(1), 11–32.

Bal, A., & Gutiérrez, C. (2015). Taxation of the digital economy. International tax structures in the BEPS era: An analysis of anti-abuse measures. Amsterdam, The Netherlands: IBFD. pp. 249-280.

Bacache-Beauvallet, M., & Bloch, F. (2018). Special issue on taxation in the digital economy. *Journal of Public Economic Theory*, *20*(1), 5–8. doi:10.1111/jpet.12285

Baskakova, M., & Soboleva, I. (2019). New dimensions of functional illiteracy in the digital economy. Voprosy Obrazovaniya / Educational Studies Moscow, (1), 244–263.

Budanov, V., Aseeva, I., & Zvonova, E. (2018). Industry 4.0.: Socio-economic junctures. *Economic Annals-XXI*, *168*(11–12), 33–37.

Bull, R., & Azennoud, M. (2016). Smart citizens for smart cities: participating in the future. *Proceedings of the Institution of Civil Engineers - Energy*, *169*(3), 93–101. 10.1680/jener.15.00030

Curran, D. (2018). Risk, innovation, and democracy in the digital economy. *European Journal of Social Theory*, *21*(2), 207–226. doi:10.1177/1368431017710907

Gamma, R., Knight, C., & Figueiredo, E. (1999). New business strategies in the context of the digital economy. Manufacturing industry and internet. Geography Notebooks, Special No. 29-38.

Garousi, V. (2015). A bibliometric analysis of the Turkish software engineering research community. *Scientometrics*, *105*(1), 23–49. doi:10.100711192-015-1663-x

Gazzola, P., Colombo, G., Pezzetti, R., & Nicolescu, L. (2017). Consumer empowerment in the digital economy: Availing sustainable purchasing decisions. *Sustainability (Switzerland)*, *9*(5), 1–19.

Herscovici, A., & Bolaño, C. (2005). The critique of the political economy of information and knowledge. Article presented at the national meeting of the Brazilian Society of Political Economy, Campin.

Holford, W. D. (2019). The future of human creative knowledge work within the digital economy. *Futures, 105*(October, 2018), 143–154.

Kostakis, V., Roos, A., & Bauwens, M. (2016). Towards a political ecology of the digital economy: Socio-environmental implications of two competing value models. *Environmental Innovation and Societal Transitions*, *18*, 82–100. doi:10.1016/j.eist.2015.08.002

Lemes, D. O., Tomaselli, F. C., & Camarotti, S. R. B. (2012). The digital economy and the mobile gaming market. In: XI SB Games - Brasilia - DF - Brazil, Nov. 2 - 4.

Li, F., Nucciarelli, A., Roden, S., & Graham, G. (2016). How smart cities transform operations models: A new research agenda for operations management in the digital economy. *Production Planning and Control*, *27*(6), 514–528. doi:10.1080/09537287.2016.1147096

Lopes, D. P. T., Santos, S. R. M., Siva, V. H. R., & Martins, G. S. (2018). Determinant factors of managerial innovation. [September / December.]. *Electronic Journal Management & Society*, *12*(33), 2541–2563.

da Silva Macedo, M. A., de Castro Casa Nova, S. P., & de Almeida, K. (1999). Mapping and bibliometric analysis of the use of data envelopment analysis (DEA) in accounting and administration studies. In Proceedings of 23 ENANPAD. Foz do Iguacu: ANPAD.

Mašić, B., Vladušić, L., & Nešić, S. (2018). Challenges in creating transformative growth for companies in digital economy. *Economics*, *6*(2), 37–48.

OECD. (2013). *The digital economy (2012)*. Organization for Economic Co-operation and Development.

Okubo, Y. (1997). Bibliometric indicators and analysis of research systems: methods and examples, OECD Science, Technology and Industry Working Papers, 1997/01, OECD Publishing, Paris.

Ratzinger, D., Amess, K., Greenman, A., & Mosey, S. (2018). The impact of digital start-up founders' higher education on reaching equity investment milestones. *The Journal of Technology Transfer*, *43*(3), 760–778. doi:10.100710961-017-9627-3 PMID:31258242

Rostaing, H. (1997). *Bibliometrics and technical techniques Toulouse: Sciences of the Society*. Marseille, France: Research Center Retrospective of Marseille.

Ruggieri, R., Savastano, M., Scalingi, A., Bala, D., & D'Ascenzo, F. (2018). The impact of digital platforms on business models: An empirical investigation on innovative start-ups. *Management and Marketing*, *13*(4), 1210–1225. doi:10.2478/mmcks-2018-0032

Silva, M. R. (2004). Bibliometric analysis of the teaching scientific production of the special education graduate program / UFSCar. (Master's Dissertation, Federal University of Sao Carlos, Brazil).

Sui, D. Z., & Rejeski, D. W. (2002). Environmental impacts of the emerging digital economy: The e-for-environment e-commerce? *Environmental Management*, *29*(2), 155–163. doi:10.100700267-001-0027-X PMID:11815820

Teece, D. J. (2018). Profiting from innovation in the digital economy: Enabling technologies, standards, and licensing models in the wireless world. *Research Policy*, *47*(8), 1367–1387. doi:10.1016/j.respol.2017.01.015

Ting, A., & Gray, S. J. (2019). The rise of the digital economy: Rethinking the taxation of multinational enterprises. *Journal of International Business Studies*. doi:10.105741267-019-00223-x

Tranos, E., Reggiani, A., & Nijkamp, P. (2013). Accessibility of cities in the digital economy. *Cities (London, England)*, *30*(1), 59–67. doi:10.1016/j.cities.2012.03.001

Zhao, F., Wallis, J., & Singh, M. (2015). E-government development and the digital economy: A reciprocal relationship. *Internet Research*, *25*(5), 734–766. doi:10.1108/IntR-02-2014-0055

Chapter 11
Social Network Sites (SNS) and Their Irrepressible Popularity:
Can They Really Cause an Addiction?

Tuğba Koç
Sakarya University, Turkey

Adem Akbıyık
https://orcid.org/0000-0001-7634-4545
Sakarya University, Turkey

ABSTRACT

Popularity of social media is increasing day by day and there are thousands of social media platforms on the internet with different features. This chapter discusses the term social media in general and examines its evolution in detail from the beginning of the first e-mail to today. Authors explore the terms pertaining to the domain of Social Network Sites (SNS) which are considered as one of the most used forms of social media. Authors present a discussion about a popular topic "SNS addiction" and examine its characteristics with a brief literature review. Accordingly, despite the fact that excessive use of social network sites cannot be formally accepted as a behavioral addiction; shy and young, extroverted, and neurotic women with no relationship are more likely to develop addictive behaviors towards social media.

INTRODUCTION

The reputation of social media is increasing day by day, and this popularity changes our daily lives and business environments in both negative and positive ways. For example one study claims that proper use of social media helps family members

DOI: 10.4018/978-1-7998-2185-4.ch011

to increase their connection and to strengthen their family bonds (Williams & Merten, 2011); whereas other has investigated that divorce rates have increased with developing technology (Greenwood, Guner, Santos, & Kocharkov, 2016). Moqbel and Kock (2018) has admitted that excessive use of social media has negative impacts on the personal and work environment by means of decreasing positive emotions, increasing health problems and task distraction. However, their strong evidence about the harmful effects of social media on personal environment is as strong as the impact on the work environment, Greengard (2012) believes that social media can be a way for achieving our life experiences. Indeed, some previous studies have clearly proved that using social media can enhance academic success (Ainin, Naqshbandi, Moghavvemi, & Jaafar, 2015), increase students' engagement (Junco, Heiberger, & Loken, 2011) as well as having more interactive customer relationship performance (Trainor, Andzulis, Rapp, & Agnihotri, 2014), creating more trusted products and customers (Laroche, Habibi, & Richard, 2013). Social media brings to our life not only performance-based positive outcomes; it may also offer some emotional gifts. For example, results have shown that getting positive feedback on the profiles enhance self-esteem and subjective well-being (Valkenburg, Peter, & Schouten, 2006). Similarly, Wang, Jackson, Gaskin, and Wang (2014) have also found that social use of social networking sites is positively related to well-being. These contradictory examples can be reproduced even further, but the most critical point in here is that there is no generalizable effect of social media. Although literature is agreed that some people are more inclined to use social media and exposed its negative effects such as young individuals (Kalpidou, Costin, & Morris, 2011) and females (Andreassen et al., 2013a), the situation depends on who you are, what are your individual characteristics and other unpredictable factors. Effects may be different even when the same person uses social media for different purposes. Baek, Bae, and Jang (2013) have found that social activities (based on reciprocity between the user and his/her friends such as chatting) decrease the feeling of loneliness; however para-social activities (based on unilateral activities such as commenting a celebrity's photo) show opposite effect. Because of these reasons, understanding social media is crucial to get benefit from it without being harmed. For this purpose, the present chapter has two main objectives (1) to present the outline of social media (Section 1), (2) to define social network sites (SNS) with examples of their potential effects, and (3) to discuss a relatively new concept "SNS addiction."

UNDERSTANDING SOCIAL MEDIA

In this section, first, we try to define social media with different definitions made by different point of view and touch on the evolution of social media.

What is Social Media?

According to Oberst (2010), the online world started gaining prominence with the social media after the year of 2000, and since then people have started to share their feelings, information, videos, and pictures at an astounding rate. According to their massive global compendium of stats, We Are Social has currently released that among 4.338 billion internet users worldwide 3.484 of them have already active social media users (We Are Social, 2019). This simply proves that 75% of internet users are also a member of social media. The reason why social media has become popular is that; it is always up to date, be able to multiple use (can be used for so many people at the same time), and is an open-source platform (Akıncı Vural & Bat, 2010). Although literature builds consensus about social media has changed our lives in many ways, there is no common sense what actually it is. Kaplan and Haenlein (2010) have stated that the terms social media and Web 2.0 are generally used interchangeably, but this situation is contradictory. According to them Web 2.0 can be considered as an ideological and technological foundation for the evolution of social media. More precisely, social media is an intimate and natural platform created by its users who come together based on their shared interests and ideas (Evans, 2008). Odabaşı (2010) has stated that social media is a way of connecting with our friends or/and strangers via sharing our experiences, ideas, and opinions on an online platform. Lusk (2010) has also agreed the idea that social media is a platform and it provides communication and sharing opportunities to its users. From another researcher perspective, social media is not just a platform, but it also consists applications, services, and systems that allows to create and share related contents (Junco, 2014). Boyd and Ellison (2007), who are recognized as the important contributors to the social media literature have claimed that the term social media captures all the services including internet-based and mobile ones that allow people to engage and participate in exchanges, joining and contributing to communities. Kietzmann, Hermkens, McCarthy and Silvestre (2011) have also admitted that social media captures mobile and web-based technologies to create interactive platforms through which users and communities share, discuss, co-create, and modify the contents. Despite the slight differences in the definitions of social media, there are some similarities that can be clearly seen. According to Mayfield (2010), there are five common characteristics that each social media platform has to be assured. These are:

1. **Participation**: Encourages becoming an active user.
2. **Openness**: Be accessible for everyone.
3. **Conversation**: Removes from being a broadcast.
4. **Community**: Creates groups that share common values and interests.

5. **Connectedness**: Increases interactions with other sites and potential users. Besides common features, the term social media also involves seven functional blocks such as sharing, conversations, groups, reputation, relationships, presence, and identity which are called by "the honeycomb of social media" (Kietzmann et al., 2011). Along the same line, Akkaya (2013) has emphasized four main aspects of social media that differ from traditional media:
    1. In traditional media, contents can be produced by only publishers, whereas in social media all users can create contents using tools which are mostly free or at small costs.
    2. In traditional media, contents are shaped by expert and dominated with their experiences; however in social media users are free to create and share regardless of their skills, knowledge or background.
    3. Social media is faster than traditional media for getting feedback.
    4. Once the content is published in traditional media, it is hard to revise. However, it is one click job correcting your mistakes in social media.

As Kuhn (1962) has propounded, Pink (2005) has agreed, and finally, Dawley (2009) has corroborated, new communication technologies such as printing press, internet, and social media play a role in epistemological and ontological development because of their functionality. In her inspirational study, Dawley (2009) has proposed a social network knowledge construction model (Figure 1) and tried to define how communication patterns could be shaped in the technology age for a student.

Based on this model, it can be indicated that networking through social media provides multi-channel communication opportunities that mass media cannot guarantee it. Before social media has penetrated our lives, constructors generally access

Figure 1. Social network knowledge construction model (Dawley, 2009)

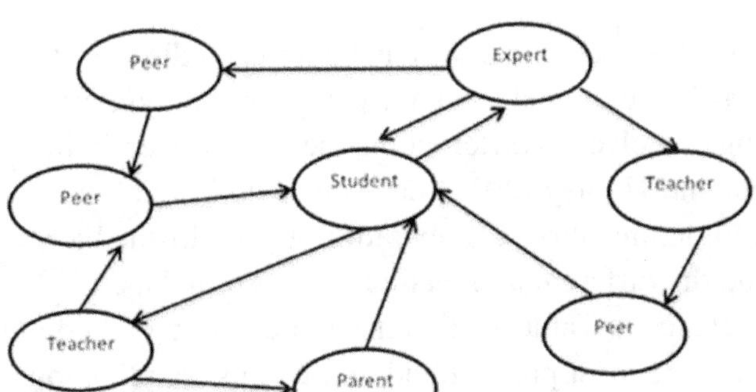

their students and share their knowledge to them with face to face communication whereas the interaction between them is a continuous process nowadays. Of course, this situation is not to be limited to the educational context but also encompasses people's daily lives. Rettberg (2009) has admitted that social media lends a hand us to craft the narratives of our own story. According to her, social media can organize our data and create an aspect of our life so that we can stay away from the clichés of mass media. For example, at certain times of the year Facebook prepares a customized video that includes the photos you shared.

Similarly, Dopplr (offline now) creates a colored timeline travel plan -so that its users can plan everything in detail- and marks correlations with friends –so that they can receive alerts when they would be in the same place-. Businesses can also get the advantage of social media by having a comprehensive platform (https://www.clarabridge.com) to engage better their customers -who also probably have at least one social media account- in real-time. Marwick (2013) has indicated that social media encourages people to promote themselves as a brand like businesses do; however majority of them abstain from monetizing through their account. Besides these enthusing features of social media, not all people may want to have this experience. The main issue is that people use social media willingly and choose what they represent in there. There are three modes of self-representation which generally overlap in social media: visual, written, and quantitative (Rettberg, 2017). Visual self-presentation captures all the images that we share on social media whereas the way of expressing yourself via the words called written self-presentation. Quantitative self-presentation comes to mean as depicting our self-portrait with numerical statements such as self-tracking and showing how many steps you have walked today. Rettberg (2017) has also stated:

Self-representations in social media are often mocked as vapid, self-obsessed, frivolous – or simply boring ... on the other hand, self-presentation shows a certain aspect of ourselves ... and it never can share everything.

The definitions, features, and issues that have been discussed so far about social media, it seems as if social media can only use for communication to other people or/and expressing ourselves in different manners. However, in their research report Cann, Dimitriou, and Hooley (2011) have classified social media tools into three groups namely; communication, collaboration, and multi-media. Table 1 shows their classification and the different applications each group has.

If we have a glance at Table 1, it comes to our mind that communication tools are the ones which are most popular and ready to use applications. Literature also has agreed that social networking is the most attractive tool for communication in our modern age (Aghazamani, 2010). In Figure 2, a recent report's statistics have

Table 1. Classification of social media tools (Cann, Dimitriou, & Hooley, 2011)

GROUP 1 COMMUNICATION TOOLS	Blogging	Blogger, LiveJournal, TypePad, WordPress Twitter, Yammer, Google Buzz
	Microblogging	Foursquare, Gowalla, Facebook Places Facebook, LinkedIn, MySpace
	Location	Google Reader, Netvibes, Pageflakes, iGoogle
	Social networking	Blogger, LiveJournal, TypePad, WordPress Twitter, Yammer, Google Buzz
	Aggregators	Foursquare, Gowalla, Facebook Places Facebook, LinkedIn, MySpace
GROUP 2 COLLABORATION TOOLS	Conferencing	Adobe Connect, GoToMeeting, Skype PBworks, Wetpaint, Wikia Delicious, Diigo, BibSonomy CiteULike, Mendeley Digg, Reddit, Newsvine
	Wikis	Google Docs, Dropbox, Zoho Bamboo, Basecamp, Huddle
	Social bookmarking	Adobe Connect, GoToMeeting, Skype PBworks, Wetpaint, Wikia Delicious, Diigo, BibSonomy CiteULike, Mendeley Digg, Reddit, Newsvine
	Social bibliography	Google Docs, Dropbox, Zoho Bamboo, Basecamp, Huddle
	Social news	Adobe Connect, GoToMeeting, Skype PBworks, Wetpaint, Wikia Delicious, Diigo, BibSonomy CiteULike, Mendeley Digg, Reddit, Newsvine
	Social documents	Google Docs, Dropbox, Zoho Bamboo, Basecamp, Huddle
	Project management	Adobe Connect, GoToMeeting, Skype PBworks, Wetpaint, Wikia Delicious, Diigo, BibSonomy CiteULike, Mendeley Digg, Reddit, Newsvine
GROUP 3 MULTI MEDIA TOOLS	Photographs	Flickr, Picasa, SmugMug Viddler, Vimeo, YouTube
	Video	Justin.tv, Livestream, Ustream Scribd, SlideShare, Sliderocket
	Live streaming	OpenSim, Second Life, World of Warcraft
	Presentation sharing	Flickr, Picasa, SmugMug Viddler, Vimeo, YouTube
	Virtual worlds	Justin.tv, Livestream, Ustream Scribd, SlideShare, Sliderocket

proved the increasing trend of social media usage all around the world. Likewise, a study's result has shown that college students spend approximately 18 hours a week on social networking which almost corresponds to 3 hours per day (Huang & Capps, 2013). Raice (2012) has also admitted customers pass the time of their day more on Facebook (6 hours average for the day) compare to Google and Youtube. Similarly, Wu, Cheung, Ku and Hung (2013) have also stated that nearly one-fourth of them their participants among Chinese smartphone users spend their time on social networking for more than three hours a day.

Figure 2. Time per day spent on social media (We Are Social, 2019)

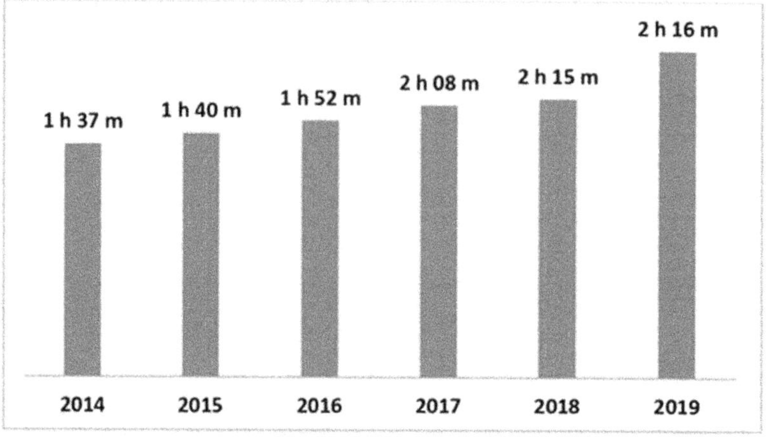

Because of exponential growth and rapid penetration of social media, it is crucial to understand the nature of these platforms, the reasons pushing people to use, and the consequences of using them should carefully investigate. Based on this inspiration, we will discuss the evolution of social media, most popular platforms, and their features –mainly focus on social network sites-, and the concept of social network sites addiction.

The Evolution of Social Media

In web 1.0, people get the information they need and nothing more. A few writers create the pages, and a vast number of people make use of them. Web 1.0 is described as "read-only web," whereas there is another way of reaching the web called "read-write" or more commonly known as Web 2.0. Although Web 2.0 is recognized as the most significant development for social media evolution, three milestones that should not be passed without mentioning since they can be recognized as the foundations of social media. The first one is the first **e-mail** sent between two computers by Raymond Samuel Tomlinson. The second one is the first **data transmission via telephone lines** between two users. The third one is a discussion system called **User Network (Usenet)** created by Tom Truscott and Jim Ellis which allows internet users to send instant messages. These three pioneering developments cover the period of 1970 to 1988 which we call "Foundation Age."

After the idea of transformable-information has been introduced by Tim Burners-Lee in 1989 at first, people have realized that they could do more than search and read (Getting, 2007). The idea of participating in the information has dramatically changed the ecosystem of the web. In 1996, **ICQ** (I Seek You) has been established by an Israeli company called Mirabilis. It is similar to Usenet, but ICQ also provides several privacy features for its users (Heim & Hansen, 1999) and it is the first stand-alone instant messenger. Two years later, the client of ICQ was bought by American Online (AOL) and then Mail.Ru Group in 2010 (Hollars & Lew, 2010). As of 2019, iOS and Android applications of are also available for ICQ. In 1997, AOL has launched its messenger called AOL Instant Messenger (**AIM**) which allows data transfer as well as instant messaging. Despite its growing popularity until the late 2000s, it has not failed to close in 2017. The same year with the AIM, **SixDegrees** formerly known as MacroView has also been established which is accepted as the first social network site. The idea behind this web site is "everybody is linked with everybody else via six degrees of separation" (Boyd & Ellison, 2008). Although ICQ and AIM offered lists of friends, they are not visible to others. SixDegress is the first web site that combined the popular features of social media as we discussed in the previous section such as profiles, friends list, and school affiliation. Another early social networking site which is called **Open Diary** has been introduced by Susan and Bruce Abelson in 1998. It is also accepted as the first blog. Although the web site has been hacked twice time in 2004 and 2008, it has managed to reach more than 561.000 blogs with 77 different countries by years 2008. In 2014 it has gone offline; however it has been activated in 2018 again. When it comes to millennium, **Wikipedia** has been introduced by Jimmy Donal Wales. It is the first collaborative online encyclopedia and has been adopted "anyone can edit" as a slogan (Bruns, 2006). From individual social connections to professional social connections, **Ryze** is the first platform to help people to leverage their professional networks. It has established in 2001 and recognized as the precursor to LinkedIn, but never gained mass popularity. As a social complement to Ryze, **Friendster** has started its life in 2002. Jonathan Abrams who is one of the owners of Friendster stated that this dating site focus on friends-of-friends meets instead of gathering strangers with similar interests. A motto "How can be lovers if we cannot be Friendsters?" has been started to spread (Boyd, 2006). According to Abrams, people create stronger ties and have better romantic relationship with the people that they have been known for a while (Boyd & Ellison, 2008). Thus, Friendster allowed its users to access at most four degrees away ("friends-of-friends-of-friends-of-friends"). At first, he was right, and Friendster got 300,000 users through word of mouth before it was founded as newsworthy (O'Shea, 2003); however, in the end, the site flamed out because of some technical and social difficulties (Boyd, 2006). In 2011, the site has transitioned into a virtual gaming community. Chafkin (2007) has evaluated the Friendster's rise and fall as the biggest disappointments in Internet history. The years between 1989 and 2002 has been introduced as "Exploration Age" which has started with the foundation of ICQ and ending with Friendster's succumbs.

As people realize the possibilities of socializing in the digital environment, new social networking sites have begun to evolve. As can be seen in Figure 3*, the expansion age of social media has begun in 2003, and it is still going on. In 2003, two important platforms have established called LinkedIn and MySpace.

*Figure 3. Timeline of social media (*only the most groundbreaking developments are listed for the consideration of the authors)*

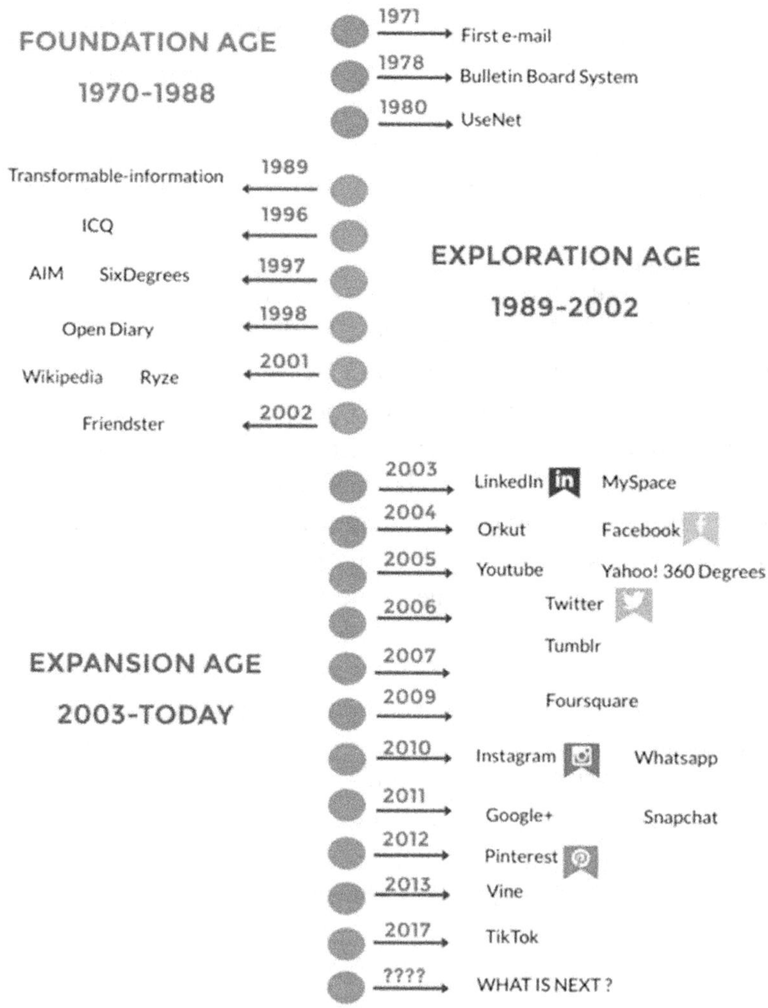

Unlike Ryze, **LinkedIn** has become an essential site for professionals. It has never stopped to evolve and always updated itself with new features like hiring solutions for businesses. In 2011, LinkedIn has been gone to public and now it is accepted the biggest initial public offering for a web company after Google (CBSNews, 2019). **MySpace** is a kind of dating site and has adopted an aggressive market strategy. They have focused on users who were the estranged users of Friendster. After the Friendster were fee-based system, MySpace has succeeded its mission and overgrown with its unique features (Boyd & Ellison, 2008). MySpace is the one which allows its users to personalize their profiles and pay regard their suggestions to update the site. Although MySpace has kept its leading position and remained as the most visited social networking site until 2008, Facebook has surpassed it after then. At the beginning of its history, **Facebook** has started out as a private sharing platform only for Harvard University students. As of September 2006, it has extended beyond universities to public (Phillips, 2007). Recently, Facebook is considered as one of the most prestigious companies in the world with its more than 2.3 billion monthly active users (Gebel, 2019). In addition to self-representation opportunities such as sharing photos, videos, ideas; Facebook also offers the Like button which enables users to confirm themselves and to get the appreciation of the other. According to Hayes, Carr, and Wohn (2016), the Like button is a kind of "paralinguistic digital affordance" which gives a communication chance without any word. Because of the array of potential meanings and ease of use, this button is one of the characteristic features of Facebook and contributes as trigger to Facebook's appeal to more people both teenagers and adults (Figure 4). How Facebook has left behind its rivals and why is still the most popular social network site? Actually, the answer is simple: Facebook provides a relatively easy way to access social connections (Ellison, Steinfield, & Lampe, 2011), contains time-saving cues (Walther & Ramirez, 2009), and targeting a global audience so that users can reach and comments on anybody with minimum efforts and without limitation.

Figure 4. Age18-34 and age 35+ digital audience penetration vs. engagement of leading social networks (Comsource, 2018)

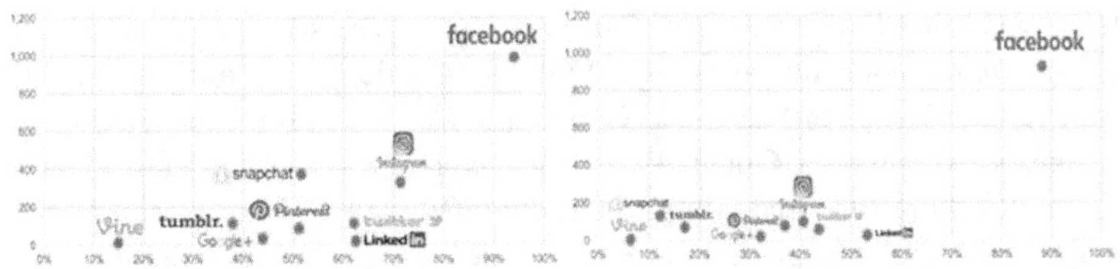

Although the original Yahoo! Company has been established in 1995, it has succeeded to adopt to technology age in 2005 with the foundation of **Yahoo! 360 Degrees**. This special module has launched with its unique services such as Flickr, Yahoo! Music, and Messenger. However Yahoo has slowly declined in the late 2000s and its core businesses have been bought by Verizon in 2017 (McGoogan, 2016). In 2005, a video sharing platform -**Youtube**- has hit the headlines and be one of the leading web sites around the world. In 2006, Google has bought Youtube, and now it operates as one of Google's subsidiaries. In 2006, something has changed with a little whisper. Jack Dorsey wrote a sentence "Just setting up my Twttr." via his platform and announced that **Twitter** (formerly known as Twttr) -a microblogging web site- has officially founded. Besides Facebook popularity, Twitter has begun experiencing a massive growth because the web-site has been a user-driven (hashtags are the idea of Twitter's users) and more suitable for an ongoing public dialogue (Junco et al., 2011). Currently, there are more than 321 million active users on Twitter (Molina, 2017). In 2007, another microblogging web site **Tumblr** has been created. The site has not been achieved its mission and made an agreement with Yahoo just before Verizon bought it in 2017. Currently, Tumblr is one of the subsidiaries of Verizon. In 2009, **Foursquare** has been founded which is a location-based service that allows its users to share their location-specific information with their real-time updates. In 2010, a photo and video-sharing website -**Instagram**- has owned by Facebook. According to the literature, these two platforms have similar features however the motives for using them are different. People tend to use Facebook to fulfill their need for belonging and need for self-presentation whereas Instagram focuses on self-expression and social interaction (Kircaburun, Demetrovics, & Tosuntaş, 2018). It is also stated although the widespread acceptance of Facebook all around the world with 2.5 billion active users, it has admitted that young people have started to move into another social media platforms such as Instagram (Sweney & De Liz, 2018; Utz, Muscanell, & Khalid, 2015). The same year with Instagram, another popular platform -**Whatsapp**-has been founded by Brian Acton and Jan Koum who were the former employees of Yahoo. Four years later it has owned by Facebook because the owner of Facebook has thought Whatsapp would be their major rivals in the near future. Whatsapp is a free, cross-platform messaging for individual uses, and since 2018 it has launched for small business use, too (Ong, 2018). According to the statistics of January 2019, Whatsapp has the most active user accounts among the messenger/VOIP applications (We are Social, 2019). Given the dominance of Facebook, Google has also made some attempts to catch social networking trends. **Google+** has launched in 2011 which is a fairly standard social networking site. According to Ovadia (2011), there is no reason to expect Google+ win the first place; however so many people are curious about what Google can do about social networking. In the end, Google+ can't manage to get rid of calling as a "ghost place" and more than 99% users of it cannot satisfy with it (Denning, 2015). As Pariser has stated that Google is undeniably good at managing relationships among data; whereas Facebook is good at managing relationships among people (Pariser, 2011). In 2011, **Snapchat** has been released as a photo-sharing app. What makes it different from Facebook and Instagram is that Snapchat offers its users more private communication opportunities with a feature of immediately disappearing posts. A report results' has indicated that college students think Snapchat is the safest web-site for photo-sharing (Bennett, 2014). The rapid acceleration of Snapchat annoyed Facebook and the acquisition attempt has occurred in 2013. Unlike Instagram and Whatsapp, Snapchat has rejected $3 billion offer from Facebook (Rusli & MacMillan, 2014). Although, Facebook remains its popularity among young adults; however adolescences and teens have already started to Instagram and Snapchat (Alhabash & Ma, 2017). Currently, the market value of Snap is estimated by nearly $15 billion (Feiner, 2019). In 2012, a new kind of social media called visual bookmarking has been created by the name of **Pinterest**. Users can discover, achieve, and share any web image or personal digital image in their scrapbook. Since most posted pictures are of products and brands, Pinterest offers many opportunities to brand advertisers as well as individuals (Phillips, Miller, & McQuarrie, 2014). As of the second quarter of 2019, Pinterest had 300 million monthly active users (Statista, 2019a). In 2013, **Vine** -a Twitter-owned service- has started its journey. Similar with few seconds appearing photos in Snapchat, Vine offers to create and share six-second videos. After Vine has shut down, another similar video sharing application has been offered which is called **TikTok**. Currently, TikTok has more than 500 million monthly active users which is more than Twitter (Langford, 2019).

Consequently, it can be stated that social media is an umbrella term which consists tools that provide several communication opportunities via connecting and retrieving features that include blogs (OpenDiary), wikis (Wikipedia), social bookmarking (Pinterest), media sharing (YouTube) virtual communities (all social network sites such as Facebook, Instagram), and collaborative tools (Google+) (Taylor, King, & Nelson, 2012).

SOCIAL NETWORK SITES (SNS)

After defining social media and its evolution in Section 1, we are going to focus on the most popular forms of social media which are called social network sites (SNSs). First, we try to clarify the concept of SNS. Then, we are going to have a look at the effects of using SNS both an individual and business level.

The Concept of SNS

Although there are many attempts to describe what social media sites refer to, Boyd and Ellison (2008)'s approach is the most cited one. According to them three major components that each SNS should have but the nature of them could be different from one website to another. They have stated that SNSs allows people to (1) create a personal page within a bounded system, (2) have a list of people with whom they are agreed to share a connection, and (3) view and change their friend's list. Boyd and Ellison (2008) have also stated that SNSs are unique communication platforms which offer users to articulate their networks as well as meeting with strangers.

According to Whiting and Williams (2013), people use SNS for ten reasons: passing time, information seeking, social interaction, communicatory utility, relaxation, entertainment, expression of opinion, information sharing, convenience utility, surveillance of knowledge about others (Alhabash & Ma, 2017). Curran and Lennon (2011) have proposed a research model to explain social networking behaviors. They have indicated that ease of use, usefulness, enjoyment, social influence and drama are the five main antecedents of SNS usage behavior. To put into more general, we can plausibly state that people want to use SNS for two main reasons: First one is about enhancing an individual's network size by means of meeting strangers. The second one is maintaining current relationships and having more strong-ties (Boyd & Ellison, 2008). One recent study's result has shown that young people generally prefer to use social media for creating new friendships, whereas older users tend to use these platforms to sustain their relationships (Munzel, Meyer-Waarden, & Galan, 2018). Besides motives for using SNS habits differ according to age, literature suggests that there are also some gender-specific patterns. For example, Sharp, Coatsworth, Darling, Cumsille and Ranieri (2007) have admitted that being social on SNS is more important for females compared to males. Similarly, Hargittai and Hsieh (2010) have also proved that males are more likely to join SNS for gaining new friends whereas females tend to develop more strong-tie activities such as chatting with close friends or press the like button for someone's picture whom they have been already introduced. With this line, Stanley (2015) has also found that females are mostly online in Facebook and Snapchat in order to monitor their siblings and parents status; whereas males go online in Facebook to meet new people.

Regardless of who uses them for what purposes, SNSs become more and more people day by day. According to the current statistics, 2.65 billion people have used social media in 2018 and will reach almost 3.1 billion in 2012 (Statista, 2019b). These numbers are reasonably enough to claim that SNS usage moves towards addiction. This claim will be discussed in more detail in Section 3.

Positive and Negative Effect of SNSs

It is stated that people - especially young adults (18-35 years) - do not realize how much time they spend on these platforms (Meena, Soni, Jain & Paliwal, 2015). A master thesis' results from Johnson & Wales University have indicated that 45% of their participants spent 6-8 hours a day in SNSs, while 23% of them have admitted that they have spent more than 8 hours a day (Wang, Chen, & Liang, 2011). A more recent report has indicated that the average time a user spends on Facebook is 58 minutes, in Youtube 60 minutes, in LinkedIn 10 minutes, and in Snapchat 25 minutes which is dominated by young adults (Stout, 2019). As a result of excessive use of these platforms, people face with some hassles in their daily lives. For example, Moqbel and Kock (2018) have expressed that high-frequency usage of social media causes health problems and low task performance as well as having more negative emotions. The negative effects of SNSs are more common among young individuals because they are more engaged with social media (Baker & Moore, 2008; Kalpidou et al., 2011). A study conducting with young adults has admitted that there is a positive relationship between the usage of SNS and sleep disturbance (Levenson, Shensa, Sidani, Colditz, & Primack, 2016). Gerson, Plagnol, and Corr (2016) have admitted that excessive use of SNS causes low well-being, especially for high goal-driven users since they are more inclined to develop negative social comparison. Besides daily life problems, time spent on Facebook and checking the notifications frequently are negatively related to students' academic success (Junco, 2012). Benson, Hand, and Hartshorne (2019) have stated that compulsive use of SNS is positively and significantly related to low academic performance.

Despite SNSs can have negative consequences they can offer some advantages such as enhanced social capital (Ellison, Steinfield, & Lampe, 2007) and sense of belonging (Davis, 2012), public individuation and user innovativeness (Choi & Kim, 2016), and increased well-being (Magsamen-Conrad, Billiotte-Verhoff, & Greene, 2014). Magsamen-Conrad et al. (2014) have aware that not all people have to feel comfortable in face-to-face communication. According to them several communication opportunities on SNS may reverse the negative effects of self-concealment on well-being, especially for the isolated and shy young individuals. A more recent study's results has showed that higher number of Facebook friends is positively related with subjective happiness and negatively related with loneliness (Phu & Gow, 2019). Beyond daily life, social media provides many unpredictable opportunities in the educational context, too. Using SNSs as an educational tool and integrating them with course content may increase the efficiency of lessons and motivation of learners. In their study, Lim & Richardson (2016) found out that, students used online social networking platforms for various reasons and their perceptions were usually positive when the SNSs were used as an educational tool. Junco et al.

(2011) conducted a study to reveal if Twitter has an impact on students' engagement in the USA, where the instructors can also participate. Results showed that Twitter has a significant impact by the way of offering to students being more active and the ability to engage. Another study looked into the impact of Facebook usage on students' academic performance and found that there was a positive correlation among them (Ainin et al., 2015). Besides academic related jobs, usage of Facebook also beneficial to predict time spent in co-curricular activities (Junco, 2012).

There is no denying that social media platforms are inevitable for the majority of people to share their knowledge and interests. However, that is not all. These platforms can be unique in the way of improving the businesses performance. Businesses are fostered to use SNSs for increasing their relationships in order to have more trusted products and more loyal customers (Laroche, Habibi, & Richard, 2013). The term 'social media marketing' has increased its popularity by means of placing brand posts on the brand fan pages on SNSs. One study results showed that positioning the brand post on the right SNS affect the popularity of the brand in a positive way (de Vries et al., 2012). Although SNSs are generally considered an easy way to participate in Computer-Mediated-Communication (CMC), Treem and Leonardi (2013) have pointed out that social media differs from computer-mediated communication in some ways namely visibility, persistence, editability, and association. Thanks to these affordances businesses may alter their socialization, knowledge sharing, and power processes.

IRREPRESSIBLE POPULARITY OF SNSs

In this section, we try to define what SNS addiction it is and what features it consists of. We have also briefly examined the reasons for SNS usage and the consequences of it. After, we have briefly examined the previous studies about the related subject.

Term Of SNS Addiction

Addiction is a complex concept, and it is tough to define it accurately. Generally speaking, there are two kinds of addiction exists; substance addiction and non-substance addiction. Former one expresses the fondness for certain substances such as alcohol or drug. The later one comes into our lives with the advancement of technology and more related to individuals' behavior. That is why it is also called behavioral addiction (Alavi et al., 2012). Marlatt, Baer, Donovan, and Kivlahan (1988, p. 224), who have defined addictive behavior as: "…a repetitive habit pattern that increases the risk of disease and/or associated personal and social problems. Addictive behaviors are often experienced subjectively as 'loss of control' – the behavior contrives to occur despite volitional attempts to abstain or moderate use. These habit patterns are typically characterized by immediate gratification (short term reward), often coupled with delayed deleterious effects (long term costs). Attempts to change addictive behavior (via treatment or self-initiation) are typically marked with high relapse rates." More specifically, Walker (1989, p.185) has defined a behavioral addiction as "a persistent behavioral pattern characterized by: a desire or need to continue the activity which places it outside voluntary control; a tendency to increase the frequency or amount of the activity over time; psychological dependence on the pleasurable effects of the activity; and, a detrimental effect on the individual and society." In 1990, Goodman has identified the diagnostic criteria for behavioral addictions as can be seen in Figure 5. Griffiths (2005) has concluded topic with his 'components' model of addiction. He has identified six features that each addiction consists of. These are:

1. **Salience**: A particular activity becomes the most important thing in person's life.
2. **Mood Modification**: Consequences of participating in a regular activity.
3. **Tolerance**: Requests more and more from a particular activity.
4. **Withdrawal Symptoms**: Unpleasant feelings in the absence of a particular activity.
5. **Conflict**: Chaos between the addict himself and also those around him.
6. **Relapse**: Be unable to stop doing an undesirable behavior.

Young (1999) have classified internet addiction into five groups namely computer addiction, information overload, net compulsions, cyber-sexual addiction and cyber-relationship; however, only one behavioral addiction called pathological gambling –falls into the net compulsion group- has been formally accepted as a diagnostic disorder (American Psychiatric Association, 1987). Although the idea of behavioral addictions is based in scientific knowledge, the concept is still controversial (Grant, Odlaug, & Chamberlain, 2016), researchers aware the other possible behavioral addiction with the evolution of social media and there is an increasing interest in this topic (Andreassen et al., 2013b). In this context, Kuss and Griffiths (2011) have claimed that a rising addiction called SNS addiction has emerged. Andreassen (2015) has also stated that excessive and compulsive behaviors on SNSs can be regarded as an addiction. It should be noted here that excessive usage an activity alone is not enough to accept any behavior as an addiction (Griffiths, 2010). There are many people who use Internet for more than 10 hours a day but have few negative consequences. Griffiths, who is a popular psychologist on behavioral addictions, also believe that being addicted to social media and being addicted to social media

Figure 5. Diagnostic criteria for behavioral addictions (Goodman, 1990)

A. Recurrent failure to resist impulses to engage in a specified behaviour.
B. Increasing sense of tension immediately prior the initiation of behaviour.
C. Pleasure or relief at the time of engaging in the behaviour.
D. A feeling of a lack of control while engaging in the behaviour.
E. At least five of the following:
   1. Frequent preoccupation with the behaviour or preparatory activities
   2. Frequent engaging in the behaviour to a greater extent or over a longer period than intended
   3. Repeated efforts to reduce, control or stop the behaviour
   4. A great deal of time spent in activities necessary for the behaviour, engaging in the behaviour or recovering from its effects
   5. Frequent engaging in the behaviour when expected to fulfil occupational, academic, domestic or social obligations
   6. Important social, occupational or recreational activities given up or reduced because of the behaviour
   7. Continuation of the behaviour despite knowledge of having a persistent or recurrent social, financial, psychological or physical problem that is caused or exacerbated by the behaviour
   8. Tolerance: need to increase the intensity or frequency of the behaviour in order to achieve the desired effect or diminished effect with continued behaviour of the same intensity
   9. Restlessness or irritability if unable to engage in the behaviour
F. Some symptoms of the disturbance have persisted for at least 1 month or have occurred repeatedly over a longer period of time.

are two different things. Just as alcoholics are addicted to alcohol, not the bottle, social media users may be addicted to the activities, not the SNS, itself. Phu and Gow (2019) have also stated that actual time spends on a specific SNS is not a clear indication of being addicted to it since there could be different reasons to use these platforms. Because of these reasons, someone should be carefully evaluated as she or he is addicted to the SNS or not.

Andreassen and Pallesen (2014, p.2) have defined SNS addiction as "being overly concerned about SNSs, driven by a strong motivation to log on to or use SNSs, and to devote so much time and effort to SNSs that it impairs other social activities, studies/job, interpersonal relationships, and/or psychological health and well-being." SNS addiction takes part in the cyber-relationship category since the primary purpose of using these platforms is communication (Kuss & Griffiths, 2011).

Research Topics in SNS Addiction

For a while, researchers have tried to find an answer to one question: What types of person are most likely to use SNS? In literature, there is some evidence that excessive use of SNS is more common in certain groups. For example, Ehrenberg, Juckes, White, and Walsh (2008) have conducted a survey-based study and indicated that more neurotic and low self-esteem individuals have spent more time on social networking activities. They have also stated that people who prefer online communication instead of face to face conversation can be regarded as more anxious and socially insecure. Low self-esteem has been also found to be positively related to SNS addiction in other studies (Bányai et al., 2017; Lou, Yan, Nickerson, & McMorris, 2012). Addictive tendencies appear more common in extroverted and less common in conscientious individuals (Wilson, Fornasier, & White, 2010). Another study has revealed that openness to new experiences, extraversion, and neuroticism are all positively related to SNS addiction (Correa, Hinsley, & De Zuniga, 2010). Impulsivity has been found as another indicator of high usage of SNS (Rothen et al., 2018). Similarly, a more recent study with a convenient cross-sectional sample of 23,532 Norwegians has found that people who are more narcissist with low self-esteem are more likely to use SNS (Andreassen, Pallesen, & Griffiths, 2017). The same study has also indicated that women may tend to develop more addictive habits towards SNS. Although there are some other studies which have admitted that social media addiction is more commonly appears among men (Çam & Işbulan, 2012), research has more consistently suggested that women are more prone to developing addictive SNS use (Andreassen et al., 2013; Kuss, Griffiths, Karila, & Billieux, 2014; Mariko Kasahara, 2017; Tartory, 2019). Kuss et al. (2014) have also investigated that people with no relationship are more willing to use SNS. In the same line but more exciting finding is that married men generally prefer to stay away from social media, whereas women actively engage in social network activities whether they are married or not (Lennon, Rentfro, & Curran, 2012). In addition to gender differences, there is undeniably the dominance of young population in social media. As previous studies have proved that Internet addiction is negatively related to age (Carbonell, Chamarro, Oberst, Rodrigo, & Prades, 2018; Neverkovich et al., 2018), SNS addiction has also been found a negative relationship with the age. In their inspiring scale construction study, Andreassen, TorbjØrn, Brunborg and Pallesen (2012) have admitted that neurotic and extraverted young people are more inclined to develop addictive habits towards Facebook. Turel and Serenko (2012) have investigated the benefits and dangers of enjoyment with SNS and found that age is a significant control variable with negative effect on habit.

CONCLUSION AND FUTURE DIRECTIONS

In our modern world, having a profile and surfing on social media are accepted as normal behaviors (Andreassen, 2015). While there are some gender and age-specific patterns that affect the SNS usage habits, it is stated that internet access or parental education have no longer been concerned as a predictors of social media because people always get a way to be online (Ahn, 2011). Considering that older users have the highest proportion of newly registered users rather than younger ones in recent years (Benson et al., 2019), it can be plausibly asserted that the spread of social media does not lose its speed. This chapter focuses on this popular topic and presents the outline of social media since its early years to state-of-art issues.

As a result of our study, we have agreed on Allen et al. (2014) who have stated that how social media can use its capacity to provide a real benefit?" is still a controversial issue. It is clearly seen that excessive and problematic use of social media -especially SNSs- has several effects on our lives, it is critical to get benefit from these platforms without being addicted to them. Although gambling is the only behavioral addiction that formally accepted (American Psychiatric Association, 1987), there are strong pieces of evidence that problematic use of SNSs can also be an addiction (Körmendi, Brutóczki, Végh, & Székely, 2016). Thus, people get aware about the current situation and take some precautions before they get addicted to them. Regarding positive and negative concerns, successful integration of social media is challenging. Having content with what you already desire entails you moving away from current technological development and becomes you just an audience when your rivals do something more creative.

Our study is not without its limitations. First, the timeline of social media (Figure 3) is a great effort by putting together with the main developments; however we aware that there are also other platforms and events which should be discussed about. Thus, we encourage researchers to design more detailed and comparative visualizations so that evolution of social media can be deeply understood. Second, we have briefly presented the concept of SNS addiction and related literature. We suggest other researchers make empirical researches about this topic since there is emerging literature about this relatively new area.

REFERENCES

Aghazamani, A. (2010). How do university students spend their time on Facebook? An exploratory study. *The Journal of American Science*, *6*, 730–735.

Ahn, J. (2011). Digital divides and social network sites: Which students participate in social media? *Journal of Educational Computing Research*, *45*(2), 147–163. doi:10.2190/EC.45.2.b

Ainin, S., Naqshbandi, M. M., Moghavvemi, S., & Jaafar, N. I. (2015). Facebook usage, socialization and academic performance. *Computers & Education*, *83*, 64–73. doi:10.1016/j.compedu.2014.12.018

Akıncı Vural, Z. B., & Bat, M. (2010). Yeni Bir İletişim Ortamı Olarak Sosyal Medya: Ege Üniversitesi İletişim Fakültesine YönelikBir Araştırma. *Journal of Yaşar University*, *20*(5), 3348–3382. doi:10.19168/jyu.65130

Akkaya, D. T. (2013). *Sosyal Medya Reklamlarında Tüketici Algılarının Tutum, Davranış ve Satın Alma Niyeti Üzerine Etkisi*. Trakya Üniversitesi.

Alavi, S. S., Ferdosi, M., Jannatifard, F., Eslami, M., Alaghemandan, H., & Setare, M. (2012). Behavioral addiction versus substance addiction: correspondence of psychiatric and psychological views. *International Journal of Preventive Medicine*, *3*(4), 290–294. PMID:22624087

Alhabash, S., & Ma, M. (2017). A tale of four platforms: motivations and uses of Facebook, Twitter, Instagram, and Snapchat among college students? *Social Media and Society*, *3*(1). doi:10.1177/2056305117691544

Allen, K. A., Ryan, T., Gray, D. L., McInerney, D. M., & Waters, L. (2014). Social media use and social connectedness in adolescents: The positives and the potential pitfalls. *Australian Educational and Developmental Psychologist*, *31*(1), 18–31. doi:10.1017/edp.2014.2

American Psychiatric Association. (1987). *Diagnostic and statistical manual of mental disorders*. Washington, DC.

Andreassen, C. S. (2015). Online social network site addiction: a comprehensive review. *Current Addiction Reports*, *2*(2), 175–184. doi:10.100740429-015-0056-9

Andreassen, C. S., Griffiths, M. D., Gjertsen, S. R., Krossbakken, E., Kvam, S., & Pallesen, S. (2013a). The relationships between behavioral addictions and the five-factor model of personality. *Journal of Behavioral Addictions*, *2*(2), 90–99. doi:10.1556/JBA.2.2013.003 PMID:26165928

Andreassen, C. S., Griffiths, M. D., Gjertsen, S. R., Krossbakken, E., Kvam, S., & Pallesen, S. (2013b). The relationships between behavioral addictions and the five-factor model of personality. *Journal of Behavioral Addictions*, *2*(2), 90–99. doi:10.1556/JBA.2.2013.003 PMID:26165928

Andreassen, C. S., & Pallesen, S. (2014). Social network site addiction-an overview. *Current Pharmaceutical Design*, *20*(25), 1–9. Retrieved from http://freepsychologypdf.com/wp-content/uploads/2018/07/Andreassen-2014-Social-network-site-addiction-An-overview.pdf. doi:10.2174/13816128113199990616 PMID:24001298

Andreassen, C. S., Pallesen, S., & Griffiths, M. D. (2017). The relationship between addictive use of social media, narcissism, and self-esteem: Findings from a large national survey. *Addictive Behaviors*, *64*, 287–293. doi:10.1016/j.addbeh.2016.03.006 PMID:27072491

Andreassen, C. S., Torsheim, T., Brunborg, G. S., & Pallesen, S. (2012). Development of a facebook addiction scale. *Psychological Reports*, *110*(2), 501–517. doi:10.2466/02.09.18.PR0.110.2.501-517 PMID:22662404

Baek, Y. M., Bae, Y., & Jang, H. (2013). Social and parasocial relationships on social network sites and their differential relationships with users' psychological well-being. *Cyberpsychology, Behavior, and Social Networking*, *16*(7), 512–517. doi:10.1089/cyber.2012.0510 PMID:23697533

Bányai, F., Zsila, Á., Király, O., Maraz, A., Elekes, Z., Griffiths, M., ... Demetrovics, Z. (2017). Problematic social media use: Results from a large-scale nationally representative adolescent sample. *PLoS One*, *12*(1), 10–14. doi:10.1371/journal.pone.0169839 PMID:28068404

Bennett, S. (2014). 70% of college students post to Snapchat daily (Twitter: 46%, Facebook: 11%). Retrieved from https://www.adweek.com/digital/snapchat-facebook-twitter-instagram-privacy/

Benson, V., Hand, C., & Hartshorne, R. (2019). How compulsive use of social media affects performance: Insights from the UK by purpose of use. *Behaviour & Information Technology*, *38*(6), 549–563. doi:10.1080/0144929X.2018.1539518

Boyd, D. (2006). Friendster lost steam. Is MySpace just a fad? Retrieved from https://www.danah.org/papers/FriendsterMySpaceEssay.html

Boyd, D. M. (2006). Friends, friendsters, and top 8: Writing community into being on social network sites. *First Monday*, *11*(12). doi:10.5210/fm.v11i12.1418

Boyd, D. M., & Ellison, N. B. (2007). Social network sites: definition, history, and scholarship. *Journal of Computer-Mediated Communication*, *13*(1), 210–230. doi:10.1111/j.1083-6101.2007.00393.x

Boyd, D. M., & Ellison, N. B. (2008). Social network sites: Definition, history, and scholarship. *Journal of Computer-Mediated Communication*, *13*(1), 210–230. doi:10.1111/j.1083-6101.2007.00393.x

Bruns, A. (2006). *Blogs, Wikipedia, second life, and beyond: from production to produsage*. New York, NY: Peter Lang.

Çam, E., & Işbulan, O. (2012). A new addiction for teacher candidates: Social networks. *Turkish Online Journal of Educational Technology*, *11*(3), 14–19.

Cann, A., Dimitriou, K., & Hooley, T. (2011). *Social media: A guide for researchers. Research Information Network*. London, UK. Retrieved from https://derby.openrepository.com/bitstream/handle/10545/196715/social media guide for screen.pdf?sequence=6&isAllowed=y

Carbonell, X., Chamarro, A., Oberst, U., Rodrigo, B., & Prades, M. (2018). Problematic use of the internet and smartphones in university students: 2006–2017. *International Journal of Environmental Research and Public Health*, *15*(3). doi:10.3390/ijerph15030475

CBSNews. (2019). *Then and now: a history of social networking sites.* Retrieved from https://www.cbsnews.com/pictures/then-and-now-a-history-of-social-networking-sites/5/

Chafkin, M. (2007). *How to kill a great idea!* Retrieved from https://www.inc.com/magazine/20070601/features-how-to-kill-a-great-idea.html

Choi, J., & Kim, H. J. (2016). Influence of SNS user innovativeness and public individuation on SNS usage patterns and social capital development: the case of Facebook. *International Journal of Human-Computer Interaction*, *32*(12), 921–930. doi:10.1080/10447318.2016.1220067

Comsource. (2018). *Understand and evaluate audiences and advertising everywhere.* Retrieved from https://www.comscore.com/Products/Ratings-and-Planning

Correa, T., Hinsley, A. W., & De Zuniga, H. (2010). Who interacts on the Web? The intersection of users' personality and social media use. *Computers in Human Behavior*, *26*(2), 247–253. doi:10.1016/j.chb.2009.09.003

Curran, J., & Lennon, R. (2011). Participating in the conversation: exploring adoption of online social media networks. *Academy of Marketing Studies*, *15*(1), 21–38.

Dawley, L. (2009). Social network knowledge construction: Emerging virtual world pedagogy. *On the Horizon*, *17*(2), 109–121. doi:10.1108/10748120910965494

Denning, S. (2015). *Has Google+ really died?* Retrieved from https://www.forbes.com/sites/stevedenning/2015/04/23/has-google-really-died/#10b77352466c

Ehrenberg, A., Juckes, S., White, K. M., & Walsh, S. P. (2008). Personality and self-esteem as predictors of young people's technology use. *Cyberpsychology & Behavior, 11*(6), 739–741. doi:10.1089/cpb.2008.0030 PMID:18991531

Ellison, N. B., Steinfield, C., & Lampe, C. (2007). The benefits of Facebook "friends:" Social capital and college students' use of online social network sites. *Journal of Computer-Mediated Communication, 12*(4), 1143–1168. doi:10.1111/j.1083-6101.2007.00367.x

Ellison, N. B., Steinfield, C., & Lampe, C. (2011). Connection strategies: Social capital implications of Facebook-enabled communication practices. *New Media & Society, 13*(6), 873–892. doi:10.1177/1461444810385389

Evans, D. (2008). *Social media marketing an hour a day*. Indiana: Wiley Publishing.

Feiner, L. (2019). *Snap has nearly doubled its stock price since the beginning of 2019 — here's why.* Retrieved from https://www.cnbc.com/2019/04/04/why-snap-stock-has-nearly-doubled-since-the-beginning-of-2019.html

Gebel, M. (2019). *In 15 years Facebook has amassed 2.3 billion users — more than followers of Christianity.* Retrieved from https://www.businessinsider.com/facebook-has-2-billion-plus-users-after-15-years-2019-2

Gerson, J., Plagnol, A. C., & Corr, P. J. (2016). Subjective well-being and social media use: Do personality traits moderate the impact of social comparison on Facebook? *Computers in Human Behavior, 63*, 813–822. doi:10.1016/j.chb.2016.06.023

Getting, B. (2007). *Basic definitions: Web 1.0, Web. 2.0, Web 3.0.* Retrieved from https://www.practicalecommerce.com/Basic-Definitions-Web-1-0-Web-2-0-Web-3-0

Goodman, A. (1990). Addiction: definition and implications. *British Journal of Addiction, 85*(11), 1403–1408. doi:10.1111/j.1360-0443.1990.tb01620.x PMID:2285834

Grant, J. E., Odlaug, B. L., & Chamberlain, S. R. (2016). *What is a behavioral addiction?* Retrieved from https://www.psychologytoday.com/intl/blog/why-cant-i-stop/201606/what-is-behavioral-addiction

Greengard, S. (2012). Digitally possessed. *Communications of the ACM, 55*(5), 14–16. doi:10.1145/2160718.2160725

Greenwood, J., Guner, N., Santos, C., & Kocharkov, G. (2016). Technology and the changing family: A unified model of marriage, divorce, educational attainment and marred female labor-force participation. *American Economic Journal. Macroeconomics*, *8*(1), 1–41. doi:10.1257/mac.20130156

Griffiths, M. (2005). A "components" model of addiction within a biopsychosocial framework. *Journal of Substance Use*, *10*(4), 191–197. doi:10.1080/14659890500114359

Griffiths, M. D. (2010). The role of context in online gaming excess and addiction: Some case study evidence. *International Journal of Mental Health and Addiction*, *8*(1), 119–125. doi:10.100711469-009-9229-x

Hargittai, E., & Hsieh, Y. (2010). Predictors and consequences of differentiated practices on social network sites. *Information Communication and Society*, *13*(4), 515–536. doi:10.1080/13691181003639866

Hayes, R. A., Carr, C. T., & Wohn, D. Y. (2016). One click, many meanings: interpreting paralinguistic digital affordances in social media. *Journal of Broadcasting & Electronic Media*, *60*(1), 171–187. doi:10.1080/08838151.2015.1127248

Heim, J., & Hansen, G. (1999). *Free stuff for sewing fanatics on the internet*. Lafayette, CA: C&T Publishing.

Hollars, K., & Lew, A. (2010). Digital sky technologies to acquire AOL's ICQ instant messaging service. Retrieved from https://www.businesswire.com/news/home/6268204/en

Huang, S.-H., & Capps, M. (2013). Impact of online social network on american college students' reading practices. *The College Quarterly*, *16*(1). Retrieved from http://collegequarterly.ca/2013-vol16-num01-winter/huang-capps.html

Junco, R. (2012). The relationship between frequency of Facebook use, participation in Facebook activities, and student engagement. *Computers & Education*, *58*(1), 162–171. doi:10.1016/j.compedu.2011.08.004

Junco, R. (2012). Too much face and not enough books: The relationship between multiple indices of Facebook use and academic performance. *Computers in Human Behavior*, *28*(1), 187–198. doi:10.1016/j.chb.2011.08.026

Junco, R. (2014). *Engaging students through social media: evidence-based practices for use in student affairs*. San Francisco, CA: Jossey-Bass.

Junco, R., Heiberger, G., & Loken, E. (2011). The effect of Twitter on college student engagement and grades. *Journal of Computer Assisted Learning, 27*(2), 119–132. doi:10.1111/j.1365-2729.2010.00387.x

Kalpidou, M., Costin, D., & Morris, J. (2011). The relationship between Facebook and the well-being of undergraduate college students. *Cyberpsychology, Behavior, and Social Networking, 14*(4), 183–189. doi:10.1089/cyber.2010.0061 PMID:21192765

Kaplan, A. M., & Haenlein, M. (2010). Users of the world, unite! The challenges and opportunities of Social Media. *Business Horizons, 53*(1), 59–68. doi:10.1016/j.bushor.2009.09.003

Kietzmann, J. H., Hermkens, K., McCarthy, I. P., & Silvestre, B. S. (2011). Social media? Get serious! Understanding the functional building blocks of social media. *Business Horizons, 54*(3), 241–251. doi:10.1016/j.bushor.2011.01.005

Kircaburun, K., Demetrovics, Z., & Tosuntaş, Ş. B. (2018). Analyzing the links between problematic social media use, dark triad traits, and self-esteem. *International Journal of Mental Health and Addiction*. doi:10.100711469-018-9900-1

Körmendi, A., Brutóczki, Z., Végh, B. P., & Székely, R. (2016). Smartphone use can be addictive? A case report. *Journal of Behavioral Addictions, 5*(3), 548–552. doi:10.1556/2006.5.2016.033 PMID:27599674

Kuhn, T. (1962). *The structure of scientific revolutions*. Chicago, IL: University of Chicago Press.

Kuss, D. J., Griffiths, M., Karila, L., & Billieux, J. (2014). Internet addiction: A systematic review of epidemiological research for the last decade, *1*(4), 397–413.

Kuss, D. J., & Griffiths, M. D. (2011). Online social networking and addiction-A review of the psychological literature. *International Journal of Environmental Research and Public Health, 8*(9), 3528–3552. doi:10.3390/ijerph8093528 PMID:22016701

Langford, S. (2019). Junk explained: What the hell is TikTok, and is it the new vine? Retrieved from https://junkee.com/tiktok-app-vine-challenge/188567

Laroche, M., Habibi, M. R., & Richard, M. O. (2013). To be or not to be in social media: How brand loyalty is affected by social media? *International Journal of Information Management, 33*(1), 76–82. doi:10.1016/j.ijinfomgt.2012.07.003

Lennon, R., Rentfro, R. W., & Curran, J. M. (2012). Exploring relationships between demographic variables and social networking use. *Journal of Management and Marketing Research, 11*, 1–17.

Levenson, J. C., Shensa, A., Sidani, J. E., Colditz, J. B., & Primack, B. A. (2016). The association between social media use and sleep disturbance among young adults. *Preventive Medicine*, *85*, 36–41. doi:10.1016/j.ypmed.2016.01.001 PMID:26791323

Lim, J., & Richardson, J. C. (2016). Exploring the effects of students' social networking experience on social presence and perceptions of using SNSs for educational purposes. *Internet and Higher Education*, *29*, 31–39. doi:10.1016/j.iheduc.2015.12.001

Lou, L. L., Yan, Z., Nickerson, A., & McMorris, R. (2012). An examination of the reciprocal relationship of loneliness and Facebook use among first-year college students. *Journal of Educational Computing Research*, *46*(1), 105–117. doi:10.2190/EC.46.1.e

Lusk, B. (2010). *Digital natives and social media behaviors: an overview.* Retrieved from https://teachandtechassign3.weebly.com/uploads/1/4/2/0/14202725/digital_natives_and_social_media_behaviour.pdf

Magsamen-Conrad, K., Billiotte-Verhoff, C., & Greene, K. (2014). Technology addiction's contribution to mental wellbeing: The positive effect of online social capital. *Computers in Human Behavior*, *40*, 23–30. doi:10.1016/j.chb.2014.07.014 PMID:25568591

Mariko Kasahara, G. (2017). *Gender differences in social media use and cyberbullying in Belize.* Retrieved from https://cornerstone.lib.mnsu.edu/etdsOtherCapstoneProjects.753.https://cornerstone.lib.mnsu.edu/etds/753

Marlatt, G. A., Baer, J. S., Donovan, D. M., & Kivlahan, D. R. (1988). Addictive behaviors: Etiology and treatment. *Annual Review of Psychology*, *39*(1), 223–252. doi:10.1146/annurev.ps.39.020188.001255 PMID:3278676

Marwick, A. (2013). *Status update: Celebrity, publicity, and branding in the social media age.* New Haven: Yale UP.

Mayfield, A. (2010). What is social media? doi:10.12968/bjom.2014.22.12.896

McGoogan, C. (2016). *Yahoo: 9 reasons for the internet icon's decline.* Retrieved from https://www.telegraph.co.uk/technology/2016/07/25/yahoo-9-reasons-for-the-internet-icons-decline/

Meena, P. S., Soni, R., Jain, M., & Paliwal, S. (2015). Social networking sites addiction and associated psychological problems among young adults: A study from North India. *Sri Lanka Journal of Psychiatry*, *6*(1), 14. doi:10.4038ljpsyc.v6i1.8055

Molina, B. (2017). *Twitter overcounted active users since 2014, shares surge on profit hopes.* Retrieved from https://www.usatoday.com/story/tech/news/2017/10/26/twitter-overcounted-active-users-since-2014-shares-surge/801968001/

Moqbel, M., & Kock, N. (2018). Unveiling the dark side of social networking sites: Personal and work-related consequences of social networking site addiction. *Information & Management, 55*(1), 109–119. doi:10.1016/j.im.2017.05.001

Munzel, A., Meyer-Waarden, L., & Galan, J. P. (2018). The social side of sustainability: Well-being as a driver and an outcome of social relationships and interactions on social networking sites. *Technological Forecasting and Social Change, 130*(July 2017), 14–27. doi:10.1016/j.techfore.2017.06.031

Neverkovich, S. D., Bubnova, I. S., Kosarenko, N. N., Sakhieva, R. G., Sizova, Z. M., Zakharova, V. L., & Sergeeva, M. G. (2018). Students' internet addiction: Study and prevention. *Eurasia Journal of Mathematics, Science, and Technology Education, 14*(4), 1483–1495. doi:10.29333/ejmste/83723

O'Shea, W. (2003). Six degrees of sexual frustration -- connecting the dates with Friendster.com. Retrieved from http://www.freerepublic.com/focus/f-news/924322/posts

Oberst, L. (2010). The 6S social network. Retrieved from http://www.sciepub.com/reference/167008

Odabaşı, Y. (2010). Tüketicilikte Dönüşümler. In *Bilgi ve İletişim Teknolojileri Işığında Dönüşümler*. Ankara, Turkey: Nobel Yayıncılık.

Ong, T. (2018). *Whatsapp launches a separate app for small businesses.* Retrieved from https://www.theverge.com/2018/1/19/16908810/whatsapp-business-app-launch-small-businesses

Ovadia, S. (2011). Internet connection: an early introduction to the Google+ social networking project. *Behavioral & Social Sciences Librarian, 30*(4), 259–263. doi: 10.1080/01639269.2011.622258

Pariser, E. (2011). *The filter bubble*. New York, NY: Penguin Press.

Phillips, B. J., Miller, J., & McQuarrie, E. F. (2014). Dreaming out loud on pinterest: New forms of indirect persuasion. *International Journal of Advertising, 33*(4), 633–655. doi:10.2501/IJA-33-4-633-655

Phillips, S. (2007). A brief history of Facebook. Retrieved from https://www.theguardian.com/technology/2007/jul/25/media.newmedia

Phu, B., & Gow, A. J. (2019). Facebook use and its association with subjective happiness and loneliness. *Computers in Human Behavior, 92*(June 2018), 151–159. doi:10.1016/j.chb.2018.11.020

Pink, D. (2005). *A whole new mind: why right-brainers will rule the future*. New York, NY: Riverhead Books.

Raice, S. (2012). *Days of wild user growth appear over at Facebook.* Retrieved from https://www.wsj.com/articles/SB10001424052702303296604577454970244896342

Rettberg, J. W. (2009). Freshly generated for you, and Barack Obama: How social media represent your life. *European Journal of Communication*, *24*(4), 451–466. doi:10.1177/0267323109345715

Rettberg, J. W. (2017). Self representation in social media. In J. Burgess, A. Marwick, & T. Poell (Eds.), *SAGE handbook of social media* (pp. 1–30). Retrieved from http://dspace.uib.no/bitstream/handle/1956/13073/Self-Representation_in_Social_Media.pdf?sequence=1&isAllowed=y

Rothen, S., Briefer, J. F., Deleuze, J., Karila, L., Andreassen, C. S., Achab, S., ... Billieux, J. (2018). Disentangling the role of users' preferences and impulsivity traits in problematic Facebook use. *PLoS One*, *13*(9), 1–13. doi:10.1371/journal.pone.0201971 PMID:30183698

Rusli, E. M., & MacMillan, D. (2014). Snapchat fetches $10 billion valuation. Retrieved from https://www.wsj.com/articles/snapchat-fetches-10-billion-valuation-1409088794

Sharp, E. H., Coatsworth, J. D., Darling, N., Cumsille, P., & Ranieri, S. (2007). Gender differences in the self-defining activities and identity experiences of adolescents and emerging adults. *Journal of Adolescence*, *30*(2), 251–269. doi:10.1016/j.adolescence.2006.02.006 PMID:16600358

Social, W. A. (2019). *Global social media research summary.* Retrieved from https://www.smartinsights.com/social-media-marketing/social-media-strategy/new-global-social-media-research/

Stanley, B. (2015). *Uses and gratifications of temporary social media: A comparison of Snapchat and Facebook.* Fullerton, CA: California State University.

Statista. (2019a). *Number of monthly active Pinterest users worldwide from 1st quarter 2016 to 2nd quarter 2019 (in millions).* Retrieved from https://www.statista.com/statistics/463353/pinterest-global-mau/

Statista. (2019b). *Number of social network users worldwide from 2010 to 2021 (in billions).* Retrieved from https://www.statista.com/statistics/278414/number-of-worldwide-social-network-users/

Stout, D. W. (2019). Social media statistics 2019: top networks by the numbers. Retrieved from https://dustinstout.com/social-media-statistics/

Sweney, M., & De Liz, A. (2018). *"Parents killed it": why Facebook is losing its teenage users.* Retrieved from https://www.theguardian.com/technology/2018/feb/16/parents-killed-it-facebook-losing-teenage-users

Tartory, R. (2019). Gender-associated behavior of Jordanians on Facebook. *International Journal of English Linguistics, 9*(2), 383. doi:10.5539/ijel.v9n2p383

Taylor, R., King, F., & Nelson, G. (2012). Student learning through social media. *Journal of Sociological Research, 3*(2), 29–35. doi:10.5296/jsr.v3i2.2136

Trainor, K. J., Andzulis, J., Rapp, A., & Agnihotri, R. (2014). Social media technology usage and customer relationship performance: A capabilities-based examination of social CRM. *Journal of Business Research, 67*(6), 1201–1208. doi:10.1016/j.jbusres.2013.05.002

Treem, J. W., & Leonardi, P. M. (2013). Social media use in organizations: exploring the affordances of visibility, editability, persistence, and association. *Annals of the International Communication Association, 36*(1), 143–189. doi:10.1080/23808985.2013.11679130

Turel, O., & Serenko, A. (2012). The benefits and dangers of enjoyment with social networking websites. *European Journal of Information Systems, 21*(5), 512–528. doi:10.1057/ejis.2012.1

Utz, S., Muscanell, N., & Khalid, C. (2015). Snapchat elicits more jealousy than Facebook: A comparison of Snapchat and Facebook use. *Cyberpsychology, Behavior, and Social Networking, 18*(3), 141–146. doi:10.1089/cyber.2014.0479 PMID:25667961

Valkenburg, P. M., Peter, J., & Schouten, A. P. (2006). Friend networking sites and their relationship to adolescents' well-being and social self-esteem. *Cyberpsychology & Behavior, 9*(5), 584–590. doi:10.1089/cpb.2006.9.584 PMID:17034326

Walker, M. B. (1989). Some problems with the concept of "gambling addiction". Should theories of addiction be generalized to include excessive gambling? *Journal of Gambling Studies, 5*(3), 179–200. doi:10.1007/BF01024386

Walther, J. B., & Ramirez, A. (2009). New technologies and new direction in online relating. In S. Smith, & S. Wilson (Eds.), *New directions in interpersonal communication* (pp. 189–214). Thousand Oaks, CA: Sage.

Wang, J. L., Jackson, L. A., Gaskin, J., & Wang, H. Z. (2014). The effects of Social Networking Site (SNS) use on college students' friendship and well-being. *Computers in Human Behavior*, *37*, 229–236. doi:10.1016/j.chb.2014.04.051

Wang, Q., Chen, W., & Liang, Y. (2011). *The impact of social media on college students. Journal of College and Character*. Johnson & Wales University. doi:10.1515/jcc-2013-0004

Whiting, A., & Williams, D. (2013). Why people use social media: A uses and gratifications approach. *Qualitative Market Research*, *16*(4), 362–369. doi:10.1108/QMR-06-2013-0041

Williams, A. L., & Merten, M. J. (2011). iFamily: Internet and social media technology in the family context. *Family and Consumer Sciences Research Journal*, *40*(2), 150–170. doi:10.1111/j.1552-3934.2011.02101.x

Wilson, K., Fornasier, S., & White, K. M. (2010). Psychological predictors of young adults' use of social networking sites. *Cyberpsychology, Behavior, and Social Networking*, *13*(2), 173–177. doi:10.1089/cyber.2009.0094 PMID:20528274

Wu, A. M. S., Cheung, V. I., Ku, L., & Hung, E. P. W. (2013). Psychological risk factors of addiction to social networking sites among Chinese smartphone users. *Journal of Behavioral Addictions*, *2*(3), 160–166. doi:10.1556/JBA.2.2013.006 PMID:25215198

Young, K. (1999). Internet addiction: Evaluation and treatment. *Student BMJ*, *7*, 351–352.

Compilation of References

Agarwal, N., Liu, H., Tang, L., & Yu, P. S. (2008). *Identifying the influential bloggers in a community*. WSDM. doi:10.1145/1341531.1341559

Aghazamani, A. (2010). How do university students spend their time on Facebook? An exploratory study. *The Journal of American Science*, *6*, 730–735.

Ahmad, N. S., Musa, R., & Harun, M. H. M. (2016). The impact of social media content marketing (SMCM) towards brand health. *Procedia Economics and Finance*, *37*, 331–336. doi:10.1016/S2212-5671(16)30133-2

Ahn, J. (2011). Digital divides and social network sites: Which students participate in social media? *Journal of Educational Computing Research*, *45*(2), 147–163. doi:10.2190/EC.45.2.b

Ainin, S., Naqshbandi, M. M., Moghavvemi, S., & Jaafar, N. I. (2015). Facebook usage, socialization and academic performance. *Computers & Education*, *83*, 64–73. doi:10.1016/j.compedu.2014.12.018

Akar, E., & Topçu, B. (2011). An examination of the factors influencing consumers' attitudes toward social media marketing. *Journal of Internet Commerce*, *10*(1), 35–67. doi:10.1080/15332861.2011.558456

Akıncı Vural, Z. B., & Bat, M. (2010). Yeni Bir İletişim Ortamı Olarak Sosyal Medya: Ege Üniversitesi İletişim Fakültesine YönelikBir Araştırma. *Journal of Yaşar University*, *20*(5), 3348–3382. doi:10.19168/jyu.65130

Akkaya, D. T. (2013). *Sosyal Medya Reklamlarında Tüketici Algılarının Tutum, Davranış ve Satın Alma Niyeti Üzerine Etkisi*. Trakya Üniversitesi.

Akram, W. (2018). A study on positive and negative effects of social media on society. *International Journal on Computer Science and Engineering*, *5*. doi:10.26438/ijcse/v5i10.351354

Al Khalili, M. (2018). *Barriers impacting social media marketing in industrial B2B* (Unpublished doctoral dissertation, Robert Morris University, Pennsylvania).

Alameddine, A. (2013). *Perceptions of executives from seven selected companies of the use of social media in marketing practices* (Doctoral dissertation, Pepperdine University, California).

Alavi, S. S., Ferdosi, M., Jannatifard, F., Eslami, M., Alaghemandan, H., & Setare, M. (2012). Behavioral addiction versus substance addiction: correspondence of psychiatric and psychological views. *International Journal of Preventive Medicine*, *3*(4), 290–294. PMID:22624087

Alexander, P., Schallert, D., & Reynolds, R. (2009). What is learning anyway? A topographical perspective considered. *Educational Psychologist*, *44*(3), 176–192. doi:10.1080/00461520903029006

Alexandrov, A., Lilly, B., & Babakus, E. (2013). The effects of social- and self-motives on the intentions to share positive and negative word of mouth. *Journal of the Academy of Marketing Science*, *41*(5), 531–546. doi:10.100711747-012-0323-4

Alhabash, S., & Ma, M. (2017). A tale of four platforms: motivations and uses of Facebook, Twitter, Instagram, and Snapchat among college students? *Social Media and Society*, *3*(1). doi:10.1177/2056305117691544

Ali, M. A., Hoque, M. R., & Alam, K. (2018). An empirical investigation of the relationship between e-government development and the digital economy: The case of Asian countries. *Journal of Knowledge Management*, *22*(5), 1176–1200. doi:10.1108/JKM-10-2017-0477

Allen, K. A., Ryan, T., Gray, D. L., McInerney, D. M., & Waters, L. (2014). Social media use and social connectedness in adolescents: The positives and the potential pitfalls. *Australian Educational and Developmental Psychologist*, *31*(1), 18–31. doi:10.1017/edp.2014.2

Ally, M., & Prieto-Blázquez, J. (2014). What is the future of mobile learning in education? *Revista de Universidad y Sociedad del Conocimiento*, *11*(1), 142–151. doi:10.7238/rusc.v11i1.2033

AlSuwaidan, L., & Ykhlef, M. (2016). Toward information diffusion model for viral marketing in business. *Int. J. Adv. Comput. Sci. Appl*, *7*(2), 637–646.

Aluri, A., Slevitch, L., & Larzelere, R. (2015). The effectiveness of embedded social media on hotel websites and the importance of social interactions and return on engagement. *International Journal of Contemporary Hospitality Management*, *27*(4), 670–689. doi:10.1108/IJCHM-09-2013-0415

Amaral, F., Tiago, T., & Tiago, F. (2014). User-generated content: Tourists' profiles on Tripadvisor. *International Journal of Strategic Innovative Marketing*, *1*(3), 137–145.

American Psychiatric Association. (1987). *Diagnostic and statistical manual of mental disorders*. Washington, DC.

Ananda, A. S., Hernández-García, Á., & Lamberti, L. (2016). N-REL: A comprehensive framework of social media marketing strategic actions for marketing organizations. *Journal of Innovation & Knowledge*, *1*(3), 170–180. doi:10.1016/j.jik.2016.01.003

Anderson, L., & Wladawsky-Berger, I. (2016). The 4 things it takes to succeed in the digital economy. Harvard Business Review. Available at https://hbr.org/2016/03/the-4things-it-takes-to-succeed-in-the-digital-economy

Andreassen, C. S. (2015). Online social network site addiction: a comprehensive review. *Current Addiction Reports*, *2*(2), 175–184. doi:10.100740429-015-0056-9

Andreassen, C. S., Griffiths, M. D., Gjertsen, S. R., Krossbakken, E., Kvam, S., & Pallesen, S. (2013a). The relationships between behavioral addictions and the five-factor model of personality. *Journal of Behavioral Addictions*, *2*(2), 90–99. doi:10.1556/JBA.2.2013.003 PMID:26165928

Andreassen, C. S., & Pallesen, S. (2014). Social network site addiction-an overview. *Current Pharmaceutical Design*, *20*(25), 1–9. Retrieved from http://freepsychologypdf.com/wp-content/uploads/2018/07/Andreassen-2014-Social-network-site-addiction-An-overview.pdf. doi:10.2174/13816128113199990616 PMID:24001298

Andreassen, C. S., Pallesen, S., & Griffiths, M. D. (2017). The relationship between addictive use of social media, narcissism, and self-esteem: Findings from a large national survey. *Addictive Behaviors*, *64*, 287–293. doi:10.1016/j.addbeh.2016.03.006 PMID:27072491

Andreassen, C. S., Torsheim, T., Brunborg, G. S., & Pallesen, S. (2012). Development of a facebook addiction scale. *Psychological Reports*, *110*(2), 501–517. doi:10.2466/02.09.18.PR0.110.2.501-517 PMID:22662404

Andrews, D., & Preece, J. (2001). A conceptual framework for demographic groups resistant to online community interaction. *Proceedings of the 34th Annual Hawaii International Conference on System Sciences (HICSS-34)*-Vol. 7, *00*(c), 7013. 10.1109/HICSS.2001.927044

Andriushchenko, K., Rudyk, V., Riabchenko, O., Kachynska, M., Marynenko, N., Shergina, L., & Kuchai, O. (2019). Processes of managing information infrastructure of a digital enterprise in the framework of the «Industry 4.0» concept. *Eastern-European Journal of Enterprise Technologies*, *1*(3), 97. doi:10.15587/1729-4061.2019.157765

Anonymous. (2016, Nov. 24). *Careers in communication*. Retrieved from https://study.com/articles/careers_in_social_networking.html

Araújo, C. A. (2006). Bibliometria: Evolução histórica e questões atuais. *EmQuestão, Porto Alegre*, *12*(1), 11–32.

Ariel, Y., & Avidar, R. (2015). *Information, Interactivity, and Social Media.*, *23*, 19.

Arif, I., Aslam, W., & Ali, M. (2016). Students' dependence on smartphones and its effect on purchasing behavior. *South Asian Journal of Global Business Research*, *5*(2), 285–302. doi:10.1108/SAJGBR-05-2014-0031

Ariganello, M. (2016). *Creating the brands we trust: How organizations in the lifestyle category build consumer trust through effective branding and content marketing in the 21st century* (Master's thesis, University of Southern California, California).

Armstrong, A., & Hagel, J. (1997). Net gain: expanding markets through virtual communities. Retrieved from http://www.techsoc.com/netgain.htm

Ashley, C., & Tuten, T. (2015). Creative strategies in social media marketing: An exploratory study of branded social content and consumer engagement. *Psychology and Marketing*, *32*(1), 15–27. doi:10.1002/mar.20761

Ayeh, J. K., Au, N., & Law, R. (2013). "Do we believe in TripAdvisor?" Examining credibility perceptions and online travelers' attitude toward using user-generated content. *Journal of Travel Research*, *52*(4), 437–452. doi:10.1177/0047287512475217

Bacache-Beauvallet, M., & Bloch, F. (2018). Special issue on taxation in the digital economy. *Journal of Public Economic Theory*, *20*(1), 5–8. doi:10.1111/jpet.12285

Baek, Y. M., Bae, Y., & Jang, H. (2013). Social and parasocial relationships on social network sites and their differential relationships with users' psychological well-being. *Cyberpsychology, Behavior, and Social Networking*, *16*(7), 512–517. doi:10.1089/cyber.2012.0510 PMID:23697533

Bagozzi, R. P., Gopinath, M., & Nyer, P. U. (1999). The role of emotions in marketing. *Journal of the Academy of Marketing Science*, *27*(2), 184–206. doi:10.1177/0092070399272005

Bakkurt, A. T. (2004). *Hizmet İşletmelerinde Güvenilirlik Güvencesi Programları ve Bir HTEA Uygulaması.*

Bal, A., & Gutiérrez, C. (2015). Taxation of the digital economy. International tax structures in the BEPS era: An analysis of anti-abuse measures. Amsterdam, The Netherlands: IBFD. pp. 249-280.

Balaji, M. S., Khong, K. W., & Chong, A. Y. L. (2016). Determinants of negative word-of-mouth communication using social networking sites, Information & Management, 53(4), 528.

Bandura, A. (1989). Human agency in social cognitive theory. *The American Psychologist*, *44*(9), 1175–1184. doi:10.1037/0003-066X.44.9.1175 PMID:2782727

Bányai, F., Zsila, Á., Király, O., Maraz, A., Elekes, Z., Griffiths, M., ... Demetrovics, Z. (2017). Problematic social media use: Results from a large-scale nationally representative adolescent sample. *PLoS One*, *12*(1), 10–14. doi:10.1371/journal.pone.0169839 PMID:28068404

Barak, M., & Levenberg, A. (2016). Flexible thinking in learning: An individual differences measure for learning in technology-enhanced environments. *Computers & Education*, *99*, 39–52. doi:10.1016/j.compedu.2016.04.003

Barefoot, D., & Szabo, J. (2010). *Friends with benefits: A social media marketing handbook.* San Francisco, CA: No Starch Press.

Barefoot, D., & Szabo, J. (2010). *Friends with benefits: A social media-marketing handbook.* San Francisco, CA: No Starch Press.

Barger, V., Peltier, J. W., & Schultz, D. E. (2016). Social media and consumer engagement: Areview and research agenda. *Journal of Research in Interactive Marketing, 10,* 4. pp. 268-287. doi:10.1108/JRIM-06-2016-0065

Barker, A., Krull, G., & Mallinson, B. (2009). A proposed theoretical model for m-learning adoption in developing countries. In mLearn 2005-4th World conference on mLearning, Cape Town. In M. Pagani (Ed.), *Mobile and wireless systems beyond 3G: Managing new business opportunities.* Hershey, PA: IGI Global.

Barnes, N. G., & Daubitz, C. (2017, February). *The 2017 Inc 500 and social media: time for reevaluation?* University of Massachusetts Dartmouth Center for Marketing Research. Retrieved from http://www.umassd.edu/cmr/

Bart, Y., Shankar, V., Sultan, F., & Urban, G. L. (2005). Are the drivers and role of online trust the same for all web sites and consumers?: a large-scale exploratory empirical study. *Journal of Marketing, 69*(4), 133–152. doi:10.1509/jmkg.2005.69.4.133

Bashir, M. A., Ayub, N., & Jalees, T. (2017). The impact of the firm generated contents and the user generated contents through social media on brand equity elements. *Pakistan Business Review, 19*(3), 744–760.

Baskakova, M., & Soboleva, I. (2019). New dimensions of functional illiteracy in the digital economy. Voprosy Obrazovaniya / Educational Studies Moscow, (1), 244–263.

Batum, T., & Ersoy, N. (2016). The use of social media in B2B marketing communications: An explatory study on Turkish companies. *Afyon Kocatepe Üniversitesi İktisadi ve İdari Bilimler Fakültesi Dergisi, 18*(2), 139–151.

Bauerly, R. J. (2009). Online auction fraud and eBay. *Marketing Management Journal, 19*(1), 133–143. Retrieved from http://www.mmaglobal.org/publications/MMJ/MMJ-Issues/2009-Spring/MMJ-2009-Spring-Vol19-Issue1-Bauerly-pp133-143.pdf

Benamar, A., Belkhatir, N., & Bendimerad, F. (2013). Adaptive and context-aware scenarios for pervasive technology-enhanced learning system. *Int. Arab J. e-Technol., 3*(1), pp. 58-67.

Bennett, S. (2014). 70% of college students post to Snapchat daily (Twitter: 46%, Facebook: 11%). Retrieved from https://www.adweek.com/digital/snapchat-facebook-twitter-instagram-privacy/

Bennett, M. M. (1993). Information technology and travel agency: A customer service perspective. *Tourism Management, 14*(4), 259–266. doi:10.1016/0261-5177(93)90060-X

Benson, V., Hand, C., & Hartshorne, R. (2019). How compulsive use of social media affects performance: Insights from the UK by purpose of use. *Behaviour & Information Technology, 38*(6), 549–563. doi:10.1080/0144929X.2018.1539518

Berger, J., & Iyengar, R. (2013). Communication channels and word of mouth: how the medium shapes the message. *The Journal of Consumer Research, 40*(3), 567–579. doi:10.1086/671345

Bergström, A., & Wadbring, I. (2010). The contribution of free dailies and news on the web: implications of media structural changes for the Swedish newspaper readership market. *Northern Lights, 8*(1), 139–155. doi:10.1386/nl.8.139_1

Bhattacharya, R., Devinney, T. M., & Pillutla, M. M. (1998). A formal model of trust based on outcomes. *Academy of Management Review, 23*(3), 459–472. doi:10.5465/amr.1998.926621

Bicen, H., & Cavus, N. (2010). The most preferred social network sites by students. *Procedia: Social and Behavioral Sciences, 2*(2), 5864–5869. doi:10.1016/j.sbspro.2010.03.958

Blau, P. M. (1964). *Exchange and power in social life*. Transaction Publishers.

Boghossian, P. (2006). Behaviorism, constructivism, and Socratic pedagogy. *Educational Philosophy and Theory, 38*(6), 713–722. doi:10.1111/j.1469-5812.2006.00226.x

Bolton, R. N., Parasuraman, A., Hoefnagels, A., Migchels, N., Kabadayi, S., Gruber, T., ... Solnet, D. (2013). Understanding Generation Y and their use of social media: A review and research agenda. *Journal of Service Management, 24*(3), 245–267. doi:10.1108/09564231311326987 doi:10.1108/09564231311326987

Botsman, R., & Rogers, R. (2010). *What's mine is yours: the rise of collaborative consumption*. Harper Business.

Bowden, J. L.-H. (2009). The process of customer engagement: a conceptual framework. *Journal of Marketing Theory and Practice, 17*(1), 63–74. doi:10.2753/MTP1069-6679170105

Boyd, D. (2006). Friendster lost steam. Is MySpace just a fad? Retrieved from https://www.danah.org/papers/FriendsterMySpaceEssay.html

Boyd, D. M. (2006). Friends, friendsters, and top 8: Writing community into being on social network sites. *First Monday, 11*(12). doi:10.5210/fm.v11i12.1418

Boyd, D. M., & Ellison, N. B. (2007). Social network sites: definition, history, and scholarship. *Journal of Computer-Mediated Communication, 13*(1), 210–230. doi:10.1111/j.1083-6101.2007.00393.x

Brennan, R., & Croft, R. (2012). The use of social media in B2B marketing and branding: An exploratory study. *Journal of Customer Behaviour, 11*(2), 101–115. doi:10.1362/147539212X13420906144552

Brieger, C. (2013). *Exploring new communication strategies for a global brand – Transmedia storytelling and gamification* (Master's thesis, Norwegian School of Economics, Norway).

Brin, S., & Page, L. (1998). The anatomy of a large-scale hypertextual Web search engine. *Computer Networks and ISDN Systems, 30*(1-7), 1–7. doi:10.1016/S0169-7552(98)00110-X

Brown, H. G., Poole, M. S., & Rodgers, T. L. (2004). Interpersonal traits, complementarity, and trust in virtual collaboration. *Journal of Management Information Systems, 20*(4), 115–138. doi:10.1080/07421222.2004.11045785

Browning, L., Gerlich, R., & Westermann, L. (2011). The new HD classroom: A "Hyper Diverse" approach to engaging with students. *Journal Of Instructional Pedagogies,* 1-10. Retrieved from http://www.aabri.com/manuscripts/10701.pdf

Bruns, A. (2006). *Blogs, Wikipedia, second life, and beyond: from production to produsage*. New York, NY: Peter Lang.

Budanov, V., Aseeva, I., & Zvonova, E. (2018). Industry 4.0.: Socio-economic junctures. *Economic Annals-XXI, 168*(11–12), 33–37.

Bughin, J., Chui, M., & Manyika, J. (2010). Clouds, big data, and smart assets: Ten tech-enabled business trends to watch. *The McKinsey Quarterly*, *56*(1), 75–86.

Bulduklu, Y. (2017). Mobile games on the basis of uses and gratifications approach: A comparison of the mobile game habits of university and high school students. *The International Journal of Research into New Media Technologies*, 1–17. doi:. doi:10.1177/1354856517748159

Bull, R., & Azennoud, M. (2016). Smart citizens for smart cities: participating in the future. *Proceedings of the Institution of Civil Engineers - Energy, 169*(3), 93–101. 10.1680/jener.15.00030

Bullock, D. H. (1982). Behaviorism and NSPI: The erratically applied discipline. *Performance & Instruction, 21*(3), 4–11. doi:10.1002/pfi.4170210306

Burnett, L. (2014). *The sharing economy - where we go from here.* Leo Burnett Inc.

Busscher, N. M. (2013). *Social media: Their role as marketing tools in B2B marketing* (Bachelor's Thesis, University of Twente).

Çabuk, S. DOĞAN SÜDAġ, H., Zeren, D., Kelimeler, A., ĠletiÇimi, P., KarÇıtlığı, T., & PaylaÇımı, O. (2000). Sahip Olmak Yerine Paylaşmak: Tüketicilerin Paylaşma Davranışlarının Unsurlarını Belirlemeye Yönelik Bir Çalışma Sharing versus having: a study of determining the factors of consumer sharing behaviour. *Çankırı Karatekin Üniversitesi Sosyal Bilimler Enstitüsü Dergisi Cankiri Karatekin University Journal of Institute of Social Sciences, 6*(61), 151–168. Retrieved from https://pdfs.semanticscholar.org/6f12/7e35044fcef9d04d628a15a614d74d74cda3.pdf

Çam, E., & Işbulan, O. (2012). A new addiction for teacher candidates: Social networks. *Turkish Online Journal of Educational Technology, 11*(3), 14–19.

Cann, A., Dimitriou, K., & Hooley, T. (2011). *Social media: A guide for researchers. Research Information Network.* London, UK. Retrieved from https://derby.openrepository.com/bitstream/handle/10545/196715/social media guide for screen.pdf?sequence=6&isAllowed=y

Cappel, J. J., & Zhenyu, H. (2017). An analysis of social media presentation at company websites. *Journal of International Business Disciplines, 12*(1), 1–17.

Carah, N., & Shaul, M. (2015). Brands and Instagram: Point, tap, swipe, glance. *Mobile Media & Communication, 4*(1), 69–84. doi:10.1177/2050157915598180

Carbonell, X., Chamarro, A., Oberst, U., Rodrigo, B., & Prades, M. (2018). Problematic use of the internet and smartphones in university students: 2006–2017. *International Journal of Environmental Research and Public Health, 15*(3). doi:10.3390/ijerph15030475

Carlile, O., & Jordan, A. 2005. It works in practice but will it work in theory? The theoretical underpinnings of pedagogy. *Emerging issues in the practice of university learning and teaching, 1*, pp. 11-26. Retrieved from http://www.aishe.org/readings/2005-1/

Caron, J., & Brennaman, K. (2009). *Symbiosis: co-evolution of emerging technology, learning theory, and instructional design.* Retrieved from https://sites.google.com/a/boisestate.edu/edtechtheories/caron_brennaman

Carter, S., & Yao, A. (2016). Mobile apps usage by Malaysian business undergraduates and postgraduates: Implications for consumer behaviour theory and marketing practice. *Internet Research, 26*(3), 733–757. doi:10.1108/IntR-10-2014-0273

CBSNews. (2019). *Then and now: a history of social networking sites.* Retrieved from https://www.cbsnews.com/pictures/then-and-now-a-history-of-social-networking-sites/5/

Ceballos, M., Crespo, Á. G., & Cousté, N. L. (2016). Impact of firm-created content on user-generated content: Using a new social media monitoring tool to explore Twitter. In *Proceedings 2015 Academy of Marketing Science (AMS) World Marketing Congress Rediscovering the Essentiality of Marketing* (pp. 303-306). Cham, Switzerland: Springer. 10.1007/978-3-319-29877-1_61

Cha, M., Haddadi, H., Benevenuto, F., & Gummadi, K. P. (2010): Measuring user influence in Twitter: the million follower fallacy. In 4th International AAAI Conference on Weblogs and Social Media, ICWSM (2010).

Chafkin, M. (2007). *How to kill a great idea!* Retrieved from https://www.inc.com/magazine/20070601/features-how-to-kill-a-great-idea.html

Chang, H. H., & Wu, L. H. (2014). An examination of negative e-Wom adoption: Brand commitment as a moderator. *Decision Support Systems, 59*, 206–218. doi:10.1016/j.dss.2013.11.008

Charlesworth, A. (2015). *An introduction to social media marketing*. New York, NY: Routledge.

Charlton, J. (2002). A factor-analytic investigation of computer 'addiction' and engagement. *British Journal of Psychology, 93*(3), 329–344. doi:10.1348/000712602760146242 PMID:12230834

Chen, G. M. (2011). Tweet this: A uses and gratifications perspective on how active Twitter use gratifies a need to connect with others. *Computers in Human Behavior, 27*(2), 755–762. doi:10.1016/j.chb.2010.10.023

Cheng, T. L. (2013). Applying networked learning to improve learner interactions: A new paradigm of teaching and learning in ODL. *Asian Association of Open Universities Journal, 8*(2), 67–85. doi:10.1108/AAOUJ-08-02-2013-B006

Chen, Z., & Berger, J. (2016). How content acquisition method affects word of mouth. *The Journal of Consumer Research, 43*(1), 86–102. doi:10.1093/jcr/ucw001

Cheong, H. J., & Morrison, M. A. (2008). Consumers' reliance on product information and recommendations found in UGC. *Journal of Interactive Advertising, 8*(2), 38–49. doi:10.1080/15252019.2008.10722141

Cheung, C. M. K., Lee, M. K. O., & Thadani, D. R. (2009). The impact of positive electronic word-of-mouth on consumer online purchasing decision. In *Proceedings Visioning and Engineering the Knowledge Society. A Web Science Perspective. WSKS 2009* (pp. 501-510). Berlin, Germany: Springer. 10.1007/978-3-642-04754-1_51

Cheung, C., Xiao, B., & Liu, I. (2014). Do actions speak louder than voices? The signaling role of social information cues in influencing consumer purchase decisions. *Decision Support Systems, 65*, 50–58. doi:10.1016/j.dss.2014.05.002

Chih-Yu, C., Hsi-Peng, L. U., & Chao-Ming, W. U. (2015). Facebook users' motivation for clicking the "Like" button. *Social Behavior and Personality, 43*(4), 579–592. doi:10.2224bp.2015.43.4.579

Chiu, C. M., Hsu, M. H., & Wang, E. T. G. (2006). Understanding knowledge sharing in virtual communities: An integration of social capital and social cognitive theories. *Decision Support Systems, 42*(3), 1872–1888. doi:10.1016/j.dss.2006.04.001

Choi, J., & Kim, H. J. (2016). Influence of SNS user innovativeness and public individuation on SNS usage patterns and social capital development: the case of Facebook. *International Journal of Human-Computer Interaction, 32*(12), 921–930. doi:10.1080/10447318.2016.1220067

Christodoulides, G., Jevons, C., & Bonhomme, J. (2012). Memo to marketers: Quantitative evidence for change: How user-generated content really affects brands. *Journal of Advertising Research, 52*(1), 53–64. doi:10.2501/JAR-52-1-053-064

Chung, K., & Shin, J. (2010). The antecedents and consequents of relationship quality in internet shopping. *Asia Pacific Journal of Marketing and Logistics, 22*(4), 473–491. doi:10.1108/13555851011090510

Cialdini, R. B. (2009). *The psychology of persuasion*. Retrieved from http://elibrary.bsu.az/books_400/N_232.pdf

Cicek, M., & Eren-Erdogmus, I. (2013). Social media marketing: Exploring the user typology in Turkey. *International Journal of Technology Marketing, 8*(3), 254–271. doi:10.1504/IJTMKT.2013.055343

Coelho, R. L. F., Oliveira, D. S. D., & Almeida, M. I. S. D. (2016). Does social media matter for post typology? Impact of post content on Facebook and Instagram metrics. *Online Information Review, 40*(4), 458–471. doi:10.1108/OIR-06-2015-0176

Cohen, R. (2014). Social media marketing: Creating a successful commercial campaign targeting women in their '30-'40. (Master's thesis, Long Island University, New York).

Coleman, J. (1990). *Foundations of social theory*. Cambridge, MA: Harvard University Press.

Coles, L. (2015). *Marketing with social media: 10 easy steps to success for business*. Australia: John Wiley & Sons.

Compeau, D. R., & Higgins, C. A. (1995). Computer self-efficacy: development of a measure and initial test. *Management Information Systems Quarterly, 19*(2), 189–211. doi:10.2307/249688

Comsource. (2018). *Understand and evaluate audiences and advertising everywhere*. Retrieved from https://www.comscore.com/Products/Ratings-and-Planning

Constant, D., Kiesler, S., & Sproull, L. (1994). What's mine is ours, or is it? A study of attitudes about information sharing. *Information Systems Research*, *5*(4), 400–421. doi:10.1287/isre.5.4.400

Constantinides, E. & Fountain, S. J. (2008). Web 2.0: Conceptual foundations and marketing issues. *Journal of direct, data and digital marketing practice, 9*(3), 231-244.

Constantinides, E. (2014). Foundations of social media marketing. *Procedia: Social and Behavioral Sciences*, *148*, 40–57. doi:10.1016/j.sbspro.2014.07.016

Conte, C. (2016). *The triangular trust in the sharing economy.* (Bachelor's thesis, Università Ca'Foscari Venezia).

Content Marketing Institute (CMI). (2018). *Benchmarks, budgets, and trends: North America.* Retrieved from https://contentmarketinginstitute.com/wpcontent/uploads/2017/09/2018

Correa, T., Hinsley, A. W., & De Zuniga, H. (2010). Who interacts on the Web? The intersection of users' personality and social media use. *Computers in Human Behavior*, *26*(2), 247–253. doi:10.1016/j.chb.2009.09.003

Coulter, K. S., Bruhn, M., Schoenmueller, V., & Schäfer, D. B. (2012). Are social media replacing traditional media in terms of brand equity creation? *Management Research Review*, *35*(9), 770–790. doi:10.1108/01409171211255948

Cronin, J. (2016). Teach students to communicate a brand story with transmedia storytelling. *Journal of Research in Interactive Marketing*, *10*(2), 86–101. doi:10.1108/JRIM-01-2015-0004

Cui, G., Lui, H. K., & Guo, X. (2012). The effect of online consumer reviews on new product sales. *International Journal of Electronic Commerce*, *17*(1), 39–58. doi:10.2753/JEC1086-4415170102

Curran, D. (2018). Risk, innovation, and democracy in the digital economy. *European Journal of Social Theory*, *21*(2), 207–226. doi:10.1177/1368431017710907

Curran, J., & Lennon, R. (2011). Participating in the conversation: exploring adoption of online social media networks. *Academy of Marketing Studies*, *15*(1), 21–38.

Curran, K., O'Brien, S., & O'Hara, K. (2011). The role of Twitter in the world of business. *International Journal of Business Data Communications and Networking*, *7*(3), 14. doi:10.4018/jbdcn.2011070101

Cvijikj, I. P., & Michahelles, F. (2013). Online engagement factors on Facebook brand pages. *Social Network Analysis and Mining*, *3*(4), 843–861. doi:10.100713278-013-0098-8

da Silva Macedo, M. A., de Castro Casa Nova, S. P., & de Almeida, K. (1999). Mapping and bibliometric analysis of the use of data envelopment analysis (DEA) in accounting and administration studies. In Proceedings of 23 ENANPAD. Foz do Iguacu: ANPAD.

Dahlstrom, E., Grunwald, P., de Boor, T., & Vockley, M. (2011). ECAR national study of students and information technology in higher education. *EDUCAUSE Center for Applied Research.* Retrieved from http://www. educause. edu

Daiya, A., & Roy, S. (2016). User and firm generated content on online social media: A review and research directions. [IJOM]. *International Journal of Online Marketing*, *6*(3), 34–49. doi:10.4018/IJOM.2016070103

Das, T. K., & Teng, B.-S. (1998). Between trust and control: developing confidence in partner cooperation in alliances. *Academy of Management Review*, *23*(3), 491–512. doi:10.5465/amr.1998.926623

Daugherty, T., Eastin, M. S., & Bright, L. (2008). Exploring consumer motivations for creating user-generated content. *Journal of Interactive Advertising*, *8*(2), 16–25. doi:10.1080/15252019.2008.10722139

Daugherty, T., & Hoffman, E. (2014). eWOM and the importance of capturing consumer attention within social media. *Journal of Marketing Communications*, *20*(1-2), 82–102. doi:10.1080/13527266.2013.797764

Davis, P. (2012). Trust is #1 barrier to sharing I Deskmag I Coworking. Retrieved from http://www.deskmag.com/en/trust-is-1-barrier-to-sharing-coworking-shareable-491

Dawley, L. (2009). Social network knowledge construction: Emerging virtual world pedagogy. *On the Horizon*, *17*(2), 109–121. doi:10.1108/10748120910965494

De Vries, L., Gensler, S., & Leeflang, P. S. H. (2012). Popularity of brand posts on brand fan pages: an investigation of the effects of social media marketing. *Journal of Interactive Marketing*, *26*(2), 83–91. doi:10.1016/j.intmar.2012.01.003

Deci, E. L. (1971). Effects of externally mediated rewards on intrinsic motivation. *Journal of Personality and Social Psychology*, *18*(1), 105–115. doi:10.1037/h0030644

Deepa, N., & Deshmukh, S. (2013). Social media marketing: The next generation of business engagement. *International Journal of Management Research and Reviews*, *3*(2), 2461.

Demircan, N., & Ceylan, A. (2003). Örgütsel Güven Kavram : Nedenleri ve Sonuçlar. *Yönetim ve Ekonomi*, *10*(2). Retrieved from http://webcache.googleusercontent.com/search?q=cache:http://www2.bayar.edu.tr/yonetimekonomi/dergi/pdf/C10S22003/ndac.pdf

Deng, L., & Poole, M. S. (2012). Aesthetic design of e-commerce web pages – Webpage Complexity, Order and preference. *Electronic Commerce Research and Applications*, *11*(4), 420–440. doi:10.1016/j.elerap.2012.06.004

Denning, S. (2015). *Has Google+ really died?* Retrieved from https://www.forbes.com/sites/stevedenning/2015/04/23/has-google-really-died/#10b77352466c

Dessart, L., Veloutsou, C., & Morgan-Thomas, A. (2016). Capturing consumer engagement: Duality, dimensionality and measurement. *Journal of Marketing Management*, *32*(5-6), 399–426. doi:10.1080/0267257X.2015.1130738

Deutsch, M. (1958). Trust and suspicion. *The Journal of Conflict Resolution*, *2*(4), 265–279. doi:10.1177/002200275800200401

Dhar, V., & Chang, E. A. (2009). Does chatter matter? The impact of user-generated content on music sales. *Journal of Interactive Marketing*, *23*(4), 300–307. doi:10.1016/j.intmar.2009.07.004

Dholakia, U. M., Bagozzi, R. P., & Pearo, L. K. (2004). A social influence model of consumer participation in network- and small-group-based virtual communities. *International Journal of Research in Marketing*, *21*(3), 241–263. doi:10.1016/j.ijresmar.2003.12.004

Dictionary, O. (2018). Trust I Definition of trust in English by Oxford Dictionaries. Retrieved from https://en.oxforddictionaries.com/definition/trust

Dijkmans, C., Kerkhof, P., & Beukeboom, C. J. (2015). A stage to engage: Social media use and corporate reputation. *Tourism Management*, *47*, 58–67. doi:10.1016/j.tourman.2014.09.005

Ding, Y., Phang, C. W., Lu, X., Tan, C. H., & Sutanto, J. (2014). The role of marketer-and user-generated content in sustaining the growth of a social media brand community. In *Proceedings 2014 47th Hawaii International Conference on System Sciences* (pp. 1785-1792). New York: IEEE. 10.1109/HICSS.2014.226

Divsalar, M., & Azgomi, M. A. (2010). A computational trust model for e-commerce systems. *Lecture Notes of the Institute for Computer Sciences, Social-Informatics and Telecommunications Engineering, 21 LNICST*, 9–18. doi:10.1007/978-3-642-11532-5_2

Dolan, R., Conduit, J., Fahy, J., & Goodman, S. (2016). Social media engagement behaviour: A uses and gratifications perspective. *Journal of Strategic Marketing*, *24*(3-4), 261–277. doi:10.1080/0965254X.2015.1095222

Downes, S. (2007). What connectivism is [Web log post]. Retrieved from http://halfanhour.blogspot. co.uk/2007/02/what-connectivism-is.html.

Drahošová, M., & Balco, P. (2017). The analysis of advantages and disadvantages of use of social media in European Union. *Procedia Computer Science*, *109*, 1005–1009. doi:10.1016/j.procs.2017.05.446

Du Plessis, C. (2015). *An exploratory analysis of essential elements of content marketing*. In *Proceedings ECSM 2015 2nd European Conference on Social Media*, (pp. 122-129). UK: Academic Conferences Publisher International.

Duarte, J., Siegel, S., & Young, L. (2012). Trust and credit: the role of appearance in peer-to-peer lending. *Review of Financial Studies*, *25*(8), 2455–2484. doi:10.1093/rfs/hhs071

Durkheim, E. (1964). *The rules of sociological method*. Retrieved from http://www.worldcat.org/title/rules-of-sociological-method/oclc/220073686

Ehrenberg, A., Juckes, S., White, K. M., & Walsh, S. P. (2008). Personality and self-esteem as predictors of young people's technology use. *Cyberpsychology & Behavior*, *11*(6), 739–741. doi:10.1089/cpb.2008.0030 PMID:18991531

Eisenberg, B. (2008, Nov. 7). *Understanding and aligning the value of social media*. Retrieved from www.clickz.com

Ellison, N. B., Steinfield, C., & Lampe, C. (2007). The benefits of Facebook "friends:" Social capital and college students' use of online social network sites. *Journal of Computer-Mediated Communication, 12*(4), 1143–1168. doi:10.1111/j.1083-6101.2007.00367.x

Ellison, N. B., Steinfield, C., & Lampe, C. (2011). Connection strategies: Social capital implications of Facebook-enabled communication practices. *New Media & Society, 13*(6), 873–892. doi:10.1177/1461444810385389

Erkan, I. (2015). Electronic word of mouth on Instagram: Customers' Engagements with Brands in Different Sectors. *International Journal of Management, Accounting, and Economics, 2*(12), 1435–1444.

Erkan, I., & Evans, C. (2016). The influence of eWOM in social media on consumers' purchase intentions: An extended approach to information adoption. *Computers in Human Behavior, 61*, 47–55. doi:10.1016/j.chb.2016.03.003

Ert, E., Fleischer, A., & Magen, N. (2016). *Trust and reputation in the sharing economy: The role of personal photos in Airbnb*. doi:10.1016/j.tourman.2016.01.013

Evans, D. (2008). *Social media marketing an hour a day*. Indiana: Wiley Publishing.

Falls, J., & Deckers, E. (2012). *No bullshit social media: The all-business, no-hype guide to social media marketing*. United States of America: Pearson Education.

Feiner, L. (2019). *Snap has nearly doubled its stock price since the beginning of 2019 — here's why*. Retrieved from https://www.cnbc.com/2019/04/04/why-snap-stock-has-nearly-doubled-since-the-beginning-of-2019.html

Felix, R., Rauschnabel, P. A., & Hinsch, C. (2017). Elements of strategic social media marketing: A holistic framework. *Journal of Business Research, 70*, 118–126. doi:10.1016/j.jbusres.2016.05.001

Fernández-López, Á., Rodríguez-Fórtiz, M. J., Rodríguez-Almendros, M. L., & Martínez-Segura, M. J. (2013). Mobile learning technology based on iOS devices to support students with special education needs. *Computers & Education, 61*, 77–90. doi:10.1016/j.compedu.2012.09.014

Finley, K. (2012). *Trust in the sharing economy: an exploratory study*.

Fischer, E., & Reuber, A. R. (2011). Social interaction via new social media: (How) can interactions on Twitter affect effectual thinking and behavior? *Journal of Business Venturing, 26*(1), 1–18. doi:10.1016/j.jbusvent.2010.09.002

Flanagin, A. J., & Metzger, M. J. (2001). Internet use in the contemporary media environment. *Human Communication Research, 27*(1), 153–181. doi:10.1093/hcr/27.1.153

Flanigan, R. L., & Obermier, T. R. (2016). An assessment of the use of social media in the industrial distribution business-to-business market sector. *The Journal of Technology Studies, 42*(1), 18–28. doi:10.21061/jots.v42i1.a.2

Fotis, J., Buhalis, D., & Rossides, N. (2011). Social media impact on holiday travel planning: The case of the Russian and the FSU markets. [IJOM]. *International Journal of Online Marketing*, *1*(4), 1–19. doi:10.4018/ijom.2011100101

Foux, G. (2006). Consumer-generated media: Get your customers involved. *Brand Strategy*, *8*(202), 38–39.

Freedman, S., & Jin, Z. G. (2008). *Do social networks solve information problems for peer-to-peer lending? Evidence from Prosper.com**. Retrieved from www.netinst.org

Fukuyama, F. (1995). *Trust: the social virtues and the creation of prosperity*. Retrieved from https://www.worldcat.org/title/trust-the-social-virtues-and-the-creation-of-prosperity/oclc/32547174

Funk, T. (2011). *Social media playbook for business: Reaching your online community with Twitter, Facebook, LinkedIn, and more:* Santa Barbara, CA*:* ABC- *Clio*, LLC.

Galuba, W., Aberer, K., Chakraborty, D., Despotovic, Z., & Kellerer, W. (2010): Outtweeting the Twitterers - predicting information cascades. In Microblogs 3rd Workshop on Online Social Networks, WOSN (2010).

Gambarov, V. (2014). *Elektronik Ticarette Güven Oluşturan Faktörler Ve Satınalma Niyetine Etkileri Üzerine Bir Araştırma*. doi:10.1192/bjp.205.1.76a

Gambetta, D. (1988). *Can we trust trust?* Retrieved from https://philpapers.org/rec/GAMCWT

Gambetti, R., & Grafigna, G. (2010). The concept of engagement: A systematic analysis of the ongoing marketing debate. *International Journal of Market Research*, *52*(6), 801–826. doi:10.2501/S147078531020166

Gamma, R., Knight, C., & Figueiredo, E. (1999). New business strategies in the context of the digital economy. Manufacturing industry and internet. Geography Notebooks, Special No. 29-38.

Garbarino, E., & Johnson, M. S. (1999). The different roles of satisfaction, trust, and commitment in customer relationships. *Journal of Marketing*, *63*(2), 70–87. doi:10.1177/002224299906300205

Garcia, L., & Ferreira, M. J. (2014). The impact of chaos and connectivism in the collaborative/cooperative learning. [RJOPES]. *Research Journal in Organizational Psychology and Educational Studies*, *3*(2), 76.

Garousi, V. (2015). A bibliometric analysis of the Turkish software engineering research community. *Scientometrics*, *105*(1), 23–49. doi:10.100711192-015-1663-x

Garrison, D. R., & Kanuka, H. (2004). Blended learning: Uncovering its transformative potential in higher education. *The Internet and Higher Education*, *7*(2), 95–105. doi:10.1016/j.iheduc.2004.02.001

Gavilan, D., Avello, M., & Martinez-Navarro, G. (2018). The influence of online ratings and reviews on hotel booking consideration. *Tourism Management*, *66*, 53–61. doi:10.1016/j.tourman.2017.10.018

Gazzola, P., Colombo, G., Pezzetti, R., & Nicolescu, L. (2017). Consumer empowerment in the digital economy: Availing sustainable purchasing decisions. *Sustainability (Switzerland), 9*(5), 1–19.

Gebel, M. (2019). *In 15 years Facebook has amassed 2.3 billion users — more than followers of Christianity.* Retrieved from https://www.businessinsider.com/facebook-has-2-billion-plus-users-after-15-years-2019-2

Gefen, D. (2000). *E-commerce : the role of familiarity and trust. 28*, 725–737. doi:10.1016/S0305-0483(00)00021-9

Gefen, D., & Straub, D. W. (2004). Consumer trust in B2C e-Commerce and the importance of social presence: Experiments in e-Products and e-Services. *Omega, 32*(6), 407–424. doi:10.1016/j.omega.2004.01.006

Gerson, J., Plagnol, A. C., & Corr, P. J. (2016). Subjective well-being and social media use: Do personality traits moderate the impact of social comparison on Facebook? *Computers in Human Behavior, 63*, 813–822. doi:10.1016/j.chb.2016.06.023

Getting, B. (2007). *Basic definitions: Web 1.0, Web. 2.0, Web 3.0.* Retrieved from https://www.practicalecommerce.com/Basic-Definitions-Web-1-0-Web-2-0-Web-3-0

Ghazali, Saadiah&Sulaiman, Nor Intan, & Zaibidi, Nerda, & Omar, MohdFaizal, & Alias, Rose. (2016). The impact of knowledge sharing through social media among academia. doi:. doi:10.1063/1.4966060

Gironda, J. T., & Korgaonkar, P. K. (2014). Understanding consumers' social networking site usage. *Journal of Marketing Management, 30*(5–6), 571–605. doi:10.1080/0267257X.2013.851106

Global Web Index. (2018). *Global web index's flagship report on the latest trends in social media.* Retrieved from https://www.globalwebindex.com/hubfs/Downloads/Social-H2-2018-report.pdf

Godey, B., Manthiou, A., Pederzoli, D., Rokka, J., Aiello, G., Donvito, R., & Singh, R. (2016). Social media marketing efforts of luxury brands: Influence on brand equity and consumer behavior. *Journal of Business Research, 69*(12), 5833–5841. doi:10.1016/j.jbusres.2016.04.181

Go, E., & Bortree, D. S. (2017). What and how to communicate CSR? The role of CSR fit, modality interactivity, and message interactivity on social networking sites. *Journal of Promotion Management*, 1–21.

Goh, K. Y., Heng, C. S., & Lin, Z. (2013). Social media brand community and consumer behavior: Quantifying the relative impact of user- and marketer-generated content. *Information Systems Research, 24*(1), 88–107. doi:10.1287/isre.1120.0469

Goodman, A. (1990). Addiction: definition and implications. *British Journal of Addiction, 85*(11), 1403–1408. doi:10.1111/j.1360-0443.1990.tb01620.x PMID:2285834

Grant, J. E., Odlaug, B. L., & Chamberlain, S. R. (2016). *What is a behavioral addiction?* Retrieved from https://www.psychologytoday.com/intl/blog/why-cant-i-stop/201606/what-is-behavioral-addiction

Green, D. T., & Pearson, J. M. (2011). Integrating website usability with the electronic commerce acceptance model. *Behaviour & Information Technology*, *30*(2), 181–199. doi:10.1080/01449291003793785

Greengard, S. (2012). Digitally possessed. *Communications of the ACM*, *55*(5), 14–16. doi:10.1145/2160718.2160725

Greenwood, J., Guner, N., Santos, C., & Kocharkov, G. (2016). Technology and the changing family: A unified model of marriage, divorce, educational attainment and marred female labor-force participation. *American Economic Journal. Macroeconomics*, *8*(1), 1–41. doi:10.1257/mac.20130156

Griffiths, M. (2005). A “components” model of addiction within a biopsychosocial framework. *Journal of Substance Use*, *10*(4), 191–197. doi:10.1080/14659890500114359

Griffiths, M. D. (2010). The role of context in online gaming excess and addiction: Some case study evidence. *International Journal of Mental Health and Addiction*, *8*(1), 119–125. doi:10.100711469-009-9229-x

Grifiths, M. (2010). Internet abuse and internet addiction in the workplace. *Journal of Workplace Learning*, *22*(7), 463–472. doi:10.1108/13665621011071127

Gupta, M., Esmaeilzadeh, P., Uz, I., & Tennant, V. M. (2019). The effects of national cultural values on individuals’ intention to participate in peer-to-peer sharing economy. *Journal of Business Research, 97*(September 2017), 20–29. doi:10.1016/j.jbusres.2018.12.018

Hacıhasanoglu, B. (2017). *Sosyal Medyada Pazarlama Stratejilerinin Oluşturulması ve Telekomünikasyon Sektörüne İlişkin Bir Uygulama* (Unpublished Master’s Thesis, Istanbul Commerce University, Turkey).

Hall, H. (2003). Borrowed theory: Applying exchange theories in information science research. *Library & Information Science Research*, *25*(3), 287–306. doi:10.1016/S0740-8188(03)00031-8

Hanna, R., Rohm, A., & Crittenden, V. L. (2011). We’re all connected: The power of the social media ecosystem. *Business Horizons*, *54*(3), 265–273. doi:10.1016/j.bushor.2011.01.007

Hargittai, E., & Hsieh, Y. (2010). Predictors and consequences of differentiated practices on social network sites. *Information Communication and Society*, *13*(4), 515–536. doi:10.1080/13691181003639866

Hassan, O. A. B. (2011). Learning theories and assessment methodologies – an engineering educational perspective. *European Journal of Engineering Education*, *36*(4), 327–339. doi:10.1080/03043797.2011.591486

Hayes, R. A., Carr, C. T., & Wohn, D. Y. (2016). One click, many meanings: interpreting paralinguistic digital affordances in social media. *Journal of Broadcasting & Electronic Media*, *60*(1), 171–187. doi:10.1080/08838151.2015.1127248

Hazari, S., Bergiel, B. J., & Sethna, B. N. (2016). Hedonic and utilitarian use of user-generated content on online shopping websites. *Journal of Marketing Communications*, 1–20.

Heim, J., & Hansen, G. (1999). *Free stuff for sewing fanatics on the internet*. Lafayette, CA: C&T Publishing.

Hennig-Thurau, T., Gwinner, K. P., Walsh, G., & Gremler, D. D. (2004). Electronic word-of-mouth via consumer-opinion platforms: What motivates consumers to articulate themselves on the Internet? *Journal of Interactive Marketing*, *18*(1), 38–52. doi:10.1002/dir.10073

Herscovici, A., & Bolaño, C. (2005). The critique of the political economy of information and knowledge. Article presented at the national meeting of the Brazilian Society of Political Economy, Campin.

Hess, T., Lang, K. R., & Xu, S. X. (2011). Social embeddedness and online consumer behavior. *Electronic Markets*, *21*(3), 157–159. doi:10.100712525-011-0071-1

Ho, J. Y. C., & Dempsey, M. (2010). Viral marketing: Motivations to forward online content. *Journal of Business Research*, *63*(9–10), 1000–1006. doi:10.1016/j.jbusres.2008.08.010

Hojeghan, S. B., & Esfangareh, A. N. (2011). Digital economy and tourism impacts, influences and challenges. *Procedia: Social and Behavioral Sciences*, *19*, 308–316. doi:10.1016/j.sbspro.2011.05.136

Holford, W. D. (2019). The future of human creative knowledge work within the digital economy. *Futures*, *105*(October, 2018), 143–154.

Hollars, K., & Lew, A. (2010). Digital sky technologies to acquire AOL's ICQ instant messaging service. Retrieved from https://www.businesswire.com/news/home/6268204/en

Hollebeek, L. D., Glynn, M. S., & Brodie, R. J. (2014). Consumer brand engagement in social media: conceptualization, scale development and validation. *Journal of Interactive Marketing*, *28*(2), 149–165. doi:10.1016/j.intmar.2013.12.002

Holliman, G., & Rowley, J. (2014). Business to business digital content marketing: Marketers' perceptions of best practice. *Journal of Research in Interactive Marketing*, *8*(4), 269–293. doi:10.1108/JRIM-02-2014-0013

http://www.economist.com/node/10650775

http://www.gsma.com/publicpolicy/wp-content/uploads/2012/11/gsma-deloitte-impact-mobile-telephony-economic-growth.pdf

Huang, H. H., & Mitchell, V. (2014). The role of imagination and brand personification in brand relationships. *Psychology and Marketing*, *31*(1), 38–47. doi:10.1002/mar.20673

Huang, S.-H., & Capps, M. (2013). Impact of online social network on american college students' reading practices. *The College Quarterly*, *16*(1). Retrieved from http://collegequarterly.ca/2013-vol16-num01-winter/huang-capps.html

Huang, Y. M., Huang, Y. M., Huang, S. H., & Lin, Y. T. (2012). A ubiquitous English vocabulary learning system: Evidence of active/passive attitudes vs. usefulness/ease-of-use. *Computers & Education*, *58*(1), 273–282. doi:10.1016/j.compedu.2011.08.008

Huang, Z., & Benyoucef, M. (2013). From e-commerce to social commerce: A close look at design features. *Electronic Commerce Research and Applications*, *12*(4), 246–259. doi:10.1016/j.elerap.2012.12.003

Hwang, G. J., & Wu, P. H. (2014). Applications, impacts, and trends of mobile technology-enhanced learning: A review of 2008–2012 publications in selected SSCI journals. *International Journal of Mobile Learning and Organisation*, *8*(2), 83–95. doi:10.1504/IJMLO.2014.062346

Iankova, S., Davies, I., Archer-Brown, C., Marder, B., & Yau, A. (2018). A comparison of social media marketing between B2B, B2C and mixed business models. *Industrial Marketing Management*. doi:10.1016/j.indmarman.2018.01.001

Inglehart, R. (1999). Trust, well-being, and democracy. In M. E. Warren (Ed.), *Democracy and trust* (pp. 88–120). doi:10.1017/CBO9780511659959.004

Ioanăs, E., & Stoica, I. (2014). Social media and its impact on consumers behavior. *International Journal of Economic Practices and Theories*, *4*(2).

Islam, Y. M., Ashraf, M., Rahman, Z., & Rahman, M. (2005). *Mobile telephone technology as a distance learning tool* (pp. 226–232). ICEIS.

Jansen, B., Zhang, M., Sobel, K., & Chowdury, A. (2009). Twitter power: Tweets as electronic word of mouth. *Journal of the American Society for Information Science and Technology*, *60*(11), 2169–2188. doi:10.1002/asi.21149

Jarvenpaa, S. L., Tractinsky, N., & Saarinen, L. (2000). Consumer trust in an internet store: a cross-cultural validation. *Journal of Computer-Mediated Communication, 5*(2), 0–0. doi:10.1111/j.1083-6101.1999.tb00337.x

Jayasuriya, N., Azam, S. M., Khatibi, A., & Dharmaratne, I. (2018). The role of social media marketing on brand equity-a literature review. *Global Journal of Management and Business Research*, XVIII.

Jeong, H., & Hmelo-Silver, C. E. (2016). Seven affordances of computer-supported collaborative learning: how to support collaborative learning? How can technologies help? *Educational Psychologist*, *51*(2), 247–265. doi:10.1080/00461520.2016.1158654

Jha, B. (2019). The role of social media in communication: Empirical study of online purchasing intention of financial products. *Global Business Review*. pp. 1-17.

Jin, L., & Huang, Y. (2014). When giving money does not work: The differential effects of monetary versus in-kind rewards in referral reward programs. *International Journal of Research in Marketing*, *31*(1), 107–116. doi:10.1016/j.ijresmar.2013.08.005

Jonassen, D. H. (1991). Objectivism versus constructivism: Do we need a new philosophical paradigm? *Educational Technology Research and Development*, *39*(3), 5–14. doi:10.1007/BF02296434

Jones, K., & Leonard, L. N. K. (2008). *Trust in consumer-to-consumer electronic commerce*. doi:10.1016/j.im.2007.12.002

Jones, Q., & Rafaeli, S. (2000). Time to split, virtually: 'discourse architecture' and 'community building' create vibrant virtual publics. *Electronic Markets*, *10*. doi:10.1080/101967800750050326

Jones, Q., Ravid, G., & Rafaeli, S. (2004). Information overload and the message dynamics of online interaction spaces. *Information Systems Research*, *15*(2), 194–210. doi:10.1287/isre.1040.0023

Junco, R. (2012). The relationship between frequency of Facebook use, participation in Facebook activities, and student engagement. *Computers & Education*, *58*(1), 162–171. doi:10.1016/j.compedu.2011.08.004

Junco, R. (2012). Too much face and not enough books: The relationship between multiple indices of Facebook use and academic performance. *Computers in Human Behavior*, *28*(1), 187–198. doi:10.1016/j.chb.2011.08.026

Junco, R. (2014). *Engaging students through social media: evidence-based practices for use in student affairs*. San Francisco, CA: Jossey-Bass.

Junco, R., Heiberger, G., & Loken, E. (2011). The effect of Twitter on college student engagement and grades. *Journal of Computer Assisted Learning*, *27*(2), 119–132. doi:10.1111/j.1365-2729.2010.00387.x

Jussila, J. (2015). *Social media in business-to-business companies' innovation*. Tampere, Finland: Tampere University of Technology.

Jussila, J. J., Kärkkäinen, H., & Aramo-Immonen, H. (2014). Social media utilization in business-to-business relationships of technology industry firms. *Computers in Human Behavior*, *30*, 606–613. doi:10.1016/j.chb.2013.07.047

Kalpidou, M., Costin, D., & Morris, J. (2011). The relationship between Facebook and the well-being of undergraduate college students. *Cyberpsychology, Behavior, and Social Networking*, *14*(4), 183–189. doi:10.1089/cyber.2010.0061 PMID:21192765

Kam, M., Kumar, A., Jain, S., Mathur, A., & Canny, J. (2009, April). Improving literacy in rural India: Cellphone games in an after-school program. In *2009 International Conference on Information and Communication Technologies and Development (ICTD),* (pp. 139-149). IEEE.

Kandell, J. (1998). Internet addiction on campus: The vulnerability of college students. *Cyberpsychology & Behavior*, *1*(1), 11–17. doi:10.1089/cpb.1998.1.11

Kang, M., & Schuett, M. A. (2013). Determinants of sharing travel experiences in social media. *Journal of Travel & Tourism Marketing*, *30*(1-2), 93–107. doi:10.1080/10548408.2013.751237

Kaplan, A. M., & Haenlein, M. (2010). Users of the world, unite! The challenges and opportunities of social media. *Business Horizons*, *53*(1), 59–68. doi:10.1016/j.bushor.2009.09.003

Karikari, S., Osei-Frimpong, K., & Owusu-Frimpong, N. (2017). Evaluating individual level antecedents and consequences on social media use in Ghana. *Technological Forecasting and Social Change*, *123*, 68–78. doi:10.1016/j.techfore.2017.06.023

Karjaluoto, H., Ulkuniemi, P., & Mustonen, N. (2015). The role of digital channels in industrial marketing communications. *Journal of Business and Industrial Marketing*, *30*(6), 703–710. doi:10.1108/JBIM-04-2013-0092

Kearney, M., Schuck, S., Burden, K., & Aubusson, P. (2012). Viewing mobile learning from a pedagogical perspective. *Research in Learning Technology*, 20.

Keegan, B. J., & Rowley, J. (2017). Evaluation and decision making in social media marketing. *Management Decision*, *55*(1), 15–31. doi:10.1108/MD-10-2015-0450

Keller, K. L. (2009). Building strong brands in a modern marketing communications environment. *Journal of Marketing Communications*, *15*(2-3), 139–155. doi:10.1080/13527260902757530

Kemmerer, K. (2013). *Unleashing the power of social media marketing within the non-profits, through the lens of social cognitive theory* (Master's thesis, Liberty University, Virginia).

Keskin, N. O., & Metcalf, D. (2011). The current perspectives, theories, and practices of mobile learning. *TOJET: The Turkish Online Journal of Educational Technology, 10*(2).

Khan, M. L. (2017). Social media engagement: What motivates user participation and consumption on YouTube? *Computers in Human Behavior*, *66*, 236–247. doi:10.1016/j.chb.2016.09.024

Kho, N. D. (2008). B2B gets social media. *EContent (Wilton, Conn.)*, *31*(3), 26–30.

Kietzmann, J. H., Hermkens, K., McCarthy, I. P., & Silvestre, B. S. (2011). Social media? Get serious! Understanding the functional building blocks of social media. *Business Horizons*, *54*(3), 241–251. doi:10.1016/j.bushor.2011.01.005

Kietzmann, J. H., Silvestre, B. S., McCarthy, I. P., & Pitt, L. F. (2012). Unpacking the social media phenomenon: Towards a research agenda. *Journal of Public Affairs*, *12*(2), 109–119. doi:10.1002/pa.1412

Kim, A. (2014). The curious case of self-interest: inconsistent effects and ambivalence toward a widely accepted construct. *Journal for the Theory of Social Behaviour*, *44*(1), 99–122. doi:10.1111/jtsb.12032

Kim, B., & Kim, Y. (2017). College students' social media use and communication network heterogeneity: Implications for social capital and subjective well-being. *Computers in Human Behavior*, *73*, 620–628. doi:10.1016/j.chb.2017.03.033

Kim, C., & Yang, S.-U. (2017). Like, comment, and share on Facebook: How each behavior differs from the other. *Public Relations Review*, *43*(2), 441–449. doi:10.1016/j.pubrev.2017.02.006

Kim, D. J., Ferrin, D. L., & Rao, H. R. (2009). Trust and satisfaction, two stepping stones for successful e-commerce relationships: a longitudinal exploration. *Information Systems Research*, *20*(2), 237–257. doi:10.1287/isre.1080.0188

Kim, D., & Benbasat, I. (2009). Trust-assuring arguments in B2C e-commerce: impact of content, source, and price on trust. *Journal of Management Information Systems*, *26*(3), 175–206. doi:10.2753/MIS0742-1222260306

Kim, J. K., & Hull, K. (2017). How fans are engaging with baseball teams demonstrating multiple objectives on Instagram. *Sport, Business, and Management International Journal (Toronto, Ont.)*, *7*, 216–232.

Kim, S. J., Wang, R. J.-H., Maslowska, E., & Malthouse, E. C. (2016). "Understanding a fury in your words": The effects of posting and viewing electronic negative word-of-mouth on purchase behaviors. *Computers in Human Behavior*, *54*, 511–521. doi:10.1016/j.chb.2015.08.015

Kim, W. G., Lim, H., & Brymer, R. A. (2015). The effectiveness of managing social media on hotel performance. *International Journal of Hospitality Management*, *44*, 165–171. doi:10.1016/j.ijhm.2014.10.014

Kircaburun, K., Demetrovics, Z., & Tosuntaş, Ş. B. (2018). Analyzing the links between problematic social media use, dark triad traits, and self-esteem. *International Journal of Mental Health and Addiction*. doi:10.100711469-018-9900-1

Kiriakidis, S. P., & Kavoura, A. (2010). A review of the literature on harassment through the internet and other electronic means. *Family & Community Health*, *11*(2), 82–93. doi:10.1097/FCH.0b013e3181d593e4 PMID:20216351

Klopfer, E., Squire, K., & Jenkins, H. (2002). Environmental detectives: PDAs as a window into a virtual simulated world. In *International Workshop on Wireless and Mobile Technologies in Education, 2002. Proceedings. IEEE* (pp. 95-98). IEEE.

Knack, S., & Keefer, P. (1997). Does social capital have an economic payoff? A cross-country investigation. *Quarterly Journal of Economics 112*(4), 1251-1288 | socialcapitalgateway.org. Retrieved from http://www.socialcapitalgateway.org/content/paper/knack-s-keefer-p-1997-does-social-capital-have-economic-payoff-cross-country-investiga

Koç, E. (2015). *Tüketici Davranışı ve Pazarlama Stratejileri: Global ve Yerel Yaklaşım.*

Koçgar, M. E. (2013). *Tüketici Davranışlarını Etkileyen Faktörler Ve Kültür: Eskişehir'de Kültürün Tüketim Tercihleri Üzerine Etkisi.*

Körmendi, A., Brutóczki, Z., Végh, B. P., & Székely, R. (2016). Smartphone use can be addictive? A case report. *Journal of Behavioral Addictions*, *5*(3), 548–552. doi:10.1556/2006.5.2016.033 PMID:27599674

Kostakis, V., Roos, A., & Bauwens, M. (2016). Towards a political ecology of the digital economy: Socio-environmental implications of two competing value models. *Environmental Innovation and Societal Transitions*, *18*, 82–100. doi:10.1016/j.eist.2015.08.002

Koufaris, M., & Hampton-Sosa, W. (2004). The development of initial trust in an online company by new customers. *Information & Management*, *41*(3), 377–397. doi:10.1016/j.im.2003.08.004

Krumm, J., Davies, N., & Narayanaswami, C. (2008). User-generated content. *IEEE Pervasive Computing*, *7*(4), 10–11. doi:10.1109/MPRV.2008.85

Kuhn, T. (1962). *The structure of scientific revolutions*. Chicago, IL: University of Chicago Press.

Kumar, A., Bezawada, R., Rishika, R., Janakiraman, R., & Kannan, P. K. (2016). From social to sale: The effects of firm-generated content in social media on customer behavior. *Journal of Marketing*, *80*(1), 7–25. doi:10.1509/jm.14.0249

Kumar, V., Aksoy, L., Donkers, B., Venkatesan, R., Wiesel, T., & Tillmanns, S. (2010). Undervalued or overvalued customers: Capturing total customer engagement value. *Journal of Service Research*, *13*(3), 297–310. doi:10.1177/1094670510375602

Kurti, A., Spikol, D., & Milrad, M. (2008). Bridging outdoors and indoors educational activities in schools with the support of mobile and positioning technologies. *International Journal of Mobile Learning and Organisation*, *2*(2), 166–186. doi:10.1504/IJMLO.2008.019767

Kuss, D. J., Griffiths, M., Karila, L., & Billieux, J. (2014). Internet addiction: A systematic review of epidemiological research for the last decade, *1*(4), 397–413.

Kuss, D. J., & Griffiths, M. D. (2011). Online social networking and addiction-A review of the psychological literature. *International Journal of Environmental Research and Public Health*, *8*(9), 3528–3552. doi:10.3390/ijerph8093528 PMID:22016701

Ladhari, R., & Michaud, M. (2015). eWOM effects on hotel booking intentions, attitudes, trust, and website perceptions. *International Journal of Hospitality Management*, *46*, 36–45. doi:10.1016/j.ijhm.2015.01.010

Lai, B. S. T. (2003). *Trust in online trading systems*. (Doctoral dissertation, University of Auckland).

Lambe, C. J., Wittmann, C. M., & Spekman, R. E. (2001). Social exchange theory and research on business-to-business relational exchange. *Journal of Business-To-Business Marketing*, *8*(3), 1–36. doi:10.1300/J033v08n03_01

Langford, S. (2019). Junk explained: What the hell is TikTok, and is it the new vine? Retrieved from https://junkee.com/tiktok-app-vine-challenge/188567

Lan, Y. F., Tsai, P. W., Yang, S. H., & Hung, C. L. (2012). Comparing the social knowledge construction behavioral patterns of problem-based online asynchronous discussion in e/m-learning environments. *Computers & Education*, *59*(4), 1122–1135. doi:10.1016/j.compedu.2012.05.004

Laroche, M., Habibi, M. R., & Richard, M. O. (2013). To be or not to be in social media: How brand loyalty is affected by social media? *International Journal of Information Management*, *33*(1), 76–82. doi:10.1016/j.ijinfomgt.2012.07.003

Law, R., Leung, K., & Wong, R. (2004). The impact of the Internet on travel agencies. *International Journal of Contemporary Hospitality Management*, *16*(2), 100–107. doi:10.1108/09596110410519982

Lee, H., & Park, H. (2013). Testing the impact of message interactivity on relationship management and organizational reputation. *Journal of Public Relations Research*, *25*(2), 188–206. doi:10.1080/1062726X.2013.739103

Lee, H.-Y., Ahn, H., Kim, H. K., & Lee, J. (2014). Comparative analysis of trust in online communities. *Procedia Computer Science*, *31*, 1140–1149. doi:10.1016/j.procs.2014.05.370

Lee, M., & Youn, S. (2009). Electronic word of mouth (eWOM): How eWOM platforms influence consumer product judgement. *International Journal of Advertising*, *28*(3), 473–499. doi:10.2501/S0265048709200709

Lemes, D. O., Tomaselli, F. C., & Camarotti, S. R. B. (2012). The digital economy and the mobile gaming market. In: XI SB Games - Brasilia - DF - Brazil, Nov. 2 - 4.

Lennon, R., Rentfro, R. W., & Curran, J. M. (2012). Exploring relationships between demographic variables and social networking use. *Journal of Management and Marketing Research*, *11*, 1–17.

Leskovec, J., Adamic, L. A., & Huberman, B. A. (2006). The dynamics of viral marketing. In *Proceedings of the 7th ACM Conference on Electronic Commerce (pp. 228-237).*

Levenson, J. C., Shensa, A., Sidani, J. E., Colditz, J. B., & Primack, B. A. (2016). The association between social media use and sleep disturbance among young adults. *Preventive Medicine*, *85*, 36–41. doi:10.1016/j.ypmed.2016.01.001 PMID:26791323

Lewis, J. D., & Weigert, A. (1985). Trust as a social reality. *Social Forces*, *63*(4), 967–985. doi:10.2307/2578601

Liang, T. P., & Lai, H. J. (2002). Effect of store design on consumer purchases: An empirical study of on-line bookstores. *Information & Management*, *39*(6), 431–444. doi:10.1016/S0378-7206(01)00129-X

Liang, T. P., Li, X., Yang, C. T., & Wang, M. (2015). What in consumer reviews affects the sales of mobile apps: A multifacet sentiment analysis approach. *International Journal of Electronic Commerce*, *20*(2), 236–260. doi:10.1080/10864415.2016.1087823

Liao, Z., & Cheung, M. T. (2002). Internet-based e-banking and consumer attitudes: An empirical study. *Information & Management*, *39*(4), 283–295. doi:10.1016/S0378-7206(01)00097-0

Li, F., Nucciarelli, A., Roden, S., & Graham, G. (2016). How smart cities transform operations models: A new research agenda for operations management in the digital economy. *Production Planning and Control*, *27*(6), 514–528. doi:10.1080/09537287.2016.1147096

Lim, J. (2016). Effects of social media users attitudes and perceptions of the attributes of news agency content and their intention to purchase digital subscriptions. *New Media & Society, 18*(8), 1403–1421. doi:10.1177/1461444814558669

Lim, J., & Richardson, J. C. (2016). Exploring the effects of students' social networking experience on social presence and perceptions of using SNSs for educational purposes. *Internet and Higher Education, 29*, 31–39. doi:10.1016/j.iheduc.2015.12.001

Lin, Z., & Goh, K. Y. (2011*). Measuring the business value of online social media content for marketers*. Paper presented at Thirty Second International Conference on Information Systems, Shanghai (1-13). Atlanta, GA: Association for Information Systems (AIS).

Ling, C., & Salvendy, G. (2013). Prioritising usability considerations on B2C websites. *Theoretical Issues in Ergonomics Science, 14*(1), 69–98. doi:10.1080/1464536X.2011.573012

Lin, M.-J. J., Hung, S.-W., & Chen, C.-J. (2009). Fostering the determinants of knowledge sharing in professional virtual communities. *Computers in Human Behavior, 25*(4), 929–939. doi:10.1016/j.chb.2009.03.008

Lin, T. J., Duh, H. B. L., Li, N., Wang, H. Y., & Tsai, C. C. (2013). An investigation of learners' collaborative knowledge construction performances and behavior patterns in an augmented reality simulation system. *Computers & Education, 68*, 314–321. doi:10.1016/j.compedu.2013.05.011

Liu, H. W., & Huang, H. C. (2015). Tradeoff between push and pull strategy: The moderating role of brand awareness. In H. Spotts (Ed.), *Marketing, technology and customer commitment in the new economy* (pp. 259–264). Cham, Switzerland: Springer. doi:10.1007/978-3-319-11779-9_98

Liu, J., Li, C., Ji, Y. G., North, M., & Yang, F. (2017). Like it or not: The Fortune 500's Facebook strategies to generate users' electronic word-of-mouth. *Computers in Human Behavior, 73*, 605–613. doi:10.1016/j.chb.2017.03.068

Liu, L., Cheung, C. M. K., & Lee, M. K. O. (2016). An empirical investigation of information sharing behavior on social commerce sites. *International Journal of Information Management, 36*(5), 686–669. doi:10.1016/j.ijinfomgt.2016.03.013

Lock, J. V., & Johnson, C. (2018). Playing together: designing online music courses using a social constructivist framework. In Pedagogy development for teaching online music (pp. 183-201). Hershey, PA: IGI Global.

Lopes, D. P. T., Santos, S. R. M., Siva, V. H. R., & Martins, G. S. (2018). Determinant factors of managerial innovation. [September / December.]. *Electronic Journal Management & Society, 12*(33), 2541–2563.

Lopez, M., & Sicilia, M. (2014). eWOM as source of influence: The impact of participation in eWOM and perceived source trustworthiness on decision making. *Journal of Interactive Advertising, 14*(2), 86–97. doi:10.1080/15252019.2014.944288

Lou, L. L., Yan, Z., Nickerson, A., & McMorris, R. (2012). An examination of the reciprocal relationship of loneliness and Facebook use among first-year college students. *Journal of Educational Computing Research*, *46*(1), 105–117. doi:10.2190/EC.46.1.e

Luo, W., Lu, Y., Zhao, D., & Jiang, H. (2017). On location and trace privacy of the moving object using the negative survey. IEEE Transactions on Emerging Topics in Computational Intelligence, 1(2), 125-134.

Luo, X., & Zhang, J. (2013). How do consumer buzz and traffic in social media marketing predict the value of the firm? *Journal of Management Information Systems*, *30*(2), 213–238. doi:10.2753/MIS0742-1222300208

Lusk, B. (2010). *Digital natives and social media behaviors: an overview.* Retrieved from https://teachandtechassign3.weebly.com/uploads/1/4/2/0/14202725/digital_natives_and_social_media_behaviour.pdf

Lu, Y., Zhao, L., & Wang, B. (2010). From virtual community members to C2C e-commerce buyers: Trust in virtual communities and its effect on consumers' purchase intention. *Electronic Commerce Research and Applications*, *9*(4), 346–360. doi:10.1016/j.elerap.2009.07.003

Ma, M. (2005). *It design for sustaining virtual communities: an identity-based approach.* (Doctoral dissertation).

Mago, Z. (2015). Games on social networks and the promotion within. Studia Ekonomiczne: Marketing communication – selected issues, 14. 49-58.

Magsamen-Conrad, K., Billiotte-Verhoff, C., & Greene, K. (2014). Technology addiction's contribution to mental wellbeing: The positive effect of online social capital. *Computers in Human Behavior*, *40*, 23–30. doi:10.1016/j.chb.2014.07.014 PMID:25568591

Maier, S. (2016). Learn from these 3 ways AirBNB won the trust it needed to succeed. Retrieved from https://www.entrepreneur.com/article/280224

Malthouse, E. C., Calder, B. J., Kim, S. J., & Vandenbosch, M. (2016). Evidence that user-generated content that produces engagement increases purchase behaviours. *Journal of Marketing Management*, *32*(5-6), 427–444. doi:10.1080/0267257X.2016.1148066

Mangold, W. G., & Faulds, D. J. (2009). Social media: The new hybrid element of the promotion mix. *Business Horizons*, *52*(4), 357–365. doi:10.1016/j.bushor.2009.03.002

Marais, N. (2010). Connectivism as learning theory: The force behind changed teaching practice in higher education. *Education, Knowledge & Economy*, *4*(3), 173–182.

Mariko Kasahara, G. (2017). *Gender differences in social media use and cyberbullying in Belize.* Retrieved from https://cornerstone.lib.mnsu.edu/etdsOtherCapstoneProjects.753.https://cornerstone.lib.mnsu.edu/etds/753

MARKETO. (2010). *The definitive guide to B2B social media.* Retrieved from http://designdamage.com/wp-content/uploads/2009/04/The-Definitive-Guide-to-B2B-SM.pdf

MARKETO. (2016). *The definitive guide to social media marketing*. Retrieved from http://www.workforcelink.com/library/The-Definitive-Guide-to-Social-Media-Marketing-Marketo.pdf

Marlatt, G. A., Baer, J. S., Donovan, D. M., & Kivlahan, D. R. (1988). Addictive behaviors: Etiology and treatment. *Annual Review of Psychology*, *39*(1), 223–252. doi:10.1146/annurev.ps.39.020188.001255 PMID:3278676

Martínez-Navarro, J., & Bigné, E. (2017). The value of marketer-generated content on social network sites: Media antecedents and behavioral responses. *Journal of Electronic Commerce Research*, *18*(1), 52.

Marwick, A. (2013). *Status update: Celebrity, publicity, and branding in the social media age*. New Haven: Yale UP.

Mašić, B., Vladušić, L., & Nešić, S. (2018). Challenges in creating transformative growth for companies in digital economy. *Economics*, *6*(2), 37–48.

Mayer, R. C., Davis, J. H., & Schoorman, D. F. (1995). An integrative model of organizational trust. *Academy of Management Review*, *20*(3), 709–734. doi:10.5465/amr.1995.9508080335

Mayfield, A. (2010). What is social media? doi:10.12968/bjom.2014.22.12.896

Mazzella, F., Sundararajan, A., Butt d'Espous, V., & Möhlmann, M. (2016). How digital trust powers the sharing economy: the digitization of trust. *IESE Insight*, (30), 24–31. doi:10.15581/002.ART-2887

McCloskey, D. (2006). *The bourgeois virtues: ethics for an age of commerce*. Retrieved from http://www.deirdremccloskey.com/docs/bv_selection.pdf

McGoogan, C. (2016). *Yahoo: 9 reasons for the internet icon's decline*. Retrieved from https://www.telegraph.co.uk/technology/2016/07/25/yahoo-9-reasons-for-the-internet-icons-decline/

Meeker, M. (2014). Internet trends 2014–code conference.

Meena, P. S., Soni, R., Jain, M., & Paliwal, S. (2015). Social networking sites addiction and associated psychological problems among young adults: A study from North India. *Sri Lanka Journal of Psychiatry*, *6*(1), 14. doi:10.4038ljpsyc.v6i1.8055

Mesch, G. S. (2009). Parental mediation, online activities, and cyberbullying. *Cyberpsychology & Behavior*, *12*(4), 387–393. doi:10.1089/cpb.2009.0068 PMID:19630583

Mesch, G., & Talmud, I. (2006). The quality of online and offline relationships: the role of multiplexity and duration of social relationships. *The Information Society*, *22*(3), 137–148. doi:10.1080/01972240600677805

Michaelidou, N., Siamagka, N. T., & Christodoulides, G. (2011). Usage, barriers and measurement of social media marketing: An exploratory investigation of small and medium B2B brands. *Industrial Marketing Management*, *40*(7), 1153–1159. doi:10.1016/j.indmarman.2011.09.009

Miller, M. R. (2011). *YouTube for business: Online video marketing for any business*. USA: Que Publishing.

Möhlmann, M. (2015). Collaborative consumption: Determinants of satisfaction and the likelihood of using a sharing economy option again. *Journal of Consumer Behaviour, 14*(3), 193–207. doi:10.1002/cb.1512

MöhlmannM. (2016). *Trust age*.

Molina, B. (2017). *Twitter overcounted active users since 2014, shares surge on profit hopes*. Retrieved from https://www.usatoday.com/story/tech/news/2017/10/26/twitter-overcounted-active-users-since-2014-shares-surge/801968001/

Molinillo, S., Liébana-Cabanillas, F., & Anaya-Sánchez, R. (2018). A social commerce intention model for traditional e-commerce sites. *Journal of Theoretical and Applied Electronic Commerce Research, 13*(2), 80–93. doi:10.4067/S0718-18762018000200107

Mollen, A., & Wilson, H. (2010). Engagement, telepresence and interactivity in online consumer experience: Reconciling scholastic and managerial perspectives. *Journal of Business Research, 63*(9-10), 919–925. doi:10.1016/j.jbusres.2009.05.014

Molm, L. D., Collett, J. L., & Schaefer, D. R. (2007). Building solidarity through generalized exchange: A theory of reciprocity. *American Journal of Sociology, 113*(1), 205–242.

Moore, J. N., Hopkins, C. D., & Raymond, M. A. (2013). Utilization of relationship-oriented social media in the selling process: A comparison of consumer (B2C) and industrial (B2B) salespeople. *Journal of Internet Commerce, 12*(1), 48–75. doi:10.1080/15332861.2013.763694

Moqbel, M., & Kock, N. (2018). Unveiling the dark side of social networking sites: Personal and work-related consequences of social networking site addiction. *Information & Management, 55*(1), 109–119. doi:10.1016/j.im.2017.05.001

Morgan, R. M., & Hunt, S. D. (1994). The commitment-trust theory of relationship marketing. *Journal of Marketing, 58*(3), 20–38. doi:10.1177/002224299405800302

Most Popular Social Networking Sites. Top 15 Rank Report (2017). Retrieved from http://www.ebizmba.com/articles/social-networking-websites

Motlik, S. (2008). Mobile learning in developing nations. *The International Review of Research in Open and Distributed Learning, 9*(2). doi:10.19173/irrodl.v9i2.564

Munzel, A., Meyer-Waarden, L., & Galan, J. P. (2018). The social side of sustainability: Well-being as a driver and an outcome of social relationships and interactions on social networking sites. *Technological Forecasting and Social Change, 130*(July 2017), 14–27. doi:10.1016/j.techfore.2017.06.031

Murdough, C. (2009). Social media measurement: It's not impossible. *Journal of Interactive Advertising, 10*(1), 94–99. doi:10.1080/15252019.2009.10722165

Murugesan, S. (2007). Understanding Web 2.0. *IT Professional*, *9*(4), 34–41.

Nadaraja, R., & Yazdanifard, R. (2013). Social media marketing: Advantages and disadvantages. *Social Media Marketing*, 1-10.

Nadler, S. (2014). *The sharing economy: What is it and where is it going?* (Doctoral dissertation, Massachusetts Institute of Technology).

Nahapiet, J., & Ghoshal, S. (1998). Social capital, intellectual capital, and the organizational advantage. *Academy of Management Review*, *23*(2), 242. doi:10.2307/259373

Naismith, L., Lonsdale, P., Vavoula, G., & Sharples, M. (2004). NESTA Futurelab Report 11: Literature review in mobile technologies and learning. Bristol, UK: NESTA Futurelab. Retrieved from http://www.nestafuturelab.org/research/reviews/ reviews_11_and12/11_01.htm

Neverkovich, S. D., Bubnova, I. S., Kosarenko, N. N., Sakhieva, R. G., Sizova, Z. M., Zakharova, V. L., & Sergeeva, M. G. (2018). Students' internet addiction: Study and prevention. *Eurasia Journal of Mathematics, Science, and Technology Education*, *14*(4), 1483–1495. doi:10.29333/ejmste/83723

Ng'ambi, D. (2013). Effective and ineffective uses of emerging technologies: Towards a transformative pedagogical model. *British Journal of Educational Technology*, *44*(4), 652–661. doi:10.1111/bjet.12053

Ngai, E. W. T., Tao, S. S. C., & Moon, K. K. L. (2015). Social media research: Theories, constructs, and conceptual frameworks. *International Journal of Information Management*, *35*(1), 33–44. doi:10.1016/j.ijinfomgt.2014.09.004

Nieto, J., Hernández-Maestro, R. M., & Muñoz-Gallego, P. A. (2014). Marketing decisions, customer reviews, and business performance: The use of the Toprural website by Spanish rural lodging establishments. *Tourism Management*, *45*, 115–123. doi:10.1016/j.tourman.2014.03.009

Niininen, O., Buhalis, D., & March, R. (2007). Customer empowerment in tourism through consumer centric marketing (CCM). *Qualitative Market Research*, *10*(3), 265–281. doi:10.1108/13522750710754308

Nonaka, I. (1994). A dynamic theory of organizational knowledge creation. *Organization Science*, *5*(1), 14–37. doi:10.1287/orsc.5.1.14

Nortcliffe, A., & Middleton, A. (2013). The innovative use of personal smart devices by students to support their learning. Increasing student engagement and retention using mobile applications: Smartphones, Skype, and texting technologies, pp. 175-208.

Nouri, J., & Pargman, T. C. (2016, September). When teaching practices meet tablets' affordances. insights on the materiality of learning. In *European Conference on Technology Enhanced Learning* (pp. 179-192). Springer International Publishing. 10.1007/978-3-319-45153-4_14

O'Shea, W. (2003). Six degrees of sexual frustration -- connecting the dates with Friendster.com. Retrieved from http://www.freerepublic.com/focus/f-news/924322/posts

Oberst, L. (2010). The 6S social network. Retrieved from http://www.sciepub.com/reference/167008

Odabaşı, Y. (2010). Tüketicilikte Dönüşümler. In *Bilgi ve İletişim Teknolojileri Işığında Dönüşümler*. Ankara, Turkey: Nobel Yayıncılık.

Odden, L. (2012). *Optimize: How to attract and engage more customers by integrating SEO, social media, and content marketing*. Hoboken, NJ: John Wiley & Sons.

OECD. (2013). *The digital economy (2012)*. Organization for Economic Co-operation and Development.

Öğüt, H., & Taş, B. (2012). The influence of internet customer reviews on the online sales and prices in hotel industry. *Service Industries Journal*, *32*(2), 197–214. doi:10.1080/02642069.2010.529436

Oh, S., & Syn, S. Y. (2015). Motivations for sharing information and social support in social media: A comparative analysis of Facebook, Twitter, Delicious, You Tube, and Flickr. *Journal of the Association for Information Science and Technology*, *66*(10), 2045–2060. doi:10.1002/asi.23320

Okubo, Y. (1997). Bibliometric indicators and analysis of research systems: methods and examples, OECD Science, Technology and Industry Working Papers, 1997/01, OECD Publishing, Paris.

Olson, K. (2012). National study quantifies the "sharing economy" movement. Retrieved from https://www.prnewswire.com/news-releases/national-study-quantifies-the-sharing-economy-movement-138949069.html

Ong, T. (2018). *Whatsapp launches a separate app for small businesses*. Retrieved from https://www.theverge.com/2018/1/19/16908810/whatsapp-business-app-launch-small-businesses

Ovadia, S. (2011). Internet connection: an early introduction to the Google+ social networking project. *Behavioral & Social Sciences Librarian*, *30*(4), 259–263. doi:10.1080/01639269.2011.622258

Owusu-Acheaw, M., & Larson, A. G. (2015). The use of social media and its impact on academic performance of tertiary students: A study of Koforidua Polytechnic, Ghana. *Journal of Education and Practice*, *6*(6).

Owusu, R. A., Mutshinda, C. M., Antai, I., Dadzie, K. Q., & Winston, E. M. (2016). Which UGC features drive web purchase intent? A spike-and-slab Bayesian variable selection approach. *Internet Research*, *26*(1), 22–37. doi:10.1108/IntR-06-2014-0166

Ozguven, N., & Mucan, B. (2013). The relationship between personality traits and social media use. *Social Behavior and Personality*, *41*(3), 517–528. doi:10.2224bp.2013.41.3.517

Paniagua, J., & Sapena, J. (2014). Business performance and social media: Love or hate? *Business Horizons*, *57*(6), 719–728. doi:10.1016/j.bushor.2014.07.005

Pariser, E. (2011). *The filter bubble*. New York, NY: Penguin Press.

Park, C., & Lee, T. M. (2009). Information direction, website reputation and eWOM effect: A moderating role of product type. *Journal of Business Research, 62*(1), 61–67. doi:10.1016/j.jbusres.2007.11.017

Pegrum, M. (2014). *Mobile learning: Languages, literacies and cultures* (p. 5). Springer. doi:10.1057/9781137309815

Pelaprat, E., & Brown, B. (2012). Reciprocity: Understanding online social relations. *First Monday, 17*(10). doi:10.5210/fm.v17i10.3324

Phillips, S. (2007). A brief history of Facebook. Retrieved from https://www.theguardian.com/technology/2007/jul/25/media.newmedia

Phillips, B. J., Miller, J., & McQuarrie, E. F. (2014). Dreaming out loud on pinterest: New forms of indirect persuasion. *International Journal of Advertising, 33*(4), 633–655. doi:10.2501/IJA-33-4-633-655

Phillips, P., Barnes, S., Zigan, K., & Schegg, R. (2017). Understanding the impact of online reviews on hotel performance: An empirical analysis. *Journal of Travel Research, 56*(2), 235–249. doi:10.1177/0047287516636481

Phu, B., & Gow, A. J. (2019). Facebook use and its association with subjective happiness and loneliness. *Computers in Human Behavior, 92*(June 2018), 151–159. doi:10.1016/j.chb.2018.11.020

Phua, J., Jin, S. V., & Kim, J. (2017). Gratifications of using Facebook, Twitter, Instagram, or Snapchat to follow brands: The moderating effect of social comparison, trust, tie strength, and network homophily on brand identification, brand engagement, brand commitment, and membership intention. *Telematics and Informatics, 34*(1), 412–424. doi:10.1016/j.tele.2016.06.004

Pink, D. (2005). *A whole new mind: why right-brainers will rule the future*. New York, NY: Riverhead Books.

Pookulangara, S., & Koesler, K. (2011). Cultural influence on consumer's usage of social networks and its impact on online purchase intentions. *Journal of Retailing and Consumer Services, 18*(4), 348-354.

Pouezevara, S. L., & Khan, R. (2007). Learning communities enabled by mobile technology: A case study of school-based, in-service secondary teacher training in rural Bangladesh. *Innovative information and communication technology in education and its potential for reducing poverty in the Asia and Pacific region.*

Poulis, A., Rizomyliotis, I., & Konstantoulaki, K. (2019). Do firms still need to be social? Firm generated content in social media. *Information Technology & People, 32*(2), 387–404. doi:10.1108/ITP-03-2018-0134

Pradiptarini, C. (2011). Social media marketing: Measuring its effectiveness and identifying the target market. *UW-L Journal of Undergraduate Research, 14*, 45–76.

Pulizzi, J. (2010). *New research: B2B content marketing: benchmarks, trends and budgets*. Content Marketing Research, Content Marketing Institute. Retrieved from https://contentmarketinginstitute.com/wp-content/uploads/2010/09/B2B_Trends_2010.pdf

PwC. (2015). The sharing economy: how is it affecting you and your business? *PwC*, (January), 1–10. Retrieved from http://pwc.blogs.com/files/sharing-economy-final_0814.pdf

Qu, Z., Wang, Y., Wang, S., & Zhang, Y. (2013). Implications of online social activities for e-tailers' business performance. *European Journal of Marketing*, *47*(8), 1190–1212. doi:10.1108/03090561311324282

Raice, S. (2012). *Days of wild user growth appear over at Facebook*. Retrieved from https://www.wsj.com/articles/SB10001424052702303296604577454970244896342

Ratzinger, D., Amess, K., Greenman, A., & Mosey, S. (2018). The impact of digital start-up founders' higher education on reaching equity investment milestones. *The Journal of Technology Transfer*, *43*(3), 760–778. doi:10.100710961-017-9627-3 PMID:31258242

Reece, M. (2010). *Real-time marketing for business growth: How to use social media, measure marketing, and create a culture of execution*. Upper Saddle River, NJ: Pearson Education.

Reimer, T., & Benkenstein, M. (2016). Altruistic eWOM marketing: More than an alternative to monetary incentives. *Journal of Retailing and Consumer Services*, *31*, 323–333. doi:10.1016/j.jretconser.2016.04.003

Rempel, J. K., Holmes, J. G., & Zanna, M. P. (1985). *Trust in close relationships, 49*(1), 95–112. Airbnb. (2019). Airbnb Güven ve Güvenlik - Güvenliğiniz bizim önceliğimiz. Retrieved from https://www.airbnb.com.tr/trust

ReportW. A. S. J. (2017). Retrieved from https://wearesocial.com/special-reports/digital-in-2017-global-overview

Rettberg, J. W. (2009). Freshly generated for you, and Barack Obama: How social media represent your life. *European Journal of Communication*, *24*(4), 451–466. doi:10.1177/0267323109345715

Rettberg, J. W. (2017). Self representation in social media. In J. Burgess, A. Marwick, & T. Poell (Eds.), *SAGE handbook of social media* (pp. 1–30). Retrieved from http://dspace.uib.no/bitstream/handle/1956/13073/Self-Representation_in_Social_Media.pdf?sequence=1&isAllowed=y

Ridings, C. M. (2000). *Determinants of trust and use in virtual communities*. Drexel University.

Ridings, C. M., Gefen, D., & Arinze, B. (2002). Some antecedents and effects of trust in virtual communities. *The Journal of Strategic Information Systems*, *11*(3-4), 271–295. doi:10.1016/S0963-8687(02)00021-5

Roberts, R. R., & Kraynak, J. (2008). *Walk like a giant, sell like a madman*. Hoboken, NJ: Wiley.

Rostaing, H. (1997). *Bibliometrics and technical techniques Toulouse: Sciences of the Society*. Marseille, France: Research Center Retrospective of Marseille.

Rothen, S., Briefer, J. F., Deleuze, J., Karila, L., Andreassen, C. S., Achab, S., ... Billieux, J. (2018). Disentangling the role of users' preferences and impulsivity traits in problematic Facebook use. *PLoS One*, *13*(9), 1–13. doi:10.1371/journal.pone.0201971 PMID:30183698

Rotter, J. B. (1967). A new scale for the measurement of interpersonal trust1. *Journal of Personality*, *35*(4), 651–665. doi:10.1111/j.1467-6494.1967.tb01454.x PMID:4865583

Roy, A. (2015). *A typology of virtual communities on the internet: contingency marketing approaches*. 22–24.

Rubin, A. M. (2009). Uses-and-gratifications perspective on media effects. In J. Bryant & M. B. Oliver (Eds.), *Media effects: Advances in theory and research*. Routledge.

Ruggieri, R., Savastano, M., Scalingi, A., Bala, D., & D'Ascenzo, F. (2018). The impact of digital platforms on business models: An empirical investigation on innovative start-ups. *Management and Marketing*, *13*(4), 1210–1225. doi:10.2478/mmcks-2018-0032

Rusli, E. M., & MacMillan, D. (2014). Snapchat fetches $10 billion valuation. Retrieved from https://www.wsj.com/articles/snapchat-fetches-10-billion-valuation-1409088794

Rutter, J. (2001). From the sociology of trust towards a sociology of "e-trust." *International Journal of New Product Development & Innovation Management*, *2*(4), 371–385. Retrieved from http://www.ncsa.uiuc.edu/SDG/Software/XMosaic/

Ryan, R. M., & Deci, E. L. (2000a). Intrinsic and extrinsic motivations: classic definitions and new directions. *Contemporary Educational Psychology*, *25*(1), 54–67. doi:10.1006/ceps.1999.1020 PMID:10620381

Ryan, R. M., & Deci, E. L. (2000b). Self-determination theory and the facilitation of intrinsic motivation, social development, and well-being. *The American Psychologist*, *55*(1), 68–78. doi:10.1037/0003-066X.55.1.68 PMID:11392867

Sabate, F., Berbegal-Mirabent, J., Cañabate, A., & Lebherz, P. R. (2014). Factors influencing popularity of branded content in Facebook fan pages. *European Management Journal*, *32*(6), 1001–1011. doi:10.1016/j.emj.2014.05.001

Sahney, S. K. (2013). "Buyer's motivation" for online buying: an empirical case of railway eticketing in Indian context. *Journal of Asia Business Studies*, pp. 43-64, doi:. doi:10.1108/JABS-07-2011-0036

Salmon, G. (2001). Changing Learning Environments. *Association of Learning Technology (ALT) Conference, 2001*. Retrieved from https://www.alt.ac.uk/search?s=salmon%20changing%20learning%20environ%2Cents

Samadi, B. (2015). Factors influencing organisational trust and knowledge sharing behaviour in MSC status companies (Doctoral dissertation, Multimedia University, Malaysia).

Samarajiva, R., & Zainudeen, A. (2008). *ICT infrastructure in emerging Asia: Policy and regulatory roadblocks*. IDRC.

Santana, J., & Parigi, P. (2015). Risk aversion and engagement in the sharing economy. *Games*, *6*(4), 560–573. doi:10.3390/g6040560

Saravanakumar, M., & Sugantha Lakshmi, T. (2012). Social media marketing. *Life Science Journal*, *9*(4), 4444–4451.

Sashi, C. M. (2012). Customer engagement, buyer-seller relationships, and social media. *Management Decision*, *50*(2), 253–272. doi:10.1108/00251741211203551

Sata, M. (2013). Factors affecting consumer buying behavior of mobile phone devices. *Mediterranean Journal of Social Sciences*, *4*(12). doi:10.5901/mjss.2013.v4n12p103

Saxton, G. D., & Wang, L. (2013). The social network effect: The determinants of giving through social media. *Nonprofit and Voluntary Sector Quarterly*, 1–19.

Schaffer, N. (2013). *Maximize your social: A one-stop guide to building a social media strategy for marketing and business success*. Hoboken, NJ: John Wiley & Sons.

Schau, H., & Gilly, M. (2003). We are what we post? Self-presentation in personal web space. *The Journal of Consumer Research*, *30*(3), 385–404. doi:10.1086/378616

Schiffman, L. G., & Kanuk, L. L. (2010). *Consumer Behaviour* (10th ed.). Prentice Hall.

Schivinski, B., & Dąbrowski, D. (2013). The impact of brand communication on brand equity dimensions and brand purchase intention through Facebook. Gdansk (Poland): Gdansk University of Technology, Faculty of Management and Economics, 4(4), 1-24.

Schivinski, B., & Dabrowski, D. (2016). The effect of social media communication on consumer perceptions of brands. *Journal of Marketing Communications*, *22*(2), 189–214. doi:10.1080/13527266.2013.871323

Schlosser, A. E. (2005). Posting versus lurking: Communication in a multiple audience context. *The Journal of Consumer Research*, *32*(2), 260–265. doi:10.1086/432235

Scott, D. (2007). *The new rules of marketing and PR*. Hoboken, NJ: John Wiley & Sons.

SEMPO. (2017, May 26). *Search engine marketing professional organization glossary*. Retrieved from http://www.sempo.org/ ?page=glossary

Sener, J. (1997, March). Constructivism: Asynchronous learning networks. *ALN Magazine*, *1*, 1.

Shankar, V., Urban, G. L., & Sultan, F. (2002). Online trust: a stakeholder perspective, concepts, implications, and future directions. *Journal of Strategic Information Systems, 11*, 325–344. Retrieved from www.elsevier.com/locate/jsis

Shao, W., & Ross, M. (2015). Testing a conceptual model of Facebook brand page communities. *Journal of Research in Interactive Marketing*, *9*(3), 239–258. doi:10.1108/JRIM-05-2014-0027

Sharp, E. H., Coatsworth, J. D., Darling, N., Cumsille, P., & Ranieri, S. (2007). Gender differences in the self-defining activities and identity experiences of adolescents and emerging adults. *Journal of Adolescence, 30*(2), 251–269. doi:10.1016/j.adolescence.2006.02.006 PMID:16600358

Sharples, M., Taylor, J., & Vavoula, G. (2005, October). Towards a theory of mobile learning. In Proceedings of mLearn (Vol. 1, No. 1, pp. 1-9).

Sharples, M. (2007). *Big issues: Report of a workshop by the Kaleidoscope Network of Excellence*. University of Nottingham.

Sheldon, P., & Bryant, K. (2016). Instagram: Motives for its use and relationship to narcissism and contextual age. *Computers in Human Behavior, 58*, 89–97. doi:10.1016/j.chb.2015.12.059

Sheth, J. N., & Sharma, A. (2005). International e-marketing: Opportunities and issues. *International Marketing Review, 22*(6), 611–622. doi:10.1108/02651330510630249

Shih, C. (2009). *The Facebook era: Tapping online social networks to build better products, reach new audiences, and well more stuff*. Boston, MA: Pearson Education.

Siamagka, N. T., Christodoulides, G., Michaelidou, N., & Valvi, A. (2015). Determinants of social media adoption by B2B organizations. *Industrial Marketing Management, 51*, 89–99. doi:10.1016/j.indmarman.2015.05.005

Siemens, G. (2004). *Connectivism. A learning theory for the digital age.* Retrieved from http:// www. elearnspace. org/Articles/connectivism. htm

Siemens, G. (2005, Jan. 1). *Connectivism: A learning theory for the digital age. International Journal of Instructional Technology and Distance Learning (ITDL).* Retrieved from http://er.dut.ac.za/bitstream/handle/123456789/69/Siemens_2005_Connectivism_A_learning_theory_for_the_digital_age.pdf?sequence=1

Siemens, G. (2005). Connectivism: A learning theory for the digital age. *International Journal of Instructional Technology and Distance Learning, 2*(1), 3–10.

Silva, M. R. (2004). Bibliometric analysis of the teaching scientific production of the special education graduate program / UFSCar. (Master's Dissertation, Federal University of Sao Carlos, Brazil).

Skinner, B. F. (1966). *BF Skinner*. Penn State Audio-Visual Services.

Smedescu, D. A. (2013). Social media marketing tools. *Romanian Journal of Marketing, 4*, 23–30.

Smith, P. R., Berry, C., & Pulford, A. (1999). *Strategic marketing communications*. London, UK: Kogan Page.

Smith, P. R., & Zook, Z. (2011). *Marketing communications: Integrating offline and online with social media*. London, UK: Kogan Page Ltd.

Social Media Marketing Industry Report (SCRIBD). (2017). Retrieved from https://tr.scribd.com/ =document/348447903/2017-Social-Media-Marketing-IndustryReport? secret_password =kpsZVgcHwVfmvTHez7rH#download&from_embed

Social, W. A. (2019). *Global social media research summary.* Retrieved from https://www.smartinsights.com/social-media-marketing/social-media-strategy/new-global-social-media-research/

Song, S., & Yoo, M. (2016). The role of social media during the pre-purchasing stage. *Journal of Hospitality and Tourism Technology*, *7*(1), 84–99. doi:10.1108/JHTT-11-2014-0067

Stanley, B. (2015). *Uses and gratifications of temporary social media: A comparison of Snapchat and Facebook*. Fullerton, CA: California State University.

STATISTA. (2019). Product brands with the most Facebook fans as of April 2019 (in millions). Retrieved from https://www.statista.com/statistics/265657/leading-product-brands-with-the-most-fans-on-facebook/

Statista. (2019a). *Number of monthly active Pinterest users worldwide from 1st quarter 2016 to 2nd quarter 2019 (in millions).* Retrieved from https://www.statista.com/statistics/463353/pinterest-global-mau/

Statista. (2019b). *Number of social network users worldwide from 2010 to 2021 (in billions).* Retrieved from https://www.statista.com/statistics/278414/number-of-worldwide-social-network-users/

Stelzner, M. A. (2015). *2015 Social media marketing industry report.* Retrieved from http://www.socialmediaexaminer.com/report/

Stelzner, M. A. (2016). *Social media marketing industry report: How marketers are using social media to grow their businesses, online social media examiner.* Retrieved from SocialMediaMarketing Industry Report2016.pdf.

Stout, D. W. (2019). Social media statistics 2019: top networks by the numbers. Retrieved from https://dustinstout.com/social-media-statistics/

Subaşı, H. H. (2012). *Elektronik Ticaret ve Güven: Bir Araştırma.*

Sui, D. Z., & Rejeski, D. W. (2002). Environmental impacts of the emerging digital economy: The e-for-environment e-commerce? *Environmental Management*, *29*(2), 155–163. doi:10.100700267-001-0027-X PMID:11815820

Sundararajan, A. (2014). *Peer-to-peer businesses and the sharing (collaborative) economy: overview, economic effects and regulatory issues.* Retrieved from http://www.collaborativeconsumption.com/directory/

Sundar, S. S., & Limperos, A. M. (2013). Uses and Grats 2.0: New gratifications for new media. *Journal of Broadcasting & Electronic Media*, *57*(4), 504–525. doi:10.1080/08838151.2013.845827

Sunil, D. (2015). Trends and practices of consumers buying online and offline: An analysis of factors influencing consumer's buying. *International Journal of Commerce and Management*, *25*(4), 442–455. Doi.org/10.1108/IJCoMA-02-2013-0012 doi:10.1108/IJCoMA-02-2013-0012

Surma, J. (2016). Social exchange in online social networks. The reciprocity phenomenon on Facebook. *Computer Communications*, *73*, 342–346. doi:10.1016/j.comcom.2015.06.017

Swain, A., & Cao, Q. (2014). Impact of online firm generated content (FGC) on supply chain performance: An empirical analysis. In *Proceedings 2014 47th Hawaii International Conference on System Sciences* (pp. 561-573). New Jersey: IEEE.

Swani, K., Brown, B. P., & Milne, G. R. (2014). Should tweets differ for B2B and B2C? An analysis of fortune 500 companies' Twitter communications. *Industrial Marketing Management*, *43*(5), 873–881. doi:10.1016/j.indmarman.2014.04.012

Swani, K., & Milne, G. R. (2017). Evaluating Facebook brand content popularity for service versus goods offerings. *Journal of Business Research*, *79*, 123–133. doi:10.1016/j.jbusres.2017.06.003

Swani, K., Milne, G. R., Brown, B. P., Assaf, A. G., & Donthu, N. (2017). What messages to post? Evaluating the popularity of social media communications in business versus consumer markets. *Industrial Marketing Management*, *62*, 77–87. doi:10.1016/j.indmarman.2016.07.006

Swani, K., Milne, G., & Brown, P., B. (. (2013). Spreading the word through likes on Facebook: Evaluating the message strategy effectiveness of Fortune 500 companies. *Journal of Research in Interactive Marketing*, *7*(4), 269–294. doi:10.1108/JRIM-05-2013-0026

Sweney, M., & De Liz, A. (2018). *"Parents killed it": why Facebook is losing its teenage users.* Retrieved from https://www.theguardian.com/technology/2018/feb/16/parents-killed-it-facebook-losing-teenage-users

Tan, F. B., & Sutherland, P. (2004). Online consumer trust : A multi-dimensional model. *Journal of Electronic Commerce in Organizations*, *2*(3), 40–58. doi:10.4018/jeco.2004070103

Tang, T., Fang, E., & Wang, F. (2014). Is neutral really neutral? The effects of neutral user-generated content on product sales. *Journal of Marketing*, *78*(4), 41–58. doi:10.1509/jm.13.0301

Tapscott, D., & Williams, A. D. (2008). *WIKINOMICS: How mass collaboration changes everything*. New York, NY: Penguin Group.

Tartory, R. (2019). Gender-associated behavior of Jordanians on Facebook. *International Journal of English Linguistics*, *9*(2), 383. doi:10.5539/ijel.v9n2p383

Taylor, R., King, F., & Nelson, G. (2012). Student learning through social media. *Journal of Sociological Research*, *3*(2), 29–35. doi:10.5296/jsr.v3i2.2136

Teece, D. J. (2018). Profiting from innovation in the digital economy: Enabling technologies, standards, and licensing models in the wireless world. *Research Policy*, *47*(8), 1367–1387. doi:10.1016/j.respol.2017.01.015

Teo, T. S. H., & Liu, J. (2007). Consumer trust in e-commerce in the United States, Singapore, and China. *Omega, 35*(1), 22–38. doi:10.1016/j.omega.2005.02.001

Ting, A., & Gray, S. J. (2019). The rise of the digital economy: Rethinking the taxation of multinational enterprises. *Journal of International Business Studies*. doi:10.105741267-019-00223-x

Tirunillai, S., & Tellis, G. J. (2012). Does chatter really matter? Dynamics of user-generated content and stock performance. *Marketing Science, 31*(2), 198–215. doi:10.1287/mksc.1110.0682

Tosuner, A. (2012). *Tüketim Davranışının Azaltılması için İnternetin Kullanılması: Ortak Kullanım Ağları. XVII.* Türkiye'de İnternet Konferansı.

Trainor, K. J., Andzulis, J., Rapp, A., & Agnihotri, R. (2014). Social media technology usage and customer relationship performance: A capabilities-based examination of social CRM. *Journal of Business Research, 67*(6), 1201–1208. doi:10.1016/j.jbusres.2013.05.002

Tranos, E., Reggiani, A., & Nijkamp, P. (2013). Accessibility of cities in the digital economy. *Cities (London, England), 30*(1), 59–67. doi:10.1016/j.cities.2012.03.001

Traxler, J. (2007). Defining, discussing and evaluating mobile learning: The moving finger writes and having writ..... *The International Review of Research in Open and Distributed Learning, 8*(2). doi:10.19173/irrodl.v8i2.346

Traxler, J., & Dearden, P. (2005, September). The potential for using SMS to support learning and organisation in sub-Saharan Africa. In *Proceedings of Development Studies Association Conference*, Milton Keynes.

Treem, J. W., & Leonardi, P. M. (2013). Social media use in organizations: exploring the affordances of visibility, editability, persistence, and association. *Annals of the International Communication Association, 36*(1), 143–189. doi:10.1080/23808985.2013.11679130

Tsao, W.-C., & Hsieh, M.-T. (2015). eWOM persuasiveness: do eWOM platforms and product type matter?, *Electronic Commerce Research, 15*(4), 509-541.

Tsao, W. C., Hsieh, M. T., Shih, L. W., & Lin, T. M. (2015). Compliance with eWOM: The influence of hotel reviews on booking intention from the perspective of consumer conformity. *International Journal of Hospitality Management, 46*, 99–111. doi:10.1016/j.ijhm.2015.01.008

Tschannen-Moran, M., & Hoy, W. K. (2000). A multidisciplinary analysis of the nature, meaning, and measurement of trust. *Review of Educational Research, 70*(4), 547–593. doi:10.3102/00346543070004547

Turel, O., & Serenko, A. (2012). The benefits and dangers of enjoyment with social networking websites. *European Journal of Information Systems, 21*(5), 512–528. doi:10.1057/ejis.2012.1

Tuten, T. L. (2008). *Advertising 2.0: Social media marketing in a Web 2.0 world: Social media marketing in a Web 2.0 world.* United States of America: Praeger Publishers.

Tuten, T., & Solomon, M. (2013). *Social media marketing*. Upper Saddle River, NJ: Pearson.

Tyler, T. (2001). Trust in society. In *The Russell Sage Foundation Series on Trust, Vol. 2*. Retrieved from https://ostromworkshop.indiana.edu/library/node/67979

Uber. (2019). *Our approach to safety.* Retrieved from https://www.uber.com/us/en/safety/

Ufford, S. (2015). *The future of the sharing economy depends on trust.* Retrieved from https://www.forbes.com/sites/theyec/2015/02/10/the-future-of-the-sharing-economy-depends-on-trust/#2648cbcf4717

Utz, S., Muscanell, N., & Khalid, C. (2015). Snapchat elicits more jealousy than Facebook: A comparison of Snapchat and Facebook use. *Cyberpsychology, Behavior, and Social Networking*, *18*(3), 141–146. doi:10.1089/cyber.2014.0479 PMID:25667961

Vaill, P. B. (1996). *Learning as a way of being: Strategies for survival in a world of permanent white water* (Vol. 216, p. 42). Jossey-Bass.

Valkenburg, P. M., Peter, J., & Schouten, A. P. (2006). Friend networking sites and their relationship to adolescents' well-being and social self-esteem. *Cyberpsychology & Behavior*, *9*(5), 584–590. doi:10.1089/cpb.2006.9.584 PMID:17034326

Valk, J. H., Rashid, A. T., & Elder, L. (2010). Using mobile phones to improve educational outcomes: An analysis of evidence from Asia. *The International Review of Research in Open and Distributed Learning*, *11*(1), 117–140. doi:10.19173/irrodl.v11i1.794

Van Doorne, J., N. Lemon, K., Mittal, V., Nass, S., Pick, D., Pirner, P., & Verhoef, P. (2010). *Customer engagement behavior: theoretical foundations and research directions.*

Verhoef, P. C., Reinartz, W. J., & Krafft, M. (2010). Customer engagement as a new perspective in customer management. *Journal of Service Research*, *13*(3), 247–252. doi:10.1177/1094670510375461

Vickery, G., & Wunsch-Vincent, S. (2007). *Participative web and user-created content: Web 2.0 wikis and social networking*. Paris, France: Organisation for Economic Cooperation and Development.

Vize, R., & Sherrett, M. (2017). Social media marketing for B2B: From information to decision to retention. In B. Rishi, & S. Bandyopadhyay (Eds.), *Contemporary issues in social media marketing* (pp. 46–59). New York: Routledge. doi:10.4324/9781315563312-4

Vlasic, G., & Kesic, T. (2007). Analysis of consumers' attitudes toward interactivity and relationship personalization as contemporary developments in interactive marketing communication. *Journal of Marketing Communications*, *13*(2), 109–129. doi:10.1080/13527260601070417

Wagner, T. F., Baccarella, C. V., & Voigt, K.-I. (2017). Framing social media communication: Investigating the effects of brand post appeals on user interaction. *European Management Journal*, *35*(5), 606–616. doi:10.1016/j.emj.2017.05.002

Walczuch, R., & Lundgren, H. (2004). *Psychological antecedents of institution-based consumer trust in e-retailing*. doi:10.1016/j.im.2003.12.009

Walker, M. B. (1989). Some problems with the concept of "gambling addiction". Should theories of addiction be generalized to include excessive gambling? *Journal of Gambling Studies*, *5*(3), 179–200. doi:10.1007/BF01024386

Walther, J. B., & Ramirez, A. (2009). New technologies and new direction in online relating. In S. Smith, & S. Wilson (Eds.), *New directions in interpersonal communication* (pp. 189–214). Thousand Oaks, CA: Sage.

Wan, F., & Ren, F. (2017). The effect of firm marketing content on product sales: Evidence from a mobile social media platform. *Journal of Electronic Commerce Research*, *18*(4), 288–302.

Wang, Q., Chen, W., & Liang, Y. (2011). *The impact of social media on college students. Journal of College and Character*. Johnson & Wales University. doi:10.1515/jcc-2013-0004

Wang, D., & Fesenmaier, D. R. (2013). Transforming the travel experience: The use of smartphones for travel. In *Information and communication technologies in tourism 2013* (pp. 58–69). Berlin, Germany: Springer. doi:10.1007/978-3-642-36309-2_6

Wang, J. L., Jackson, L. A., Gaskin, J., & Wang, H. Z. (2014). The effects of Social Networking Site (SNS) use on college students' friendship and well-being. *Computers in Human Behavior*, *37*, 229–236. doi:10.1016/j.chb.2014.04.051

Wang, R., Kim, J., Xiao, A., & Jung, Y. J. (2017). Networked narratives on Humans of New York: A content analysis of social media engagement on Facebook. *Computers in Human Behavior*, *66*, 149–153. doi:10.1016/j.chb.2016.09.042

Wang, S., Cunningham, N. R., & Eastin, M. S. (2015). The impact of eWOM message characteristics on the perceived effectiveness of online consumer reviews. *Journal of Interactive Advertising*, *15*(2), 151–159. doi:10.1080/15252019.2015.1091755

Wang, Z., Chen, L., & Anderson, T. (2014). A framework for interaction and cognitive engagement in connectivist learning contexts. *The International Review of Research in Open and Distributed Learning*, *15*(2). doi:10.19173/irrodl.v15i2.1709

Watson, R. P., Leyland, F. P., Berthon, P., & Zinkham, G. (2002). U-commerce: Expanding the universe of marketing. *Journal of the Academy of Marketing Science*, *30*(4), 333–347. doi:10.1177/009207002236909

Webb, P. K. (1980). Piaget: Implications for teaching. *Theory into Practice*, *19*(2), 93–97. doi:10.1080/00405848009542880

Wei, K., Zha, Y., & Sun, H. (2014). *A comparative study of buyers' and sellers' transaction intentions in consumer-to-consumer emarketplaces*. Retrieved from http://aisel.aisnet.org/pacis2014/103

Weisberg, J., Te'eni, D., & Arman, L. (2011). *Past purchase and intention to purchase in e-commerce: The mediation of social presence and trust Article information, 21*(1), 82–96. doi:10.1108/10662241111104893

Welch, M. R., Rivera, R. E. N., Conway, B. P., Yonkoski, J., Lupton, P. M., & Giancola, R. (2005). Determinants and consequences of social trust. *Sociological Inquiry, 75*(4), 453–473. doi:10.1111/j.1475-682X.2005.00132.x

Wendlandt, L. B. (2012). *Return on investment concerns in social media marketing: An examination of recent cases* (Master's thesis, The College of St. Scholastica, Minnesota).

Weng, J., Lim, E.-P., Jiang, J., & He, Q. (2010, February). Twitterrank: finding topic-sensitive influential twitterers. In Proceedings of the third ACM international conference on Web Search and Data Mining (pp. 261-270). ACM.

Wenger, E. (1998). *Communities of practice: Learning, meaning, and identity*. Cambridge University Press. doi:10.1017/CBO9780511803932

Wenger, E., McDermott, R. A., & Snyder, W. (2002). *Cultivating communities of practice: A guide to managing knowledge*. Harvard Business Press.

West, D. M. (2013). Mobile learning: Transforming education, engaging students, and improving outcomes. *Brookings Policy Report.*

Westrøm, H., Kristjansson, S., Investigation, A., Behaviour, C., Westrøm, H., & Kristjansson, S. (2015). Sharing economy in Denmark. An investigation of consumer behaviour.

Whiting, A., & Deshpande, A. (2014). Social media marketing: A myth or a necessity. *Journal of Applied Business & Economics, 16*(5), 74–81.

Whiting, A., & Williams, D. (2013). Why people use social media: A uses and gratifications approach. *Qualitative Market Research, 16*(4), 362–369. doi:10.1108/QMR-06-2013-0041

Williams, A. L., & Merten, M. J. (2011). iFamily: Internet and social media technology in the family context. *Family and Consumer Sciences Research Journal, 40*(2), 150–170. doi:10.1111/j.1552-3934.2011.02101.x

Wilson, K., Fornasier, S., & White, K. M. (2010). Psychological predictors of young adults' use of social networking sites. *Cyberpsychology, Behavior, and Social Networking, 13*(2), 173–177. doi:10.1089/cyber.2009.0094 PMID:20528274

Witman, P. (2013). Social media for social value. *Computer, 46*(7), 82–85. doi:10.1109/MC.2013.247

Wong, K., Wong, A., Yeung, A., Fan, W., & Tang, S.-K. (2014). Trust and privacy exploitation in online social networks. *IT Professional, 16*(5), 28–33. doi:10.1109/MITP.2014.79

Wong, L. H. (2012). A learner-centric view of mobile seamless learning. *British Journal of Educational Technology, 43*(1), E19–E23. doi:10.1111/j.1467-8535.2011.01245.x

Wong, L. H., & Looi, C. K. (2011). What seams do we remove in mobile-assisted seamless learning? A critical review of the literature. *Computers & Education*, *57*(4), 2364–2381. doi:10.1016/j.compedu.2011.06.007

Wood, R., & Bandura, A. (1989). Social cognitive theory of organizational management. *Academy of Management Review*, *14*(3), 361–384. doi:10.5465/amr.1989.4279067

Wu, D. M. (2010). *Culture, trust, and security – an empirical study of consumer attitudes towards B2C e-commerce in Chinese societies*. (Doctoral dissertation, Edinburgh Napier University).

Wu, A. M. S., Cheung, V. I., Ku, L., & Hung, E. P. W. (2013). Psychological risk factors of addiction to social networking sites among Chinese smartphone users. *Journal of Behavioral Addictions*, *2*(3), 160–166. doi:10.1556/JBA.2.2013.006 PMID:25215198

Wu, J. J., Chen, Y. H., & Chung, Y. S. (2010). Trust factors influencing virtual community members: A study of transaction communities. *Journal of Business Research*, *63*(9), 1025–1032. doi:10.1016/j.jbusres.2009.03.022

Xiang, Z., & Gretzel, U. (2010). Role of social media in online travel information search. *Tourism Management*, *31*(2), 179–188. doi:10.1016/j.tourman.2009.02.016

Xie, K. L., Zhang, Z., & Zhang, Z. (2014). The business value of online consumer reviews and management response to hotel performance. *International Journal of Hospitality Management*, *43*, 1–12. doi:10.1016/j.ijhm.2014.07.007

Xun, J., & Guo, B. (2017). Twitter as customer's eWOM: An empirical study on their impact on firm financial performance. *Internet Research*, *27*(5), 1014–1038. doi:10.1108/IntR-07-2016-0223

Yamagishi, T., & Yamagishi, M. (1994). Trust and commitment in the United States and Japan. *Motivation and Emotion*, *18*(2), 129–166. doi:10.1007/BF02249397

Yang, L. (2017). *Effect of product review, interactivity, social inequality, and culture on trust in online retailers: a comparison between China and the U.S.* (Doctoral dissertation, Bowling Green State University). doi:10.2202/1935-6226.1069

Ye, C. (2013). *Toward an integrated understanding of online trust*. Retrieved from https://vpn.utm.my/docview/1448297657?accountid=41678

Ye, Q., Law, R., Gu, B., & Chen, W. (2011). The influence of user-generated content on traveler behavior: An empirical investigation on the effects of e-word-of-mouth to hotel online bookings. *Computers in Human Behavior*, *27*(2), 634–639. doi:10.1016/j.chb.2010.04.014

Yıldırım, L. (2017). *Online Alışveriş Sitelerinde Uygulanan Canlı Destek Sistemlerinin Tüketicilerde Oluşturduğu Güvene Etkisi: Bir Araştırma.*

Yoo, C. W., Sanders, G. L., & Moon, J. (2013). Exploring the effect of e-Wom participation on e-Loyalty in e-commerce. *Decision Support Systems*, *55*(3), 669–678. doi:10.1016/j.dss.2013.02.001

Yoo, K.-H., & Gretzel, U. (2011). Influence of personality on travel-related consumer-generated media creation. *Computers in Human Behavior*, *27*(2), 609–621. doi:10.1016/j.chb.2010.05.002

Yoon, H. S., & Occeña, L. G. (2015). Influencing factors of trust in consumer-to-consumer electronic commerce with gender and age. *International Journal of Information Management*, *35*(3), 352–363. doi:10.1016/j.ijinfomgt.2015.02.003

Yoon, S. J. (2002). The antecedents and consequences of trust in online-purchase decisions. *Journal of Interactive Marketing*, *16*(2), 47–63. doi:10.1002/dir.10008

Young, K. (1999). Internet addiction: Evaluation and treatment. *Student BMJ*, *7*, 351–352.

Zahay, D. (2014). Beyond interactive marketing. *Journal of Research in Interactive Marketing*, *8*(4), 32–46. doi:10.1108/JRIM-08-2014-0047

Zahay, D. (2015). *Digital marketing management: A handbook for the current (or Future) CEO*. New York: Business Expert Press.

Zak, P. J., & Knack, S. (2001). Trust and growth. *Economic Journal (London)*, *111*(470), 295–321. doi:10.1111/1468-0297.00609

Zeng, D., Chen, H., Lusch, R., & Li, S. (2010). Social media analytics and intelligence. *IEEE Intelligent Systems*, *25*(6), 13–16. doi:10.1109/MIS.2010.151

Zhang, Y., Trusov, M., Stephen, A. T., & Jamal, Z. (2017). Online shopping and social media: friends or foes. *Journal of Marketing*, *81*(6), 24–41. doi:10.1509/jm.14.0344

Zhao, F., Wallis, J., & Singh, M. (2015). E-government development and the digital economy: A reciprocal relationship. *Internet Research*, *25*(5), 734–766. doi:10.1108/IntR-02-2014-0055

Zhao, J. J., Truell, A. D., Alexander, M. W., Sharma, S., & Smith, S. M. (2013). Strategic use of social media on companies' e-commerce sites. *The Journal of Research in Business Education*, *55*(2), 50–68.

Zhu, Y.-Q., & Chen, H.-G. (2015). Social media and human need satisfaction: implications for social media marketing. *Business Horizons*, *58*(3), 335–345. doi:10.1016/j.bushor.2015.01.006

Zimmerman, J., & Ng, D. (2017). *Social media marketing all-in-one for dummies*. Hoboken, NJ: John Wiley & Sons.

Zurita, G., & Nussbaum, M. (2004). Computer supported collaborative learning using wirelessly interconnected hand-held computers. *Computers & Education*, *42*(3), 289–314. doi:10.1016/j.compedu.2003.08.005

About the Contributors

Shirin Alavi has about 13 years of experience across the academia and corporate sector. She is currently working as an Assistant Professor with Jaypee Institute of Information Technology, Noida. She has earlier worked with the Standard Chartered Bank and has work experience in the domain of CRM operations and International Business and Marketing. She has conducted research in the domains of customer relationship management, online communities, marketing, social media and mobile apps and has several years of research experience. She has published several manuscripts in International and National Journals and also serves on the Editorial Review Board of International Journals. She has completed one PhD guidance and is guiding PhD students in the domain of digital marketing, green marketing and consumer behaviour. She is member of NBA and NAAC accreditation committee of the institute.

Vandana Ahuja works as a Professor at Amity Business School, Amity University and has over 20 years of experience. Prior to Amity, she has worked with Jaypee Business School and IILM as a faculty where she has researched the domain of the collaborative web, with focus on its contributions to the fields of Marketing and CRM and has several years of research experience. She has published several manuscripts in International and National Journals and also serves on the Editorial Board of several International scopus indexed Journals as an Associate Editor, Guest Editor and Editorial Review Board member. These include Journal of Global Marketing (Taylor and Francis), Procedia Computer Science (Elsevier), International Journal of Human Capital and Information Technology Professionals(IGI Global), International Journal of Computers, Communication and Control, International Journal of Management Practise (Inderscience), International Journal of Information Technology and Management (Inderscience). At Jaypee Business School, she was Area-Chair, Marketing and Program Director and taught Sales and Distribution Management, Social Media and E-Marketing, and Services Marketing. She has organised and chaired several National and International conferences and has guided PhD students in the domain of CRM, Branding and Online Marketing. At IILM, she was Dean-Research, and was instrumental in introducing the practice of combining faculty teaching and research by sharing of perspectives, paradigms and debates in the regular pedagogical practices of the faculty in the classrooms and was the head of the accreditation processes for NBA and AACSB. She has authored several books, the most significant being her textbook on Digital Marketing, published by Oxford University Press.

* * *

Adem Akbıyık is an assistant professor of Management Information Systems. Dr. Akbiyik completed his Ph.D. at Sakarya University, followed by a post-doctoral fellowship at the McMaster Digital Transformation Research Centre (MDTRC) at the DeGroote School of Business, McMaster University. His research is focused on consumer analytics, hr analytics, and social media analysis. He has taught courses focusing on text mining, requirements management, and IS project management.

Lydia Andoh-Quainoo has a background in both Psychology and Marketing. She holds an MPhil Psychology from the University of Ghana and a Professional Postgraduate Diploma in Marketing from the Chartered Institute of Marketing, UK. She is a lecturer of Marketing and Psychology, Faculty of Business Administration in the Pentecost University College.

Sofia Balio attended the Master in Management in the School of Economics and Management in the University of Porto, including a semester abroad on Kedge Business School. Currently works as a Project Manager and Business Analyst in Retail.

Luciana Barbieri da Rosa graduated in Business Administration - Bachelor from the São Luis School of Education - FESL (2007) and Full Degree from the Special Graduate Program for Teacher Education for Professional Education - PEG / UFSM. Specialist in Environmental Education from the Federal University of Santa Maria / RS (UFSM-2009) and Specialist in Public Management from the Federal University of Santa Maria (UAB / UFSM - 2015). Master in Business Administration from the Postgraduate Program in PPGA Administration (UFSM - 2013). Acted as substitute professor at the Department of Administrative Sciences - UFSM (2013-2015) and Tutor of the Specialization in Public Management UAB / UFSM (2017-2018) and professor at Palotina College - FAPAS (2018). She is currently a PhD student in Business Administration from the PPGA / UFSM Graduate Program in Business Administration. Works in the areas of: Innovation, Sustainability, Strategy, Marketing and Production. Editorial Advisor of ReA - UFSM Administration Magazine.

Gülay Erol Boyaci is a research assistant of International Trade Department at Başkent University. She is a Ph.D. candidate in marketing management at Hacettepe University where she also holds a Bachelor of Business Administration. Her current research interests are in ethical behaviors of online retailers and online consumer behaviors.

Waleska Yamakawa Zavatti Campos graduated in Pedagogy from the University of São Paulo - FFCLRP-USP (2008). Master's degree in Administration from the Pontifical Catholic University of Rio de Janeiro/IAG Business School (in progress). Postgraduate in External Control and Public Governance (2017). Postgraduate in Public Administration (2014). MBA in People Management (2012).

Beatriz Casais has a PhD in Business and Management Studies - specialization in Marketing and Strategy by University of Porto, Faculty of Economics. Professor at University of Minho and IPAM Porto. Integrated researcher at CiTUR.

Monica Chaudhary is PhD in Management (Marketing) and double Masters in Management and Economics with more than fourteen years' experience in Academics, Research, Consulting and Industry. She has been part of big MNCs and worked in the area of Data analytics & intelligence. She is an expert in Marketing Analytics and Consumer Behaviour areas with good understanding of Economics. She has authored several refereed research papers in reputed research journals (SSCI & SCOPUS indexed, ABDC listed) with academic citations. She is also Editorial Board Member & Reviewer for leading peer reviewed research journals and conferences. She has chaired many conferences sessions, delivered talks, conducted workshops and is an active researcher. She can be contacted at monicarana@gmail.com

Priyanka Garg is a research scholar at Jamia Milia Islamia University. She has done her MBA in area of Marketing. She has more than nine years of academic and corporate experience. She has presented papers in International conferences and has many publication to her credit in refereed national and international journals. Her core area of teaching and research is Advertising, consumer behaviour, brand management and social media.

Tais Pentiado Godoy currently, PhD student in Business Administration from the Federal University of Santa Maria (2016). Graduated in Business Administration at UFSM (2017). Master in Production Engineering from the Federal University of Santa Maria (2013). Has Administration Technician; Technological axis: Management and Business by UFSM (2013). Bachelor of Laws from Santa Maria Methodist College (2010). Has experience in the area of Law, with emphasis on Social Security Law.

Bahtışen Kavak is a professor of Marketing at Hacettepe University in Ankara, Turkey. She received MS and PhD degrees in business administration from Hacettepe University, Ankara, Turkey. She has been head of marketing departmant in Hacettepe University since 2009. She has been interested in marketing research, industrial marketing, international marketing and consumer behavior.

Tuğba Koç is a research assistant in the Department of Management Information Systems at Sakarya University. Currently, she is a Ph.D. candidate in the field of MIS. Her interests include interdisciplinary research areas such as IT occupational subculture, educational technologies, and cultural issues about information systems. She has more than 15 international conference articles including AMCIS which is one of the state of art events.

Maria Carolina Martins-Rodrigues International PhD in Management, University of Extremadura, Spain Post-graduate in Knowledge management, University of Belgrano, Buenos Aires, Argentina, and a research fellow of CIEO (Algarve University). Her research interests currently are Sustainability, innovation, Knowledge Management, Entrepreneurship, Social Responsibility and Business Management. Has co-authored over 20 articles and book chapters and published in several scientific journals. She has also organized Iberian Conference on Entrepreneurship and international Conferences of Sustainability and Innovation. Founder member and vice-president of the direction of Empreend - Portuguese Association for Entrepreneurship. Was Professor in University Aberta (UAb) and University Moderna. In TAX Administration was Tax Administration Technician Advisor acting as coordinator in the International Relations Services Directorate (DSRI). and was Head of the Tax Service.

Niti Mittal is Senior Research Fellow at Jaypee Institute of Information Technology, Noida (India). She has Masters in Organic Chemistry and in Education. She qualified prestigious UGCNET in the subject of Education. Her major research interest area is technology enabled learning and mobile learning. Email: nitimittalster@gmail.com

Neslişah Özdemir is a research assistant of Business Administration at Kastamonu University. She is a Ph.D candidate in Business Administration Department in Hacettepe University. She has been interested in marketing research, industrial marketing and consumer behaviour.

Saloni Pahuja is working as Assistant Professor in Amity School of Business, Amity University, Sector- 125, Noida, Uttar Pradesh, India. She is a Computer Engineer and completed her masters in the area of Human Resource Management. She has more than nine years of experience in academics and in corporate. She has published many research papers in National and International journals of high repute. She has supervised more than hundred training and research projects at the graduate and postgraduate level. Her teaching and research interests lies in the area of Human Resource Management, Business Research, Strategic HRM, Industrial Relations, and Human Resource Planning & Acquisition. She is Gold Medalist-Awarded with Late Shri Amitabh Khandelwal Memorial Medal (Gold Medal) for being the Topper in MBA and also awarded for best research paper presentations at International level.

Niray Tuncel is an Assistant Professor at Hacettepe University, Department of Business Administration. She holds a BA in Business Administration from Bilkent University. She earned her MSc in Marketing from Bahçeşehir University and her PhD in Business Administration from Hacettepe University. After receiving her PhD, she conducted a research at University of Mannheim as a visiting fellow. Her research interests include Consumer Behavior, Consumer Ethics, Digital Marketing, and Collaborative Consumption.

Nihan Yilmaz is a Research Assistant of Family and Consumer Sciences at Hacettepe University Faculty of Economics and Administrative Sciences (Ankara, Turkey). She received the M.Sc. degree and the Ph.D. degree in Family and Consumer Sciences from the Hacettepe University. She has participated in many international conferences. She has been involved in many collaborative research projects financed by Hacettepe University. Her research interests include Consumer Behavior, Family Economics and Independent Life among Elderly. She has been published in a variety of national and international scientific journals, including Turkish Journal of Geriatrics, The International Journal of the Humanities, International Journal of Arts & Sciences, Australian Academy of Business and Economics Review etc.

Index

www.ingramcontent.com/pod-product-compliance
Lightning Source LLC
LaVergne TN
LVHW061548290926
849162LV00004B/942

9781799821854